To Improve the Academy

To Improve the Academy

*Resources for Faculty, Instructional,
and Organizational Development*

Volume 23

Sandra Chadwick-Blossey, Editor
Rollins College

Douglas Reimondo Robertson, Associate Editor
Eastern Kentucky University

Professional and Organizational Development Network in Higher Education

ANKER PUBLISHING COMPANY, INC.
Bolton, Massachusetts

To Improve the Academy
Resources for Faculty, Instructional, and Organizational Development

Volume 23

Copyright © 2005 by Anker Publishing Company, Inc. All rights reserved. Printed in the United States of America. No part of this publication may be reproduced or distributed in any form or by any means, electronic or mechanical, including photocopying, recording, or by any information storage or retrieval system, without the prior written consent of the publisher or the individual authors.

ISBN 1-882982-76-2

Composition by Deerfoot Studios
Cover design by Boynton Hue Studio

Anker Publishing Company, Inc.
P.O. Box 249
Bolton, MA 01740-0249 USA

www.ankerpub.com

To Improve the Academy

To Improve the Academy is published annually by the Professional and Organizational Development Network in Higher Education (POD) through Anker Publishing Company, and is abstracted in ERIC documents and in Higher Education Abstracts.

Ordering Information

The annual volume of *To Improve the Academy* is distributed to members at the POD conference in the autumn of each year. To order or to obtain ordering information, contact:

Anker Publishing Company, Inc.
P.O. Box 249
Bolton, MA 01740-0249
Voice   (978) 779-6190
Fax   (978) 779-6366
Email   info@ankerpub.com
Web   www.ankerpub.com

Permission to Copy

The contents of *To Improve the Academy* are copyrighted to protect the authors. Nevertheless, consistent with the networking and resource-sharing functions of POD, readers are encouraged to reproduce articles and cases from *To Improve the Academy* for educational use, as long as the source is identified.

Instructions to Contributors for the Next Volume

Anyone interested in the issues related to instructional, faculty, and organizational development in higher education may submit manuscripts. Manuscripts are submitted to the current editors in December of each year and sent through a blind peer review process. Correspondence, including requests for information about guidelines and submission of manuscripts for Volume 24, should be directed to:

Sandra Chadwick-Blossey
Director, Christian A. Johnson Institute for Effective Teaching
Rollins College
Campus Box 2636
Winter Park, FL 32789
Voice   (407) 628-6353
Fax   (407) 646-1581
Email   schadwick@rollins.edu

MISSION STATEMENT

As revised and accepted by the POD Core Committee on April 2, 2004

Statement of Purpose

The Professional and Organizational Development Network in Higher Education is an association of higher education professionals dedicated to enhancing teaching and learning by supporting educational developers and leaders in higher education.

POD encourages the advocacy of the ongoing enhancement of teaching and learning through faculty, TA, instructional, and organizational development. To this end, it supports the work of educational developers and champions their importance to the academic enterprise.

Vision Statement

During the 21st century, the Professional and Organizational Development Network in Higher Education will expand its guidelines for educational development, build strong alliances with sister organizations, and encourage developer exchanges and research projects to improve teaching and learning.

Values

The Professional and Organizational Development Network in Higher Education is committed to:

- Personal, faculty, instructional, and organizational development

- Humane and collaborative organizations and administrations

- Diverse perspectives and a diverse membership

- Supportive educational development networks on the local, regional, national, and international levels

- Advocacy for improved teaching and learning in the academy through programs for faculty, administrators, and graduate students

- The identification and collection of a strong and accessible body of research on development theories and practices

- The establishment of guidelines for ethical practice

- The increasingly useful and thorough assessment and evaluation of practice and research

Programs, Publications, and Activities

The Professional and Organizational Development Network in Higher Education offers members and interested individuals the following benefits:

- An annual conference designed to promote professional and personal growth, nurture innovation and change, stimulate important research projects, and enable participants to exchange ideas and broaden professional networks

- An annual membership directory and networking guide

- Publications in print and electronic form

- Access to the POD web site and listserv

Membership, Conference, and Programs Information

For information contact:
Frank and Kay Gillespie, Executive Directors
The POD Network
P.O. Box 271370
Fort Collins, CO 80527-1370
Voice   (970) 377-9269
Fax   (970) 377-9282
Email   podnetwork@podweb.org

About the Authors

THE EDITORS

Sandra Chadwick-Blossey is director of the Christian A. Johnson Institute for Effective Teaching at Rollins College. She teachers undergraduate and graduate courses in organization development and learning organizations. Prior to her eight years at Rollins, she was director of the Learning Assistance Program at Wake Forest University. She can be reached at schadwick@rollins.edu.

Douglas Reimondo Robertson is professor and director of the Teaching and Learning Center at Eastern Kentucky University (EKU). He has helped to start three university faculty development centers (Portland State University, University of Nevada–Las Vegas [UNLV], and Eastern Kentucky University), and has served as founding director at two (UNLV and EKU). His most recent book is *Making Time, Making Change: Avoiding Overload in College Teaching* (New Forums Press, 2003). He can be reached at douglas.robertson@eku.edu.

THE CONTRIBUTORS

Sally S. Atkins is professor of human development and psychological counseling at Appalachian State University, where she teaches in the graduate program in community counseling. A licensed psychologist, she has 16 years' experience in faculty and organizational development work through the Hubbard Center for Faculty and Staff Support. She can be reached at atkinsss@appstate.edu.

Steven A. Beebe is professor and chair of the Department of Communication Studies and associate dean of the College of Fine Arts and Communication at Texas State University–San Marcos. He is the author or coauthor of 10 widely used communication books and more than 100 book chapters, articles, and professional papers. He has also been a visiting scholar at both Oxford University and Cambridge University. He was an American Council on Education Fellow in 2002–2003, serving both on his home campus and at Southwestern University. He can be reached at SBeebe@txstate.edu.

Laurie Bellows is senior lecturer and director of graduate student professional development in the Office of Graduate Studies at the University of Nebraska–Lincoln (UNL). In her work supporting graduate students at UNL, she organizes the campus-wide TA orientation, administers the Institute for International Teaching Assistants, conducts professional development workshops, and consults individually with graduate students on professional development issues. In addition, she co-directs the Preparing Future Faculty program. She earned her Ph.D. at the University of Nebraska. She has served on the executive board for the Professional and Organizational Development Network in Higher Education and is a current member of the TA developers subcommittee. She can be reached at lbellows1@unl.edu.

Phyllis Blumberg is professor and director of the Teaching and Learning Center at the University of the Sciences in Philadelphia. Her main roles include collaboration with faculty to improve their teaching, promoting more learning-centered teaching within the university, and assisting faculty to engage in scholarly teaching. Her research interests include program evaluation, problem-based learning, and self-directed learning. She can be reached at p.blumbe@usip.edu.

Kathleen T. Brinko is director of faculty and academic development at the Hubbard Center for Faculty and Staff Support at Appalachian State University. For the past 20 years she has worked with teaching assistants and faculty on teaching and quality of life issues. She can be reached at brinkokt@appstate.edu.

JoAnn Canales is professor of education at Texas A&M University–Corpus Christi. She currently chairs the Faculty Renaissance Center (FRC) Council, a faculty development initiative with a mantra of By Faculty, For Faculty. She was selected as the Inaugural Assessment Fellow of the Faculty Renaissance Center in 2004, a position created by the FRC to assist the university community with issues related to assessment, program review, and accreditation initiatives. She was an American Council on Education Fellow in 2002–2003, serving both on her home campus and at Pace University. She can be reached at jcanales@falcon.tamucc.edu.

Nancy Van Note Chism is associate vice chancellor for professional development and associate dean of the faculties at Indiana University–Purdue University Indianapolis, as well as associate professor of higher education at Indiana University. She is past president of the Professional and Organizational Development Network in Higher Education and currently co-chairs the research subcommittee. She can be reached at nchism@iupui.edu.

Christine M. Cress is associate professor in the postsecondary, adult, and continuing education program at Portland State University. Her scholarship is focused on learning communities, community-based learning experiences, and the impact of campus climate on student development outcomes and faculty morale. She directed a comprehensive campus climate study of faculty work life at the University of Arizona (www.u.arizona.edu/~millen) and has consulted on learning, leadership, and assessment projects at institutions across the country. She can be reached at cressc@pdx.edu.

Robert M. Diamond is president of the National Academy for Academic Leadership. He is Research Professor Emeritus at Syracuse University, where he was assistant vice chancellor and director of the Center for Institutional Development, which was awarded the 1996 Theodore M. Hesburgh Award for Faculty Development to Enhance Undergraduate Learning. He is the editor of *Field Guide to Academic Leadership* (Jossey-Bass, 2002). He can be reached at r.m.diamond@verizon.net.

Patricia M. Dwyer is dean of teaching, learning, and instructional resources at Shepherd College. She received her undergraduate degree in English from Chestnut Hill College and attended the Bread Loaf School of English (Middlebury College) for her M.A., studying at both the Vermont and Oxford campuses. She completed her Ph.D. in American Literature at George Washington University in 1995. She can be reached at pdwyer@shepherd.edu.

Justin Everett is assistant professor and director of the Writing Center at the University of the Sciences in Philadelphia. His primary function is to oversee the tutoring program in the areas of writing and literacy, including the tutoring services associated with the university's writing proficiency examination. His areas of research include composition studies, cooperative learning, and the English renaissance. He is currently coauthoring a textbook in the area of rhetoric and argumentation. He can be reached at j.everet@usip.edu.

Traci Fordham is assistant professor of communication studies at St. Lawrence University, where she teaches courses in interpersonal, gender, small group, and intercultural communication. She is a co-facilitator of St. Lawrence University's Oral Communication Institute, and is the co-director of the National Dialogue Project, a grant-funded initiative sponsored by the American Association of Colleges and Universities and Campus Compact to cultivate civic engagement through dialogue. Her research includes dialogue and pedagogy, gender and communication, and travel, communication, and cultural adaptation. She can be reached at tracifordham@stlawu.edu.

Alan C. Frantz is faculty assistant for special projects (academic affairs) and associate professor of educational leadership at Idaho State University. His current projects include working with the university honors program, first-year seminar, and C.L.A.S.S. program in the Center for Teaching and Learning, and assisting in the Office of Graduate Studies. An American Council on Education Fellow in 2002–2003, he selected Portland State University for the fellowship year. Provost Mary Kay Tetreault and President Daniel O. Bernstine served as his mentors, and Devorah Lieberman served as a role model for leadership in faculty development. He can be reached at franalan@isu.edu.

Lion F. Gardiner is associate professor of zoology at Rutgers University, Campus at Newark. His books include *Planning for Assessment: Mission Statements, Goals, and Objectives,* developed in connection with a New Jersey statewide outcome assessment program (1989), *Redesigning Higher Education: Producing Dramatic Gains in Student Learning* in the ASHE-ERIC Higher Education Report series (Jossey-Bass, 1996), and, as co-editor, *Learning Through Assessment: A Resource Guide for Higher Education,* published by the American Association for Higher Education (1999). He has served on the Professional and Organizational Development Network in Higher Education's board of directors and as an associate editor of *To Improve the Academy,* and is a member of the editorial board of *Innovative Higher Education.* He is a founding principal of the National Academy for Academic Leadership and is an active consultant. He can be reached at gardiner@andromeda.rutgers.edu.

Mary Rose Grant is assistant professor in the School for Professional Studies at Saint Louis University, where she teaches courses in the biological and life sciences. She is the director of the core curriculum and chairs the general curriculum committee. She is also the director of faculty development for the school and implemented a comprehensive development program specific to the needs of part-time faculty. As a member of the university Reinert Center for Teaching Excellence Advisory Board, she serves on both the program and faculty enhancement mentoring committees. She is a founding member of the Missouri-Illinois Faculty Developers consortium. She can be reached at grantmr@slu.edu.

Kathleen A. Harper is an instructional consultant with Faculty & TA Development at The Ohio State University. She earned a B.S.E. in electrical engineering and applied physics and an M.S. in physics from Case Western Reserve University, and a Ph.D. in physics from The Ohio State University, specializing in physics education. Her primary research area is student problem solving, although she has also published articles on cooperative learning, laboratory teaching, and reflective journaling. She can be reached at harper.217@osu.edu.

Jennifer L. Hart is assistant professor in the higher education and continuing education emphasis in the Department of Educational Leadership and Policy Analysis at the University of Missouri–Columbia. Her scholarly agenda centers on the professions, organizational transformation, and gender issues within academe. She is interested in shaping policy and addressing issues about how professions emerge and transform within the academy and how gender plays a role in the development of professional academic work, including teaching and learning. She can be reached at hartjl@missouri.edu.

Judi Hetrick is assistant professor of journalism at Miami University in Oxford, Ohio. She was a professional journalist for many years, and she earned both her M.A. and Ph.D. in folklore from Indiana University. Her research blends her interests in everyday vernacular culture and mass media. She is working on a book called *America's Serious Home Videos.* Miami's new journalism curriculum—which will incorporate print, broadcast, and online traditions within a liberal arts framework—begins in fall 2004. She can be reached at hetricjl@muohio.edu.

Richard A. Holmgren is associate dean of the college at Allegheny College. As associate dean, he is involved in faculty development, programs for first-year students, and academic support for students. He also teaches courses in writing, speaking, and mathematics. His primary professional interest is fostering the development of a campus culture that supports learning and teaching. He can be reached at richard.holmgren@allegheny.edu.

Virginia S. Horvath is interim dean for academic and student services, regional campuses, and professor of English at Kent State University. She has been active in faculty development at her home institution, where she is a member of the Faculty Professional Development Center Council, and in several projects with the American Association for Higher Education. As an American Council on Education Fellow in 2002–2003, she was placed at Mount Union College, where she worked with President Jack Ewing and Dean Richard Marriott. She can be reached at vhorvat1@kent.edu.

Libby Falk Jones is professor of English and founding director of the Center for Learning, Teaching, Communication, and Research at Berea College. At Berea since 1988, she has directed several faculty-staff development programs and seminars for new faculty and taught a variety of writing and general studies courses. She has written and spoken on teaching and learning infrastructure, writing and teaching, women's academic vocations and feminist pedagogies, writing centers, and critical thinking and workplace literacy. She currently co-chairs the National Council of Teachers of English Assembly for Expanded Perspectives on Learning and serves as Berea's campus contact for the American Association for Higher Education's Carnegie Academy for the Scholarship of Teaching and Learning. She can be reached at libby_jones@berea.edu.

Alan Kalish is director of Faculty & TA Development and adjunct assistant professor of education policy and leadership at The Ohio State University. He previously served as the founding director of the Center for Teaching and Learning at California State University–Sacramento, and associate director of the Teaching Resources Center at Indiana University–Bloomington, where he also earned his Ph.D. in English. His research interests include how people negotiate the transition from graduate school to faculty lives, and his publications include articles on this topic, as well as on other issues in college teaching. He can be reached at kalish.3@osu.edu.

Rona J. Karasik is professor of community studies and director of the gerontology program at St. Cloud State University. Her current research interests include intergenerational service-learning, aging in the community, and housing for older adults. She is an active advocate of expanding service-learning opportunities in gerontology, as well as more broadly throughout the university. She can be reached at karasik@stcloudstate.edu.

Valerie D. Lehr is professor of government and gender studies at St. Lawrence University. She has extensive experience with faculty development work as a result of a four-year term as associate dean of the first year, a number of years as coordinator of the gender studies program, and her work with the Oral Communication Institute. Her scholarship focuses on lesbian and gay politics and feminist theory. She can be reached at vlehr@stlawu.edu.

Marian E. Miller is a graduate student in the community counseling program at Appalachian State University. She also served as faculty development assistant in the Hubbard Center for Faculty and Staff Support. She can be reached at mm47819@appstate.edu.

Kim M. Mooney is the founding director of the Center for Teaching and Learning at St. Lawrence University. The center was established in 2001 during her five-year term as associate dean for faculty affairs. She is an associate professor of psychology and teaches courses in social and health psychology. Her research interests include the effects of gender on health-related attitudes and behavior, the effects of food choices on impression formation, and the teaching and research experiences of feminist psychologists in small college environments. She can be reached at kmooney@stlawu.edu.

Cathie J. Peterson has been an administrator at Johnson County Community College since 1985 and earned an Ed.D. from the University of Kansas–Lawrence in 2003. She has taught in the areas of English as a second language and adult basic education. She received the Research Award in 2003 from Johnson County Community College and is interested in faculty vitality and the factors that contribute to faculty renewal, revitalization, and enthusiasm. She can be reached at cpeters@jccc.net.

Kathryn M. Plank is associate director of Faculty & TA Development and an adjunct assistant professor in the School of Educational Policy and Leadership at The Ohio State University (OSU). She joined OSU after several years at Penn State, where she was associate director of the Center for Excellence in Learning and Teaching and an affiliate assistant professor of English. Her interests include assessment, teaching with technology, gender issues in higher education, and literature and medicine. She can be reached at plank.28@osu.edu.

Stephanie V. Rohdieck is an instructional consultant for the Graduate Teaching Associates Program at The Ohio State University and has worked at Faculty & TA Development for over four years. She has a master's degree in social work administration and earned her B.A. in psychology and women's studies. Her current interests are graduate teaching preparation, diversity issues in higher education, and writing reflectively about teaching. She can be reached at rohdieck.1@osu.edu.

Connie M. Schroeder is assistant director of the Center for Instructional and Professional Development at the University of Wisconsin–Milwaukee. Through the Classroom Assessment Program she has designed a three-month process to spark inquiry into student learning, and designed faculty learning communities to advance inquiry, renewal, and connection. She is involved with the campus and University of Wisconsin System scholarship of teaching and learning program, facilitates monthly interactive dialogues with new and seasoned faculty/teaching academic staff, and coordinates the Freshman Seminar Retreat. She serves as lead instructor for the graduate course, Teaching and Learning in College: Reflection on Theory and Practice, and is committed to enhancing diversity awareness through a new faculty program, Dialogues in Diversity. Her research interests center on organizational change in higher education, particularly within the context of academic departments. She can be reached at connies@uwm.edu.

David E. Swee is professor and chair of family medicine at the University of Medicine and Dentistry of New Jersey–Robert Wood Johnson Medical

School. For 2002–2003, he was one of two F. Marian Bishop Fellows in the American Council on Education Fellowship Program, during which he worked with Dean Craig Brater at the Indiana University School of Medicine on the Indiana University–Purdue University Indianapolis campus. He has a long-standing interest in educational support and faculty development, serving for nine years as the chair of the medical school's curriculum committee. He continues to be actively involved with accreditation agencies as a surveyor of medical schools for the Liaison Committee on Medical Education and of continuing medical education programs for the Accreditation Council for Continuing Medical Education. He can be reached at swee@umdnj.edu.

Patricia Hanrahan Valley is founding director of the Center for Teaching and Learning Effectiveness at Embry-Riddle Aeronautical University (ERAU). In this role she is responsible for the orientation and instructional development of over 3,000 full- and part-time faculty members. A strong advocate for the use of technology in the classroom and in faculty development, she has developed an online faculty orientation, provides educational technology training for faculty, teaches online courses, and is currently involved with the BETA Project for online student ratings of instruction. She is also an assistant professor at ERAU, teaching graduate research methods and managerial communications, as well as undergraduate management and communications courses. Her research interests include adult learning, student writing in the disciplines, the effective use of technology in education, and institutional issues in the employment of part-time faculty. She can be reached at valleyp@erau.edu.

Catherine M. Wehlburg is director of the Center for Teaching Excellence at Texas Christian University. She received her Ph.D. in educational psychology from the University of Florida in 1992. Her research interests include learning, student engagement in the learning process, and the assessment of student learning. She can be reached at c.wehlburg@tcu.edu.

Ellen Weissinger is executive associate dean of graduate studies and professor of educational psychology at the University of Nebraska–Lincoln. She previously served as associate director of the Buros Institute for Mental Measurements and associate dean of Teachers College at UNL. Her expertise areas include psychological measurement, research methodology, and evaluation design. She taught doctoral-level research methods courses for many years and served as a member of over 100 doctoral supervisory committees. She earned her Ph.D. at the University of Maryland, her M.A. at the University of Iowa, and her undergraduate degree at the University of Nebraska. She can be reached at eweissinger1@unl.edu.

Table of Contents

Section III: Best Practices for Faculty Development

Preface

To Improve the Academy is the annual publication of POD, the Professional and Organizational Development Network in Higher Education. This growing alliance of professionals promotes excellence in teaching and learning through faculty and organizational development. Members of POD include college and university administrators, faculty developers, instructional technologists, educational consultants, and full- and part-time faculty from all disciplines who are involved in research and teaching. Each fall, POD members gather for the annual meeting. Some of the chapters in this volume were inspired by presentations or conversations at the 2003 meeting held in Denver, Colorado. More information about POD can be found at podnetwork.org.

The production of *To Improve the Academy, Volume 23* was a yearlong process involving collaboration of ideas, thoughtful writing, submission of manuscripts, peer review, multiple revisions, and careful editing. More than 100 people were involved and all were volunteers who care about the improvement of teaching and learning. I particularly want to thank Associate Editor Douglas Reimondo Robertson, whose wisdom, dedication, and diligence added immeasurably to the quality of this volume. The initial decisions concerning the appropriateness and choice of chapters were made by the reviewers. For their thoughtful and timely work, I would like to thank Mary J. Allen, Danilo Baylen, Donna Bird, Peter Bishop, Phyllis Blumberg, Debra Busacco, Darcey Cuffman, Cynthia Desrochers, Michele DiPietro, Sally Barr Ebest, Peter Felton, Tara Gray, Eric Hobson, Wayne Jacobson, Trish Kalivoda, Heidi Holst Knudsen, Emily Lardner, Jean Layne, Vilma Mesa, Sue Neeley, Megan Palmer, Judy Silvestrone, Margaret Snooks, Lydia Soleil, David Starrett, Ian Stewart, and Patricia Valley. Ultimately, the decisions among many excellent manuscripts regarding inclusion and arrangement were mine.

Carolyn Dumore, of Anker Publishing, was most responsive and helpful with my many questions. I want to thank President Rita Bornstein and Dean Roger Casey of Rollins College for encouraging me to work on this volume. And, as always, I am grateful for the good ideas and constant support of my husband, Professor Erich C. Blossey, D. J. and J. M. Cram Chair of Chemistry at Rollins College.

Sandra Chadwick-Blossey
Rollins College
Winter Park, FL
April 2004

Introduction

Although the primary audience for this publication is the membership of the Professional and Organizational Development Network in Higher Education, individuals and groups outside of the organization do purchase the book. Indeed, we are happy to learn that one or more volumes have been used as texts in graduate-level courses. A primary goal of the editor for *To Improve the Academy, Volume 23* is to increase the readership of this important publication by selecting high-quality chapters of wide appeal to academic administrators, faculty developers, full- and part-time faculty, instructional technologists, educational consultants, and institutional researchers.

For certain, a climate of change is the backdrop for all concerns and constituents of higher education in the new century. In Section I: Faculty Development in a Climate of Change, Lion F. Gardiner and Robert M. Diamond, with academic leaders in mind, collaborated on the opening two chapters. Gardiner presents a compelling case for the urgency of change and the societal demands for quality outcomes, prescribing steps for transforming institutions and effectively managing learning. Diamond further describes the elements of a successful change process and suggests that the expanded role of academic support centers is similar to that of an internal change agency. Using compatible theoretical underpinnings, Patricia Dwyer in Chapter 3 describes an institutional process at a small college that evolved into a culture of assessment. In Chapter 4, Connie M. Schroeder gives evidence of the transformational dimensions of the scholarship of teaching and learning through the eyes of SoTL scholars. To complete Section I, Alan C. Frantz and his colleagues (all ACE Fellows), Steven A. Beebe, Virginia S. Horvath, JoAnn Canales, and David E. Swee, describe their findings from a survey of teaching and learning centers. Their report outlines organizational, accountability, assessment, and implementation strategies practiced across the country on college and university campuses.

Section II: Quality of Work Life for Faculty and Faculty Developers is composed of four chapters. To lead this area of inquiry, Kathleen T. Brinko, Sally S. Atkins, and Marian E. Miller present in Chapter 6 the responses to their survey on the quality of work life for faculty development professionals. In Chapter 7, Christine M. Cress and Jennifer L. Hart demonstrate different work life experiences for faculty of color and white faculty by providing qualitative and quantitative data from their systematic study at a large research university. By contrast, Libby Falk Jones describes in Chapter 8 the dialogue process and outcomes of a yearlong study group on teaching as a vocation at a small college. In Chapter 9, Cathie J. Peterson discusses her findings from an investigation of faculty vitality at a large community college.

Section III: Best Practices for Faculty Development provides a wide range of best practices for the development of full- and part-time faculty, as well as graduate students at large universities, small colleges, and community colleges. Former TIA editor Catherine M. Wehlburg demonstrates in Chapter 10 how course and departmental assessment data can be used for faculty development. In Chapter 11, Kathryn M. Plank, Alan Kalish, Stephanie V. Rohdieck, and Kathleen A. Harper discuss their strategies for creating an integrated data system for teaching centers. In Chapter 12, Phyllis Blumberg and Justin Everett describe a successful process for achieving campus consensus on learning-centered teaching. Richard A. Holmgren outlines in Chapter 13 a successful program at his small college that resulted in a culture change that promotes open discussions about teaching and learning. Another unique example of a successful faculty development program is presented by Kim M. Mooney, Traci Fordham, and Valerie D. Lehr in Chapter 14 that promotes engaged classroom dialogue. In Chapter 15, Rona J. Karasik forewarns faculty new to service-learning of some of the challenges and pitfalls and then offers realistic approaches for successful outcomes. Judi Hetrick describes in Chapter 16 the appropriate and inappropriate roles for new faculty to take in campus-wide curricular change. Two authors from a large university, Laurie Bellows and Ellen Weissinger, tell us in Chapter 17 what they have learned about the needs and wants of graduate students who are looking forward to college teaching professions. In Chapter 18, a model for developing part-time faculty at community colleges is presented by Mary Rose Grant. Patricia Hanrahan Valley describes her successful practices in providing for the development needs of part-time faculty in Chapter 19. Nancy Van Note Chism promotes a sound process for teaching awards programs conducted by faculty development centers in Chapter 20.

Section I

Faculty Development in a Climate of Change

1

Transforming the Environment for Learning: A Crisis of Quality

Lion F. Gardiner
Rutgers University

This chapter addresses academic leaders and summarizes research findings on the conditions needed to produce learning and student development in higher education at the level required by society, and our relative success in doing this. It attempts to make clear the urgency for change that exists in the way in which we conduct our educational affairs. It describes the causes of less-than-optimal learning, outlines 10 key elements for effectively managing learning in complex institutions, presents eight steps required to lead a successful transformation in an institution or unit, and provides resources with detailed information and guidance.

FOCUSING ON LEARNING: OUR CORE MISSION

Among other missions a college or university may have, as a *school* its learning mission is paramount. Schools exist to develop people; producing learning is their raison d'être. For at least two decades businesspeople, political leaders, and experts in human development have been asking us to produce graduates who are skilled in higher-order cognition, such as critical thinking and complex problem solving; behave in a principled ethical fashion; can accept and work harmoniously and productively with people unlike themselves; have the ability to adapt to diverse and changing situations; and take responsibility, work hard, and show initiative (e.g., Carnevale, Gainer, & Meltzer, 1990; Van Horn, 1995).

Modern colleges and universities are complex organizations. Producing these essential outcomes is not a simple matter. This discussion will focus on four key organizational components that contribute powerfully to learning and student development: curriculum, instruction, campus climate, and academic

advising. The contribution each can and should make to learning and development and the research evidence concerning its current capacity to do this well
in most institutions are examined. (A more extensive review of this research, together with citations to specific sources, appears in *Redesigning Higher Education: Producing Dramatic Gains in Student Learning* [Gardiner, 1996]; see Resources below.)

CURRICULUM

Curricula should provide students with balanced learning plans composed of
diverse experiences such as courses, projects, student organizations, employment, and travel that will effect their learning and development in an orderly
fashion appropriate to each person's developmental stage, prerequisite knowledge and skills, and future needs. A student's general education curriculum,
together with a disciplinary major field curriculum, are ordinarily intended to
contribute heavily to his or her development. If learning is the goal, these curricula must provide a carefully planned developmental map of relevant learning experiences appropriate to each person's needs.

Students are dependent on their curricular plans to guide them though
the college experience. A set of specific intended learning outcomes—what
graduates should know and be able to do—for each curriculum is a sine qua
non of good practice. These statements of intended outcomes direct curricular design and implementation, assessment of each student's learning, and
evaluation of curricular effectiveness. An examination of curricula, however,
reveals that most lack, and thus cannot be not aligned with, intended outcomes. In addition, well over 90% of general education curricula and most
major field curricula use a distribution format that provides only minimal
guidance to students. These curricula require students merely to choose from
lists of approved courses and accumulate a requisite number of credit hours to
be authorized to graduate. The standard is fulfillment of a specified number of
hours of seat time rather than demonstrating specific, important knowledge,
skills, and values—the intended learning outcomes. This situation is consistent with the conclusions of an Association of American Colleges report that
"there is a notable absence of structure and coherence in college and university
curricula" (Zemsky, 1989, p. 7) and other reports from the Association of
American Colleges (1985) and the Association of American Colleges and Universities (2002).

Research has established, at least for general education curricula, that
most of these resemble each other closely. In addition, they may have relatively
little impact on the outcomes achieved by students regardless of the specific

courses, breadth of courses available, or degree of freedom to choose among them (Astin, 1993). On the other hand, a core curriculum where students take courses in common does positively affect learning outcomes, satisfaction with a student's college experience, and persistence on campus. Therefore, students' approach to a curriculum and how a faculty utilizes the curriculum for educational purposes may be more significant in producing learning than the curriculum's formal features. Other research also has failed to support the developmental power of distributional curricula (Jones & Ratcliff, 1990).

There is evidence that some vocationally focused programs, in contrast with liberal arts programs, can actually retard or even decrease, sometimes significantly, development of valuable outcomes (Altemeyer, 1988; McNeel, 1994; Self & Baldwin, 1994; Self, Olivarez, & Baldwin, 1994). A study of university students showed that after pre-college learning was removed statistically from their post-college "general learned abilities" as measured by the Graduate Record Exam, neither high- nor low-scoring students demonstrated high-level gains from their work at the university (Jones & Ratcliff, 1990). Fife (1991) states that "the curriculum is no longer achieving its intended purpose" (p. xiii).

INSTRUCTION

Our students' learning in their courses forms the core of their intellectual experience in college. Their courses are intended to introduce them to new ideas and help them develop mature, complex, and powerful ways of thinking about the world, such as critical thinking and principled ethical reasoning. These complex skills and the dispositions to engage in them that society requires necessitate intentionally planning and explicitly teaching for them, providing sustained practice with corrective feedback throughout a course. This is necessary across the entire curriculum, general education and major field alike.

Intellectual Experiences in Class

What is the level of our students' intellectual experiences in their courses? In spite of what their teachers may think, study after study over the years has shown that in a large percentage of their classes, students experience a focus on low-level cognition such as facts and concepts rather than critical thinking and disciplinary problem solving (Ellner & Barnes, 1983). Information is what we tend to transmit to our students in lectures, and this is also what we tend to require them to reproduce or recognize on assessments. Therefore, memorizing information is what they think is most important and what they try to do.

Active Involvement in Class

A requisite for effective learning is sustained active engagement with what is being studied: societally important issues, disciplinary content, and problems requiring critical thinking or other types of higher-order cognition. However, many studies reveal that more often than not faculty lecture to their classes, dominating their students' attention and providing relatively little opportunity for them to assume an active rather than passive, note-taking role (Ellner & Barnes, 1983). In many classes few students say anything or have the opportunity to work with peers on disciplinarily important issues. The amount of student talk in class can occupy less than 1% of time available. Extended lectures are also problematic given students' limited 10- to 20-minute attention span. Research has shown that for about 50% of the time in their lectures, students are off task, thinking about things other than the class (Bonwell & Eison, 1991). The result is that relatively little of lecture content can be recalled even immediately after a class, with rapid diminution of memory thereafter (McLeish, 1968).

Most students, when asked, seem to have difficulty remembering much from many of their previous courses. The media regularly report studies showing that college students lack knowledge of basic facts concerning American history and government and geography, and simple abilities in practical day-to-day matters such as using transportation schedules and making supermarket calculations.

A problem stemming from inadequate learning in college is the persistence of misconceptions concerning basic concepts, even in their own major fields of study, and the lack of ability to solve problems. Studies of students in physics, biology, and anthropology courses in leading private and public universities and selective private institutions show a low level of comprehension of basic disciplinary concepts such as force, momentum, and organic evolution (e.g., Fuerst, 1984; Hake, 1998; Mazur, 1997; Zimmerman, 1986).

Out-of-Class Learning

Most of what students learn they have to learn outside of formal classes. Classes are far too short to permit the extensive cognition and practice required for synaptic remapping of the brain. Although students' quality of effort and level of engagement have been established as key factors in learning, studies consistently show that most students do far less work outside of their classes than the average of two hours or more per hour spent in class expected by their teachers for adequate learning. Yet this low level of effort and the learning it produces in most cases does not result in failure or dismissal from the institution. One reason may be the well-known low cognitive demand of many or most teacher-made assessments. Most students can achieve passing scores using a *surface learning approach* that focuses on memorizing isolated facts that are soon forgotten. (A *deep approach* seeks understanding and meaning and permits deep cognitive processing that engages all important regions of the brain. It thus can result in thorough comprehension and long-term retention of new knowledge and the ability to use it.) Teacher-made tests in most cases are also of unknown validity and reliability, two technical requirements necessary to ensure the credibility and usefulness of assessment results.

Grades

Although grades are the main means by which we signify the level of learning to our students, their parents, and other stakeholders, for almost a century researchers have criticized grades as an ineffectual means for representing learning. Single letters cannot communicate much information about the various kinds of complex cognitive, affective, and motor learning we want our students to achieve. End users of grades usually have no idea what information was used to determine a grade. For example, how much of the grade represents learning, rather than, say, attendance or participation in class activities? Or what type of cognitive achievement does it signify: number of facts memorized or level of critical thinking skill demonstrated? Added to the defects of grades as devices for describing knowledge and skills developed is their potential contamination by the very high percentage of college students who admit to various types of cheating as reported by numerous researchers.

CAMPUS CLIMATE

Climate is the emotional feel of a campus, department, or course. Do students feel welcome, intellectually stimulated to a high level, and emotionally and socially supported, or do they experience their institution as cold, indifferent to them, or even hostile and rejecting? Research strongly supports the importance of each person's social and emotional integration into a campus community. The quality of campus psychological climate correlates not only with student learning, but with persistence on campus and satisfaction with their college experience. Given the vast cultural diversity of college students and their needs, together with the special needs of the overwhelming majority of students who live off campus and thus miss out on the significant potential intellectual and social benefits from residence life, clearly, the campus climate needs to be managed deliberately and carefully if it is to become a valuable tool for supporting learning among all of our students.

Research also demonstrates that many students experience their college or university as an unsupportive environment (Astin, 1993; Boyer, 1989). Many students from noncollege or ethnic minority backgrounds find our campuses strange and threatening places. Women and members of ethnic and sexual minority groups often suffer severe indignities from their peers and, at times, even members of the faculty. Entirely aside from our significant ethical responsibility to ensure our students are treated well and have their worth affirmed when in our care, condoning an alienating or abusive environment undermines their learning, our core mission.

ACADEMIC ADVISING

Given the broad cultural diversity of our students, their commonly inadequate academic preparation for higher education, the loose organization of our curricula, their parents' frequent inability to guide them when making important academic decisions, and an unfamiliar and sometimes threatening campus climate, the quality of the academic advising they receive is of paramount importance. We must ensure they adapt successfully to college, learn at a high level, enjoy their college experience, and accomplish the developmental changes society requires. Appropriately, modern academic advising is developmental rather than prescriptive (Gordon, Habley, & Associates, 2000). Each person develops a relationship with a faculty academic advisor who gets to know the student and helps him or her develop a learning plan based on his or her individual values and life goals.

Only students can learn for themselves. A high level of student effort is necessary to carry this out. Therefore, student motivation to learn is at the root of accomplishing our education mission. Yet students often seem far less animated by a love of learning and thirst for knowledge and self-development than complying with bureaucratic regulations—registration rituals, curricular graduation requirements, and course policies—after all, this has been the experience of many of them throughout their K–12 years. If learning is the intended outcome, we need a systematic process for resocializing our students as they enter the institution, to reignite their childhood love of learning. An institution serious about learning will invest significant resources and effort in modern developmental academic advising relationships to guide development, monitor attitude and effort, and ensure that significant learning is occurring for each person.

The research consistently shows, however, that the academic advising received by most college students—of that minority of students who receive *any* advising—is of an insufficient amount and quality (Habley & Crockett,

1988). All too often academic advising is more clerical or bureaucratic than developmental, having to do with picking courses from lists to fulfill graduation requirements, and most students spend little time with their advisors. They end up advising themselves, depending on lists of requirements to fulfill and student scuttlebutt.

Research shows high-quality academic advising has a positive impact on students' learning, social and vocational development, and satisfaction with college and therefore persistence on campus (Saunders & Ervin, 1984). Persistence and satisfied alumni, and their lifelong financial contributions, are not insubstantial benefits to an institution in times of scarcity.

The Roles of Institutional Management and Leadership in Producing High-Quality Learning

Management and leadership are two distinct concepts; both are essential in higher education. As currently practiced, both are criticized as often being insufficiently sophisticated to produce the high-quality learning society requires. Management can be thought of as dealing with first-order change: routine technical problems that are well understood and for whose solution accepted methods exist (Heifetz, 1994; Waters, Marzano, & McNulty, 2003). Examples are scheduling classes, registering students, and keeping track of grades. Leadership, on the other hand, deals with second-order change: problems where solutions are not well understood and that require adaptation to new realities through changes in people's values, beliefs, and behavior. "Leadership defines what the future should look like, aligns people with that vision, and inspires them to make it happen despite the obstacles" (Kotter, 1996, p. 25). Our example here is significantly improving an institution's capacity to produce the high-quality learning that our society requires.

Managing Learning: 10 Key Elements

Consider 1) the diverse and complex types of knowledge, skills, and other specific outcomes our students must acquire, 2) the difficult developmental transformations they need to undergo so they can become effective and committed critical thinkers and problem solvers, and 3) the diversity of our populations of students and academic staff members. Clearly, leaving this potpourri of processes to chance and players to their own devices, as we now so often do, has to give us the wholly unimpressive outcomes that research suggests we now produce compared to what society requires and what the state of the educator's art can now achieve. Why would we assume a faculty that

lacks almost any effective communication among its members about its educational work, as is so often the case, could produce any desired outcome reli-
ably, particularly those that require high levels of planning, coordination, and
monitoring? Learning in our complex organizations must be deliberately and
expertly managed. Our success in fostering high-level learning in all of our
students across an institution or unit requires using the findings of research
and developed best practices. The task is much too complex and societally too
important for us to continue using the methods of the past and neglecting the
professional literature in this business.

Because of the importance of specific prerequisite knowledge stored in
long-term memory as a necessary foundation for further learning through
neuronal networking (Zull, 2002), to be effective and cost-efficient, each student's sequence of learning must be carefully planned, implemented, and
monitored, taking into consideration his or her current knowledge, skills, and
level of development. Researchers and expert practitioners in higher education
have identified and described key management functions and tools to address
issues of organizational complexity that any college, university, or unit can use
to help it produce learning at a high level (Gardiner, 1996).

1) Have well-constructed and inspiring mission statements at all levels in the
   organization, from institution to course, that are closely aligned with each
   other and provide clear guidance for decision-making, such as for developing statements of intended learning outcomes for all curricula.

2) Have well-constructed statements of *intended* outcomes for both curricula and their courses that are understood and routinely used by academic
   staff and students to focus attention, set high expectations for everyone,
   and are a basis for planning and improving academic programs.

3) Use systematic assessment research everywhere that is aligned with statements of intended outcomes so that everyone knows the *actual* outcomes
   (the results of learning), understands the processes that have produced
   them, and uses the results of assessment for decision-making and to continuously improve the quality of learning and to create a culture of evidence that permeates the organization.

4) Have coherent curricula that are closely aligned with their intended outcomes and that integrate all aspects of learning and student development.

5) Use instructional methods that are consistently aligned with their intended outcomes and that are at all points consistent with research on
   brain function and learning and are known to work.

6) Deliberately design and manage a campus climate that consistently supports learning, starting with the classroom.

7) Ensure that all students know how to take a deep approach to learning, have the skills of effective learning, and understand the amount of time required for deep, brain-changing learning and the importance of sustained hard effort, high standards, and taking responsibility for their own learning and development.

8) Have a high-quality developmental academic advising program that is a focal point of the institution's and its units' connections with their students and that plans and builds supporting relationships between individual faculty members and every student.

9) Ensure that every administrator and faculty and staff member is fully competent to perform the tasks he or she is responsible for as a manager of learning and leader of change, and participates in continuous, never-ending, high-quality professional development as appropriate to these tasks.

10) Compensate, promote, and otherwise reward all members of the staff appropriately for their contributions to the institution's learning mission.

How effectively are you managing your students' learning in your organization? You can use this list of 10 management elements as a checklist to help you take stock. What percentage of the 10 points are present, and how do you know? Where are the weak points? Each may indicate an opportunity for improving your organizational capacity to produce learning and a need for first-order change.

STAFF DEVELOPMENT: FOUNDATION OF INSTITUTIONAL COMPETENCE

Clearly, many students learn effectively and see their lives significantly changed through their experience on our campuses. This transformation occurs because of their own high motivation and effort to learn, together with the efforts of innumerable committed and hard-working members of the academic staff. The accumulated research available today and the perceptions of many astute observers both on and off campus, however, make equally clear the widespread lack of effectiveness and inefficiency—even dysfunction—of learning in many institutions and units for many of their students (Gardiner, 1996). Their test results and grades provide only an illusion of learning.

Our Investment in Staff Competence

To what can be attributed the striking limitations of contemporary curriculum, instruction, and academic advising, and the problems associated with the unsupportive campus climates described earlier? There are many factors both internal and external to an institution that influence its effectiveness. Central to its competence in producing learning among its students, however, are the knowledge, skills, and dispositions of its academic staff. "If we know anything from research over a 30-year period about what affects student achievement, it's teacher quality" (Bradley, 1999, p. 51). In striking contrast to business enterprise, however, higher education continues its longstanding custom of investing little in the preparation of its teachers for their work as educators, not in graduate school and not as working professionals after they secure their faculty appointments. Where faculty and staff professional development programs exist, more often than not they are weak, participation in them is voluntary, and they are given only desultory moral and financial support by senior administrators. Consequently, they reach relatively few members of the staff. For those who do participate, their involvement is often episodic and disjointed rather than progressing systematically through coherent professional curricula relevant to their specific needs.

Critical Thinking: A Prime Example of the Problem

Because of lack of preparation, teaching in higher education is all too often reduced to orally explaining in a traditional lecture what a *teacher* has learned rather than engaging *students* in activities that will cause learning by *their* brains. Critical thinking is one of the most societally important outcomes we can produce that should be at the center of most curricula. It is a complex concept and involves many discrete cognitive skills and affective dispositions, and requires the skilled use of specific intellectual criteria and standards. A study by Paul, Elder, and Bartell (1997) starkly illustrates the impact of lack of preparation for our complex work of brain development. These researchers studied 140 faculty members from education and liberal arts and science disciplines in 30 California public and private colleges and universities. Eighty-nine percent of these faculty members said critical thinking was "a primary objective of their instruction" (p. 18). "Most claimed that they permeated their instruction with an emphasis on critical thinking" (p. 22). Seventy-eight percent of them also said their "students lacked appropriate intellectual standards . . . to use in assessing their thinking" (p.18) but "that their department's graduates develop a good or high level of critical thinking ability while in their program" (p. 19).

However, only 20% of these teachers "said that their departments had a shared approach to critical thinking" (p. 19). "[O]nly 9%...were clearly teaching for critical thinking on a typical day in class" (p. 18). Relatively few (19%) "gave a clear explanation of what critical thinking is" or gave "any intellectual criteria or standards they required of students" (8%; p. 18). "Only 8% clearly differentiated between an assumption and an inference, and only 4% differentiated between an inference and an implication" (p. 19). "When asked how they conceptualized truth, a surprising 41% of those who responded...said that knowledge, truth and sound judgment are fundamentally a matter of personal preference or subjective taste" (p. 19).

The researchers concluded that "we can infer that comparatively few faculty have thought seriously about critical thinking" (p. 21). "Few...have had in-depth exposure to research on the concept. Most appear to have only a vague understanding of what critical thinking is and what is involved in bringing it successfully into instruction" (p. 31). The researchers concluded further that it is unlikely that the graduates of these programs would understand how to reason about complex issues in their disciplines or that "moral issues and problems require as much disciplined reasoning and clarity of definition as does reasoning in any other domain" (p. 32).

Today, the old assumption that disciplinary competence or skill as a researcher or scholar will translate into success as a teacher seems naïve. The profession of college educator requires knowledge of the research on learning and student development, curriculum design and assessment, instructional design and mental measurement, the wide array of instructional strategies now available that can produce durable learning, classroom management, developmental academic advising, management of staffs of graduate and undergraduate TAs and others, and leadership for change at various institutional levels.

Administrators from the level of department chair to president require this same knowledge, the type and amount of detail depending on their roles. They too typically receive little professional education for the demanding work of managing learning and leading change. Therefore, instituting a high-quality program of professional development for all academic staff to ensure their technical competence to teach, manage learning, and lead change throughout their careers is a key management responsibility and a sine qua non of any attempt to ensure effectiveness in a college or university. In Chapter 2 of this volume, Robert M. Diamond discusses staff development and academic support centers—change agencies—in detail.

Leadership for Change: A Process

As we have seen, knowing in detail what your institution *should* be doing and *is* doing, and continuously improving the quality of the learning it produces, are essential to mission accomplishment. These are tasks of the management process—making sure things get done the right way. If all management tasks are accomplished at a high level in a professional fashion by everyone involved, most students will probably learn the right things at the right level and in the right sequence. Given what we have seen, however, the accumulated research suggests chances are excellent your institution has a long way to go to ensure best practice is pervasive throughout the organization and all of your students are learning well. How can you engineer the transformation—the second-order, adaptive change—that may be required for your institution or unit? This is a different level of organizational change than guiding improvements in management. This is about leadership, leadership for change. "Successful transformation is 70 to 90 percent leadership and only 10 to 30 percent management" (Kotter, 1996, p. 26). And leadership for change requires different knowledge, skills, and dispositions than effective management. "The literature is replete with examples of bright, powerful, well-intentioned leaders who fail in their leadership initiatives because they simply did not understand what they needed to know, how to proceed with implementation, or when they needed to use various practices and strategies" (Waters, Marzano, & McNulty, 2003, p. 13). Based on their meta-analysis of 30 years of research, these authors have identified 21 different leadership responsibilities and practices significantly correlated with students' learning in their schools (see the Resources section at the end of the chapter).

Because of the need for transformation in so many, perhaps most, organizations, considerable research and thought have been devoted to understanding the characteristics of effective organizations and what steps must be taken to reform those that are dysfunctional or underperforming. Lick (2002) describes several comprehensive change models. Kotter (1996) provides a widely admired model of organizational transformation. He suggests there are eight steps or processes required for leading any successful organizational change. Each step addresses a leadership error commonly made during change efforts that can cause them to fail. The steps must be carried out in this order, no steps can be skipped, several or even all may be worked on simultaneously, but new ones begun only after the groundwork has been properly laid, and all must be constantly reinforced.

Steps 1 Through 4: Softening the Status Quo; Laying a Solid Foundation for Transformation

Step 1. Develop a sense of urgency for change. Effecting change is difficult. The most important error when initiating change is permitting complacency to lull people and keep them from focusing sharply on what needs to happen. People are busy with their daily work, they think the quality of their work is pretty good, change is threatening, they can sense this will be a lot of extra work, some may believe the new ideas are profoundly in error, and who knows what the results will be anyway? Their attention must be sharply focused on the needed changes for the duration of the project, a difficult but essential step. No one leader can bring about change; the cooperation of many others is required. Kotter estimates that sustaining a major change effort requires a majority of the people and 75% of people in management roles to believe change must happen, and 15% to 25% percent of the people must be willing to work very hard.

Today in higher education complacency seems pervasive. Relatively few institutions have responded vigorously to two decades of appeals to reform or to engage in systematic assessment research to understand themselves. Public relations offices churn out a torrent of institutional self-congratulation. The first part of this chapter has been devoted to persuading you that fundamental change is required throughout higher education and that given the pervasive conditions of low performance revealed by research, there is a good chance your institution shares some of these same problems and you need to act to determine if that is so. You may be different, but do you have credible evidence of high-level learning of the right sort among all of your students?

Kotter identifies nine different factors that can contribute to complacency:

- There is no widely perceived crisis that threatens the institution and its members.

- The institution's physical surroundings communicate success. The buildings are beautiful, the landscaping elegant, the catered dinners sumptuous.

- Standards of performance are low. Intended learning outcomes are easy to achieve or, more likely, have never even been defined, or if they have, are unused for planning or evaluation. Graduation is based on seat time (accumulated credits) not demonstrated competence through challenging assessments. Faculty do their own thing in their classrooms with little supervision or specific integration of their courses into a coherent curricular whole.

- People are concentrating on their own narrow, day-by-day tasks rather than on whether the institution or unit as a whole is effective in accomplishing its mission. Perhaps only the president has ultimate responsibility for the learning mission, and she is preoccupied with raising money and dealing with the state government.

- Formal internal planning and assessment are set up so goals are easy for everyone to achieve. Offer a new course, develop a new initiative, teach so many hours, get your grades in on time.

- Feedback on people's work is all based on the inadequate internal assessment systems with little input from external stakeholders. A new course gets offered or there are new initiatives, you taught your courses; everything is hunky dory. People do not have to confront angry parents, businesspeople who find your graduates cannot add, let alone think independently, or have a poor work ethic, or the governor or legislators who do have to deal with these complaints.

- Individual faculty and staff members who display initiative and who do collect data demonstrating problems are ignored—or even punished—and the data are suppressed, their reports becoming classic shelf documents.

- People deny the validity of and ignore the evidence that contradicts a rosy picture of the institution or unit. "We're not that bad."

- Senior administrators and faculty opinion leaders produce a steady stream of narcotic happy talk. "We are wonderful here; all of us are highly accomplished." "This is a truly distinguished institution, on the verge of joining the first rank of institutions in our sector. In fact, we're world class." Celebrations are held, awards are presented, medals are struck. "Although happy talk is sometimes insincere, it is often the product of an arrogant culture that, in turn, is the result of past success. . . . Big egos and arrogant cultures reinforce the nine sources of complacency" (Kotter, 1996, p. 41).

Although having copious, accurate, and relevant information from high-quality assessment research is essential, data and their interpretation are not enough to move most people to change. The specific causes of complacency must be identified and eliminated or significantly weakened. How many of these conditions are present in your institution or unit, and how do you know?

Step 2. Construct a leadership team. No single person can provide the force required to overcome the summed complacency, lethargy, and active resistance of an entire organization. A team of informed, committed, and credible members is required to guide implementation of the change effort. Composition of the team is critical to ensure high-quality decisions. The team should include the most senior administrators with their authority and power to implement change, people with essential technical expertise, and others who can communicate various perspectives from around the institution or unit on the issues the team will deal with. Members must be well regarded throughout the institution to enhance the credibility of the team's diagnoses and decisions. Mutual trust among members and their deep commitment to a shared team goal is essential. They must effectively communicate essential information to key decision-makers.

Step 3. Create a vision and a strategy. A vision describes the desired future state and why it is important to achieve it. The vision reduces numerous decisions into a single idea of the future; serves to energize everyone to action toward that end, helping overcome barriers of personal inconvenience and effort; and helps organize the efforts of large numbers of people toward the changes required. The strategy articulates the logic of the desired change and provides some initial information on how it can be achieved.

Step 4. Communicate the vision for change to everyone. Understanding the new strategic vision will be an intellectual challenge for everyone, and many will experience emotional stress when required to give up current ways of doing things. Understanding this is often difficult for the leadership team members who have been concentrating on the issues for a considerable time. Communicating with everyone else in the institution or unit requires close attention and often considerable time and effort.

Steps 5 Through 7: Introducing New Ways of Doing Things

Step 5. Empower everyone for action across the institution or unit. Effecting a major transformation can be extremely difficult; everyone is needed. In many institutions, faculty and staff members do not feel as though they can have an impact on the institution. They may feel blocked by a lack of current, research-based knowledge and skill concerning learning, student development, or managing and leading, they may lack specific information about their students or the organization, or be hemmed in by rules, organizational structures, or by the behavior of senior administrators that is inconsistent with the strategic vision. They need to be empowered.

Step 6. Engineer short-term successes. Ensure there are performance improvements demonstrating that current change activities will lead to positive results, and inform people about them. Solid evidence of the effectiveness of the new way, such as good assessment data and information on costs will lend credibility to the message. This step is important to let people judge the effectiveness of new methods versus costs, build morale to stay the course, effectively refute those who may attempt to undermine the change process, recognize change agents, keep everyone, including top administrators, focused on change, and help develop momentum.

Step 7. Solidify improvements and engender additional change. Ensure that celebration of short-term gains does not lead back to complacency and slow or stop progress. Additional changes can be added now that the change process has begun to prove its worth and political support is available. Various change-oriented projects already underway may be continued but require leadership from administrators and faculty and staff members throughout the institution or unit, not just at the top. At this point there may be an enhanced recognition of and desire to prune away unnecessary bureaucratic interdependencies among units.

Step 8: Institutionalizing the Transformation

Step 8. Embed innovations in the organization's culture. Changes must be grounded in the institution's culture: its shared values, assumptions, and behavioral expectations. A vigorous change effort that has successfully brought research-based methods of learning to a campus may ultimately founder if it does not forthrightly confront a clash with an underlying culture that places relatively little value on students and their development and overwhelmingly favors the pursuit of prestige among academicians elsewhere through idiosyncratic faculty research activities. Such a clash may quickly undermine advances made and derail the change effort. The organization reverts to being focused on itself—its image—rather than its student customers. This process of connecting change with culture—changing the culture where necessary—occurs only after changes have produced credible results. Success depends on copious discussion, may require staff changes, and necessitates care when promoting people into new positions so old cultural values and expectations are not reintroduced.

CONCLUSION

Based on numerous studies and the observations of countless members of the academy and its external stakeholders, the quality of learning in higher education is far lower than we might like to believe and that society requires and is technically possible today. Unless you have convincing evidence to the contrary, there is likely opportunity for significant improvement in learning on your campus and in your unit. Central to improvement is effective management of the organization and, specifically, management of learning. You and your staff can lead the change required to produce this improvement.

The professional literatures in education and management are clear about the kinds of changes that will be required. Methods now exist to help you determine specifically what is needed on your campus. You will need to accept the challenge of leadership, educate yourself and your staff concerning the knowledge and skills required to take the lead in the change effort, develop an inspiring vision of the future, take risks, and employ best practice for learning at all points. These actions can lead to increased, perhaps transformed, learning for your students and their impact on their families and society.

RESOURCES

Diamond, R. M. (Ed.). (2002). *Field guide to academic leadership.* San Francisco, CA: Jossey-Bass.

A handbook for effective, research-based management of learning and leadership for change. Numerous experts discuss pressures for fundamental reform and requisites for sustainable change, leadership, mission, culture, and interpersonal relationships, academic aspects of managing learning, assessment and evaluation, and relating academic issues to finance, student affairs, technology, diversity, and issues related to specific administrative positions.

Diamond, R. M. (2005). The institutional change agency: The expanding role of academic support centers. *To improve the academy: Vol. 23. Resources for faculty, instructional, and organizational development* (pp. 24–37). Bolton, MA: Anker.

Comprehensively reviews forces for change that confront colleges and universities, and describes development of the institutional change agency that can provide high-quality support for the changes most academic institutions will have to make in their capacity to produce learning.

Gardiner, L. F. (1996). *Redesigning higher education: Producing dramatic gains in student learning* (ASHE-ERIC Higher Education Report, 23[7]). San Francisco, CA: Jossey-Bass.

A review and synthesis of numerous studies on student development in college and college effects on students. Focused specifically on curriculum, instruction, campus climate, and academic advising, it reveals limitations of commonly used academic practices in producing learning and summarizes recommendations of researchers to substantially improve learning. A resource to use to raise the level of urgency for change in an institution or unit.

Gardiner, L. F. (2000, Fall). Why we must change: The research evidence. *Thought & Action, 16*(2), 121–138.

An abbreviated account of the issues raised in Gardiner (1996). Available electronically at http://www.nea.org/he/heta00/f00p121.pdf.

Kotter, J. (1996). *Leading change.* Boston, MA: Harvard Business School Press.

Based on long experience, Kotter shows why efforts to make major changes in organizations often fail, and provides an eight-step method for leading significant and successful organizational transformations.

Lucas, A. F., & Associates. (1999). *Leading academic change: Essential roles for department chairs.* San Francisco, CA: Jossey-Bass.

A handbook for leading change in the academic department. A dozen different authors address diverse aspects of effective leadership and management of learning in the department.

Tichy, N. M. (1997). *The leadership engine: How winning companies build leaders at every level.* New York, NY: HarperCollins.

A discussion of the importance of building leadership everywhere in an organization. Contains a detailed handbook for developing leaders.

Waters, T., Marzano, R. J., & McNulty, B. (2003). *Balanced leadership: What 30 years of research tells us about the effect of leadership on student achievement.* Aurora, CO: Mid-continent Research for Education and Learning.

Reports results of a meta-analysis of 70 high-quality studies culled from 5,000 conducted over three decades on the relationship between leadership and student learning in schools. Identifies 21 key leadership responsibilities and practices. Available at http://www.mcrel.org/topics/productDetail.asp?productID=144.

REFERENCES

Altemeyer, B. (1988). *Enemies of freedom: Understanding right-wing authoritarianism.* San Francisco, CA: Jossey-Bass.

Association of American Colleges. (1985). *Integrity in the college curriculum: A report to the academic community.* Washington, DC: Author.

Association of American Colleges and Universities. (2002). *Greater expectations: A new vision for learning as a nation goes to college.* Washington, DC: Author. Retrieved June 2, 2003, from http://www.greaterexpectations.org

Astin, A. W. (1993). *What matters in college? Four critical years revisited.* San Francisco, CA: Jossey-Bass.

Bonwell, C. C., & Eison, J. A. (1991). *Active learning: Creating excitement in the classroom* (ASHE-ERIC Higher Education Report No. 1). Washington, DC: George Washington University, Graduate School of Education and Human Services.

Boyer, E. L. (1989). *The condition of the professoriate: Attitudes and trends, 1989.* Princeton, NJ: Carnegie Foundation for the Advancement of Teaching.

Bradley, A. (1999, January 11). Zeroing in on teachers: Quality Counts '99 [Special issue]. *Education Week, 18*(17), 46–47, 49–52.

Carnevale, A. P., Gainer, L. J., & Meltzer, A. S. (1990). *Workplace basics: The essential skills employers want.* San Francisco, CA: Jossey-Bass.

Ellner, C. L., & Barnes, C. P. (Eds.). (1983). *Studies of college teaching: Experimental results, theoretical interpretations, and new perspectives.* Lexington, MA: D.C. Heath.

Fife, J. (1991). Foreword. In W. Toombs & W. Tierney, *Meeting the mandate: Renewing the college and departmental curriculum* (p. xiii). Washington, DC: George Washington University, School of Education and Human Development.

Fuerst, P. A. (1984). University student understanding of evolutionary biology's place in the creation/evolution controversy. *Ohio Journal of Science, 84*(5), 218–228.

Gardiner, L. F. (1996). *Redesigning higher education: Producing dramatic gains in student learning* (ASHE-ERIC Higher Education Report, 23[7]). San Francisco, CA: Jossey-Bass.

Gordon, V. N., Habley, W. R., & Associates. (2000). *Academic advising: A comprehensive handbook.* San Francisco, CA: Jossey-Bass.

Habley, W. R., & Crockett, D. S. (1988). The third ACT national survey of academic advising. In W. H. Habley (Ed.), *The status and future of academic advising: Problems and promise* (pp. 11–76). Iowa City, IA: ACT National Center for the Advancement of Educational Priorities.

Hake, R. R. (1998). Interactive-engagement versus traditional methods: A six-thousand-student survey of mechanics test data for introductory physics courses. *American Journal of Physics, 66*(1), 64–74.

Heifetz, R. A. (1994). *Leadership without easy answers.* Cambridge, MA: Harvard University Press.

Jones, E. A., & Ratcliff, J. R. (1990, April). *Is a core curriculum best for everybody? The effect of different patterns of coursework on the general education of high- and low-ability students.* Paper presented at the annual meeting of the American Educational Research Association, Boston, MA.

Kotter, J. P. (1996). *Leading change.* Boston, MA: Harvard Business School Press.

Lick, D. W. (2002). Leadership and change. In R. M. Diamond (Ed.), *Field guide to academic leadership* (pp. 27–47). San Francisco, CA: Jossey-Bass.

Mazur, E. (1997). *Peer instruction: A user's manual.* Upper Saddle River, NJ: Prentice-Hall.

McLeish, J. (1968). *The lecture method.* Cambridge, England: Cambridge Institute of Education.

McNeel, S. P. (1994). College teaching and student moral development. In J. R. Rest & D. Narváez (Eds.), *Moral development in the professions: Psychology and applied ethics* (pp. 27–49). Mahwah, NJ: Lawrence Erlbaum.

Paul, R. W., Elder, L., & Bartell, T. (1997). *California teacher preparation for instruction in critical thinking: Research findings and policy recommendations.* Sacramento, CA: California Commission on Teacher Credentialing.

Saunders, S. A., & Ervin, L. (1984). Meeting the special advising needs of students. In R. B. Winston, T. K. Miller, S. C. Ender, T. J. Grites, & Associates (Eds.), *Developmental academic advising: Addressing students' educational, career, and personal needs* (pp. 250–286). San Francisco, CA: Jossey-Bass.

Self, D. J., & Baldwin, D. C., Jr. (1994). Moral reasoning in medicine. In J. R. Rest & D. Narváez (Eds.), *Moral development in the professions: Psychology and applied ethics* (pp. 147-162). Mahwah, NJ: Lawrence Erlbaum.

Self, D. J., Olivarez, M., & Baldwin, D. C., Jr. (1994). Moral reasoning in veterinary medicine. In J. R. Rest & D. Narváez (Eds.), *Moral development in the professions: Psychology and applied ethics* (pp. 163–171). Mahwah, NJ: Lawrence Erlbaum.

Van Horn, C. E. (1995). *Enhancing the connection between higher education and the workplace: A survey of employers.* Denver, CO: State Higher Education Executive Officers and Education Commission of the States.

Waters, T., Marzano, R. J., & McNulty, B. (2003). *Balanced leadership: What 30 years of research tells us about the effect of leadership on student achievement.* Aurora, CO: Mid-continent Research for Education and Learning.

Zemsky, R. (1989). *Structure and coherence: Measuring the undergraduate curriculum.* Washington, DC: Association of American Colleges.

Zimmerman, M. (1986). The evolution-creation controversy: Opinions from students in a "liberal" liberal arts college. *Ohio Journal of Science, 86*(4), 134–139.

Zull, J. (2002). *The art of changing the brain.* Sterling, VA: Stylus.

2

The Institutional Change Agency: The Expanding Role of Academic Support Centers

Robert M. Diamond
President, National Academy for Academic Leadership

Higher education is going through significant changes stimulated by the rapid growth of the internet, the increasing globalization of higher education, and the ever-pressing question of institutional quality. New modes of educational delivery through virtual networks are breaking the traditional mold of instructional provision. New players, new pedagogies, and new paradigms are redefining higher education. The rules are changing, and there is increased pressure on institutions of higher education to evolve, adapt, or desist.

(Swail, 2002, p. 16)

ACADEMIC REFORM AND THE FORCES FOR CHANGE

There is little question that colleges and universities are confronting formidable forces for change. Critics, budget cuts, and competition have come together to challenge institutional priorities and structures—not to mention faculty, staff, and administrators' roles. Interestingly, the area that will be most directly affected by suggested changes is the one least often discussed—the design and delivery of instruction. In considering recent calls for change and the actions colleges and universities must take to respond to them, it is clear that not only are fairly fundamental changes needed in the areas of course and curricular design and pedagogy, but that these changes must be accomplished with few resources and with many factors complicating the change process (see Table 2.1). Compounding the problem are increasing demands by accrediting bodies and other external entities that these changes take place within a relatively short timeframe.

The Role of Accreditation

While many of the problems being identified are not new—ad hoc curricula, educational deficiencies among graduates, lower success rates for students of color, a disconnect between what institutions say they value and what they reward, and little use of educational research in teaching—it has been only recently that the professional and regional accrediting agencies have moved these problems to the top on their agendas. Recognizing the need for increased institutional accountability, there is concern that if colleges and universities do not deal with these problems, external mandates as seen in the K–12 sector are likely. Those responsible for accreditation have begun to address the quality of teaching and the nature of learning at colleges and universities in the United States. The approach and specific descriptions may differ, but the new standards of each of the major accrediting bodies now call for evidence of student learning, statements of intended outcomes, evidence that data on learning is being collected and used, and that attention is being paid to professional development for faculty and staff.

This shift away from a reliance on *input* variables (e.g., the number of Ph.Ds on the faculty, the number of books in the library) to *output* criteria (e.g., stated performance goals in measurable terms and collection and use of data to assess students' ability to reach identified goals), now evident in all accrediting standards, was first observed in the professionally accredited areas such as engineering (Accreditation Board for Engineering and Technology [ABET]) and business and management (Association to Advance Collegiate Schools of Business [AACSB]). An important benefit of this shift is that it allows institutions and programs to determine the specific criteria on which they will be judged rather than having an external group determine the specific structure and content of the curriculum. (For a review of these changes, see www.ou.edu/idp/materials/accrediting.htm.)

In requiring clear and measurable goals for student learning, a cohesive curriculum should be designed to provide students with the opportunity to reach these goals. Courses should include assessment to determine the extent to which these goals are reached. In addition, a professional development program that provides faculty, administrators, and staff with the knowledge and skills required to reach stated goals is essential. These standards require a focus on teaching and learning that does not exist on many campuses. Thus, while this new emphasis would seem to be good news, the problem at most institutions is that faculty and staff may not be adequately prepared for these roles in the new learning paradigm (Tagg, 2003).

TABLE 2.1

Forces for Change: Impacts on Academic Affairs

Forces for Change	Possible Institutional Responses
I. Fiscal/Financial	
Decreasing state and federal support	Restructure academic programs to be cost efficient while improving academic quality
Decreasing foundation assistance	
Increasing operating costs	Eliminate duplication of programs and courses
Increasing or decreasing enrollments in the institution or in specific programs	Eliminate low-enrollment and low-priority programs
	New configurations of academic units (combining departments or schools/colleges)
Decreasing enrollments	Limit expensive faculty research to high-priority areas
Increased costs of nonfunded federal mandates	Place higher priority on faculty and staff activities that support institutional priorities
Increased costs of technology	More efficient scheduling of teaching/classes
Increased cost of deferred maintenance	Expand the use of technology to reduce instructional cost per student
	Restructure budget systems to support instructional priorities
	Increase emphasis on fundraising to support academic priorities
	Increase collaboration/resource sharing between institutions (i.e., academic programs, libraries, and other service areas)
II. Teaching and Learning	
Demands for improved quality	Redesign of courses and curricula with intended learning outcome statements and associated data collection and use
Demands for increased accountability	
Demands for increased community involvement	Increase emphasis on faculty development
Accreditation standards for learning outcome and performance indicators	Direct the relationship between stated intended outcome goals and student assessment
	Expand the use of technology to improve instructional effectiveness
	Increase application of research on learning, student development, and pedagogy

Forces for Change	Possible Institutional Responses
	Expand scope of scholarship to support research on new approaches to learning, teaching, course/curriculum design
	Expand individualization of instruction
	Expand students' opportunities for internships and professional/job related experiences
	Increase use of peer teaching and small group interactions

Forces for Change	Possible Institutional Responses
III. Students	
Increasing enrollment	Increase cooperation and integration between student affairs and academic affairs
Increasing diversity	
Increasing number of under-prepared students	Increase attention paid to prerequisites and students with advanced study or work experience
Increasing percentage of adult and part-time students	Increase in credit and time flexibility
	Improve use of available student time
Increasing numbers taking courses from two or more institutions	Develop systems that facilitate the transferring of credit
Increased number of students taking college-level courses in high school	Increase use of nontraditional courses, including web-based or distance formats
Increased number of students with work experience	More flexibility in course requirements and use of exemptions

Forces for Change	Possible Institutional Responses
IV. Faculty	
More diversity, including more women	Increase faculty grants to support instruction-related activities
Changing priorities of faculty with more emphasis on non-institution-related activities	Increase attention to interpersonal relations, team building
Continuing growth in part-time positions	Increase flexibility in the tenure system and the use of part-time tenure positions for designated periods
Increasing number of retirements	Increase part-time positions with longer term appointments and improved benefits
	Restructure reward systems to relate more directly to the mission and vision of the institution, and to school, college, and academic unit priorities

Forces for Change	Possible Institutional Responses
	Changing faculty roles, more time spent in community with professional development viewed as an integral part of assignment
	Reduce reliance on lecturing, more contact with students, with small groups, on assessment, and on course and curriculum design
	Scope of scholarly activities expanded. Greater attention paid to the quality and significance of scholarly activities

V. Competition and Technology

Increased competition from the for-profit sector	Increase in off-campus programs and learning opportunities
Increased competition from other institutions	Reduce cost of income-producing programs with associated use of technology
Increased availability of technology	Increase attention paid to the benefits of direct contact with faculty and other students in traditional residential institutions
	Increase emphasis on quality of programs and deliverable outcomes
	Increase emphasis on skills and knowledge needed for success after graduation
	Identify institution's unique strengths and establish priorities accordingly
	Increase in use of distance learning and nontraditional delivery options

The Elements of a Successful Change Process

The significant kind of organizational change required to implement the various initiatives described in Table 2.1 is not beyond the reach of colleges and universities. However, it will require effort and commitment on the part of administrators, faculty, and staff—and attention to shifting priorities and the change process. Fortunately, the research on change, and on teaching and learning, provides guidelines about prerequisite conditions, steps in the change process, and the characteristics of the campus climate that must be established if change initiatives are to be successful. These include:

- The importance of a clearly articulated institutional mission and vision statement that addresses the needs of students and society and is supported by administrators, faculty, and staff of the institution

- Departmental or divisional priority statements that specifically support the institution's mission and vision

- Students' learning and development at the center of the institution (while the research mission of major universities will remain a priority, it must be balanced with the institution's teaching mission)

- Research on change and leadership, learning and teaching, and knowledge of the institution's culture taken into account in all decision-making

- Leadership for change effectively integrated throughout the institution (see the following section)

- Institutional leaders with a vision for their institution and a clear understanding of their specific roles in the change process

- Administrative and faculty leaders who are knowledgeable and skilled in such areas as institutional change, teaching, learning, leadership, and technology, and clear about their own strengths and weaknesses

- Rewards and recognition for those units and individuals who are successful in meeting the stated institutional priorities

- Decision-making based on continuous monitoring of the quality of learning through the collection and use of assessment data

- Professional development of faculty and staff to support institutional initiatives

- Academic leaders working collaboratively to explore new structures, procedures, and relationships

- A willingness to test all previous assumptions

- Commitment to change at all levels of the institution—faculty, administrators, students, and staff[1]

Without attention to these conditions, lasting reform will be a struggle with an all too predictable outcome. Campus leaders must lead the way and take key steps to determine the actions that will lead to a successful and lasting change initiative. Fortunately, on most campuses, talents and resources abound that, if used well, can play important roles in this process.

An Integrated Model of Academic Reform

As noted, fundamental and long-lasting changes require that 1) campus leaders at all levels of the institution (trustees, president, vice presidents, deans, chairs, directors, and faculty leaders) have both a clear set of common goals and priorities and the knowledge and skills necessary to provide the leadership their roles require, and 2) all units of the institution (academic affairs, student affairs, development, budget, and physical plant) are willing to work together toward these common goals. This is a tall order, to be sure.

GETTING STARTED

Establishing a Sense of Urgency and Setting Priorities

While each of the forces for change identified in Table 2.1 may affect all colleges and universities to some degree, it is important to note that the significance will differ from institution to institution. Budget cuts in some states are far more drastic than in others, private institutions have to address different challenges than those in the public sector, the academic backgrounds of students vary considerably across institutions, and deadlines for meeting the new accreditation standards can be quite different from institution to institution and from professional program to professional program.

Because institutions routinely pursue multiple agendas simultaneously, campus leaders must determine which specific forces for change need to be addressed, by whom, and in what priority. Once these decisions are made, it is the further responsibility of this group to assign responsibility and to communicate a sense of urgency throughout the institution. Unless the need to change is clearly understood by faculty and staff, there will be little chance of any initiative being successful. Also keep in mind that the hard work associated with dealing directly with most of these forces will need to be done at the school, college, or department level, or in the support unit where alternative solutions will need to be explored and specific actions will need to be taken.

Developing an Action Plan

There are few institutions that will need to start from scratch to address these issues. A significant body of literature exists to assist in the change process. Once problems are identified and priorities are established, the next step that leadership should take is to review the literature on organizational change and leadership as a background for developing an institutional action plan. A list of recommended resources will be found at the end of this chapter. Review of the literature should be followed by a careful analysis of existing campus resources such as academic support offices and faculty expertise that could be used effectively to facilitate and implement the change process. Academic leaders must keep in mind that implementing major reform requires action on their part, but they cannot do it alone, since they may not have either the time or the depth of expertise needed in key areas. Delegating the responsibility for implementation to key offices and focusing on their roles as campus leaders is an important challenge for administrators. The very fact that priorities are established and communicated and that leadership responsibilities are assigned at a high level in the institution also plays a key role in establishing a sense of urgency for initiatives that follow.

The Institutional Change Agency

Although the first response to the need for advice and guidance may be to turn to national experts, it is important to keep in mind that outside consultants can help an institution develop an action plan, communicate a sense of urgency, and provide specialized assistance in a number of areas, but they are often unavailable for sustained involvement and are far too expensive to rely on for the day-to-day activities that will be required. In addition, consultants are often perceived by faculty and staff as outsiders to institutions, significantly limiting their ability to participate in many of the difficult conversations that will be required. It makes good sense for institutions to establish their own agencies (offices, departments, or units) to provide the coordination, facilitation, and technical assistance that administrators, faculty, and staff will need. It may be tempting to appoint a committee or task force for such initiatives, but, in fact, change is an ongoing process and establishing a centralized location for work in this area clearly signals that change is here to stay.

A single coordinating agency is suggested for a number of other reasons. First, it cuts down on duplication of effort and competition for scarce resources. Second, it makes it easier for faculty and staff to identify and use the services that are provided, and third, it enhances your outcome by allowing for a combination of related talents and expertise. Although the size of this office will be directly related to the size of the institution, there are key services that should be available through this agency.

- *Professional development.* Offering workshops, leadership seminars, and consultation to faculty, administrators, and staff with a focus on using the research on learning and student development, change, and pedagogy. Programs to focus on include such topics as technology, new forms of instruction, writing learning outcomes, leadership, and assessment.

- *Course and curriculum design.* Assisting faculty in reviewing existing programs, curricula, and courses, in designing new offerings, and in writing and evaluating outcome statements for all courses and programs.

- *Assessment and evaluation.* Assisting faculty, administrators, and staff in the design of data collection strategies and in reporting and interpretation of data.

- *Facilitation.* As experts with process skills and as neutral chairs of key committees and task forces, this role allows institutions to avoid the problems associated with having chairs of these groups also advocate for a particular unit or approach. A neutral approach provides objectivity and expertise in group process, which are important when emotionally charged changes are being explored.

Locating the Center

Where the unit responsible for such work resides in the organizational structure is an important variable and signals to the campus community the relative importance of the change process and initiatives. Ideally, the unit would be located in the office of the provost or chief academic officer. This location not only recognizes the importance of the work of the agency but can eliminate institutional red tape by reducing competition among service providers. Such affiliation also allows the chief academic officer of the institution to directly establish its priorities and determine its scope of work.

Staffing the Center

Fortunately, much of the expertise to support change already exists on most campuses in the faculty, instructional, or teaching center; in the office of institutional research, library, or technology center; and within the faculty. What this chapter proposes is that all of these talents can be located in a single unit charged specifically with facilitating and implementing the desired actions. Ideally, this unit has two important characteristics. First, its staff are perceived as professional support personnel to the entire institution. Second, new programs and initiatives that are cooperatively developed with faculty or staff from other units of the institution are not placed within this agency or center once they are operational but within their appropriate academic home. This is essential if the unit is to be perceived as an office whose primary goal is to help others to be successful. It also allows the staff of the unit to move on to other priorities when a project is completed. This office becomes, in effect, the campus "strike force" for organizational change. If additional support funds for such an office are limited, and they often are, it may make sense to explore a combination of a full-time leadership and clerical staff with part-time faculty and technical appointments in specialized areas.

Expanding the Role of Faculty, Instructional, or Teaching Centers

Most campuses today include a center or office for teaching, academic excellence, or instruction. As one option, institutions can expand the role of this office that exists on many campuses. This approach has a number of advantages.

- The unit most likely is already located in the academic affairs office.

- The unit is already perceived as a source of support by faculty and staff.

- The unit most likely already includes a staff of professionals knowledgeable about research on teaching, learning, assessment, and evaluation, who have experience in helping faculty write learning outcomes and in offering workshops and seminars, and on some campuses, expertise with use of technology. In addition, most units include staff with the process skills that are ideal for facilitating working groups.

- These units may also have support and production staff to assist with such activities as editing, graphic design, and technology.

While few units will have all of the needed competencies or the number of staff members that may be required, these offices, by their very nature, are ideally staffed and located to serve in the role of change agents. While some of the required staff may currently be housed part-time in the technical support offices, the library, or on the faculty, a central unit has the potential to significantly reduce competition between support offices by facilitating an open discussion before major, and often quite expensive, instructional options are identified. The individual chosen to lead such a unit must have high-level process skills, a focus on organizational change, and most importantly, not be an advocate of any single solution. This person must also be respected both by faculty and institutional leaders.

Staff Development

Many of the skills and much of the knowledge that will be required for an institutional change agency can already be found on most campuses; however, some important skills may need to be developed or refreshed. As a result, early attention must be paid to staff development. This should not be surprising, since the full range of potential initiatives described in Table 2.1 will be relatively new to most institutions. The need for planned staff training becomes even more important when key activities need to be undertaken simultaneously across an institution, requiring the use of other faculty and staff on a part-time basis—individuals who will need to be carefully selected and then prepared for their specific assignment.

Table 2.2 is a checklist that can be used to help determine any gaps in essential knowledge and skills on your campus, the first step in designing a professional development program for agency staff. Keep in mind that no one individual can be expected to have all the needed knowledge and specialized skills identified, and that while some of the knowledge and skills are appropriate for all staff members, others, requiring specialization, must exist but not in every staff member. Much of the knowledge required is available in the references identified in the Resource section at the end of this chapter, but some specific skill development may be needed for some staff. Workshops and seminars addressing many of these skill areas are available through the Professional and Organizational Development Network in Higher Education (POD) and the American Association for Higher Education (AAHE), and via a number of entities that offer workshops on leadership and change. In some cases, it may be most cost effective to offer specific topic workshops for staff and faculty on your own campus.

TABLE 2.2

A Checklist for Change Agency Staff

	Level of Proficiency			
Area	High	Medium	Low	Do Not Have
I. Knowledge				
An understanding of the literature and research on:				
• Organizational theory as it applies to colleges and universities	☐	☐	☐	☐
• Mission and vision development	☐	☐	☐	☐
• Leadership (motivation and change)	☐	☐	☐	☐
• Leadership (management and governing)	☐	☐	☐	☐
• Teaching, learning, and teaching techniques	☐	☐	☐	☐

	Level of Proficiency			
Area	High	Medium	Low	Do Not Have
• Technology	☐	☐	☐	☐
• Course and curriculum design	☐	☐	☐	☐
• Evaluation and assessment	☐	☐	☐	☐
• Group processes	☐	☐	☐	☐
• Advising	☐	☐	☐	☐
• Grant writing	☐	☐	☐	☐

II. Skills

The ability to effectively:

	High	Medium	Low	Do Not Have
• Select, manage, and implement priority projects	☐	☐	☐	☐
• Participate as a member of a team	☐	☐	☐	☐
• Lead groups	☐	☐	☐	☐
• Select members of a team	☐	☐	☐	☐
• Assist faculty in designing courses/curricula	☐	☐	☐	☐
• Assist faculty in writing learning outcomes	☐	☐	☐	☐
• Design, administer, and interpret surveys, tests, and other data collection instruments	☐	☐	☐	☐
• Assist faculty in selecting appropriate instructional approaches and technologies	☐	☐	☐	☐
• Assist faculty in the design of instructional materials, both media and print based	☐	☐	☐	☐
• Edit materials	☐	☐	☐	☐
• Design workshops, seminars	☐	☐	☐	☐
• Assist faculty and administrators in grant writing	☐	☐	☐	☐
• Assist in budge preparation	☐	☐	☐	☐

IN SUMMARY

Colleges and universities are increasingly being confronted by forces that call for major changes in their structures, their priorities, and the roles of faculty, students, and staff. At the same time, more students with greater needs must be served with fewer resources. While those in top leadership positions have the responsibility for establishing and communicating a sense of mission and vision and for providing direction and priorities, they certainly do not have the time and may lack the professional expertise needed for facilitating and directing the many campus-wide initiatives that will be required. For this reason, a centrally located unit charged with facilitating and supporting the various interrelated change activities is proposed.

Without such a cost-effective office, major institutional reform will remain a troublesome challenge with all the related accreditation problems. The problems every institution will face in the next decade are both urgent and complex, and we cannot delay any longer in addressing them. We have the knowledge and skills to do what needs to be done. Whether each campus has the willingness, the leadership, and the dedication to do so is another matter.

ENDNOTE

[1]Modified from Diamond, R. M. (2002). *Field guide to academic leadership*. San Francisco, CA: Jossey-Bass. Pages xxx–xxxi.

RESOURCES

The Academic Change Library

Basic Resources: There are two references that are recommended for reading by decision makers as they begin to develop an action plan for their institution and for those in leadership roles at the school, college, department, and unit levels as well as those in the institutional change agency.

Kotter, J. (1996). *Leading change*. Boston, MA: Harvard Business School Press.

> This easy-to-read, practical volume describes an excellent model for change that can be easily adapted to higher education. Academic leaders who have used it have found it to be extremely helpful.

Diamond, R. M. (Ed.). (2002). *Field guide to academic leadership*. San Francisco, CA: Jossey-Bass

> This book, from the National Academy for Academic Leadership, is designed to provide basic information on a range of key topics. National leaders address topics and issues of interest to academic leaders at all levels: administrative issues and leadership; institutional culture; mission and vision statements; the latest research on learning, student development, and teaching; course and curriculum design and evaluation; faculty roles and rewards; technology; advising; diversity; collaboration between academic affairs and student affairs; and supportive budget structures. Also included are chapters addressing specific leadership issues by position, a number of checklists for change agents, and annotated bibliographies of references for additional information.

Other key resources for anyone involved in rethinking educational processes.

Research on Teaching and Learning
Gardiner, L. F. (1996). *Redesigning higher education: Producing dramatic gains in student learning* (ASHE-ERIC Higher Education Report, 23[7]). San Francisco, CA: Jossey-Bass.

Assessment
Palomba, C. A., & Banta, T. W. (1999). *Assessment essentials: Planning, implementing, and improving assessment in higher education.* San Francisco, CA: Jossey-Bass.

Teaching
McKeachie, W. J., & Associates. (2002). *Teaching tips: Strategies, research, and theory for college and university teachers* (11th ed.). Boston, MA: Houghton Mifflin.

Course and Curriculum Design—The Process
Diamond, R.M. (1997). *Designing & assessing courses & curricula: A practical guide* (Rev. ed.). San Francisco, CA: Jossey-Bass

Promotion, Tenure, Scholarship, and Faculty Rewards
See the wide range of publications on these topics from Anker Publishing (www.ankerpub.com), including materials and guide books on serving on promotion and tenure committees, preparing institutional and department guidelines, preparing personal professional portfolios, and for faculty preparing for review.

REFERENCES

Swail, W. S. (2002, July/August). Higher education and the new demographics: Questions for policy. *Change, 34*(4), 15–23.

Tagg, J. (2003). *The learning paradigm college.* Bolton, MA: Anker.

3

Leading Change: Creating a Culture of Assessment

Patricia M. Dwyer
Shepherd College

In Leading Change, *John Kotter (1996) outlines an eight-step process to effect major organizational change. At Shepherd College, the assessment process that evolved into a culture of assessment mirrors the steps that Kotter describes. In 1998, Shepherd College found itself in a predicament that many colleges and universities can relate to: slated for an accreditation visit in 2002 with campus assessment efforts stalled at every turn. A new director organized an assessment task force, established a template for assessment plans and reports, and began grassroots education about assessment. Over the four years, a vision that aligned assessment with improving student learning effected dramatic changes in attitudes about assessment.*

INTRODUCTION

Shepherd College is part of the public school system of West Virginia. Located in the historic eastern panhandle of West Virginia and perched on the Potomac River, the school attracts students primarily from West Virginia, Virginia, Maryland, Washington, D.C., and Pennsylvania. Approximately 4,000 students are enrolled in 197 undergraduate majors, minors, and concentrations. The college also has a community college component and is currently developing selected graduate programs.

LEADING CHANGE

How does one lead change? Is change a top-down initiative, a grassroots movement, or some combination of the two? Successful assessment programs and organizations that have experienced transformation point to a model of leadership that taps the resources and talents of the group. The outcome is a common sense of purpose and responsibility—a vision that can be embraced by the entire community. In *The Dance of Change,* Senge et al. (1999) define this kind of leadership "as the capacity of the human community to shape its future, and specifically to sustain the significant processes of change required to do so" (p. 6). The human community that Senge describes sustains a certain "creative tension, [that is,] energy generated when people articulate the vision and tell the truth (to the best of their ability) about current reality" (p.16). Creative tension is at the heart of the scenario that Loacker and Mentkowski (1993) explore in their essay "Creating a Culture Where Assessment Improves Student Learning." They describe Alverno College President Sister Joel Read's call for the faculty to engage in a process of critical inquiry to inform curricular change. The key to success in moving through these turbulent waters was asking the critical questions—what kind of person are we as educators seeking to develop?—and involving both faculty and administrators in formulating the answers. Loacker and Mentkowski point to the sense of co-responsibility that contributed to the college's transformation.

KOTTER'S THEORIES ON EFFECTING CHANGE

At the 2002 Professional and Organizational Development Network in Higher Education conference in Atlanta, I was fortunate to participate in Dr. Ann Lucas's workshop on nurturing leadership skills in department chairs. In her presentation, Dr. Lucas presented John Kotter's theoretical model for understanding ways that change takes hold and becomes effective in an organization. As I listened to her exploration of Kotter's eight-step process, I was struck with how similar the process was to the incorporation of our assessment program at Shepherd College. At the outset of this chapter, let me thank Ann for introducing me to Kotter's theory.

Kotter's eight-stage process of creating major change is outlined in his book *Leading Change* (1996). These are:

Step 1. Establishing a Sense of Urgency

- Examining the market and competitive realities

- Identifying and discussing crises, potential crises, or major opportunities

Step 2: Creating a Guiding Coalition

- Putting together a small group with enough power to lead the change
- Getting the group to work together like a team

Step 3: Developing a Vision and a Strategy

- Creating a vision to help direct the change effort
- Developing strategies for achieving that vision

Step 4: Communicating the Change Vision

- Using every vehicle possible to constantly communicate the change vision
- Having the guiding coalition role model the behavior expected of employees

Step 5: Empowering Broad-Based Action

- Getting rid of obstacles
- Changing systems or structures that undermine the change vision
- Encouraging risk taking and nontraditional ideas, activities, and actions

Step 6: Generating Short-Term Wins

- Planning for visible improvements in performance, or "wins"
- Creating those wins
- Visibly recognizing and rewarding those people who made the wins possible

Step 7: Consolidating Gains and Producing More Change

- Using increased credibility to change all systems, structures, and policies that don't fit together and don't fit the vision
- Hiring, promoting, and developing people who can implement the change vision
- Reinvigorating the process with new projects, themes, and change agents

Step 8: Anchoring New Approaches in the Culture

- Creating better performance through customer- and productivity-oriented behavior

- Articulating the connections between new behaviors and organizational success

- Developing a means to ensure leadership development and succession

The eight-step process that Kotter identifies interfaces with the assessment process implemented on Shepherd's campus and helps to explain why the assessment process succeeded, that is, that a true culture of assessment developed over time, and more importantly, has been sustained beyond the accreditation visit that created the initial urgency. The following section describes the connections between Kotter's steps and the successful process for implementing assessment at Shepherd College.

MAKING THE CONNECTIONS

Step 1. Establishing a Sense of Urgency

- Examining the market and competitive realities

- Identifying and discussing crises, potential crises, or major opportunities

Facing an accreditation visit was all the urgency we at Shepherd College needed. But the major opportunities cited in this stage can provide a more positive spin to the urgency that gets a campus to move forward with an assessment process. Some opportunities may include a call to major curricular reform as in the case of Alverno College, a realignment of schools or programs, outside funding for a particular project that demands assessment, and so forth. Urgency does not have to be equated with panic. Integral to a good assessment program is collection of data and reflection on the learning goals of a program. Often faculty and administrators need a jump-start to make these activities a priority.

Step 2: Creating a Guiding Coalition

- Putting together a small group with enough power to lead the change

- Getting the group to work together like a team

Shepherd College had formed a plethora of assessment committees, but very little action had been taken. When putting together a guiding coalition, the director invited selected faculty and staff members who would work well together and would be good ambassadors for the assessment program. In addition, the name change to Assessment Task Force contributed to the different tone that the group hoped to communicate. Unlike other committees that tend to be top-heavy with administrators, the task force had one dean who represented the other administrators. Staff, faculty, and, most importantly, students were invited to participate. The task force met once a month and planned assessment workshops, helped departments construct assessment plans and reports, and generally offered assistance where needed.

Step 3: Developing a Vision and a Strategy

- Creating a vision to help direct the change effort

- Developing strategies for achieving that vision

This step was perhaps the most important in the assessment process. Our vision took the form of connecting assessment to improving student learning. That was the mantra whenever the director was discussing assessment issues with chairs or faculty, staff or students. The assessment office became Assessment of Student Learning—the secretary answered the phone with that phrase, the office stationery communicated that message, every newsletter and announcement always linked assessment and student learning. At this same time, the director proposed that a statement be added to the institutional mission that would highlight the importance of improving student learning. The following was added to the college mission statement in 2000: "Student learning is central to the culture of our institution, finding ways to improve student learning is a continuous process."

Strategies for achieving the vision included yearly assessment plans and reports from each department and unit. While this cycle demanded a quick turnaround to complete the assessment loop, it also provided more immediate feedback (and deadlines) for departments who were starting assessment activities for the first time. In addition, departments identified three—and only three—learning goals to be assessed each year. This kept the process from seeming overwhelming, especially for beginners.

To support assessment efforts, the director invited departments to go off campus for an assessment retreat. The Office for Assessment of Student Learning made arrangements and paid for meals, and the director offered to facilitate a discussion with the department about program learning goals. Throughout the academic year, the director organized grassroots faculty development opportunities to continue educating the campus about assessment.

Step 4: Communicating the Change Vision

- Using every vehicle possible to constantly communicate the change vision

- Having the guiding coalition role model the behavior expected of employees

In communicating the vision, the Office for Assessment of Student Learning created a newsletter, *Assessment of Student Learning at Shepherd*, that showcased assessment's link to student learning; initiated a speaker series, Focus on Student Learning, with faculty and staff as guest speakers presenting topics of interest; and organized a brown-bag lunch discussion group, Food for Thought, on issues of teaching and learning.

The guiding coalition, our Assessment Task Force, served as support for the campus, and in communicating with departments or individuals, it always linked assessment with student learning. The task force members reviewed yearly plans and gave feedback and advice about the format of the plan. Thus, they made sure that each plan was linked to the mission, had three learning outcomes to be assessed, had two means of assessing each outcome (both direct and indirect), and had a benchmark to determine success. Task force members would not comment on the actual outcomes being assessed but only gave feedback on the components of a good plan.

Step 5: Empowering Broad-Based Action

- Getting rid of obstacles

- Changing systems or structures that undermine the change vision

- Encouraging risk taking and nontraditional ideas, activities, and actions

Getting rid of obstacles? Perhaps a more accurate description on our campus was working around the obstacles. For example, the director called her team a task force rather than a committee. This kept the group from stepping on the toes of already established assessment committees who were not moving the process forward. In addition, the task force was housed under strategic planning rather than the faculty senate, known for its propensity to stall or obfuscate important issues.

Early on in the assessment process, the task force wanted to encourage departments to assess those outcomes that would be more risky; in other words, departments should not assess only those outcomes that felt safe or ones that were guaranteed to produce good numbers. Thus, the task force created a campus philosophy of assessment in which it asserted that assessment results would not be used for punitive purposes.

Initially, each department was automatically awarded $500 to defray the cost of assessment materials. At the end of the first year under the new director, very little of the money had been utilized; other than ordering tests, most departments did not know how to use the money. In the second year, the director shifted to mini-grant applications and encouraged departments to apply for projects. After the first year of awards, projects were advertised to the general campus population as a way to generate more ideas for using assessment funds.

Step 6: Generating Short-Term Wins

- Planning for visible improvements in performance, or "wins"

- Creating those wins

- Visibly recognizing and rewarding those people who made the wins possible

Our "wins" in the first year were simply getting assessment plans and reports completed for each department/program. While they weren't perfect, the completion of the assessment loop gave departments some data to work with—and department members discovered that they could learn something about their programs that could be very valuable. As assessment cycles afforded more information to the departments, they were encouraged to use results in seeking budget increases.

We visibly recognized these wins by showcasing departments' assessment efforts in the newsletter or through the speaker series. In addition, we started a student achievement day; here students submitted proposals to present projects or papers to the school community.

Step 7: Consolidating Gains and Producing More Change

- Using increased credibility to change all systems, structures, and policies that don't fit together and don't fit the vision

- Hiring, promoting, and developing people who can implement the change vision

- Reinvigorating the process with new projects, themes, and change agents

Increased credibility for our assessment process came with the commendation we received on our assessment efforts from our North Central accreditation team. In 2002, the college also restructured and created the position of dean of teaching, learning, and instructional resources to expand on assessment activities and to develop a center for teaching and learning. New activities included student and faculty learning communities and a reinvigorated writing-across-the-curriculum program.

Step 8: Anchoring New Approaches in the Culture

- Creating better performance through customer- and productivity-oriented behavior

- Articulating the connections between new behaviors and organizational success

- Developing a means to ensure leadership development and succession

Our better performance included changes in the curriculum, prompted by assessment, to better meet student needs. Organizational success in our accreditation visit contributed to making assessment more a part of the fabric of the institution. New leadership has emerged through the faculty learning communities, the in-house speaker series, the interdisciplinary student learning communities that bring faculty together in teaching initiatives, and a summer teaching institute for faculty to revise a course based on active learning strategies.

CONCLUSION

Kotter's eight-step process of change provides a dynamic framework for adopting new programs like the assessment process at Shepherd College. Forming a guiding coalition and a vision provides the foundation and the inspiration for action; aligning resources to that vision and creating wins ensures that the change will last. Two years beyond our accreditation, departments and academic support units continue to explore ways to revise curriculum or change teaching strategies to improve student learning. While we were not aware of Kotter's theory at the outset of our process, we are gratified to know why it was successful.

REFERENCES

Kotter, J. P. (1996). *Leading change.* Boston, MA: Harvard Business School Press.

Loacker, G., & Mentkowski, M. (1993). Creating a culture where assessment improves learning. In T. W. Banta (Ed.), *Making a difference: Outcomes of a decade of assessment in higher education* (pp. 5–24). San Francisco, CA: Jossey-Bass.

Senge, P., Kleiner, A., Roberts, C., Ross, R., Roth, G., & Smith, B. (1999). *The dance of change: The challenges to sustaining momentum in learning organizations.* New York, NY: Currency Doubleday.

4

Evidence of the Transformational Dimensions of the Scholarship of Teaching and Learning: Faculty Development Through the Eyes of SoTL Scholars

Connie M. Schroeder
University of Wisconsin–Milwaukee

This analysis began from two unlikely starting points: a favorite Marcel Proust quote below that has nothing to do with faculty development, but could, and Pat Hutchings (2000) descriptive quote, "The scholarship of teaching and learning [SoTL] is characterized by a transformational agenda" (p. 8). Do SoTL faculty development programs foster transformation? Is there evidence of a transformational process and transformative learning? The project summaries of eight SoTL scholars were analyzed for evidence of transformation. The evidence for transformation of landscapes of learning, teaching, scholarship, and self are explored from SoTL scholars' perspectives in a faculty development program, providing insight into and support for transformational faculty development.

> The only real voyage of discovery . . . consists not in seeing new land-
> scapes but in having new eyes . . .
>
> —Marcel Proust

This captivating metaphor contains elements of transformation and a living paradox that we know to be true in our lives. Without going anywhere, we can journey someplace new. Careful unpacking of its meanings reveals principles relevant to the work of faculty development and the experience of transformative learning.

Marcel Proust claims that discovery through fresh eyes surpasses traveling to new surroundings. First, we acquire fresh eyes, and second, once we get the new eyes, we'll not only see differently, but actually make the voyage of discovery. His adage implies choice—that we can choose to have new eyes, or else what would be the point in admonishing us to do so? His challenge also implies a result—two transformations occur—in the one who sees, and that which is now seen. The shift in the seer precedes the shifting landscapes, and is required to make the real voyage of discovery. The transformations are so powerful that the experience surpasses actually being in a new place with new surroundings. The paradox, however, is in the result, in staying where we are and yet voyaging beyond what we already see. The earth has not moved under our feet and we have not gone anywhere. Yet somehow we have changed. What we see has changed, and these changes make as much difference as if we had physically traveled from where we originally stood and looked. Our vision shifts; the familiar landscapes transform; we voyage; and we discover.

It would be no small stretch to consider scholarship as a voyage of discovery—a voyage that may not take us very far physically. Familiar landscapes can become new through the journey of inquiry. The scholarship of teaching and learning calls the scholar to discover and make the voyage of inquiry. But does it call for transformation? When Pat Hutchings (2000) said, "The scholarship of teaching and learning [SoTL] is characterized by a transformational agenda" (p. 8), we can imagine transformation resulting along broad, institutional dimensions, or transformation of the individual. If we consider individual transformation, might Proust's paradox offer any insight into the process and outcomes of transformation through scholarly inquiry into teaching and learning? Though Proust surely was not speaking to faculty developers in higher education, perhaps he has something to say to us.

TRANSFORMATION THROUGH NEW EYES

We are familiar with the experience of acquiring new eyes in our daily lives that emerges out of intentional choice or through sudden flashes of insight. For example, when we experience "new eyes" unexpectedly, with little choice or effort, sudden insight may appear as an "aha" moment. We feel like we are seeing an old idea for the first time. It seems to strike us, as in a bolt of lightning. For example, on our walk home, the streetlight on the snow or wet pavement catches our eye in a way that seems to transform our predictable, once familiar street into a picturesque, European hamlet. At other times, in an instant, our close partner or child appears to us as if we are seeing them for the first time. A sense of wonder is evoked, and we gaze in surprise with rapt attention. We are mesmerized, if not transported, by a nuance or trait that hadn't shown itself before or in quite the same way. We are able to discover something novel among the myriad familiar characteristics we've already seen and looked at many times. This experience of acquiring new eyes may be more abstract and occur less visually when transforming familiar ideas, perspectives, and feelings. These sudden flashes and glimpses bring wonder, and delight, and color our all too familiar world with fresh scenery, texture, dimension, and hue, almost jarring us physically. We are moved. We have traveled. We discover.

Our acquisition of new eyes may emerge also from our hard work or intentional effort. For example, through sheer determined and fixed attention, we stare at a hologram trying desperately to see what is before us in a different way. We try to *will* a new perspective by looking intently. Similarly, in personal and professional situations, most of us have had an occasion in which we intentionally stepped back physically or emotionally in order to distance ourselves and gain a new perspective or renew the visual anatomy of our mind's eye. These acts are intentional as we free ourselves from familiar constraints in order to see differently than before, and may take more time.

FACULTY DEVELOPMENT AND TRANSFORMATION

The voyage occurs then, in living the paradox, in that mysterious intersection between the new seeing on the part of the viewer, observer, or participant, and that which is already there but able to be newly seen. We should not be surprised that learning about learning may require new eyes cast on the very familiar terrain of our teaching and learning in order to see new possibilities and begin new voyages of discovery. Does this happen in our faculty development programs or in how we approach faculty development? Is transformation an explicit goal when we think of improving teaching and learning? More importantly, what is transformation and how would we know it occurred?

A common goal in faculty development is to engage faculty in effective teaching. However, all too often, we direct our resources toward instructional improvement that aims to train faculty in new techniques through a primary focus on cognitive learning. Levinson-Rose and Menges (1981) reviewed literature on faculty development programs spanning the late 1960s until 1980. Most programs were technique oriented and prescriptive "without consideration of the faculty member's teaching or his or her prior knowledge and experience" (Cranton, 1994, p. 727). Traditional approaches may ignore the perspectives and beliefs faculty already have formed. Cranton (1994) claims it is unlikely that faculty have made explicit their assumptions about teaching and learning or the consequences of acting on those assumptions.

Robertson (1997) contrasts simple learning that "further elaborates the learner's existing paradigm, systems of thinking, feeling, or doing relative to the topic" with transformative learning that "causes the learner's paradigm to become so fundamentally different in its structure as to become a new one" (p. 42). Sokol and Cranton (1998) concur that adult educators have often assumed that learning about teaching is instrumental. This can lead to "forming practices rather than transforming practices" (Cranton, 1994, p. 734). Even participatory programs do not necessarily incorporate transformative learning processes. Our directive methods often include brief workshops and teaching tips as we aim to be both effective and efficient while imparting new knowledge and building new skills. These efforts can improve teaching and student learning and provide vital resources. However, brief exposure to how-to strategies, while important, do not provide the trusting and reflective contexts for critical discourse in which teaching and learning assumptions are challenged.

TRANSFORMATIVE LEARNING THEORY

Transformative learning was introduced by Mezirow (1997) as a change process that transforms frames of reference (Imel, 1998). His theory defines frames of reference as "the structures of assumptions through which we understand our experiences. They selectively shape and delimit expectations, perceptions, cognition, and feelings" (Mezirow, 1997, p. 5). According to this view, "actions and behaviors will be changed based on the changed perspective (Cranton, 1994, p. 730).

Several key elements of the transformational learning process are cited frequently in the literature. Initially, a disorienting dilemma, or "an activating event that typically exposes a discrepancy between what a person has always assumed to be true and what has just been experienced, heard or read" (Cranton, 2002, p. 66) and may contribute to a readiness for change (Taylor, 2000). Cranton (2002) describes this as a "catalyst for transformation" (p. 66). It could be a single event or a series of events that occur over a much longer period as in "an accretion of transformation in points of view" (Mezirow, 1997, p. 7). For example, engaging in problem solving may challenge and expose discrepancies (Mezirow, 1997; Taylor, 2000).

The literature highlights the central importance of cultivating a process of critical reflection with certain key elements (Mezirow, 1991; Sokol & Cranton, 1998). "Critical reflection is the means by which we work through beliefs and assumptions, assessing their validity in the light of new experiences or knowledge, considering their sources, and examining underlying premises" (Cranton, 2002, p. 65). Cranton (1994) explains, "Transformative learning theory leads us to view learning as a process of becoming aware of one's assumptions and revising these assumptions" (p. 730). Cranton (1994) simply states, "If basic assumptions are not challenged, change will not take place" (p. 739), and elaborates that we are more likely to have sets of assumptions that guide teaching practices. Sokol and Cranton (1998) further explain, "As transformative learners, they question their perspectives, open up new ways of looking at their practice, revise their views, and act based on new perspectives" (p. 14). Mezirow (1997) cautions, "learners need practice in recognizing frames of reference and using their imaginations to redefine problems from a different perspective" (p. 10). Several authors point out the necessity of making the time necessary for critical reflection (Pohland & Bova, 2000).

In addition to critical reflection that challenges assumptions, transformative learning calls for a trusting, social context for the dialogue referred to as reflective discourse (Mezirow, 2000) or critical discourse (Grabove, 1997). Cranton (1994) argues that the most promising transformative learning potential in faculty development work is long-term work with others, including "a group of faculty genuinely interested in teaching" (p. 735). Taylor (2000) found that the key ingredient most common in the process of transformational learning was the context of relationships. Imel (1998) concurs with the importance of establishing a community among learners.

Several sources emphasize individual agency; learners having their own design (Taylor, 2000); autonomous thinking; and control and choice (Grabove, 1997; Mezirow, 1997). Mezirow (1997) suggests that the educator serve as a facilitator or *provocateur,* in order to foster the self-direction and control needed for transformative learning. The role of the educator or faculty developer in transformative learning processes changes from that of a directive expert by shifting power, responsibility, and decision-making to the faculty (Cranton, 1994). Robertson (1997) writes extensively on the importance of creating a helper relationship. According to Baumgartner (2001), action on the new perspective, as in "living the new perspective" (p. 17), is critical for transformative learning to occur.

As opposed to the elements critical for the process of transformative learning, the outcomes indicative of transformation may include Cranton's (1992) framework of three types of change: change in assumptions, change in perspective, and change in behavior. Boyd (1989) claims an outcome of transformative learning includes a change in self.

Mezirow's theory and ideas have been expanded upon by several theorists in order to address his emphasis on the rational and linear aspects of transformation (Boyd, 1991; Grabove, 1997; Robertson, 1997). Baumgartner (2001) argues that "transformational learning is a complex process involving thoughts and feelings" (p. 18), and compares Dirkx's (1998) extrarational emphasis in which transformation involves soul-based learning that is not constrained by rational and cognitive learning. Grabove (1997) further emphasizes the potential for integration of self and other, renewal and rebirth as themes indicative of the nonrational dimensions of transformative learning. She suggests the transformative learner "moves in and out of the cognitive and the intuitive, of the rational and the imaginative, of the subjective and the objective, of the personal and the social" (Grabove, 1997, p. 95).

We might ask ourselves as faculty development professionals, do we offer programs that incorporate the processes that enable deeper understanding, discovery, or transformative change? Are we aiming for increasing knowledge and skills as primary program outcomes, but falling short of creating opportunities in which faculty can critically reflect, reconceptualize, and engage in soul learning? Wouldn't it make sense to imagine that at some point, in some faculty members' careers, they will seek deeper understanding and affective as well as cognitive transformation? Are we considering how, and are we willing to offer a palette of opportunities that include a broader array of learning and development? Though time and budgetary resources are stretched, must we provide only the most popular programs, and not venture into opportunities that may promise a different kind of development? Certainly not all faculty at all points in their careers would have the interest or time to invest in transformative change programs and, given time constraints, may prefer brief exposure to new techniques in order to improve their teaching. But the question facing faculty developers is not necessarily how to appeal to the masses, but rather, how to offer a diverse array of opportunities for improving teaching and learning that meet the needs of faculty at a variety of levels of involvement and development. What type of programs produce this type of transformation, and how would we determine evidence of transformation?

This empirical analysis of a SoTL program examines the experience of SoTL from the scholars' perspectives, in light of the theoretical literature on the process and outcomes of transformation. Looking at evidence of transformative learning through SoTL may help us to consider investing in programs soundly linked to individual change and which may better prepare faculty to advance sustained departmental and structural changes in teaching and learning that have not been able to occur in higher education (Lazerson, Wagener,

& Shumanis, 2000). Perhaps we have been selling learning and change short by investing in quick fixes in our faculty development efforts. In order to transform not only teaching and learning, but institutions and their structures, have we considered the value of transforming individuals, or individuals transforming themselves?

A SoTL PROGRAM AS A MODEL OF TRANSFORMATIVE LEARNING

Each year at the University of Wisconsin–Milwaukee (UWM), a Midwestern research intensive urban university, five center scholars are selected by the Center for Instructional and Professional Development (CIPD). The SoTL scholars submit proposals to participate in a yearlong SoTL program. Each individual scholar identifies an initial focus of inquiry around student learning, designs a rigorous research question and project, implements it, and reports and disseminates the results. Each scholar receives an $8,000 grant to use as he or she deems appropriate, and may choose to arrange a course buyout, for example, or hire a research assistant.

The group of center scholars meets three times over the summer for extended sessions to refine their questions and discuss articles about SoTL, their SoTL methodology, and preparation for the institutional review board (IRB) process. The group also meets previous center scholars and hears of their projects in detail. The extended summer sessions allowed the scholars to reflect on and discuss articles that challenged their assumptions about student learning and teaching, or to gain a clearer understanding of SoTL. Most of the discussions with the center scholars were informal, leisurely, and lively, involving personal exchanges over lunch and establishment of rapport. Toward the end of summer, we delved further into their research designs and problems with methodology. During the academic year, we focused on updates of their projects and discussed their emerging findings. Inevitably, stemming from a scholars' project focus, our conversation would hone in on some aspect of student learning, such as motivation or student expectations. As a group, we would explore our assumptions and their connection to the articles we read and to our teaching. The scholars often arranged additional one-on-one consultations with the CIPD staff on qualitative methods and finding relevant literature.

In the spring we attend the national conference of the American Association for Higher Education (AAHE), and the scholars submit a summary of their work in progress for conference dissemination. The year winds down with the scholars vigorously engaged in collecting and analyzing their data, or writing up their project summaries or articles for their disciplinary journals. Interestingly, the scholars frequently lamented ending our monthly meetings, expressing regret at no longer having the group experience, and were very willing to participate in our ongoing CIPD programs as facilitators, disseminators of their study, or as guest speakers at the future center scholar monthly meetings.

At the completion of their SoTL project, scholars prepare a five- to ten-page project summary that describes their SoTL project and findings, the process they undertook to begin and complete their project, and their reflections on the process. Each scholar uses similar standard headings as were used most to present the case studies in Hutchings (2000) including Framing the Question, The Context, Gathering the Evidence, Emergent Findings and Broader Significance, Conditions for Doing the Scholarship of Teaching and Learning, Benefits of the Work, and Lessons Learned. Clearly, the content and format of the project summaries differ from the format of the articles the scholars may submit to their disciplinary journals. Each year the newest center scholars submit their project summaries to be compiled into a monograph by the CIPD. Although the headings remain the same each year, a new monograph title is selected for each annual monograph. The monograph is distributed to faculty and teaching academic staff at campus teaching and learning events focused on SoTL (Schroeder & Ciccone, 2002, 2003).

As SoTL projects vary in their completion time, the annual monograph produced may contain summaries from several of the current SoTL scholars, as well as the previous year's center scholars, in order to provide at least five summaries in each monograph. In addition, one of the UWM project summaries in the second monograph was from a scholar in the University of Wisconsin Teaching Scholars Program designed for faculty and teaching academic staff with 10 or more years of outstanding teaching experience. With a primary focus on the scholarship of teaching, participants at mid-career can approach teaching and student learning in a scholarly way by designing a major course revision during the yearlong program. The teaching scholars meet several times a year for extended programs, institutes, and conferences. Therefore, the eight scholars in the monographs whose SoTL work was analyzed for this study are called SoTL scholars for the purposes of this study.

As assistant director of the CIPD at UWM, I assist the director in coordinating the Center Scholar Program and provide consultations to the scholars. I collect and co-edit the monograph, and consequently, I become very familiar with their individual experiences as well as their written project summaries.

My interest in transformational change through faculty development originates from my dissertation project focused on faculty as change agents. I investigated the individual and broader organizational change that can result from participation in a sustained, transformative faculty development program (Schroeder, 2001). Through qualitative case study, I looked at the individual and organizational conditions that fostered faculty involvement as change agents within their departments and beyond, stemming from participation in sustained faculty development programs. In pursuing this earlier research, I had been immersed in the literature on individual and organizational change, including transformational change (Mezirow, 1990), individual learning (Argyris & Schon, 1978; Miles & Fullan, 1992; Kozma, 1985; Senge, 1990), and reconceptualization and transformative faculty development (Bowden, 1989; Cranton, 1994, 1996; Gravett, 1996; Ho, 1998; Pintrich, Mart, & Boyle, 1993; Prawat, 1992; Ramsden, 1992; Trigwell & Prosser, 1996). This literature helped direct me to the deeper learning and transformation necessary for change in faculty beliefs and conceptions about teaching and learning, their faculty teaching practices, and involvement as change agents in broader organizational change around teaching and learning.

Having arrived at this institution just over two years ago, I reflected on the types of programs and change produced through participation in the existing faculty development programs offered at UWM. Since I often look at university life through the lens of individual and organizational change, I began to wonder about the center scholar SoTL program and to notice that the scholars' project summaries often referred to their experience with SoTL as a powerful process touching them along deeply personal, emotional, and cognitive dimensions. I wanted to delve further into whether participation in the SoTL scholar programs was a transformative experience, and if so, in what ways. I wondered if I would be able to determine evidence of the scholars' individual transformations from their writing.

GATHERING EVIDENCE OF TRANSFORMATIVE OUTCOMES

To gather evidence, I approached the project summaries as narrative, qualitative data in which the subjects reveal the process of their SoTL experience using the language and metaphors they were comfortable using to present their experience and findings. Documents and materials that the subjects have written and that already exist serve as qualitative data and provide rich descriptions (Bogdan & Biklen, 1992). Together, the two monographs comprised 150 pages of data. I reread the completed summaries from the previous two monographs twice more, noting themes and patterns of change as they emerged (Miles & Huberman, 1984). All of the eight scholars made references to individual change. After analyzing the data, the themes of landscapes of learning, teaching, scholarship, and self emerged. I selected key excerpts to extract from the original data that demonstrated transformation. McCall and Simmons (1969) describe this type analysis as analytical description.

As an indication of transformation, I first noted comments that used language, including *change, learned, discovered, enlightenment, shifted, new*, as well as the use of metaphors that indicated change. I then noted comments that specified what had changed or the type of change, as in *I now felt*... or, *I used to, but now I*... , or, *I no longer*... , or, *I had thought*... , indicating a change in feeling, perspective, practice, or way of being. Initially, I had not realized how often the scholars employed the language of vision and voyage or journey to discuss change in their summaries, as they had not spoken so metaphorically during our discussions. However, the use of *sight, vision, journey*, and *new perspectives* are common metaphors for transformation and change and were used very frequently by the SoTL scholars as well, and brought to mind Proust's familiar verses and affirmed once again that he, indeed, had something to say to us in faculty development.

I was curious whether the scholars thought the experience had changed them in broader terms, including their practices, perspectives, and selves, and if change occurred or was expressed along both cognitive and affective dimensions.

From the collected voyages into SoTL by the scholars, it was apparent that each spoke from his or her unique point of departure within a disciplinary terrain. Yet they share the very essence of transformation through new eyes. What can we learn about SoTL from the SoTL scholars using Proust's metaphor and paradox as a guide? How did faculty experience having new eyes to cast upon the terrain of teaching and learning? How did their fantastic voyages begin? What evidence of transformation did their individual summaries provide?

Landscapes of Learning

Every time we encounter a person gazing through binoculars, a telescope, or zoom lens, we cannot help but wonder what he or she is looking at. Just what are SoTL scholars seeing with new eyes? The subjects of their intense studied gazing through their SoTL work are varied and diverse, stemming from the questions and problems in their teaching and classroom interactions.

SoTL scholar Jude Rathburn (2002) examined how the use of technology helps or hinders student learning by examining multiple intelligence theory and learning theory in the consideration of instructional design. She explained,

Each assignment or in-technology exercise gives me a window through which I can gain a glimpse of students' attitudes, triumphs, and the struggles involved with learning new technology and applying those tools in new situations ... (p. 53)

Once the instructors have begun to ask questions, to approach their teaching with inquiry, they form questions or problematize learning (Bass, 1999). This begins the deliberate charting of a voyage to unfamiliar landscapes of learning.

All learning activities and dissemination of student work occurred through the web component in public forums. In addition, there were chat rooms and bulletin board forums strictly for "socializing." I wanted to look at how a sense of community might occur if students had an additional means of interacting beyond the classroom walls. (Rathburn, 2002, p. 83)

SoTL scholar Renee Meyers (2003) described how she began to look at learning.

I wanted to know more about "what is" happening in the group discussions that occur regularly in my classroom. I examined how students' use of evidence facilitated learning in group quiz discussions. I was interested in knowing more about "how" students communicated in these groups, and how that communication affected discussion learning outcomes. ... I decided to look more closely at students' use of evidence in this persuasive process. (p. 16)

SoTL scholar Kathryn Olson (2003) chose to study the cultivation of deep understanding in the revision of a Pro-seminar course. In order to see into learning, she "chose four quite different assignments" (p. 44) in the revised Pro-seminar course to examine with new eyes. Although she had designed and taught both versions of the Pro-seminar course, her SoTL project involved engaging the students in making "transparent [the] purposes of Pro-seminar assignments, as well as the course's role as a part of a larger graduate curriculum" (Olson, 2003, p. 42).

SoTL scholar Barb Daley (2002) investigated how constructivist teaching using concept mapping influences the learning processes of adult students in higher education. In her SoTL project, she "saw really significant changes in how students learned" (p. 23) each time she used concept mapping in her courses. She further explained,

> I began to think about how I could not only teach the content in my courses, but how I could also help adults to understand their own learning processes... I started to use concept mapping in the courses I was teaching and each time I used it, I saw really significant changes in how students learned... The funding allowed me to follow students for a year and see what impact the maps had on their learning. (pp. 22–23)

SoTL scholar Elizabeth Buchanan (2002) wanted to "look at the impact of a hybrid approach on undergraduate students and their learning experiences... [to discover] an alternative educational experience and environment ... [and to] ... look at how a sense of community might occur" (pp. 11–12) through interactions outside a physical classroom space. Buchanan emphasized the importance Cross and Steadman (1996) place on observing students while they are learning.

> Observing students in the act of learning, reflecting and discussing observations and data with teaching colleagues, and reading the literature on what is already known about learning is one way teachers can implement the scholarship of teaching. (p. 2)

Rathburn (2002), too, began to see changes in learning during her SoTL project and pointed out, "I can see improvement in the depth of analysis" (p. 53). Buchanan (2002) noted how the students in her SoTL project felt more comfortable in the class and participated more enthusiastically: "This learning experience required commitment from students and once they had bought into the course, learning became transparent and seamless" (p. 15).

However, the intentional, deliberate *looking in* that changed the scholars' familiar landscape of learning was not always affirming or comfortable. Their new vision of the landscape of learning was often accompanied by expressions of disappointment, uncertainty, surprise, puzzlement, and even discomfort as they uncovered false assumptions and gathered their surprising findings. For example, several scholars admitted, "What surprised me was that I could not prompt these goals with or without the software" (O'Malley, 2002, p. 45); "My growing disappointment with the superficiality of their responses signaled a great disparity between what I expected my students to believe about their role as learners and their actual beliefs... I was shocked to realize that many people do not share my technological enthusiasm" (Rathburn, 2002, p. 51); "I was puzzled and a little disappointed" by students who indicated they hadn't sensed improvement in their analytical or critical thinking skills (Aycock, 2003, p. 29). Daley (2002) expressed her surprise that some students explained that they did not use concept mapping because they did not have the software access, despite her instructions that they could construct the maps however they chose. SoTL scholar Lisa Dieker (2002) "was shocked to learn" (p. 37) that her novice teachers were intimidated by watching videos of expert teachers and expressed confusion and uncertainty about the expected learning. These uncomfortable surprises reinforce the importance of deliberately allowing oneself to challenge assumptions, to view the familiar with fresh eyes, and the necessity of going beyond what we think we know anecdotally about learning in order to transform.

Landscapes of Teaching
The voyage of discovery for the SoTL scholars included acquiring new perspectives on their teaching as well. Why is this distinct from seeing or experiencing changes in learning? As reward systems and faculty roles have evolved to value research over teaching, most faculty are not encouraged to look into their teaching. According to Shulman (1999), "Blindness and amnesia are the state of the art in pedagogy" (p. 16). This blindness characterizes the polar opposite of having cultivated a multiplistic view of teaching and the "turning it this way and that" (Aycock, 2003, p. 27). Huber and Morreale (2002) explain that the current state in teaching as one in which "... our colleagues may care deeply about their courses, but they do not usually see their own teaching and learning as a matter for scholarly inquiry and communication" (p. 25). Bass (1999) struggled with the difficulty of framing a crisis in learning as a line of inquiry, a set of questions that originated in his teaching and concurred with Grant Wiggins's (1996) explanation, "... we find it difficult to see when our teaching isn't clear or adequate" (as cited in Bass, 1999, p. 4). If it is hard to even see our teaching with our existing eyes, how will we come to see it with new eyes?

Fortunately, changes taking place outside of higher education have found their way into our colleges and universities and are forcing us to look harder at our teaching, and in some cases "... are encouraging innovation and leading many faculty to turn a critical eye on their own assumptions and traditional teaching practices" (Huber & Morreale, 2002, p. 8). New eyes are perhaps fashioned in part from critical eyes turned to focus on how our own assumptions affect our teaching and courses, and learning within our disciplinary fields. For example, the SoTL scholars became familiar with the SoTL work of Carnegie scholar and psychologist Bill Cerbin (1996), who admitted, "I began to think of each course...as a kind of laboratory...and along the way you can watch and see if your practices are helping to accomplish your goals..." (p. 53).

Can the mind's eye begin to shift in how it sees the familiar terrain of teaching? The scholars discovered this was possible. O'Malley (2002) developed a new perspective toward the familiar assumption that simply lecturing on a topic leads to student learning, despite his colleagues' frequent support of this conclusion. Buchanan (2002) expressed her transformation in teaching in terms of enlightenment: "I have a newfound sense of what quality teaching and learning really are.... One could consider my experience a form of enlightenment" (p. 15). Similarly, Daley (2002) reported her familiar ways of teaching had changed.

> I found myself very excited about this project because it allowed me to look at my teaching and ask questions that I felt could only help me become a better teacher.

> I chose to teach two groups of students to use a constructivist strategy called concept mapping... I followed these students during semester two to see if they continued to use concept maps and to find out how the use of maps impacted their learning. (p. 29)

Rathburn (2002) described how her view of her teaching underwent serious transformation as she became a learner herself.

> Now that I view my teaching as a quasi-experiment in progress, I am not as hard on myself as I used to be when an exercise or activity flops. I still have plenty of "terrible, horrible, no good, very bad days" in the classroom, but they are much less devastating. I have learned to view those experiences as opportunities to model my own process of critical reflection as I explain to students my rationale for trying something new or changing an approach that is ineffective. (p. 55)

Meyers (2003) referred to her transformation in teaching as she, too, became a learner through the work of SoTL.

> This study taught me that I need to help my students learn "how to argue" more successfully in group discussion. If I can find a way to teach that practice so students really learn how to argue effectively,

then they have acquired a skill that they can use across their lifespan. This research project opened my eyes to that need. (p. 21)

Skeptics may claim that it is impossible to change the landscape of teaching, that the structures are too deeply embedded that support research, which in turn affect how we see teaching. How can we afford to believe that our perspectives are impossible to change? It is our perspectives that should be forming our practices and the necessary accompanying and supportive structures and practices, and they should never be beyond the reach of questioning and revision. If we are complaining that the embedded structures, values, and beliefs are difficult, if not seemingly impossible, to change, might we look to the level and depth of change we are willing to support through the types of faculty development opportunities we provide?

If we recall, before the research model became firmly embedded in academia, teaching was a clear and established priority. We transformed our vision of teaching when our values and mission shifted and we adopted a research model largely inherited from German research universities. Our own history challenges our resistance to change, our pessimism about change, and should encourage us to invent programs that help move higher education to consider broader forms of scholarship that reinforce multiple facets of our institutional missions. From our past, we learn that the landscape of teaching can shift, and through SoTL faculty development programs, we can indeed be encouraged that transformation is possible. As one SoTL scholar pointed out,

> Perhaps, the great lesson learned throughout this project is that teaching can be reframed so that it no longer resides at the bottom of one's to do list. It can become an activity one wants to talk about with her colleagues, an activity one looks forward to each week or even each day; teaching is embraced as heartily as one's research activities where student learning is always at the fore of the research questions. (Buchanan, 2002, p. 16)

Landscapes of Scholarship
The voyages taken by the SoTL scholars reveal scholarship as connected work and as collaborative work through SoTL. In contrast to the often private and autonomous efforts of teaching and research, Meyers (2003) made new connections between her multiple faculty roles, transforming how she sees her scholarly research interests.

Another lesson I learned is that with SoTL it is quite possible for a faculty member to bring together both their research and instructional interests. In the past these two activities have been quite separate in my mind. But by doing this project, it was clear that I could meld my research and teaching interests in group communication, and by doing so, I could expand and enrich both my research and teaching activities. This was one of the first projects that I have ever done where these two aspects of my career came together so seamlessly. (p. 22)

Other scholars emphasized the impact that the collaborative structure of the SoTL scholar program had on their perceptions of scholarship. One scholar commented,

Working on a SoTL project with a group of other committed, engaged, and enthusiastic faculty members, served to remind me, and reinforce for me, my beliefs about how valuable groups can be in one's own learning process . . . I think the Center Scholars group is a great framework for doing SoTL research, and helped me see how valuable such groups can be for those of us doing research a bit out of the mainstream in the academy. (Meyers, 2003, p.22)

Rathburn (2002) found both connection and community in the collaborative aspects of the SoTL program.

I also feel connected to a dedicated community of scholars who recognize that teaching is worth doing well. I no longer feel like a lone voice in the wilderness—there are others who are learning and exploring right along with me. (p. 55)

The collaborative yearlong program with lively discussions at monthly meetings created a valued and supportive group that transformed another scholar's perspective on scholarship. As one scholar admitted, "One lesson I relearned from doing this project is the power of the 'group' in the research endeavor" (Meyers, 2003, p. 22).

Landscapes of Self

Parker Palmer (1998) challenges us to explore "the inner landscape of the teaching self" (p. 4). The self is a dimension of transformation that we seldom focus on or intentionally nurture, and we rarely create a space for dialogue about deeply personal changes. However, the scholars articulated this level and type of change. Buchanan (2002) experienced deeply powerful changes.

> Finally, my teaching will never be what students called "normal." The scholarship of teaching and learning provides a foundation from which the "norm" is called into question and critiqued . . . My participation as a Center Scholar changed the way I view myself and my role in students' educational experiences . . . I had changed as a result of the experience. (pp. 15–17)

Meyers (2003) revealed the transformation of her inner landscape. "Finally, I learned (or maybe re-learned) how much I value the teaching and learning process. In doing this project, my passion for the educational enterprise was rekindled (p. 22)."

How often do we hear these kinds of statements in higher education or within the parameters of faculty development programs? Involving faculty in revising their syllabus is exciting and essential. Involving faculty in scholarly voyages of inquiry into teaching and learning where transformation is possible is incredibly exciting, for them as well as us, and raises the likelihood of involvement in broader institutional change (Schroeder, 2001). The SoTL scholars from each of the four years of the program at UWM continue to give their time, expertise, and support to ongoing programs, again and again, without compensation. A web of discoverers and voyagers is spun around teaching and learning, creating a community of inquirers who have transformed.

Gathering Evidence of a Transformative Process

When we examine the experiences of faculty engaged in the work of the scholarship of teaching and learning, we find faculty achieve some of the same important ends of traditional faculty development workshops—improvement in teaching and student learning through the acquisition of knowledge about teaching and learning new teaching techniques and strategies. However, the process of engaging in SoTL work allows faculty to develop by way of a different route than that of workshops or skill-building and technique training resulting in a very different process and set of outcomes.

Convinced that the scholars had experienced transformational outcomes, I considered further how the program at UWM created a process that illustrated elements of transformative learning. I was prompted to examine the literature in order to compare the SoTL Center Scholar Program as a transformative learning process to the theoretical underpinnings of transformative learning.

Was there an initial disorienting dilemma or catalyst, for example? Bass (1999) explains that the SoTL provides an opportunity for faculty to see in their teaching a set of problems worth pursuing as an ongoing intellectual focus. (p. 3)

> There is then a tight connection between the shift to seeing teaching as an activity over time and a belief in the visibility and viability of teaching *problems* that can be investigated as scholarship, and not merely for the purpose of "fixing them." (p. 2)

According to Bass (1999) changing the status of the problem in teaching is a transformational change and a fundamental shift. We can begin to see how the challenge of seeing into teaching and reframing questions for SoTL inquiry entails having new eyes cast on our familiar classrooms contexts. The once familiar classroom landscape now looks different when we make the fundamental shift to engage in the "problematization of learning" (Bass, 1999, p. 1). This early stage of inquiry, forming a question and peering into learning, may serve as the catalyst for transformation or disorienting dilemma in which our teaching practices or student learning aren't working as planned. Our assumptions push closer to the surface. Transformation can begin, and the real voyage of discovery calls.

As shown in Table 4.1, I compared the components of the SoTL program at UWM with the transformative learning literature. From this careful analysis, I concluded that the Center Scholar Program created a unique process that clearly involves a number of elements central to the process of transformative learning.

For example, the proposal process and intensive discussions of the research questions provide the initial articulation of the scholars' assumptions about learning and teaching. The self-designed nature of a research project creates a clear opportunity for self-direction. The articles, discussions, consultations, and elements of surprise through data collection produce an ongoing challenge of assumptions and lively, critical discourse. Pohland and Bova (2000) and Cranton (1992, 1994) point out the importance of follow-up support activities to support the transformative leader. The scholars' ongoing involvement with CIPD illustrates the element of extended support. We remained an interconnected community; former scholars stop by for coffee, update us on their involvement in their departments, and recruit new scholars. The expressed intensity of connection and longing for interaction as scholars completed their projects reinforces Mezirow's (1990) claim that transformative learning is not an individual process, but, rather, involves processing more than information in order to explore alternative perspectives and the importance of critical discourse among colleagues.

TABLE 4.1
**A Comparison of the Elements of the UWM SoTL Program
With Transformational Learning**

SoTL Program Process	Transformational Learning Process
Classroom teaching concerns/event	Disorienting dilemma; catalyst event
Write/submit SoTL proposal • Refinement of proposal with CIPD Staff • Problematize learning	Articulate assumptions • Reflection • Critical reflection/challenge assumptions
SoTL scholar extended summer meetings • Refinement of questions • SoTL articles • Discussion of proposals • Discussion of articles • IRB process discussed • Previous scholars as guests	Articulate assumptions • Critical discourse • Critical reflection • Challenge assumptions • Revise assumptions
Literature review • Disciplinary journals • General education literature	Critical reflection • Challenge assumptions • Revise assumptions
Individual project design	Self-direction, independence, autonomy
Data collection	Self-direction, independence, autonomy
Analysis of data collected	Self-direction, independence, autonomy, reflection; revise assumptions
Findings	Self-direction, independence, autonomy, reflection; revise assumptions
Written project summaries	Critical reflection
Application of findings to teaching	Taking action, implementing new practices
Dissemination of project	Ongoing support/networking
Ongoing involvement with CIPD faculty development programs	Ongoing support/networking
Outcomes	*Transformative Learning*
Seeing new landscapes in: • Teaching • Learning • Scholarship • Self	• Perspectives • Feelings • Behavior • Soul-making

The additional research elements, particularly research of the SoTL kind, illustrate another of the many ways transformative learning can be implemented. Standards of scholarship and principles of transformative learning are both satisfied and evident through the UWM SoTL program. The literature suggests there are many dimensions, not one process, (Grabove, 1997), and no single mode (Cranton, 1997) of transformative learning.

CONCLUSION

The voyages made by the SoTL scholars share common experiences in traveling the depths of transformation. Both the SoTL Center Scholar Program process and the outcomes provide evidence consistent with the transformative change literature. The unique components of rigorous scholarly research through SoTL are seamlessly woven into and support transformative learning. Their voyages to new landscapes far surpass the mere changing of scenery. Excerpts from the writings of the travelers can help demystify the transformational agenda along individual dimensions and enable us to see how the choice to transform lies waiting along our familiar and daily paths of teaching.

We do not have to search hard to find evidence of deep change in the reflections of the eight SoTL scholars on their yearlong investment in a SoTL faculty development program. In fact, most of the comments about change carry a life-changing force of passion and transformation that we may only hope to encounter occasionally in our work and leisure lives. While standing on the familiar ground of their everyday practice of teaching, they felt the surprise and wonder that signaled they were indeed *looking in* on learning and teaching with new eyes, and the familiar landscapes they have known truly became unfamiliar, wonderfully unfamiliar. Aycock (2003) fittingly reminded his readers how T. S. Eliot (1964) described poetry as the ". . . making of the familiar strange, and the strange familiar" (p. 259). Their evidence of transformation through SoTL is not easily dismissed as mere touchy-feely experiences, though they readily admit being deeply influenced both cognitively and affectively. Their evidence challenges and confronts us as faculty developers to make possible programs that offer deep change, and may indeed play a critical role in fostering the type of broader change and structural adjustments necessary to transform higher education (Schroeder, 2001). Is their transformation not unlike the deeper understanding and life-changing transformation we strive for and intend for our students? We may embrace transformational agendas in our faculty development programs armed with the evidence of voyages of discovery through SoTL, and the zest of Dr. Seuss's lyrical reminder, "Oh, the places you'll go!" (Geisel, 1990, p. 11).

REFERENCES

Argyris, C., & Schon, D. (1978). *Organizational learning: A theory of action perspective.* Reading, MA: Addison-Wesley.

Aycock, A. (2003). Serendipity and SoTL: An ethnographic narrative. In C. Schroeder & A. Ciccone (Eds.), *Learning more about learning* (pp. 26–37). Milwaukee, WI: University of Wisconsin–Milwaukee, Center for Instructional and Professional Development.

Bass, R. (1999, February). The scholarship of teaching: What's the problem? *Inventio: Creative thinking about learning and teaching, 1*(1). Retrieved April 29, 2004, from http://www.doit.gmu.edu/Archives/feb98/randybass.htm

Baumgartner, L. M. (2001). An update on transformational learning. In S. B. Merriam (Ed.), *New directions for adult and continuing education: No. 89. The new update on adult learning theory* (pp. 15–24). San Francisco, CA: Jossey-Bass.

Bogdan, R. C., & Biklen, S. K. (1992). *Qualitative research for education: An introduction to theory and methods.* Needham Heights, MA: Allyn and Bacon.

Bowden, J. (1989). *Curriculum development for conceptual change learning: A phenomenographic pedagogy.* Paper presented at the sixth annual (international) Conference of the Hong Kong Educational Research Association, Hong Kong.

Boyd, R. D. (1989). Facilitating personal transformation in small groups, Part I. *Small Group Behavior, 20*(4), 459–474.

Boyd, R. D. (1991). *Personal transformation in small groups: A Jungian perspective.* London, England: Routledge.

Buchanan, E. (2002). Examining and promoting student learning through a hybrid course environment. In C. Schroeder & A. Ciccone (Eds.), *Models in our midst* (pp. 9–19). Milwaukee, WI: University of Wisconsin–Milwaukee, Center for Instructional and Professional Development.

Cerbin, W. (1996). Inventing a new genre: The course portfolio at the University of Wisconsin–La Crosse. In P. Hutchings (Ed.), *Making teaching community property: A menu for peer collaboration and peer review* (pp. 52–56). Washington, DC: American Association for Higher Education.

Cranton, P. (1992). *Working with adult learners.* Toronto, Ontario: Wall & Emerson.

Cranton, P. (1994, November/December). Self-directed and transformative instructional development. *Journal of Higher Education, 65*(6), 726–744.

Cranton, P. (1996). Professional development as transformative learning: New perspectives for teachers of adults. *Journal of Higher Education, 65,* 726–744.

Cranton, P. (1997). *New directions for adult and continuing education: No. 74: Transformative learning in actions: Insights from practice.* San Francisco, CA: Jossey-Bass.

Cranton, P. (2002, Spring). Teaching for transformation. In J. M. Ross-Gordon (Ed.), *New directions for adult and continuing education: No. 93. Contemporary viewpoints on teaching adults effectively* (pp. 63–71). San Francisco, CA: Jossey-Bass.

Cross, K. P., & Steadman, M. H. (1996). *Classroom research: Implementing the scholarship of teaching.* San Francisco, CA: Jossey Bass.

Daley, B. (2002). Facilitating adult learning in higher education. In C. Schroeder & A. Ciccone (Eds.), *Models in our midst* (pp. 21–31). Milwaukee, WI: University of Wisconsin–Milwaukee, Center for Instructional and Professional Development.

Dieker, L. (2002). Inquiry into video streaming. In C. Schroeder & A. Ciccone (Eds.), *Models in our midst* (pp. 35–39). Milwaukee, WI: University of Wisconsin–Milwaukee, Center for Instructional and Professional Development.

Dirkx, J. M. (1998). Transformative learning theory in the practice of adult education: An overview. *PAACE Journal of Lifelong Learning, 7,* 1–14.

Eliot, T. S. (1964). *Selected essays.* New York, NY: Harcourt, Brace, & World.

Geisel, T. (1990). *Oh, the places you'll go!* New York, NY: Random House.

Grabove, V. (1997, Summer). The many facets of transformative learning theory and practice. In P. Cranton (Ed.), *New directions for adult and continuing education: No. 74. Transformative learning in action: Insights from practice* (pp. 89–95). San Francisco, CA: Jossey-Bass.

Gravett, S. (1996). Conceptual change regarding instruction: The professional enhancement of faculty. *Journal of Staff, Program, and Organizational Development, 13*(3), 207–214.

Ho, A. S. P. (1998). A conceptual change staff development programme: Effects as perceived by the participants. *International Journal for Academic Development, 3*(1), 25–38.

Huber, M. T., & Morreale, S. P. (Eds.). (2002). *Disciplinary styles in the scholarship of teaching and learning: Exploring common ground.* Washington DC: American Association for Higher Education and the Carnegie Foundation for the Advancement of Teaching.

Hutchings, P. (2000). *Opening lines: Approaches to the scholarship of teaching and learning.* Menlo Park, CA: The Carnegie Foundation for the Advancement of Teaching.

Imel, S. (1998). *Transformative learning in adulthood.* Washington, DC: Office of Educational Research and Improvement. (ERIC Document Reproduction Service No. ED42326). Retrieved April 29, 2004, from http://www.cete.org/acve/docgen.asp?tbl=digests&ID=53

Kozma, R. (1985, May/June). A grounded theory of instructional innovation in higher education. *Journal of Higher Education, 56*(3), 300–319.

Lazerson, M., Wagener, U., & Shumanis, N. (2000, May/June). Teaching and learning in higher education, 1980–2000. *Change, 32*(3), 13–19.

Levinson-Rose, J., & Menges, R. (1981). Improving college teaching: A critical review of research. *Review of Educational Research, 51,* 403–434.

McCall, G., & Simmons, J. (1969). *Issues in participant observation: A text and reader.* Reading, MA: Addison-Wesley.

Meyers, R. (2003). An examination of students' use of evidence in group quiz discussions. In C. Schroeder & A. Ciccone (Eds.), *Learning more about learning* (pp. 15–23). Milwaukee, WI: University of Wisconsin-Milwaukee, Center for Instructional and Professional Development.

Mezirow, J. (1990). *Fostering critical reflection in adulthood: A guide to transformative and emancipatory learning.* San Francisco, CA: Jossey-Bass.

Mezirow, J. (1991). *Transformative dimensions of adult learning.* San Francisco: Jossey-Bass.

Mezirow, J. (1997, Summer). Transformative learning: Theory to practice. In P. Cranton (Ed.), *New directions for adult and continuing education: No. 74. Transformative learning in action: Insights from practice* (pp. 5–12). San Francisco, CA: Jossey-Bass.

Mezirow, J. (2000). Learning to think like an adult: Core concepts of transformation theory. In J. Mezirow & Associates (Eds.), *Learning as transformation: Critical perspectives on a theory in progress* (pp. 3–34). San Francisco, CA: Jossey-Bass.

Miles, M., & Fullan, M. (1992, June). Getting reforms right: What works and what doesn't. *Phi Delta Kappa, 73*(10), 745–752.

Miles, M., & Huberman, A. (1984). *Qualitative data analysis: A sourcebook of new methods.* Beverly Hills, CA: Sage.

Olson, K. (2003). Using comparative practice to test the veracity of learning theories designed to promote "deep understanding." In C. Schroeder & A. Ciccone (Eds.), *Learning more about learning* (pp. 38–49). Milwaukee, WI: University of Wisconsin–Milwaukee, Center for Instructional and Professional Development.

O'Malley, R. (2002). SoTL reflections on efforts to find appropriate technology on pedagogy to stimulate student participation in the learning process. *Models in our midst* (pp. 41–47). Milwaukee, WI: University of Wisconsin–Milwaukee, Center for Instructional and Professional Development.

Palmer, P. J. (1997). *The courage to teach: Exploring the inner landscape of a teacher's life.* San Francisco, CA: Jossey-Bass.

Pintrich, P. R., Marx, R. W., & Boyle, R. A. (1993). Beyond cold conceptual change: The role of motivational beliefs and classroom contextual factors in the process of conceptual change. *Review of Educational Research, 63*(2), 167–199.

Pohland, P., & Bova, B. (2000). Professional development as transformational learning. *International Journal of Leadership in Education, 3*(2), 137–150.

Prawat, R. (1992, May). Teachers' belief about teaching and learning: A constructivist perspective. *American Journal of Education, 100*(3), 354–395.

Proust, M. (1948). *La prisonniere.* (J. O'Brien, Ed. & Trans.). New York, NY: Columbia University Press. (Original work published 1924)

Ramsden, P. (1992). *Learning to teach in higher education.* London, England: Routledge.

Rathburn, J. (2002). Using technology to enhance learning and understanding. In C. Schroeder & A. Ciccone (Eds.), *Models in our midst* (pp. 49–58). Milwaukee, WI: University of Wisconsin–Milwaukee, Center for Instructional and Professional Development.

Robertson, D. L. (1997). Transformative learning and transition theory: Toward developing the ability to facilitate insight. *Journal on Excellence in College Teaching, 8*(1), 105–125.

Schroeder, C. (2001). Faculty change agents: Individual and organizational factors that enable or impede faculty involvement in organizational change (Doctoral dissertation, University of Wisconsin–Madison, 2001). *Dissertation Abstracts International,* No. 0262.

Schroeder, C., & Ciccone, A. (Eds.). (2002). *Models in our midst.* Milwaukee, WI: University of Wisconsin–Milwaukee, Center for Instructional and Professional Development.

Schroeder, C., & Ciccone, A. (Eds.). (2003). *Learning more about learning.* Milwaukee, WI: University of Wisconsin–Milwaukee, Center for Instructional and Professional Development.

Senge, P. M. (1990). *The fifth discipline: The art & practice of the learning organization.* New York, NY: Currency Doubleday.

Shulman, L. S. (1999, July/August). Taking learning seriously. *Change, 31*(4), 11–17.

Sokol, A., & Cranton, P. (1998, Spring). Transforming, not training. *Adult Learning, 9*(3), 14–17.

Taylor, E. W. (2000). Analyzing research on transformative learning theory. In J. Mezirow & Associates (Eds.), *Learning as transformation: Critical perspectives on a theory in progress* (pp. 29–310). San Francisco, CA: Jossey-Bass.

Trigwell, K., & Prosser, M. (1996). Congruence between intention and strategy in university science teachers' approaches to teaching. *Studies in Higher Education, 32,* 77–87.

Wiggins, G. (1996, Winter). Embracing accountability. *New Schools, New Communities, 12*(2), 4–10.

5

The Roles of Teaching and Learning Centers

Alan C. Frantz
Idaho State University

Steven A. Beebe
Texas State University, San Marcos

Virginia S. Horvath
Kent State University

JoAnn Canales
Texas A&M University, Corpus Christi

David E. Swee
University of Medicine and Dentistry of New Jersey—Robert Wood
Johnson Medical School

> To be what we are, and to become what we are capable of becoming,
> is the only end in life.
> —Robert Louis Stevenson

This chapter shares findings from a survey of teaching and learning centers on college and university campuses in the United States. Topics addressed include organizational infrastructure, assessment and accountability, factors/challenges contributing to successful implementation, and a list of functions and program offerings found in teaching and learning centers across the country.

INTRODUCTION

For decades, American institutions of higher education have established teaching and learning centers (TLCs) to help faculty members develop, assess, and refine their teaching skills (Epper & Bates, 2001; Sorcinelli, 2002). However, as Bartlett (2002) points out in a *Chronicle* article about the closing of the 30-year-old TLC at the University of Nebraska, budget constraints can leave such centers especially vulnerable. The central questions to be asked are, "What do these centers provide to enhance and improve the teaching climate of their institution?" and "How do they achieve their goals, overcome obstacles, address accountability, and survive in times of budgetary constraints?"

In an effort to address these questions, we sought to identify specific principles, practices, and leadership strategies that would assist in decision-making about developing or enhancing a comprehensive TLC. Wright (2000), in one of the few extant survey research studies of the operation of faculty development centers, found that over 80% of the center directors report to the chief academic officer of the institution. In addition, she reported that almost two-thirds of the 33 campuses she surveyed received their funds from general, instructional, or administrative sources; the remaining third were funded from such external revenue streams as grants, contracts, student fees, gifts, endowment funds, or earned income. The costs for administering these services were quite varied. Wright reported that in the fall of 1997, when her survey was distributed, seven programs reported budgets over $300,000; six were in the $150,000–$299,000 range; four centers ranged between $75,000 and $149,000; and the remaining centers had budgets below $74,000, with six of those below $24,999.

The range of services was also quite varied. All 33 centers Wright surveyed were engaged in faculty and instructional development activities, including faculty consultation services (100%), resource rooms for faculty (98%), workshops (97%), and newsletters (63%). Other services provided by some of the centers in the survey included instructional technology support (57%), media production facilities (27%), examination services (21%), grant proposal assistance (95%), student learning skills assistance (6%), supplemental instruction learning skills (3%), teaching awards (3%), and multicultural teaching and learning services (3%).

Sorcinelli (2002) distilled 10 principles of good practice for developing and maintaining TLCs predicated on her own experience in developing two centers. She explains, "these principles are not Ten Commandments; they are guidelines for getting started. They are not perfectly linear; rather they follow a loose progression, starting from before a center exists and moving to when a center is in place" (p. 10). The 10 principles of good practice are:

1) Build stakeholders by listening to all perspectives.

2) Ensure effective program leadership and management.

3) Emphasize faculty ownership.

4) Cultivate administrative commitment.

5) Develop guiding principles, clear goals, and assessment procedures.

6) Strategically place the center within the organizational structure.

7) Offer a range of opportunities, but lead with strengths.

8) Encourage collegiality and community.

9) Create collaborative systems of support.

10) Provide measures of recognition and rewards. (pp. 10–21).

Although there appears to be a widely disseminated understanding of what teaching and learning centers are, there have been only a handful of studies that have examined the functions of TLCs and other faculty development programs (Centra, 1976; Chambers, 1998; Crawley, 1995; Diamond, 2002; Erickson, 1986; Gullatt & Weaver, 1997; Kalivoda, Broder, & Jackson, 2003; Sorcinelli, 2002). Despite the 10 guiding principles identified by Sorcinelli, campus leaders who wish to establish a center often have specific questions about how to inaugurate and sustain a TLC, particularly when expenses outside of direct instruction come under close scrutiny. This study sought to identify specific practices and programs of successful TLCs as identified by current directors of these centers, particularly best practices that could help others who are seeking to initiate a center, strengthen an existing center, or assist those who are documenting the impact of a center on the campus climate of teaching and learning.

METHODOLOGY

Five members of the American Council on Education (ACE) Fellows program collaborated on a leadership team. Fellows spend a year studying and observing the world of higher education, with a special focus on leadership. Fellows are assigned to leadership teams, in which they complete a major project. They are mentored by one or more senior administrators at a host institution.

The team members identified six areas of interest for a survey regarding faculty development centers.

- The functions or programs offered by each center

- Perceived best practices

- Obstacles to goal attainment

- Organizational or reporting structure

- Accountability measures

- Relationship between the TLC and faculty use of technology

After individually and collectively visiting a number of centers and visiting the websites of many others, our team developed an eight-item survey; one item contained 45 characteristics or offerings to be marked with an X if it applied to the faculty development center or program. With approvals from the Human Subjects Review boards at our institutions, we sent the survey electronically to 260 directors of TLCs during the spring of 2003. The survey was sent primarily to those institutions listed on the University of Kansas web site of TLCs in the United States and Canada, including universities, four-year, and two-year colleges (see http://www.ku.edu/~cte/resources/websites.html). The survey was also posted on the listserv of the Professional and Organizational Development Network in Higher Education (POD), a group with more than 1,000 faculty, administrators, and staff members, primarily in the United States. Although there was potential for duplication, we also posted the survey on the POD listserv of small colleges, as we hoped to elicit responses from smaller institutions that were not on the University of Kansas list, and where faculty may oversee some TLC functions without the presence of an actual center on their campuses.

FINDINGS

Table 5.1 presents the findings from the 109 surveys that were returned electronically. Of the 109 responses, 91 resulted from the 260 direct requests (35%), and 18 resulted from the listserv posting. The table shows the percentage and numbers of responses by institutional type for the various characteristics and offerings of faculty development centers. Of our total 109 responses, we received only two responses from public baccalaureate colleges and only one from a specialized college; thus, those three responses are represented in the total percentages given, but not depicted in the graphs (indicated by an asterisk). To read the graphs, please bear in mind the number and percentage given in parentheses after the item. The graph shows the actual number of responses, segmented by institutional type in this order: 51 public doctoral universities, 13 private doctoral universities, 19 public master's universities, 8 private master's universities, 8 private liberal arts colleges, and 7 public associate's colleges.

TABLE 5.1
Offerings of Teaching and Learning Centers

	Public Doctoral	Private Doctoral	Public Master's	Private Master's	Private Liberal Arts	Public Associate's
1) IT Support is part of the Center (49 = 45%)*	18	7	10	6	4	2
2) IT Support is a separate Center (64 = 59%)*	35	10	9	4	3	2
3) Multiple Programs report to the Center (15 = 14%)*	10			3	1	
4) Advisory Board (78 = 72%)*	34	10	12	7	6	6
5) Newsletter (68 = 62%)*	30	11	9	6	5	6
6) Resource Materials Library (99 = 91%)*	48	11	15	8	7	7
7) New Faculty Orientation (97 = 89%)*	42	12	17	8	8	7
8) Peer Tutor Training (19 = 17%)*	10	2	4	2		
9) TA or GA Training (57 = 52%)*	41	11	3	1		
10) ESL for International TAs (15 = 14%)	11	3	1			
11) Outstanding Teacher Awards (47 = 43%)*	25	6	5	3	4	3
12) Assessment Coordination at the Institutional Level (20 = 18%)	14		2	2	1	1
13) Assessment Assistance at the Course Level (79 = 72%)*	39	9	12	6	5	5

14) Community-based Learning
    (14 = 13%)

6 1 1 4 1 1

15) Community Connections
    (17 = 16%)

9 4 2 1 1

16) Service Learning
    (33 = 30%)

13 1 6 5 5 3

17) Consultation on Teaching for
    Individual Faculty (103 = 94%)*

49 13 17 8 7 6

18) Tenure/Promotion Portfolio Assistance
    (69 = 63%)*

33 10 12 7 4 2

19) Course/Instructor Evaluations
    (49 = 45%)

25 7 9 5 3

20) Public Presentation Assistance
    (48 = 44%)

20 9 10 4 3 2

21) Faculty Mentoring Program
    (60 = 55%)*

26 8 11 5 5 3

22) Faculty-in-Residence for Assessment
    (7 = 6%)

4 1 1 1

23) Faculty-in-Residence for Scholarship
    (11 = 10%)

4 1 2 1 3

24) Faculty-in-Residence for Teaching
    (15 = 14%)

7 1 2 2 3

25) Faculty-in-Residence for Technology
    (12 = 11%)

5 1 2 2 2

26) Faculty Development Grants
    (80 = 73%)*

34 9 13 7 8 7

27) Teaching with Technology Grants
    (56 = 51%)*

24 8 8 6 4 3

28) Course Redesign Grants
    (51 = 47%)*

26 7 7 5 5

29) Other Grants
    (48 = 44%)

18 6 8 5 7 5

30) Chairing a Department
    (24 = 22%)*

12 1 5 2 2 1

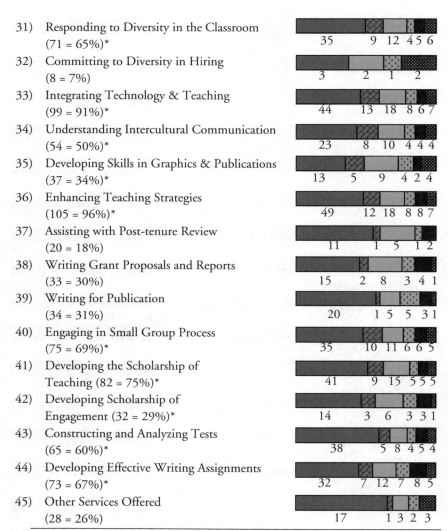

31)	Responding to Diversity in the Classroom (71 = 65%)*	35 9 12 4 5 6
32)	Committing to Diversity in Hiring (8 = 7%)	3 2 1 2
33)	Integrating Technology & Teaching (99 = 91%)*	44 13 18 8 6 7
34)	Understanding Intercultural Communication (54 = 50%)*	23 8 10 4 4 4
35)	Developing Skills in Graphics & Publications (37 = 34%)*	13 5 9 4 2 4
36)	Enhancing Teaching Strategies (105 = 96%)*	49 12 18 8 8 7
37)	Assisting with Post-tenure Review (20 = 18%)	11 1 5 1 2
38)	Writing Grant Proposals and Reports (33 = 30%)	15 2 8 3 4 1
39)	Writing for Publication (34 = 31%)	20 1 5 5 3 1
40)	Engaging in Small Group Process (75 = 69%)*	35 10 11 6 6 5
41)	Developing the Scholarship of Teaching (82 = 75%)*	41 9 15 5 5 5
42)	Developing Scholarship of Engagement (32 = 29%)*	14 3 6 3 3 1
43)	Constructing and Analyzing Tests (65 = 60%)*	38 5 8 4 5 4
44)	Developing Effective Writing Assignments (73 = 67%)*	32 7 12 7 8 5
45)	Other Services Offered (28 = 26%)	17 1 3 2 3

Note: Table 5.1 designed by Bernadette Howlett, Idaho State University
Instructional Technology Resource Center

In addition, center directors reported offerings and grant opportunities that were not among those we listed. The most common offerings appear below.

Features of Many Centers

- A wide variety of workshops
- Midterm student feedback (SGID)
- Faculty luncheon or dinner discussions
- Videotaping for teaching performance feedback
- Summer faculty development programs
- Support for research on teaching and learning

Features of Some Centers

- Classroom/media equipment loans
- Postdoctoral fellows programs
- Campus reading groups
- Preparing Future Faculty projects
- Evaluation services (grants, curriculum development, program evaluation)
- Assistance with new policy development for technology issues

Grants Offered Through Centers (in addition to technology and course redesign)

- Teaching improvement grants made to teams of faculty and staff
- Departmental learning communities
- Funding for book discussion groups
- Summer research start-up grants for faculty
- Faculty-student research collaboration grants
- Scholarship of teaching, professional development, research initiation grants
- Interdisciplinary or multicultural teaching and curriculum development grants

- Travel grants (usually to teaching and learning conferences or workshops)

- Assessment (for faculty to improve their understanding of assessment)

Best Practices

In addition to learning about the range of programs and practices at various institutions, we were also eager to learn about perceived best practices. We posed the following questions:

- What are best practices of TLCs in the United States as reported by center directors?

- What are strategies that help TLC directors achieve their goals?

- What are the obstacles that inhibit TLCs from achieving their goals?

- What organizational structure or reporting line works best to support and sustain a TLC?

The results are summarized in the following four tables. Table 5.2 presents a summary of the best practices of TLCs as identified by their directors. Response numbers are noted for each major category of response as well as selected examples that illustrate each major category of response. Table 5.3 summarizes the strategies that best help teaching and learning centers achieve their goals. The primary obstacles to achieving their goals are summarized in Table 5.4. Table 5.5 indicates the preferred reporting lines for teaching and learning center directors. It is interesting to note how consistently the responses from TLC directors track with the 10 principles of good practice outlined by Sorcinelli (2002).

TABLE 5.2
Best Practices of Teaching and Learning Centers

Identify one or more of your best practices that have made your teaching and learning center effective.

Offering Workshops (34 responses)
- Lecture series
- Workshops on topics linked to faculty needs
- Lunch discussions and lectures; provide food and refreshments
- Faculty orientations
- TA training workshops (e.g., Preparing Future Faculty workshops)

Providing Faculty Mentoring/Personal Assessment Programs (27 responses)
- Provide clear formative feedback to faculty who request feedback
- Make visits to faculty classes who request visits
- Video faculty classes and provide feedback
- Target mentoring programs (e.g., part time, senior faculty)
- Use peers to assist in providing feedback

Collaborating/Establishing Learning Communities (22 responses)
- Link people from different departments to work on joint projects
- Develop a team approach to faculty development

Adapting/Assessing Needs/Listening (20 responses)
- Distribute campus surveys
- Constantly ask faculty what they want/need
- Listen one-on-one to what faculty express as their needs for the center
- Use focus groups to assess what faculty members value/want/need
- Develop a systematic approach to assessment then implement what faculty want

Being Visible/Accessible (20 responses)
- Have director maintain a high profile on campus
- Make ourselves available for classes
- Provide campus newsletters
- Have staff visit faculty in their offices

Providing Technical Support (20 responses)
- Offer individual technical support
- Help faculty integrate technology and teaching
- Use new digital technology to assist with distance learning and Internet courses

Providing Resources (e.g., stipends, travel funds, release time) (15 responses)
- Provide summer stipends
- Provide release time for faculty teaching development projects
- Fund teaching awards

Establishing a Positive Climate for Teaching/Learning (9 responses)
- Be personally positive and supportive of faculty
- Help faculty manage stress
- Prevent perception of the TLC as remedial training for ineffective teachers

Networking (5 responses)
- Support scholarly circles for networking

Helping Write Grants (5 responses)
- Assist in preparing grant proposals
- Identify funding sources for faculty members

TABLE 5.3
Strategies for Achieving the Goals

Identify factors that have helped the teaching and learning center achieve its goals.

Strong Administrative Support (39 responses)
- Positive comments from administration to faculty
- Positive comments from administration to learning center director and staff
- Budget support for faculty fellows program
- Positive leadership from administrators who are actively interested, visible, and engaged in the center

Engaged and Supportive Faculty (28 responses)
- Faculty who recognize the value of what the TLC does
- Faculty who are personally motivated to use our services
- Faculty who have ownership of the programs, instead of a sense that they are having something imposed on them from above

Cultural Tradition of Support and Climate of Collaboration/Cooperation (20 responses)
- Faculty who value teaching
- Hiring practices that stress the value of teaching
- Positive perception of those who use the center, instead of the center as a place where "bad teachers" go to be fixed

Adequate Budget (18 responses)
- Budget support from administration

Skilled and Dedicated Staff Support (16 responses)
- Staff members who go the extra mile to provide support services
- Staff members whom faculty perceive as credible

Grant Funding (8 responses)
- Track record of helping faculty to receive and manage grant resources
- Assistance with grant proposals

Location and Physical Facilities (5 responses)
- Location near faculty members
- Appealing, inviting physical facilities

Strategic Planning and Goal Setting (4 responses)
- Collaborative goal setting
- Systematic assessment of goals

Providing Food and Refreshments (4 responses)

Student Support (3 responses)

TABLE 5.4

Obstacles to Teaching and Learning Centers

Identify one or more obstacles that have hindered the teaching and learning center from achieving its goals.

Budget Constraints and Budget Cuts (38 responses)
- New budget cuts
- Loss of grant support

Faculty Perceptions of a Research Culture Rather Than an Emphasis on Teaching Enhancement (29 responses)
- Faculty belief that research rather than teaching is rewarded
- Lip service given to teaching by administration

Lack of Adequate Staff Support (23 responses)
- Lack of staff
- Cuts in staffing due to budget cuts
- Few faculty volunteers

Lack of Faculty Time to Devote to Development Activities (16 responses)
- Faculty perception that they are too busy teaching to devote time to development
- Pressures for faculty to focus on research—publish or perish

General Lack of Administrative Support (14 responses)
- Lack of public administrative support of our program
- Lack of private, personal administrative support of our program
- Changing administrators or administrators with a short memory who do not honor their previous commitments

General Lack of Faculty Support and Interest; Faculty Inertia (12 responses)
- Faculty without a history of coming to the center
- Faculty concerns about confidentiality
- Lack of perceived connections between using the center and enhancing careers

Facility Problems: Poor Location or Lack of Space (9 responses)

TABLE 5.5
Recommended Teaching and Learning Center Reporting Line

What is the best organizational or reporting structure for a teaching and learning center director?

Report to Provost or Vice President for Academic Affairs or Chief Academic Officer (84 responses)
- Have regular meetings with the chief academic officer

Report to Vice Provost or Associate Vice President for Academic Affairs (6 responses)

Dean (5 responses)

It Depends (5 responses)
- Need for each campus to determine the best reporting line in that institution
- "Reporting" may not be the best term; the center should belong to the campus

Faculty Governing Board (1 response)

Technology

Because technology is such an important part of teaching and learning in a digital age, we were also interested in learning about the relationships between TLCs and technology. In Table 5.1, the IT support graphs show the numbers of institutions with technology as part of the faculty development center (49) and as a separate center (64). What the graph does not show is that there were 16 (15%) institutions that marked IT support as *both* part of the center *and* as a separate center, and 12 (11%) institutions marked neither. There were 12 (11%) institutions that sponsor a "faculty-in-residence for technology" position, and 56 (51%) provide specific teaching with technology faculty development grants. It is clear that technology currently plays a major role in faculty development at most institutions. The nature and level of the support for technology varies, but the important advice/patterns appeared in responses to this survey item: "If technology instruction is included in your Center's mission, please describe the nature of the technological support that you provide." Table 2.6 summarizes the various responses. One important perspective that emerged in various forms is that technology is perceived as a means to initiate discussion about teaching. It attracts faculty to sessions. Technology appears to be a carrot that helps to begin a conversation on teaching with technology, but leads to deeper issues and programs on pedagogy as it relates to faculty development.

TABLE 5.6
Responses on Teaching and Learning Centers and Technology

- Centers, even as they may teach faculty about emerging technology, emphasize pedagogy and how learning can be enhanced by technology.
- Faculty developers assist with online course or electronic classroom management tools.
- Support can include administrative costs (e.g., finance, payroll), research, technology that accompanies textbooks, distance education, software (e.g., for presentations, graphics) and hardware (e.g., scanners, CD burners).
- Methods of delivery include workshops (single or a series, some faculty-led, some led by professional staff), institutes, labs, equipment loan, one-on-one, hands-on, and studio demonstrations.
- Consultation can be provided in the form of a helpdesk, faculty fellowships, department workshops, or online (email or web based). Consultations may include advice about hardware/software purchases.
- Rewards/incentives can include arranging for workshop advertising, computer replacement linked to workshop attendance, professional leave salary enhancements, release time, travel to conferences on utilizing new technology, summer stipends, and software purchases or awards.
- Support staff includes faculty experts, instructional technology specialists, web/video developers for online courses, student technical consultants, just-in-time teaching, and instructional design consultants.
- Centers collaborate often with other campus resources and departments, especially separate technology support centers.

Accountability

Our questions about accountability may point to a significant need as many centers may find themselves in a position of justifying the investment of their expenses. Although many colleges and universities have established teaching and learning centers, only 21 of the 109 survey respondents reported any information about their accountability practices.

No clear pattern emerged from the findings, possibly due to the low response rate. Those who reported assessing their own effectiveness use a variety of practices, ranging from workshop evaluations to soliciting feedback through focus groups. Table 7 lists responses in four categories: accountability practices, frequency of review/analysis, individuals responsible for the accountability practices, and recipient(s) of accountability findings.

TABLE 5.7

Responses on Accountability in the Teaching and Learning Center

Accountability Practices
- Workshop evaluations
- Workshop learning assessments
- Satisfaction/value surveys
- Number of workshop participants
- Number of subscribers to newsletter
- Frequency of contacts with faculty
- Periodic interviews
- Focus groups
- Formal review by ACE Fellow
- Institutional needs assessments
- Strategic planning and program review

Frequency of Review/Analysis
- By Term
- Annually

Individuals Responsible for the Accountability Practices
- Center staff
- Center director
- Center director and designated staff members
- Advisory board members
- Full-time evaluator on staff
- Provost's office staff
- Advisory board subcommittee
- Council on teaching (appointed faculty members who report to the provost)
- Each workshop participant collects own data (never asked by administration for a report)

Recipient(s) of Accountability Findings
- Provost
- Center's advisory council
- Information systems and college development (a separate department within the university)
- President's cabinet following review by advisory committee
- Dean of the college

With respect to accountability, the availability of resources, coupled with the mission and the predisposition of the institution's leaders toward accountability within each institution, will, more than likely, dictate the extent of accountability measures implemented. Some parameters for consideration to ensure best practices regarding accountability address four key areas including leadership, process, communication, and funding. The leadership of a designated "chief worrier" (likely the TLC director) is needed to drive the data collection, analysis, and reporting. This individual is central to overseeing a process that employs qualitative and quantitative processes using multiple measures to yield formative and summative data, as well as the development of an evaluation cycle that is in harmony with the institution's academic assessment and strategic planning cycles. Also needed is communication of the accountability practices and the findings via the faculty development web site to ensure that the appropriate constituencies are continuously informed of the efficacy of the faculty development initiatives. Finally, adequate funding will provide the necessary leverage to effectively implement a sound accountability plan.

Striking a balance between a comprehensive accountability plan that is informative and instructive, yet not cumbersome, is a challenge faced by all institutions regardless of size and mission. Perhaps a guiding principle to keep in mind as we work toward resolving that tension lies in the words of Moliere, "It is not only for what we do that we are held responsible, but also for what we do not do."

RECOMMENDATIONS

The survey responses and our contacts with other centers lead us to eight distinct recommendations for those who are considering developing, expanding, or changing TLCs.

- The range of services provided by a TLC should be aligned with institutional mission and conceptions of faculty work. Expectations of faculty that are most important in serving the mission should be the highest priorities for the TLC.

- Administrative support for centers should include not only financial and human resources but also advocacy for the center's function in promoting high standards for teaching and learning at an institution. If administrators attend or introduce workshop sessions at least occasionally, this sends a strong message to faculty.

- If a center is intended to serve as a resource for all faculty and a means of making the teaching mission visible, administrators should be cautious about using a center as a clearinghouse for responsibilities that may have no other home (such as assessment, graduate research assistant training, or administration of course evaluations). These responsibilities are possible if the staffing and budget are sufficient; otherwise, they will detract from the core faculty development purpose of the TLC.

- Administrators should work with center directors and faculty leaders to promote the perception of the center as a site of inquiry about learning, not primarily a source of remediation for faculty who are having difficulties in the classroom. When a faculty member does receive needed assistance with teaching, the TLC ought to be known as a place where confidentiality is assured.

- Although many of the topics and services that draw faculty into a center address practical concerns of their professional lives—promotion/tenure issues, classroom management, use of instructional media and technology. Administrators should encourage the center to offer programs that also address the ways faculty can meet the learning needs of undergraduate and graduate students. Examples include learning communities, student use of technology, and diverse learning styles.

- Administrators should support center directors as they experiment with new programs that address changing ideas about students, learning, and faculty work.

- Administrators should support efforts to use emerging technology as a resource in all faculty and staff development initiatives, including a TLC. A key phrase faculty often state is the desire to learn "appropriate use of technology."

- Administrators should encourage and rely upon varied means of communicating with those within and outside the institution—newsletters, web sites, and discussions—to advertise and recognize the activities a center offers in support of the teaching mission.

FUTURE RESEARCH

The purpose of this survey research was to learn the range and varieties of offerings at TLCs, their perceived best practices, strategies for and obstacles to achievement of goals, accountability practices, and reporting lines. We consider future research questions that delve deeper into the areas we have touched upon to be of value. One such area is how small institutions approach faculty development when they do not have formal centers. Another area is the use of technology for delivering faculty development programs. We heard about institutions that are beginning to offer online faculty development and use their web sites to archive programs. This area needs especially careful analysis. Finally, it would serve TLC directors well to know how others are addressing the serious issue of assessment in a time of budget cuts. It is interesting to note that of 80 TLCs that reported involvement in assessment at the course and/or institutional level, only 21 of them reported any assessment or accountability measures of their own operations. Why is this? Are there star assessment programs in place? If so, what do their assessment plans entail? Information about best practices in assessment could be valuable to any center that needs to collect data that demonstrate its effectiveness. By the time the center's budget is being cut, it is too late to initiate an assessment plan. We do not wish to read about a repeat of the Nebraska experience in the *Chronicle*.

NOTE

Requests for copies of the survey may be directed to Alan Frantz at franalan@isu.edu.

REFERENCES

Bartlett, T. (2002, March 22). The unkindest cut. *Chronicle of Higher Education*, p. A10.

Centra, J. A. (1976). *Faculty development practices in US colleges and universities.* Princeton, NJ: Educational Testing Service.

Chambers, J. (1998). *Teaching and learning centers in US higher education: Current and projected roles and services.* Unpublished report, Florida Community College, Jacksonville, FL.

Crawley, A. (1995). Faculty development programs at research universities: Implications for senior faculty renewal. In E. Neal & L. Richlin (Eds.), *To improve the academy: Vol. 14. Resources for faculty, instructional, and organizational development* (pp. 65–90). Stillwater, OK: New Forums Press.

Diamond, R. M. (2002). Faculty, instructional, and organizational development: Options and choices. In K. H. Gillespie, L. R. Hilsen, & E. C. Wadsworth (Eds.), *A guide to faculty development: Practical advice, examples, and resources* (pp 2–8). Bolton, MA: Anker.

Epper, R., & Bates, A. (2001). *Teaching faculty how to use technology: Best practices from leading institutions.* Phoenix, AZ: Oryx Press/American Council on Education.

Erickson, G. (1986). A survey of faculty development practices. In M. Svinicki, J. Kurfiss, & J. Stone (Eds.), *To improve the academy: Vol. 5. Resources for student, faculty, and institutional development* (pp. 182–196). Stillwater, OK: New Forums Press.

Gullatt, D., & Weaver, S. (1997, October). *Use of faculty development activities to improve the effectiveness of U. S. institutions of higher education.* Paper presented at the meeting of the Professional and Organizational Development Network in Higher Education, Nines City, FL.

Kalivoda, P., Broder, J., & Jackson, W. K. (2003). Establishing a teaching academy: Cultivation of teaching at a research university campus. In C. M. Wehlburg & S. Chadwick-Blossey (Eds.), *To improve the academy: Vol. 21. Resources for faculty, instructional, and organizational development* (pp. 79–92). Bolton, MA: Anker.

Sorcinelli, M. D. (2002). Ten principles of good practice in creating and sustaining teaching and learning centers. In K. H. Gillespie, L. R. Hilsen, & E. C. Wadsworth (Eds.), *A guide to faculty development: Practical advice, examples, and resources.* Bolton, MA: Anker.

Wright, D. L. (2000). Faculty development centers in research universities: A study of resources and programs. In M. Kaplan & D. Lieberman (Eds.), *To improve the academy: Vol. 18. Resources for faculty, instructional, and organizational development* (pp. 291–301). Bolton, MA: Anker.

Section II

Quality of Work Life for Faculty and Faculty Developers

6

Looking at Ourselves: The Quality of Life of Faculty Development Professionals

Kathleen T. Brinko, Sally S. Atkins, and Marian E. Miller
Appalachian State University

Responses to a questionnaire revealed that faculty development professionals typically juggle several roles—which they find to be energizing—and typically balance multiple challenges and stressors—which they feel they handle well. These faculty developers are enthusiastic about and, in many cases, sustained by their work because they find opportunities for lifelong learning, professional growth, and meaningful work.

INTRODUCTION

As a profession, we faculty developers know very little about ourselves. The majority of the literature in our field addresses our practice, primarily the improvement of teaching. Graf and Wheeler (1996) provided us with some demographic and job-related information, and Lewis (1996) and Tiberius (2002) gave brief histories of the evolution of the practice of faculty development. However, we have no information on how faculty developers perceive their work and professional quality of life.

Over a period of 18 years, the Hubbard Center for Faculty and Staff Support at Appalachian State University has systematically studied the quality of life of several groups, including faculty (Atkins, Brinko, Butts, Claxton, & Hubbard, 2001; Hageseth & Atkins, 1988), staff (Hageseth & Atkins, 1989), new faculty (Branch, 1995), and chairpersons (Atkins & Hageseth, 1991). The university has also engaged in an ongoing examination of the psychological and philosophical issues underlying faculty and staff well-being (Hubbard

93

& Atkins, 1995; Hubbard, Atkins, & Brinko, 1998; van der Bogert, Brinko, Atkins, & Arnold, 1990). These studies, as well as hundreds of formal and informal consultations, have influenced a number of programmatic and structural changes at Appalachian State and have shaped the Hubbard Center's unique holistic approach to faculty development (Hubbard, Atkins, & Brinko, 1998). With this long-standing interest in studying quality of life issues, and prompted by conversations with colleagues in faculty development who had quality of life issues, we decided to turn our attention to those issues within our own profession.

CHANGING CONTEXTS, CHANGING ROLES

It is important to note that this study has taken place amidst tremendous changes occurring in American higher education and in the roles of the faculty development professional within these changing contexts. Changing attitudes regarding the roles of the teacher and the learner, research on the nature of learning from the cognitive sciences, and changes within organizational systems within higher education continue to shape the profession of faculty development (Lieberman & Guskin, 2003; Tiberius, 2002). From the assumptions of the 1950s, when professors were seen primarily as masters of the discipline, through the evolution of many faculty development programs and centers of the early 1970s that focused primarily upon assisting professors in understanding and mastering the complex instructional competencies of pedagogy, the role and responsibility of the faculty developer changed (Centra, 1976; Gaff, 1975; Lieberman & Guskin, 2003; Tiberius, 2002). In today's world of higher education, the role of the faculty member has become increasingly complex, as has that of the faculty developer. Shaped by the differing historical contexts and the evolution of attitudes regarding teaching and learning, faculty developers now find themselves needing to embrace multiple roles within the system of the institution (Tiberius, 2002). Increasingly, faculty developers are called upon to address faculty life and career concerns within the personal dimension, such as life stage issues, wellness programs, and retirement issues (Lewis, 1996). More than ever, faculty development professionals are called upon to work as institutional agents of transformational change, helping faculty members to design environments for learning, embracing ideas of learning communities, fostering learning organizations, and navigating faculty development as a dialectic between individuals and the organizational system (Langley, O'Connor, & Welkener, 2004; Lieberman & Guskin, 2003; Senge, 1990). These complex challenges of modern faculty development work would seem to have a major impact on faculty developers' perceived quality of life.

METHOD

Although our previous quality of life studies included in-depth interviews, we believed that this first study of faculty developers should be exploratory and should try to capture a broad overview of their quality of life. These results, then, would shape questions for later in-depth interviews.

In December 2001, we developed a paper-and-pencil questionnaire to mail to directors and assistant or associate directors of faculty development centers. After receiving approval from the university's institutional review board for human subjects research and from the university's statistician concerning coding and analyzing the data, we conducted a pilot study of our questionnaire with five professionals in the field who were no longer working as directors or who did not work in the United States. Based on the feedback from this pilot study we refined the questionnaire, and in February 2002, we mailed a 24-item questionnaire (Appendix 6.1) to 256 directors and a 23-item questionnaire (the same, minus Question 7) to 52 associate or assistant directors of faculty development programs in the United States, as listed in the *POD Membership Directory* (Professional and Organizational Development Network in Higher Education, 2001).

Each questionnaire was coded with a unique number to track returns and to follow up. However, to protect subject confidentiality, graduate assistants received the completed questionnaires, kept track of returns, and conducted the follow-up mailing. To further protect the subjects, the graduate assistants also entered all quantitative data into a database and keyboarded all handwritten responses to the qualitative questions. In total, we received 145 usable questionnaires (response rate = 57%) from the directors surveyed and 36 usable questionnaires (response rate = 69%) from the associate or assistant directors surveyed.

Using SPSS, we summarized the quantitative demographic data (Questions 1 through 9) and quality of life data (Questions 10 through 20), performed Pearson product moment correlations, and created scatter plots among possibly related factors (Questions 1, 6, and 10a, 10b, 10c). Using qualitative methods, we coded the open-ended questions (Questions 21 through 24), generating categories from the data.

DEMOGRAPHICS

Demographics of Directors

The directors ranged in age from 36 to 71 years, with a mean age of 53 years and a median age of 55 years. Of the respondents, 67% were female and 33% were male. The majority of directors (94%) held a doctorate; 34% obtained their highest degree in education, 16% in the social sciences, and 13% in the humanities. The remaining 37% obtained their highest degree in business, science, mathematics, communication, and other disciplines. Respondents earned their highest degree from 0 to 39 years prior to the survey, with the degrees fairly equally distributed over that span of time.

Respondents began as practitioners in faculty development from 0 to 33 years prior to the survey. Those who had worked in the field from 0 to 5 years comprised 39% of the sample, those who worked 6 to 10 years comprised 22% of the sample, and those who worked in the field for 11 to 33 years comprised 37% of the sample. Respondents held the position of director from less than 1 year to 26 years, with an average of 6 years. Interestingly, 60% of responding directors were relatively new, with 0 to 5 years experience in the job. Only 18% served previously as assistant or associate director before assuming the position as director, and they had served in that capacity from a few months to 10 years.

Responding directors came from public institutions (65%), private institutions (30%), and other kinds of settings (5%), such as two-year colleges, medical colleges, and system-wide faculty development offices. With regard to the classification of their institutions, 37% were directors at research I or II universities, 7% at doctoral I or II universities, 34% at comprehensive universities, 12% at liberal arts colleges, and 4% at other kinds of settings.

Less than half (47%) reported working full-time as director; an additional 14% reported that they were employed as director three-quarters time, 27% reported one-half time, and 8% reported one-third to one-quarter time. Thus, many respondents reported that in addition to their role as director, they held other roles in the institution, such as faculty member (76%), editor (14%), assistant or associate dean (3%), assistant or associate vice provost (4%), and other (23%).

Demographics of Assistant or Associate Directors

The assistant or associate directors ranged in age from 29 to 68 years, with an average age of 47 years. Of the respondents, 69% were female and 31% were male. Most (75%) held a doctorate, 47% held their highest degree in education, 19% held their highest degree in the humanities, and the remaining 34%

held degrees in a variety of disciplines, including science, mathematics, social sciences, or other. Respondents earned their highest degree from 0 to 35 years prior to the survey, with the degrees fairly equally distributed over that span of time.

Assistant or associate directors began as practitioners in faculty development from 0 to 25 years prior to the survey, with their beginning dates fairly equally distributed over that span of time. Respondents served as assistant or associate directors from 1 to 17 years prior to the survey. Sixty-nine percent of respondents held their positions for 0 to 5 years while 41% held their positions for 5 to 17 years. The mean number of years respondents spent in the position of assistant or associate director was 5.5 years.

Of the responding assistant or associate directors, 78% worked at research I or II universities, 8% at doctoral I or II institutions, 6% at comprehensive universities, 3% at liberal arts colleges, and 6% at other settings, such as a state system or national disciplinary faculty development center. The assistant or associate directors held their current positions from 1 to 17 years, with an average of 5.5 years. Interestingly, 69% of respondents were in their positions as assistant or associate directors for only 0 to 5 years. Most of the assistant or associate directors (85%) worked full-time in faculty development, while 3% were employed three-quarters time, 6% were one-half time, 3% were one-third time, and 3% were one-quarter time. Although most were employed full-time in faculty development, 50% were also teaching faculty, and 14% served as editors of publications.

Results

Directors' Quality of Life

Responding directors reported that they worked from 20 to 120 hours per week[1] in all their roles, averaging 54 hours per week. In response to questions asking them to rate themselves as excited or bored, enthusiastic or burned out, and growing or stuck, the majority of those who responded to this survey reported that they were excited (94%), enthusiastic (87%), and growing professionally (91%).[2] The majority of directors (87%) reported that their other roles (as faculty, editor, assistant or associate dean, assistant or associate provost) energized and refreshed them rather than tired and exhausted them.[3] There were no significant correlations between age, years as director, or hours worked per week and their excitement and enthusiasm for work.

Although directors were quite positive in their perceptions of their work, they also reported that their work exacted a personal toll. In response to questions regarding stress, many reported various symptoms of stress, including headache (43%), irritability (33%), and depression (33%). The most pre-dominate symptom reported was fatigue (77%). To alleviate stress and to take care of themselves personally, respondents reported a number of strategies, in-cluding regular exercise (74%), social support (50%), and healthier eating habits (42%). When asked how well they handle stress, 64% reported well or very well, 30% reported a mixed response, and only 2% reported handling not well or not well at all. Strategies for caring for oneself professionally and for staying vital included reading professional literature (87%), attending profes-sional conferences—both disciplinary (73%) and POD (71%)—and collabo-rative work (71%).

Many of these directors' faculty development centers offer at least some kind of personal support services for faculty. Seventy-one percent of the direc-tors reported that their centers sponsored workshops on personal develop-ment topics; 27% reported that their centers had support groups; 55% said that their centers had books and articles that promoted personal development.

Frequently the directors' institutions also offered some kind of personal support for faculty as well. Seventy-four percent of directors' institutions of-fered some kind of health promotion or wellness program; 60% offered coun-seling or psychotherapy; 45% offered infant or preschool childcare; 25% of-fered career counseling; 14% offered employment services for spouses or partners; 5% offered after-school care for school-aged children.

The primary professional challenge for directors included lack of re-sources (51%), including lack of funding, time, and staff. Thirty-seven per-cent of the respondents also reported that they were challenged by individual professional issues such as deciding about one's professional future, establish-ing oneself as an expert in faculty development, having responsibility without authority, keeping up with professional literature, and the like. Twenty-eight percent were challenged by programmatic issues such as engaging faculty in the center's programs, establishing a new center, working with adjunct faculty, keeping programs alive and fresh, and the like. Seven percent were challenged by a lack of administrative support and 4% were challenged by staffing issues.

Personal challenges for directors included balancing time (27%), family is-sues (12%), and mental and physical health issues (11%). A majority of direc-tors reported that they are sustained by their work (54%), particularly by the sense of faculty development being meaningful work/making a difference (28%), the challenge/change/growth of this type of work (14%), and their com-mitment and excitement about the field of teaching and learning (12%). Direc-tors also reported that they are sustained by their family and friends (33%), col-leagues (21%), teaching (14%), recreation (14%), and spiritual life (10%).

Within five years, 25% of the directors saw themselves as retiring, and 25% saw themselves as continuing as director in faculty development. Another 10% anticipated a move higher into the administration, 7% planned to return to teaching, and 12% were unsure what they would be doing professionally in five years.

Assistant or Associate Directors' Quality of Life

Most assistant or associate directors reported that they were excited (86%), enthusiastic (86%), and growing professionally (81%) in their work.[2] In all their roles, assistant or associate directors hours worked from 25 to 100 hours per week[4], with an average of 51 hours per week. Of those who worked in other roles, such as editor or teacher, most (84%) reported that the other roles energized and refreshed them.[3] There were no significant correlations between age, years as assistant or associate director, hours worked per week, and enthusiasm for work.

With regard to handling stress, the majority (64%) reported that they handled stress well or very well, while 33% reported a mixed response and 3% did not respond to this question. Symptoms of stress included fatigue (67%), lack of concentration and distractibility (47%), headache (47%), and insomnia or hypersomnia (43%).

Strategies for dealing with stress included regular exercise (69%), healthier eating habits (49%), and social support (46%). Strategies for professional self-care included attending POD conferences (89%), reading professional literature (86%), attending disciplinary conferences (60%), collaborative work (51%), and exploring new professional topics (51%).

Like the directors' centers, the assistant or associate directors' centers offered some personal support services for faculty. Twenty-five percent of the assistant or associate directors reported that their centers sponsored workshops on personal development topics; 11% reported that their centers had support groups; 14% said that their centers had books and articles that promoted personal development.

More often, the assistant or associate directors' institutions offered some kind of personal support for faculty. Sixty-four percent of assistant or associate directors' institutions offered some kind of health promotion or wellness program; 53% offered counseling or psychotherapy; 42% offered infant or preschool childcare; 31% offered career counseling; 17% offered employment services for spouses or partners; 8% offered after-school care for school-aged children.

Professional challenges for assistant or associate directors included work-load (37%), professional competency (31%), and administrative changes (26%). Personal challenges included family issues (34%) and balancing time (31%). Practices that sustained assistant and associate directors included family (43%), work itself (37%), outside interests (34%), spiritual life (31%), and colleagues (31%).

Within the next five years, 34% of the assistant or associate directors saw themselves in the same position; 20% saw themselves moving up to a higher position; 17% saw themselves retired; and 17% were not sure about future professional plans.

LIMITATIONS OF THE STUDY

Determining who was to be included in this sample was problematic in that there is no comprehensive database in the United States that identifies center directors and assistant or associate directors and their gender. To identify potential participants, we used the *POD Membership Directory* (Professional and Organizational Development Network in Higher Education, 2001) and the titles listed with each member's name. Further, we used the first names of individuals to determine gender. Thus, omissions and errors in the data are inherent in such an imprecise system.

Although there was a high response rate to our questionnaire, the participation in this study was voluntary, and we cannot be certain that the results reflect the quality of life of all directors or assistant or associate directors in faculty development. For example, no assistant or associate directors and only three directors responded that they did not handle stress well. Thus, it is unclear whether nonrespondents handle stress as well as respondents, or whether nonrespondents were not able to handle stress well and therefore chose to *not* participate in the study.

Additionally, the directors were employed by a variety of Carnegie institution types: research, doctoral, comprehensive, liberal arts, two-year, and other. However, most assistant or associate directors were employed by Carnegie Classification research I and II institutions, and this sampling may affect the generalizability of the results for assistant and associate directors.

DISCUSSION

Although our sample of assistant or associate directors is small, there are no notable differences detected between them and the directors. All faculty development professionals report that despite multiple stressors, challenges, and demands, the work itself is satisfying and rewarding. While there are many implications to be drawn from this study, overall the results suggest three broad themes regarding faculty development work.

Challenges and Stress

Whether they are full-time or part-time in their positions, faculty development professionals spend a great deal of time working. For many, the work entails multiple roles and expectations. The qualitative data collected in Questions 21 and 22 of the survey confirmed and elaborated upon their responses to earlier questions about the number of hours worked and multiple roles. For example, many respondents had comments similar to these:

- "[My biggest challenge is] balancing multiple roles."

- "Bridging the gap between teaching and administration means doing *two* jobs."

- "[There are] too many needs, too few resources."

- "[There's] too much work. Too many obligations."

- "My stress levels are due to really doing two 75% time jobs."

Further, both directors and assistant or associate directors perceive a great deal of stress in their positions. The most common challenges were lack of resources, individual professional challenges, and programmatic challenges. Respondents were very articulate in identifying and conveying the depth of their challenges.

- "[My institution's] culture does not value the scholarship of teaching."

- "[I report to a] dean who doesn't value humanity or good teaching."

- "It's the political battles that exhaust me."

- "The scope of what I can imagine is so much broader than what the institution supports."

- "I'm running out of ideas about what to do. I don't know where to take the center and how to get it there."

Almost all faculty developers reported some physical manifestation of stress, primarily fatigue, headache, lack of concentration, insomnia or hypersomnia, irritability, and depression. Yet they were quite self-aware and adept at alleviating that stress, primarily through exercise, social contacts, and healthier eating habits. Many respondents' centers offered some kind of personal development services, such as workshops, support groups, and print resources, indicating that in practice, many faculty developers are concerned about their faculty as persons and not just as teachers.

Meaningful Work

One of our earliest questions concerned the difference in level of professional satisfaction between those who had worked in faculty development for a short versus a long period of time. We were surprised that, in spite of long work hours and difficult challenges, almost all directors and assistant or associate directors—no matter how long they had been in the field—reported a high level of excitement for, enthusiasm about, and growth in their work. This enthusiasm had a lot to do with opportunities to grow, to make a difference in lives, and to do something they deeply cared about, as articulated in their responses to Question 24.

- "What sustains me is the sense that I'm growing—as a teacher, a colleague, and center coordinator."

- "I have a sense of helping advance values and ideas.

- "The sense that I am needed and have something to contribute."

- "The joy of making a difference, the exhilaration of creative work, and the intellectual stimulation of people that I come into contact with."

- "The feedback that I get that I make a difference really sustains me."

- "I love my work, which is really not work to me!"

Change and Creativity

Since there is a considerable body of literature about faculty who experience midlife burnout and boredom (e.g., Boice, 1993), we were somewhat surprised that there were no significant correlations between age, years as director, or hours worked per week and faculty developers' excitement and enthusiasm for their work. It is interesting to note that there were approximately the same number of respondents who served as directors for 5 years or less and who served over 11 (and up to 33) years. Thus, in this sample—where directors averaged 53 years of age and assistant or associate directors averaged 47 years of age—we have two very distinct populations: those who are new to the formal role of faculty development center administrator, and those have made a career as a faculty development center administrator. Yet all were equally excited and enthusiastic about their work, no matter their age. For the new directors who previously held faculty positions, we might posit that seasoned faculty take faculty development positions for professional renewal, and in essence, as an act of faculty development for themselves. If, as many writers have suggested, the challenges of midlife call for increased self knowledge, creativity, generativity, and commitment (Berquist, Greenberg, & Klaum 1993; Karpiac, 2000), then it would seem logical that a midlife career move into faculty development would provide such opportunities for challenge and new learning and challenge and for making a difference through service to colleagues and the institution. We might also posit that career faculty developers continue to find great satisfaction in their positions because, in general, they do not feel stuck but find other roles (e.g., teaching faculty, editor, or administrator) to keep vital.

FUTURE DIRECTIONS

In addition to the three broad themes outlined above, the data provided by this sample of faculty development professionals is rich with puzzles, contradiction, and nuance. It begs to be more fully understood through in-depth interviews, and is ready for a stratified sampling of institution type to discern differences in the quality of life of faculty development professionals in research, doctoral, comprehensive, and liberal arts institutions.

This first effort at characterizing the quality of life of faculty development professionals yields a portrait of very challenged, but very satisfied, individuals. However, these results contradict our experience with various members of POD. Over the years, we spoke with a number of faculty development professionals who reported that they were unhappy, isolated, and/or in crisis— which was the original impetus for the study. The fact that this study relied upon voluntary participation makes us suspect the results. Thus, additional studies are needed that employ methods to assure that the target population is adequately sampled.

Determining who was to be included in this sample was problematic in that there is no comprehensive database. Our reliance on the *POD Membership Directory* certainly missed those center directors and assistant or associate directors who do not belong to POD, and may have missed some who were center directors and assistant or associate directors who do belong to POD if their titles were omitted from the *POD Membership Directory*. Further, the titles listed may not be accurate descriptions of their true roles. For example, some faculty development centers have faculty members as the titular head while their assistant or associate directors actually perform the same functions as the directors of other centers. Additionally, we relied upon the first names of the members to determine gender—a very imprecise method.[5] Future researchers need a more accurate way of identifying faculty development professionals and their gender.

It is interesting to note that approximately two-thirds of the respondents were female, and we were pleased that this proportion paralleled the gender of the entire sample. However, this high percentage calls into question the imbalance of males and females in the profession. Like student development, is faculty development experiencing a feminization of the profession? In the past, did faculty development have more or the same percentage of males in the profession? We need more research to investigate this phenomenon, and to explore the implications for our profession and for academe.

Of special concern to us was the number of work hours per week that directors and assistant or associate directors reported. Over the past 20 years, faculty have perceived that academe—and indeed American society—has increased expectations for faculty, and that faculty do their job at great personal sacrifice (Atkins, Brinko, Butts, Claxton, & Hubbard, 2001). It appears that faculty development professionals—who often are drawn from faculty ranks—carry these expectations into their new role. Although most of our respondents reported that they handle stress well or very well, many have difficulty balancing the many tasks at work, as well as balancing work with their personal lives. An area that needs further study is the amount of time faculty spend working—actual and perceived—and if academe is encouraging workaholism (Fassel, 1990).

In our sample, the directors were employed by a variety of Carnegie institution types: research, doctoral, comprehensive, liberal arts, two-year, and other. However, most assistant or associate directors were employed by Carnegie Classification research I and II institutions. We speculate that research institutions are larger and more financially able to support a larger staff that includes assistant or associate directors. However, it is the mission of research institutions to focus on research more than teaching. We wonder, then, if research institutions are indeed giving more recognition and support to teaching than they had in the past. We need more studies on research institutions, comparing their past and present support (e.g., financial and human resources) for teaching and learning. Coupled with this effort could be the development of a "rule of thumb" ratio of faculty developers to faculty; this ratio could be used as one measure of comparison among programs.

Another intriguing finding in this study is that within five years, only one-fourth of the directors saw themselves as continuing in their positions as director in faculty development. Thus, our profession potentially will have 192 directorship positions open—and possibly more if we consider non-POD directorships. Some of these positions will be filled by the eight assistant or associate directors who wish to move into higher positions, and some will be filled by new individuals entering into the profession. However, at the least, we may be facing a shortage of faculty development professionals in the next five years; and at the most, we will be experiencing a large turnover in professional expertise. Studies are needed to measure the impact of this sea change on our profession, our professionals, and our service to our faculty clientele.

ENDNOTES

[1] It is difficult to believe that anyone would work 80, 90, or 120 hours per week. However, four respondents reported that they worked 80 hours per week, one reported 90 hours, and one reported 120 hours. It is important to note that these are the respondents' *perceptions* of how much time they spend working each week.

[2] Because many respondents marked between the Likert scales' demarcations, we converted these five-point scales into nine-point scales. Those who responded 1–5 on the nine-point scales were considered to be excited, enthusiastic, or growing. Those who responded 6–9 on the scales were considered to be bored, burned out, or stuck.

[3] The five-point Likert scale to measure this response was also converted to a nine-point scale. Respondents who reported 1–5 on the scale were considered to be energized or refreshed by their other roles; those who responded 6–9 on the scale were considered to be tired or exhausted by their other roles.

[4] One assistant or associate director reported working 100 hours per week. It is important to note that this is the respondent's *perception* of how much time he/she spends working each week.

[5] Using the list of first names in our sample of directors and of assistant or associate directors, we identified those names that are commonly assigned to males and those assigned to females. Approximately 35% of the directors were male, 63% were female, and 3% of the names were ambiguous with regard to gender. Approximately 33% of the assistant or associate directors were male, 62% were female, and 6% of the names were ambiguous with regard to gender. Future researchers also need a database that more accurately identifies gender.

REFERENCES

Atkins, S. S., Brinko, K. T., Butts, J. A., Claxton, C. S., & Hubbard, G. T. (2001). Faculty quality of life. In D. Lieberman & C. Wehlburg (Eds.), *To improve the academy: Vol. 19. Resources for faculty, instructional, and organizational development* (pp. 323–345). Bolton, MA: Anker.

Atkins, S. S., & Hageseth, J. A. (1991). The academic chairperson: Leading faculty is like herding cats. *Journal of Staff, Program, and Organizational Development, 9*(1), 29–35.

Berquist, W. H., Greenberg, E. M., & Klaum, G. A. (1993). *In our fifties: Voices of men and women reinventing their lives.* San Francisco, CA: Jossey-Bass.

Boice, R. (1993). Primal origins and later correctives for midcareer disillusionment. In M. J. Finkelstein & M. W. LaCelle-Peterson (Eds.), *New directions for teaching and learning: No. 55. Developing senior faculty as teachers* (pp. 33–41). San Francisco, CA: Jossey-Bass.

Branch, V. (1995). Teaching is "job number one": New faculty at a comprehensive university. *Journal of Staff, Program, and Organizational Development, 12*(4), 209–218.

Centra, J. A. (1976). *Faculty development practices in US colleges and universities.* Princeton, NJ: Educational Testing Service.

Fassel, D. (1990). *Working ourselves to death: And the rewards of recovery.* New York, NY: HarperCollins.

Gaff, J. G. (1975). *Toward faculty renewal: Advances in faculty, instructional, and organization development.* San Francisco, CA: Jossey Bass.

Graf, D., & Wheeler, D. (1996). *Defining the membership: The POD membership survey.* Ames, IA: Professional and Organizational Development Network in Higher Education.

Hageseth, J. A., & Atkins, S. S. (1988). Assessing faculty quality of life. In J. G. Kurfiss (Ed.), *To improve the academy: Vol. 7. Resources for student, faculty, and institutional development* (pp. 109–120). Stillwater, OK: New Forums Press.

Hageseth, J. A., & Atkins, S. S. (1989). Building university community: Where's the staff? *Journal of Staff, Program, and Organizational Development, 7*(4), 173–180.

Hubbard, G. T., & Atkins, S. S. (1995). The professor as a person: The role of faculty well-being in faculty development. *Innovative Higher Education, 20,* 117–128.

Hubbard, G. T., Atkins, S. S., & Brinko, K. T. (1998). Holistic faculty development: Supporting personal, professional, and organizational well-being. In M. Kaplan (Ed.), *To improve the academy: Vol. 17. Resources for faculty, instructional, and organizational development* (pp. 35–49). Stillwater, OK: New Forums Press.

Karpiak, I. (2000). The "second call": Faculty renewal and recommitment at midlife. *Quality in Higher Education, 6*(2), 125–134.

Langley, D. J., O'Connor, T. W., & Welkener, M. M. (2004). A transformative model for designing professional development activities. In C. M. Wehlburg & S. Chadwick-Blossey (Eds.), *To improve the academy: Vol. 22. Resources for faculty, instructional, and organizational development* (pp. 145–155). Bolton, MA: Anker.

Lewis, K. G. (1996). Faculty development in the US: A brief history. *International Journal of Academic Development, 1*(2), 26–33.

Lieberman, D. A., & Guskin, A. E. (2003). The essential role of faculty development in new higher education models. In C. M. Wehlburg & S. Chadwick-Blossey (Eds.), *To improve the academy: Vol. 21. Resources for faculty, instructional, and organizational development* (pp. 257–272). Bolton, MA: Anker.

Professional and Organizational Development Network in Higher Education. (2001). *Membership directory and networking guide.* Miami Beach, FL: Author.

Senge, P. M. (1990). *The fifth discipline: The art & practice of the learning organization.* New York, NY: Currency Doubleday.

Tiberius, R. G. (2002). A brief history of educational development: Implications for teachers and developers. In D. Lieberman & C. Wehlburg (Eds.), *To improve the academy: Vol. 20. Resources for faculty, instructional, and organizational development* (pp. 20–37). Bolton, MA: Anker.

van der Bogert, V., Brinko, K. T., Atkins, S. S., & Arnold, E. L. (1990). Transformational faculty development: Integrating the feminine and the masculine. In L. Hilsen (Ed.), *To improve the academy: Vol. 9. Resources for student, faculty, and institutional development* (pp. 89–98). Stillwater, OK: New Forums Press.

APPENDIX **6.1**

QUALITY OF LIFE SURVEY—DIRECTORS

1) In what year were you born?

2) What is your gender?   Male   Female

3) What is your highest degree and in what field?

4) In what year did you get your highest degree?

5) In what year did you begin as a practitioner in faculty development?

6) How many years have you been the director of a teaching center (present and past positions)?

7) How many years have you been the assistant or associate director (present and past positions)?

8) Current institution:
    ___ Public   ___ Research I, II
    ___ Private   ___ Doctoral I, II
                         ___ Comprehensive
                         ___ Liberal Arts
                         ___ Other:_____

9) What is your current appointment as director:
                         ___ Full-time
                         ___ 3/4 time
                         ___ 1/2 time
                         ___ 1/3 time
                         ___ 1/4 time

10) In your current position as director of a teaching center, are you:

excited   bored
L_____|_____|_____|_____|

enthusiastic   burned out
L_____|_____|_____|_____|

growing   stuck
L_____|_____|_____|_____|

11) What other titles/roles do you currently have:

<u>Other Role</u>

     ___ Faculty/teacher   ___ Assistant/associate dean

     ___ Editor   ___ Assistant/associate vice

     ___ Other: _____

12) In general, do these other roles:

energize you	refresh you		tire you	exhaust you
└───────────	───────────┴	─────────────	──────────┴	───────────┘

13) In general, how many hours per week do you work (in all your roles)?

14) As director of a teaching center (present and past positions), have you ever experienced symptoms of stress?
   If yes, please check all that apply:

☐ Headache/pain   ☐ Gastro-intestinal distress

☐ Backache/pain   ☐ Irritability/anger

☐ Fatigue   ☐ Insomnia/hypersomnia

☐ Depression   ☐ Anxiety/panic

☐ Other: _____   ☐ Difficulty concentrating/ distractible

15) What did you/are you doing now to alleviate stress? (Check all that apply.)

☐ Psychotherapy   ☐ Meditation

☐ Social support   ☐ Healthier eating habits

☐ Increased drug, smoking, or   ☐ Vitamin supplements
    alcohol consumption   ☐ Regular exercise

☐ Decreased drug, smoking, or   ☐ Creative activities
    alcohol consumption

☐ Spiritual activities

☐ Medication(s)
    (name it/them:_____)

☐ Other:

_____

16) What other things do you do to care for yourself *personally*?

17) How well do you feel that you handle stress?

    Very well   Well   Mixed   Not well   Not well at all

18) What do you do to care for yourself professionally, to remain professionally vital? Check all that apply:

☐ Read professional literature   ☐ Attend POD conference
☐ Attend disciplinary   ☐ Attend regional faculty
   conferences/events   development conferences
☐ Collaborate in teaching,   ☐ Attend conrferences/training on
   research, etc.   teaching/learning
☐ Explore new professional topics   ☐ Attend conferences/training on
☐ Other: technology

---

19) Does your *center* offer any personal development programs or services? If yes, check all that apply:

☐ Workshops (sample topics):

☐ Support groups
☐ Books and articles
☐ Other:

---

20) Does your *institution* offer any personal development programs or services?

☐ Counseling/psychotherapy (individual or group)
☐ Childcare facilities (infant/preschool)
☐ After school/holiday program (school-aged)
☐ Career counseling
☐ Health promotion/wellness program
☐ Spouse/partner employment
☐ Other:

---

21) What is the biggest *professional* challenge that you face right now as center director?

22) What is the biggest *personal* challenge you face right now?

23) Where do you see yourself five years from now?

24) What sustains you?

7

The Hue and Cry
of Campus Climate:
Faculty Strategies for Creating
Equitable Work Environments

Christine M. Cress
Portland State University

Jennifer L. Hart
University of Missouri–Columbia

Quantitative and qualitative data from faculty at a large public research university provide contrasting work life experiences for faculty of color and white faculty. Significant differences are evident regarding teaching and research, institutional priorities, individual goals, job satisfaction, and sources of stress. Specific faculty strategies for creating equitable environments are highlighted.

INTRODUCTION

Despite administrative efforts to ensure fairness and enhance diversity, faculty of color are underrepresented and continue to experience subtle and overt discrimination in the academy (Antonio, 2002; Astin & Cress, 1998; Finkelstein, Seal, & Schuster, 1998; Garcia, 2000). Prompted by concerns over high attrition rates for faculty of color, a systematic investigation was conducted to determine elements that enhance or hinder faculty work life at a large public research-intensive university in the southwest. While student demographics had shifted at the institution, the representation of diverse faculty role models continued to decline. Since perceptions of the institution are inextricably linked with behavioral outcomes, including faculty retention (Tierney & Bensimon, 1996), the present study assessed differential faculty experiences in order to solicit strategies to transform the institutional climate.

BACKGROUND LITERATURE

Recent studies indicate that faculty of color feel marginalized and undervalued in academe (Finkelstein et al., 1998; Garcia, 2000). Turner (2002) suggests that the representation of faculty of color is not only problematical but that creating a critical numerical mass is not enough. Rather, an essential element for faculty of color success is the nature of the response they feel from *majority* faculty. This includes the subtle and less tangible elements of work life such as attitudes, expectations, and stereotypes that may be manifested as disrespectful remarks and behaviors. Further, the effectiveness of individual agency is diminished for some faculty (e.g., faculty of color, women faculty, gay and lesbian faculty) who may find that asserting their own teaching and research interests into the academic culture may detrimentally impact tenure and promotion (Tierney, 1997; Tierney & Rhoads, 1993; Turner & Thompson, 1993).

Faculty of color are often assumed to be experts on issues of race and ethnicity and are frequently called upon by the administration to educate the majority, to teach courses that contribute to a multicultural curriculum, and to speak for all faculty of color on committees (Brown, 2000; Padilla, 1994). These expectations translate into what has been referred to as cultural taxation (Brown; 2000; Padilla, 1994),

> to show good citizenship toward the institution by serving its needs for ethnic representation on committees, or to demonstrate knowledge and commitment to a cultural group, which may even bring accolades to the institution but which is not usually rewarded. (Padilla, 1994, p. 26)

Equally burdensome and underrecognized is the hidden workload of student advising (Creamer, 1998; Garcia, 2000; Turner, 2002). While advising is a regular duty of faculty workload, faculty of color often feel the increased onus of informal advising. Students of color tend to seek out faculty of color because they are perceived to better understand their issues (Brown, 2000). Moreover, some faculty of color feel that research and scholarship focused on diversity or ethnic issues is viewed as nonacademic by their white majority colleagues (Creamer, 1998; Garcia, 2000; Padilla, 1994) which may detrimentally impact tenure and promotion (Tierney, 1997; Tierney & Rhoads, 1993; Turner & Thompson, 1993). Ultimately, increased out-of-class instruction load, coupled with expectations related to cultural taxation, create an environment for faculty of color where there is too much demand for work that is not rewarded and too little opportunity to produce scholarship that is valued (Turner, 2002).

CONCEPTUAL FRAMEWORK

Wilber (1998) proposes that organizations are best understood by examining individuals and groups across social/psychological and behavioral/procedural dimensions, that are either internal (known but unobservable) or external (observable). These four dimensions are 1) individual beliefs, values, attitudes, and feelings; 1) individual behaviors; 3) institutional or group beliefs, values, attitudes, and feelings; and 4) institutional or group processes and practices (see Figure 7.1). The problem, according to Wilber, is that most leadership and change efforts tend to address only one dimension. Therefore, if we want to fully understand the nature of the academic environment, we must examine the entire complement of realities.

FIGURE 7.1
An Interactive Organizational Model

	Internal	External
Individual	*Beliefs, values, attitudes, feelings*	*Behaviors*
Group or Institution	*Beliefs, values, attitudes, feelings (i.e., cultural norms)*	*Processes, practices*

Adapted from Wilber (1998)

Hurtado, Milem, Clayton-Pedersen, and Allen (1998) supplement Wilber's work by arguing that, historically, institutions have attempted to address diversity issues almost exclusively from a structural perspective (e.g., increasing the numbers of underrepresented individuals). When structural diversity is increased without consideration of other psychological and social dimensions of campus climate, interpersonal conflicts are likely to result. The consequence is that opportunities to sustain diversity are compromised.

Given that most academic leaders and administrators responsible for initiating institutional change are a part of the white majority, it is crucial that we understand the various perceptions and experiences of all faculty, but especially those of faculty of color. Existing research on faculty of color suggests that these faculty often face obstacles that make their work life qualitatively different from that of their white colleagues (Astin, Antonio, Cress, & Astin, 1997; Astin & Cress, 1998, 2002; Creamer, 1998; Garcia, 2000; Laden & Hagedorn, 2000; Padilla, 1994; Turner, 2002). This study focused on the psychological and behavioral climates at the institution using models by Wilber (1998) and Hurtado et al. (1998) to guide the analysis. These frames are particularly salient since "only when values and their effect on practice are revealed can change agents begin to transform values and modify practice" (O'Meara, 2002, p. 60).

METHODOLOGY

To examine campus climate comprehensively, the study design included collection and assessment of both quantitative and qualitative data. The quantitative data allowed for statistical analysis and comparison within the institution across race/ethnicity on a number of issues (e.g., teaching loads, publication numbers, perceptions of discrimination). The qualitative data allowed for purposive samples of faculty to share their experiences at the institution and to offer insights and suggestions for institutional improvement. Thus, the methodology provided for statistical testing of inequities, deeper insights into the daily realities of faculty work life, and the emergence of strategic suggestions for change.

Quantitative Data

Quantitative data were utilized from the university's participation in the National Survey of College and University Faculty (Higher Education Research Institute [HERI], 1999). This was the fourth in a series of national faculty surveys conducted on a triennial basis by HERI that resulted in 33,785 responses, including 837 from this institution. Statistical testing (chi-square) across gender, tenure, and academic rank indicated that the sample mimics the institution's general population of faculty.

In a first approximation (t test), the average difference was used to compare two faculty groups: faculty of color versus white faculty. While we know, for example, that African American faculty experiences may differ from Asian American faculty experiences, previous research has indicated that these differences are significantly less than for those between white faculty and faculty of color as an aggregate (Astin, Antonio, Cress & Astin, 1997). Therefore, race/ethnicity in this analysis was dichotomized.

To account for observed statistical differences between the racial/ethnic groupings that may be due to other sources of variation (e.g., gender, academic rank), the second order approximation (factorial ANOVA) analysis identified whether supplemental variables had significant predictive power. Thus, the prospect of conclusions being confounded was reduced.

Qualitative Data

While campus climate issues differentially affect faculty of color, any institutional change effort requires involvement of the broader community. Therefore, qualitative data were gathered from randomly selected individuals and from existing campus faculty groups. The total number of participants was 274, distributed relatively equally across academic ranks and representing membership in each of the university's 15 colleges and professional schools, including over 80 departments (see Figure 7.2). As noted above, faculty of color (and women faculty) were purposefully oversampled in order to fully investigate their experiences of campus climate.

FIGURE 7.2
Demographics for Faculty Participants

Gender		
Women	Men	No Response
214 (78%)	59 (22%)	1 (>1%)

Race/Ethnicity							
White (Non-Hispanic)	Hispanic	Asian American/ Pacific Islander	Native American	African American/ Black	Multi-Racial	Other	No Response
175 (75%)	20 (9%)	16 (7%)	3 (1%)	8 (3%)	5 (2%)	3 (1%)	3 (1%)

Academic Rank						
Full Professor	Associate Professor	Assistant Professor	Lecturer	Instructor	Other	No Response
58 (25%)	53 (23%)	50 (21%)	16 (7%)	3 (1%)	52 (22%)	1 (>1%)

To ensure anonymity data do not include administrative groups.

Focus groups were formed from academic clusters and ranks according to gender and race/ethnicity (e.g., male full professors, female associate professors, men of color, women of color); 165 faculty participated in these focus groups. In addition, faculty from existing on-campus groups (e.g., the Association for

Women Faculty, Faculty with Disabilities, Lesbian/Gay/Bisexual Faculty) and administrative groups (e.g., Academic Deans Council, Faculty Senate, President's Cabinet) were invited to participate since their insights and presence could prove instrumental in leveraging future change efforts. Sixty-eight faculty attended the discussion groups and 41 (21 men and 20 women) attended the administrative groups.

Participants were asked to address three general topics, guided by a semi-structured interview protocol: 1) factors at the university that have contributed to faculty success, 2) factors that have hindered or impeded faculty success, and 3) ideas, strategies, and recommendations for change. Additional questions and probes further explored faculty perspectives and experiences. While some categories and themes from the protocol framed and organized the initial analysis, all existing and emerging themes from the data were checked and compared across academic field, rank, gender, race/ethnicity, focus group type, and discussion group type.

RESULTS

Congruent with research objectives to investigate faculty experiences and identify strategies for institutional change, results are grouped according to Wilber's (1998) four-dimension organizational paradigm (shown earlier in Figure 7.1). Quantitative findings and qualitative comments illustrative of emergent themes in the data operationalize the conceptual framework and serve as the foundation for recommendations for organizational transformation and development. The findings are presented as follows: 1) individual beliefs, values, attitudes, and feelings; 2) individual behaviors; 3) institutional beliefs, values, attitudes, and feelings; and 4) institutional processes and practices.

It should be reemphasized that the interaction of *individual* beliefs and behaviors mutually shape *institutional* values and processes, so the differences are often not completely distinct. Still, since "reality is not something objective or external to participants" (Tierney, 1987, p. 64), it is perfectly congruent to use faculty perceptions of values, behaviors, and processes to understand the nature of an organization's culture and environment.

Individual Beliefs, Values, Attitudes, and Feelings

Faculty were asked to indicate their feelings about interpersonal relationships with faculty colleagues and administrators. Faculty of color are significantly more likely than their white peers to be dissatisfied with their professional counterparts (see Table 7.1). In fact, satisfaction decreases as faculty of color move up in the academic ranks, where over 15% of faculty of color who are full professors are not satisfied with their collegial relationships. In contrast, over 75% of white full professors are satisfied or very satisfied with their professional relationships. This difference may be due, in part, to the attempts of faculty of color to address multicultural and diversity issues with their resistant white colleagues.

- "We're seen as being irrational because we are angry and emotional about inequities and discrimination. They just wish we would assimilate and be quiet."

TABLE 7.1
Individual Beliefs, Attitudes, Values, Feelings (in %)

	White Faculty	Faculty of Color	Full Professor		Associate Professor		Assistant Professor	
			White Faculty	Faculty of Color	White Faculty	Faculty of color	White Faculty	Faculty of color
Satisfaction* with faculty colleagues	71.7	54.2 p<0.05	76.8	46.9	62.7	54.1	71.6	68.8
Satisfaction* with administrators	59.6	38.1 p<0.01	63.6	37.6	56	34.8	53.8	43.8
Subtle Discrimination as a source of stress**	4.8	25.7 p<0.01	3.6	28.1	7.3	17.4	4.2	33.3

(*satisfied or very satisfied, **extensive)

Nearly 60% of white faculty feel satisfied or very satisfied in their relationships with administrators. In comparison, about 25% of all faculty of color are not satisfied in their relationships with administrators. While it is unknown whether these administrators are upper-level managers or department chairs, faculty of color feel they do not have good working relationships with those who are in positions of leadership, power, and decision-making.

Further, faculty of color questioned the integrity of administrators and their commitment to diversity.

- "People tell you one thing and do another. Everything is spelled out in the books and yet the administration does exactly what they want."

- "The issues of governance and democratic practice in the faculty and administration aren't divorced from the issues for women of color. You actually have an undemocratic system. A network where decisions are made among friends. That's why it becomes very difficult for women of color to break into those decision making networks."

- "This university is still to me a white male university because that's what you see at most of the policy making positions and the idea of diversity doesn't even compute."

One in four faculty of color reported feeling "extensive" stress due to subtle discrimination (as compared to 1 in 20 white faculty). Nearly another one in four faculty of color report that they are somewhat distressed by subtle discrimination. Restated, half of all faculty of color experience some degree of stress due to subtle discrimination.

- "As minority faculty members we go through very polite discrimination. Someone said to me, 'I don't even think of you as Black.'"

- "A white professor made a statement that women and minorities undermine the ranking of the university."

- "When I was coming up for tenure the acting chair wanted me to know that the dean said that there would be no preferential treatment, not for women and not for minorities. I was so shocked that I didn't react. What does that mean? That I am here because I am a minority and a woman and not because of my qualifications. If I told this woman this is a racist statement, she would freak out. She is not aware of what she's saying. We need to find a way to sensitize people to the kind of casual comments that are really racist in a subtle manner."

In summary, when exploring individual beliefs, faculty of color feel less satisfied in their professional relationships with faculty colleagues and administrators and experience significant distress over subtle discrimination. As Wilber (1998) and others (e.g., Deci, Kasser, & Ryan, 1997; Tierney & Bensimon, 1996) have asserted, internalized feelings and attitudes are inextricably linked with externalized behaviors. These data are examined next. Specifically, the analysis focuses on the inclination of faculty to actively promote diversity in their classrooms as part of creating an inclusive campus climate.

Individual Behaviors
One of the most striking differences between white faculty and faculty of color is in their teaching behaviors. Only 45% of white faculty, as compared to 67% of faculty of color, responded affirmatively that teaching to enhance students'

knowledge and appreciation of racial/ethnic groups is essential or very important (see Table 7.2).

TABLE 7.2
Individual Behaviors* (in %)

	White Faculty	Faculty of Color	Full Professor		Associate Professor		Assistant Professor	
			White Faculty	Faculty of Color	White Faculty	Faculty of color	White Faculty	Faculty of color
Teaching knowledge and appreciation of racial/ethnic groups	44.9	66.7 p<0.01	39.8	67.8	52.5	58.3	48.4	76.5
Promote racial understanding	48.8	68.1 p<0.01	46.9	71.0	49.3	63.7	53.2	68.8

(*essential or very important)

Similarly, over two-thirds of faculty of color assert that promoting racial understanding in their classrooms is very important or essential. Perhaps the good news is that nearly half of white faculty share this behavioral perspective. Accordingly, faculty of color state that failing to facilitate racial understanding undermines student success and the academic integrity of the institution.

- "There is a level of denial about the pervasive problems of race and ethnicity in this university. It can't be divorced from the retention rates for undergraduate students and graduate students. These things are all connected to each other. The reason that somebody could get away with not grooming you for the next level, this is the same reason we allow all the Native American kids to flunk out."

- "The institution would like to have the appearance of diversity and multiculturalism while maintaining what the current faculty view as academic excellence. We're merely replicating the status quo. That is not true academic excellence."

The data evidence distinctive differences regarding attitudes and subsequent behaviors of individual faculty across race/ethnicity. As Wilber (1998) and Hurtado et al. (1998) suggest, group dynamics with respect to cultural norms and collective practices must also be examined to understand the degree of congruence or incongruence between individuals and the organization. Faculty perceptions of institutional norms and processes follow.

Institutional Beliefs, Values, Attitudes, and Feelings (Cultural Norms)

The majority of faculty indicate that there is institutional support for their research agenda. However, faculty of color are less likely than white faculty to believe that their research is valued within their department. This particularly holds true at the full professor level. Interestingly, white associate professors hold similar views to their faculty of color counterparts regarding support for their research interests. Unfortunately, about one-third of these faculty and faculty of color feel alienated from their department due to their research interests and choices (see Table 7.3).

TABLE 7.3

Institutional Beliefs, Attitudes, Values, Feelings (Cultural Norms)* (in %)

	White Faculty	Faculty of Color	Full Professor		Associate Professor		Assistant Professor	
			White Faculty	Faculty of Color	White Faculty	Faculty of color	White Faculty	Faculty of color
Research Agenda is Valued	78.4	66.2 $p<0.08$	83.0	65.7	67.9	62.5	81.8	73.4
A lot of racial conflict present	4.3	14.1 $p<0.01$	3.2	15.6	6.9	12.5	3.4	13.3

(*agree or agree strongly)

Of grave concern to faculty of color was the dismissal of their work if it related to multicultural or feminist issues. Indeed, the value of diversity-related scholarship at the institution was in question.

- "Some of the reviewers for promotion are not aware of certain specialty presses. The same manuscript that was [initially] accepted by African World Press, which is very respected, at least in my field, was turned down because somebody saw my dossier and implied that all Black people support each other and publish each other's work. So I sent this same manuscript out to [another press] which accepted it and that is what facilitated the positive decision on my promotion."

- "In spite of the talk about diversity it doesn't permeate. It's not a category or a criterion that is at all respected or implemented or articulated at any level."

Reinforcing these comments, a number of white faculty stated that they were so busy trying to survive themselves that they were unable to add "another initiative like diversity" to their "full plates."

- "We're so entrenched in just trying to get our day-to-day work done that looking to other kinds of things like diversity is difficult." (white female associate professor)

- "I just don't feel that diversity is honored here because we have this bureaucracy model. Anything that takes extra time is not going to be dealt with, which in all reality is actually antigrowth for the institution and for student learning." (white female faculty)

Like the contrasting views on institutional values and priorities related to multiculturalism, there is also differing opinion on how faculty of color and white faculty view racial conflict on campus. Faculty of color are significantly more likely than white faculty to agree that there are racial tensions.

- "I'm one of three Latino faculty in the whole college. It's not a priority and I'm the one trying to bring it to their attention. I can even feel very liberal faculty getting irritated with me. They get mad at me for bringing that up. Like how dare you. This is not something to consider. For them it's not a priority."

The culture of incivility described by faculty is likely related to earlier accounts of stress due to discrimination. Faculty highlighted exchanges where ideas were dismissed and faculty of color were left feeling voiceless and invisible.

- "I have heard from other colleagues who are Hispanic or African American that they have had students on campus talk to them in ways that I wouldn't want to be talked to. There are people on the staff who have been insulting to them, faculty who have ignored them at meetings, who have dismissed what they wanted to do."

- "If you come with an idea, it's viewed as a small-disconnected idea. Then later, a white male wants to do this and it's a great idea. Everybody's going to do this. Whatever you suggest it's not particularly good. It's a constant hammering away at your intelligence and integrity."

Hence, the organizational culture was depicted as resistant to multicultural efforts. Norms within colleges and departments appear to be reinforced through hostile and combative communications that uphold values for traditional forms of scholarship and competitive individualism. According to faculty of color, the resultant racial conflict plays into the hands of those in power as an age-old divide and conquer scheme that precludes the institution from making change. Given the existing climate, the only way to transform cultural norms is to directly address the institutional processes and procedures that reward such attitudes and behaviors.

Institutional Processes and Practices

When considering issues of race/ethnicity, female faculty of color voiced concern that their teaching load and expectations are especially heavy as compared to their colleagues.

- "I keep being told you really don't need to spend this much time working with students. We have a faculty member, a man, a white male in our department who really thinks that the only thing that you should count toward merit is publications. Not teaching or service. I think for many women teaching is an interpersonal connection that we value and the lack of university rewards is a difficult barrier to fight against all the time."

- "I find myself mentoring an inordinate number of students. I realize that I have come to be for these students somebody who will have a more understanding perspective on their problems, who will give them personalized attention. They assume because I am a woman of color I will be able to identify with some of their struggle. So I just don't see other Latino women students, I see the Native American students. I see the students with disabilities. I see African American students, all coming to me. It's an activity that I personally find rewarding but it does not translate in any way into the kinds of recognition of the service that I provide to the university."

Not surprising, then, faculty of color are significantly less likely than their white colleagues to believe that faculty of color are treated fairly on campus (see Table 7.4). Compared to almost 90% of white faculty who indicate that faculty of color are treated equitably, about half of all faculty of color do not share this perspective.

- "Quite frankly, if I want to move up I won't stay here. I've been told by white faculty on this campus that there is no administrative mobility for women of color. There is no pipeline or mentorship for women of color into administrative management."

TABLE 7.4
Institutional Processes and Practices* (in %)

	White Faculty	Faculty of Color	Full Professor		Associate Professor		Assistant Professor	
			White Faculty	Faculty of Color	White Faculty	Faculty of color	White Faculty	Faculty of color
Faculty of Color treated fairly	87.2	55.8 $p<0.01$	92.2	46.7	84.9	59.1	74.4	68.8
Women faculty treated Fairly	82.4	71.0 $p<0.01$	89.7	68.9	77.8	66.7	67.1	81.3
Gay and Lesbian faculty treated fairly	80.2	63.3 $p<0.01$	84.4	66.6	76.4	52.6	72.2	71.4

(*agree, agree strongly)

Not only do faculty of color perceive unfair treatment based upon race/ethnicity, but they affirm that faculty are treated unfairly based upon gender and sexual orientation. Faculty of color are less likely than white faculty to agree that women faculty and gay and lesbian faculty have the same opportunities as white faculty and heterosexual faculty.

DISCUSSION AND RECOMMENDATIONS

- "It's mind boggling when you think of all these intelligent and hard-working people and what could be accomplished if the barriers were removed."

Within the interviews, focus groups, and discussion groups, faculty shared their sentiments about the treatment and acceptance of various individuals and groups as a part of the campus community. They told heartbreaking stories of discrimination. They singled out examples of leadership and policies that create an inequitable work environment. They also expressed their belief in the critical historical juncture in which the institution is poised to either improve itself or face a new millennium as a disjointed and disconnected learning community.

Campus climate is not just about warm and fuzzy or hurt feelings. Instead, it is the lived experiences of faculty lives, which in turn has an impact on the academic excellence of the entire institutional community. Consistent with previous studies (Aguirre, 2000; Turner & Myers, 2000), faculty of color frequently referred to themselves as the *token* individuals. They spoke of the burdens of representing faculty of color on committees and the realities of increased advising loads since students of color often sought them out, whether or not they were their assigned adviser. Supporting existing scholarship (Brown, 2000; Finkelstein et al., 1998; Garcia, 2000; Padilla, 1994; Turner, 2002), faculty of color noted feeling marginalized and culturally taxed, having less opportunity to pursue their own research and scholarly interests, and having their work devalued by majority faculty. These factors often resulted in increased stress and diminished job satisfaction (Astin, Antonio, Cress, & Astin, 1997). Unfortunately, the outcome of raising issues of inequity and diversity can result in negative career consequences if faculty of color challenge existing social and organizational structures within the university (Foster, 1989; Giddens, 1984; Tierney, 1997; Tierney & Bensimon, 1996).

Given that positional leaders and those with decision-making authority at the university are primarily senior-level white males, their ability to empathize with faculty of color experiences may be limited. Since most individuals tend to act and behave according to their beliefs and feelings (Wilber, 1998), white faculty may be more likely to devalue the experiences of faculty of color since their perceptional realities are different. Fortunately, faculty of color are not completely alone in their concerns. For instance, one white male faculty commented:

- "The kinds of things that are the result of the lack of a salary structure and individual initiative based salary negotiating actually do magnify gender and ethnicity related inequities. To the extent that those behaviors may be asymmetric over gender and ethnic background you're going to end up getting gaps that get widened."

Creating positive institutional change will only occur if members of the institution work together toward common goals. Moreover, understanding the organizational context utilizing Wilber's framework can facilitate effective change efforts by addressing individual and institutional dimensions.

For example, specific recommendations for changing the institution emerged directly from the faculty themselves. They spoke of creating humanitarian alliances across departments and disciplines, developing mentor programs for faculty, providing leadership and professional development opportunities for faculty of color, and adjusting the reward system to value teaching and research focused on diversity and multicultural issues.

In particular, faculty of color felt that there needs to be specific incentives and disincentives if "real" and "tangible" institutional transformation is going to occur. They felt adamant that positive change would not occur spontaneously and that faculty and administrators need to be held accountable for their efforts. Faculty of color did not suggest creating quotas, but that "progress benchmarks" regarding diversity issues could be defined by faculty within individual departments as well as across schools with specific monetary and promotional consequences tied to the outcomes. As one faculty member stated:

- "How do we make the importance of people of color a priority among competing priorities? How do we express or communicate the need in a larger national interest that students in the pipeline will effect our very own survival? You must make it part of the promotion and tenure process. Part of the renewal of contracts for administrators. We have to provide perks in terms of financial support for this kind of implementation to make it worth their while. Right now they're not getting anything out of giving their time to help somebody else. Male or female, Black or White, Asian or Hispanic."

As a result of the data and faculty recommendations for change, the project constructed a series of action initiatives intended to improve the university across multiple dimensions of the organization and which address the interaction of individual values and behaviors with organizational norms and processes. The recommendations are strategies intended to influence values, behaviors, and organizational procedures in order to enhance the campus work and learning climate for academic excellence.

Strategy 1. Create Networking Opportunities for Faculty of Color

- Create a faculty mentoring program that would encourage application from interested mentors who would be supported in their mentoring roles by resources in their units and would receive additional compensation from the provost's office for their efforts.

Strategy 2. Integrate New Forms of Scholarship Into Promotion and Tenure Processes

- Educate promotion and tenure and search committees about the criteria for newly emerging research areas (e.g., feminist, race/ethnicity studies, sexuality studies, community based and applied research) and about multiple models for faculty success.

- Given the difficulty of achieving blind review through all performance review processes, develop a *second-look* review mechanism for faculty of color to ensure fair treatment of individuals in these groups.

Strategy 3. Monitor distribution of resources and Teaching/Advising Loads

- Establish an annual departmental reporting process to compare faculty teaching and service responsibilities. Pay particular attention to the workload for faculty of color, recognizing the burden of informal advising assumed by those faculty.

- Develop a college-based system of rewards, including compensatory release time and research support for faculty with extraordinary teaching and service responsibilities.

- Make internal resources for research and faculty development activities equally visible and available to all.

Strategy 4. Offer Leadership Opportunities for Faculty of Color

- Make each college and its dean accountable for increasing the numbers of faculty of color in leadership positions.

Strategy 5. Address Subtle Discrimination

- Make clear that subtle discrimination and other disrespectful behavior will not be tolerated at any level, and require administrators to take this into account for all evaluations and merit raises.

- Require training for all deans, department heads, and directors on a continuing basis, to prevent all forms of discrimination. Encourage administrators to educate their faculty in turn.

- Thoroughly investigate patterns of complaints against any administrator and discipline discriminatory administrators, removing them from positions of leadership if necessary.

CONCLUSION

Variability of experience exists from individual to individual. It is imperative, then, that we forgo stereotyping any faculty member by their affiliation with certain categorical groupings. Still, the fact remains that white faculty and faculty of color experience the institution quite differently. If we are to fully understand institutional impediments in faculty lives, we must take into consideration how faculty construct and make meaning of their experiences. For instance, what may appear to one faculty as a jovial or jocular remark, may appear to another faculty as a comment of ridicule. The co-mingling of these independent realities is what embodies faculty's daily working lives. If we fail to bring into consciousness the possibility of multiple interpretations of experience and the multiple dimensions that comprise an organization, we replicate and reinforce inequities and domination that inevitably get subsumed into the practices of our teaching, service, and research.

Further, as Wilber (1998) suggests, we can only leverage institutional change when we recognize the dynamic interdependence of individuals and organizations. To facilitate organizational transformation, we must validate individual feelings, reward (or sanction) individual behaviors, make explicit organizational culture (with respect to institutional goals and mission), and align organizational practices with institutional vision.

Faculty of color believe from their experiences and interactions that, at the very least, critical information, knowledge, and decisions are often withheld from them. Further, some faculty of color believe that their marginalization in the institution is based on active and intentional prejudice, since their race/ethnicity (and at times their gender or sexual orientation) is dissimilar from those in leadership positions. What this means for the institution is that alternative approaches to problem solving and creative initiatives are stifled, recruitment and retention of diverse faculty remain problematic, career progression is delayed or denied, and the overall climate is pervasively chilly. While the findings from this study are specific to one institution, the strategies offered here are adaptable to any organization that is genuinely committed to diversity. We hope that these insights into the academic lives of faculty of color and their specific recommendations for change will ultimately lead to equitable working and learning environments for the entire academic community.

REFERENCES

Aguirre, A., Jr. (2000). *Women and minority faculty in the academic workplace: Recruitment, retention and academic culture* (ASHE-ERIC Higher Education Report, 27[6]). San Francisco, CA: Jossey-Bass.

Antonio, A. L. (2002). Faculty of color reconsidered. Retaining scholars for the future. *Journal of Higher Education, 73*(5), 582–602.

Astin, H. S., Antonio, L. S., Cress, C. M., & Astin, A. W. (1997). *Race and ethnicity in the American professoriate, 1995–96*. Los Angeles, CA: Higher Education Research Institute, University of California Los Angles.

Astin, H. S., & Cress, C. M. (1998). *A national profile of women faculty in research universities.* Invitational Conference at Harvard University, Committee for Gender Equity, Cambridge, MA.

Astin, H. S., & Cress, C. M. (2002). Women faculty transforming research universities. In L. S. Hornig (Ed.), *Equal rites, unequal outcomes: Women in American research universities* (pp. 53–88). New York, NY: Kluwer.

Brown, M. C. (2000). Involvement with students: How much can I give? In M. Garcia (Ed.), *Succeeding in an academic career: A guide for faculty of color* (pp. 71–88). Westport, CT: Greenwood Press.

Creamer, E. G. (1998). *Assessing faculty publication productivity: Issues of equity* (ASHE-ERIC Higher Education Report, 26[2]). Washington, DC: George Washington University, Graduate School of Education and Human Development.

Deci, E., Kasser, T., & Ryan, R. (1997). Self-determined teaching: Opportunities and obstacles. In J. Bess (Ed.), *Teaching well and liking it: Motivating faculty to teach effectively* (pp. 57–71). Baltimore, MD: Johns Hopkins University Press.

Finkelstein, M. J., Seal, R. K., & Schuster, J. H. (1998). *The new academic generation: A profession in transformation.* Baltimore, MD: Johns Hopkins University Press.

Foster, W. (1989). Toward a critical practice of leadership. In J. Smyth (Ed.), *Critical perspectives on educational leadership* (pp. 39–63). London, England: Falmer Press.

Garcia, M. (2000). *Succeeding in an academic career: A guide for faculty of color.* Westport, CT: Greenwood Press.

Giddens, A. (1984). *The constitution of society.* Los Angeles, CA: University of California Press.

Higher Education Research Institute. (1999). *The American college teacher: National norms for 1998–99 HERI faculty survey.* Los Angeles, CA: University of California.

Hurtado, S., Milem, J. F., Clayton-Pedersen, A. R., & Allen, W. R. (1998). Enhancing campus climates for racial/ethnic diversity: Educational policy and practice. *Review of Higher Education, 21*(3), 279–302.

Laden, B. V., & Hagedorn, L. S. (2000). Job satisfaction among faculty of color in academe: Individual survivors or institutional transformers? In L. S. Hagedorn (Ed.), *New directions for institutional research: No. 105. What contributes to job satisfaction among faculty and staff* (pp. 57–66). San Francisco, CA: Jossey-Bass.

O'Meara, K. (2002). Uncovering the values in faculty evaluation of service as scholarship. *Review of Higher Education, 26*(1), 57–80.

Padilla, A. M. (1994). Ethnic minority scholars, research, and mentoring: Current and future issues. *Educational Researcher, 23*(4), 24–27.

Tierney, W. G. (1987). Facts and constructs: Defining reality in higher education organizations. *Review of Higher Education, 11*(1), 61–73.

Tierney, W. G. (1997). Organizational socialization in higher education. *Journal of Higher Education, 68*(1), 1–16.

Tierney, W. G., & Bensimon, E. M. (1996). *Promotion and tenure: Community and socialization in academe.* Albany, NY: State University of New York Press.

Tierney, W. G., & Rhoads, R. A. (1993). *Enhancing promotion, tenure and beyond: Faculty socialization as a cultural process* (ASHE-ERIC Higher Education Report No. 6). Washington, DC: George Washington University.

Turner, C. S. V. (2002). Women of color in academe: Living with multiple marginality. *Journal of Higher Education, 73*(1), 74–93.

Turner, C. S. V., & Myers, S. L., Jr. (2000). *Faculty of color in academe: Bittersweet success.* Needham Heights, MA: Allyn and Bacon.

Turner, C. S. V., & Thompson, R. J. (1993). Socializing women doctoral students: Minority and majority experiences. *Review of Higher Education, 16*(3), 355–370.

Wilber, K. (1998). *The marriage of sense and soul: Integrating science and religion.* New York, NY: Random House.

8

Exploring the Inner Landscape of Teaching: A Program for Faculty Renewal

Libby Falk Jones
Berea College

To improve the quality of faculty life, Berea College developed a yearlong program exploring teaching as a vocation. Sixteen faculty from different departments participated in the series of seven experiential, dialogic sessions. Participants reported experiencing increased empathy and patience, deeper engagement with their work, a stronger sense of community, and encouragement to meet the challenges of being educators.

> If a single person is teaching, the whole universe shifts and makes room.
> —Maria Harris, Berea College's
> Exploring the Inner Landscape of Teaching Seminar

INTRODUCTION

The need for faculty renewal in higher education is increasing today. As faculty face demands of heavy course loads, department and institutional responsibilities, accountability to varied constituencies, and budgetary constraints, faculty quality of life has eroded (Atkins, Brinko, Butts, Claxton, & Hubbard, 2001; Austin, Brocato, & Rohrer, 1997; Menges, 1996; Smith, 1990). Many faculty also experience a disconnect with today's students, who bring to their education a different set of learning approaches, motivation, and expectations from students of previous generations (Parks, 1986).

In response to the need for renewal, most colleges and universities have developed programs where faculty can investigate their teaching practices, experiment with new approaches, learn new skills, and share their successes and challenges. The focus of such programs may be encouraging active learning, teaching critical thinking, using instructional technology, understanding today's students, or a mixture of these important topics. At Berea, for example, our Communication Across the College Program, begun in 1989, brings together a dozen faculty and staff to form a one- to two-year learning community for comprehensive, ongoing reflection, research, and dialogue on learning and teaching topics. The success of such programs often flows largely from the development of a community in which participants build trust, speak honestly, and connect deeply with one another (Cox, 2001). Within such a community, faculty are able to gain information and develop new teaching skills and to explore themselves and their paths as teachers, an exploration on which all long-lasting faculty development must be based. What might happen, we wondered at Berea, if we offered a program for faculty renewal where inner exploration of the teaching life was not a byproduct but a center?

SEMINAR DESIGN

A yearlong program, titled Exploring the Inner Landscape of Teaching, was developed and led in 1995–1996 by three faculty. The goal of the seminar was to enable planners and a dozen colleagues to examine our callings as teachers, to explore the deep hungers leading us into and keeping us in our profession. Our hope was to understand teaching as a "graced activity...which, when dwelt in with fidelity, has the power to recreate the world" (Harris, 1987, p. xvi). If a primary goal for educators is "to bring students to a knowledge of the world within, its geography and anthropology, depths and heights, myths and primary texts" (O'Reilley, 1993, p. 32), then teachers need to mine these depths in themselves. Robertson (1999) argues that to function at the highest level of teaching, faculty need to draw on their awareness of their inner experience as it interacts with learners' inner experience. We believed that Berea College, with its historical and current commitments to educating 1,500 students primarily from Appalachia, black and white, women and men, within an inclusive Christian, liberal arts, and service tradition, offered both opportunities and challenges for our work as educators. We wanted to explore our own teaching and learning paths as a means for encountering the very hard yet crucial questions facing us today about the nature and shape of education.

Informing the seminar design were writings by several scholars: Parker J. Palmer (1983; 1991; 1998; 2000), who taught at Berea in 1993–1994, while he was writing *The Courage to Teach* (1997); Maria Harris (1987), who explores the artistry of teaching; and Mary Rose O'Reilley (1993; 1998; 2000), who probes teaching (and living) as a contemplative practice. Another important resource was the work of the Assembly for Expanded Perspectives on Learning (a division of the National Council of Teachers of English), whose publications, conferences, and workshops provided theory and practices exploring teachers' inner lives.

Simple but crucial principles undergirded the seminar's design.

- Self-exploration, sharing of experiences, and reflection must be central at every session. Short readings and theoretical materials could support each session, but our time together must draw deeply on ourselves.

- Session leaders should come from both inside and outside of the college. We wanted to ground the seminar in available talents as well as enrich it with outside expertise.

- Sessions must be involving and experiential, the pace calm and slow. The impulse to overfill the time must be resisted.

- The tone of each session must be open, honest, and supportive.

- Participation should be voluntary; the group should reflect diversity in field, gender, ethnicity, belief, and length of time at the college. Group size, including planners as full participants, should be 12–16.

- The number of sessions should be great enough to allow for the creation of community, but not so numerous as to become a burden. We settled on seven half-day sessions, spread throughout the academic year.

Thus the following seminar description appeared in the letter of invitation to faculty:

> This seminar series is designed to encourage reflection and dialogue among faculty from the four divisions of the college on the values and beliefs that inform our vision and our practice of teaching. Through readings, discussions, and exercises led by faculty and other presenters, participants will explore the inner geography of teaching—the ways our teaching informs and shapes us, nourishes or depletes our inner lives. Participants will investigate the spiritual base that underlies learning and teaching and on which we draw to meet the challenges we face as educators today. Participants will also reflect together on how as teachers we can help students meet their need for a deep learning that grounds them in their inner selves and at the same

time opens them to creative intellectual and spiritual relationships with others in community.

Twelve faculty—four men and eight women representing the departments of art, foreign languages, religion, English, music, psychology, biology, chemistry, nursing, education, business, and general studies—expressed interest in joining us in this exploration. Four of these participants were in their second or third year of teaching at Berea; four had taught at Berea more than 20 years each. We were also joined by our new president, Larry Shinn. In his inaugural address the previous spring, President Shinn had called on the campus to "find ways to be both rational and compassionate beings and nurture the whole person in our teaching and learning." In asking to participate, the president made it clear that he too was a seeker, eager to pursue this journey in the company of colleagues. We benefited throughout the seminar from his passion for learning and learners and his willingness to share his own experiences, struggles, and insights.

Funding for the program was provided by President Shinn and the Office of the Associate Dean for General Education and Faculty Development. The budget totaled $5,000, including expenses and stipends for three outside session leaders, books and articles, refreshments, and a $200 stipend for each participant.

SEMINAR PROGRAM

The half-day, three- to four-hour sessions typically occurred on Saturday mornings, occasionally on Friday evenings or Sunday afternoons, in various comfortable and private campus locales. Participants were invited to dress comfortably. Following are descriptions of five seminar sessions, illustrating the variety of means of engagement.

Our program opened with a visit by Maria Harris. After a Friday evening discussion of what had led each of us to this seminar and how each of us understood "inner landscape"—a sharing which lay the groundwork for the honest exchanges that followed—Harris invited us to explore our teaching through religious imagination, as a work of art. Teaching is artistic work, Harris argues; teachers are makers of others. Harris (1987) suggests five steps in exploring what she calls the holy work of teaching: contemplation, engagement, formgiving, emergence, and release (p. 25). The following Saturday morning, in a studio in the art building, Harris led us in an exercise she describes in *Teaching and Religious Imagination* (1987, p. 34). We were each given a glob of clay. After playing with the clay to discover its possibilities and limitations, we were blindfolded and asked to continue letting this material find a form expressing the self each of us brought to our teaching. The discussion following our display and commentary on our creations was rich indeed. At the end of the discussion, we returned our clay creations to their original form, releasing their potential to be recreated by us or others.

A local cellist, Suzanne McIntosh, made use of a different art form, music, as a means for prompting our inner journeys (Chitouras, 1993; Leviton, 1994). Experiencing a variety of sounds made by the cello led to reflections on the nature and kinds of listening central to teaching and learning. We also explored improvisation, discussing ways to create environments that give permission for our students to experience creative insights. In a closing exercise, we together produced sounds that wove into a surprising resonance, reaffirming the power of the community we were creating.

Parker Palmer led the group in a discussion of teaching as a vocation centered on Chuang Tzu's poem, "The Woodcarver" (Merton, 1965; Palmer, 1991). After two participants read the poem aloud to the group, Palmer asked us to reflect on the woodcarver's preparation for his work, the materials for his work, and his relation to the object he creates and to the master who sets him the task. How might the woodcarver's experience of his vocation enlighten us as teachers? How might his path inform our work in our classrooms? Small-group discussions of these questions yielded deepening levels of insight that were then shared with the whole group.

Robert Schneider, professor of classics and general education and one of the seminar's designers, invited us to reflect on ways we relate to our students and the personal resources we bring to various challenging pedagogical situations. He began with a short presentation, titled "Teaching as Relationship: 'Thou Shalt Love Thy Student as Thyself,'" in which he explored the historical model of the teacher-pupil relationship and narrated the teaching journey which had brought him to his understanding that we teach from the heart to the heart. Then Schneider asked the group to inventory the personal resources—qualities, life experiences, and knowledge—that each of us brought to our work as teachers. Participants' lists included such qualities as empathy, ability to stay calm in a crisis, caring and kindness, grit, toleration of ambiguity, and parenting skills. Small groups were then presented with three classroom scenarios, each embodying challenges faculty may face in exploring Biblical texts, the theory of evolution, and issues of sexual preference. Schneider asked us first to freewrite, then to share our thinking on ways our personal resources could help us respond to the intellectual and moral difficulties presented in the scenarios. (This exercise is included in Appendix 8.1.)

In a session titled "Who Are the Learners We Teach?" Larry Shinn, Berea's president and a religious studies scholar, drew on his research on the Hare Krishnas and on Sharon Parks's (1986) model of young adult faith development to help the group probe some important questions related to our college's commitment to "explore the Christian faith and its many expressions." He invited participants to respond to such questions as the following: What does it mean for faculty to encourage students to seek "safe spaces" for "inner work"? How can we promote the academy's search for "truth" and its inclusion of all ideas—including the rejection of all religions—and still nourish students' spiritual growth? Together the group discussed ways to help our college become a mentoring community inclusive of all individuals, regardless of their particular beliefs.

ASSESSMENT: TEACHING IS "NOT EASIER BUT . . . BETTER!"

At the end of the year, the group of 16 was asked to reflect individually in writing, then in dialogue, on the value of the seminar. Key questions were whether the seminar had met the needs and desires which led individuals to join, if the seminar had opened new ways of seeing teaching and learning, whether and how participants had applied any of the insights gained in the seminar, and what might help strengthen future seminars and continue this work.

All participants reported that the seminar had met at least some of their goals and needs, including needs whose existence they had not fully realized. "I viewed the seminar as an opportunity to share experiences and insights with more seasoned teachers or those in other disciplines, and I have not been disappointed," wrote a new faculty member. "What surprised me was the extent to which I became reflective on my own goals and intentions as a teacher," she noted. For several faculty, the opportunity to reflect was the key to the seminar's success. "I ended my first year at Berea disappointed and tired," wrote another new faculty member. "'Exploring the Inner Landscape' has assisted me to regroup. I have been able to find sources of quiet and renewal in the preparation for and participation in the workshops." Renewal was important for senior faculty participants as well. "I needed an opportunity to reflect upon my own teaching and search for ways to transform it," wrote one professor. "Through ideas from colleagues, session directors, and readings, I was able to engage deeply in such reflections." Another participant wrote of the power of the self-discovery she experienced in the seminar, particularly in the work with Maria Harris.

I was stunned with what I produced in clay with Maria Harris. That poor little clay bird flew out of my inner landscape with no conscious intent. It became part of me, so much so that I felt that it existed only in my hand. Strangely, I felt no loss when I returned the clay to a lump. What was it? What did it mean? Where did it come from? The whole experience has made me ponder about what else is inside me and how do I access it?

Several participants confirmed the value of the seminar in affirming their approaches to education. A senior professor noted, "The seminar endorsed the understanding that as we teach, we learn, and underlined the significance of the inner landscape of all participants in the educational transaction." He added that he was able, in class, to undergird his teaching presence "with the understood support of the premises of the seminar." A new faculty member credited the seminar for giving direction to what had been largely unconscious approaches in her teaching. Others praised the seminar for giving them the confidence to try new approaches. "The experiential exercises gave me the opportunity to be in the role of a student rather than that of teacher," wrote a senior professor. "This role reversal is essential in giving me the confidence to take more risks in the classroom and to develop more empathy," he noted. An important new idea for several participants was the concept that the material in the course guides the teaching, rather than vice versa. "I have become much more cognizant of how the subject matter functions as a teacher in the course, and I have sought to become better at facilitating students' access to the material," wrote a senior professor.

The seminar also succeeded in helping faculty to embrace the emotional, relational dimension of teaching and learning. "I find myself thinking more about the motivation and emotion behind my teaching than I have before this," wrote one professor. "I also try to listen to what my students mean, rather than what they say." Another noted, "I am a better listener today than I was in September. I listen better to others and to myself." A third faculty member wrote that the seminar had helped her develop more patience with her students and with herself.

By far, the most important value of the seminar was the development of community. One participant wrote that the seminar

internally and spiritually provided a bonding situation for us faculty (too often physically isolated in our own offices as well as on intellectual and emotional circuits).... This bonding function is the most important to me—the sense that we are an educational community of caring as well as informed individuals. I now know each participant in ways I never would have otherwise.

Others wrote and spoke of the loneliness, fear, and separation that faculty experience and the ways the seminar encouraged the connection, hope, and energy that can overcome this isolation. "Although the outside speakers were wonderful, and I gained much from their presence and presentations, it was the nurturing experiences of the seminar participants—sharing frustrations, concerns, and challenges—which really helped me to grow as a teacher," wrote a new faculty member. "I have found a sense of intimacy with colleagues that I honestly had not realized could occur," noted another professor. A senior faculty member wrote of the valuable "climate of trust and honesty" that characterized the seminar. "The value of this increased collegiality cannot be measured," wrote another professor. The seminar did not offer easy answers, noted a new faculty member, but sharing challenges with colleagues encouraged her to continue to struggle with the challenges. "Things do not seem to get easier but maybe they get better!" she concluded.

In addition to affirming the value of the seminar experience, participants also noted challenges and suggested changes. Despite our attempt not to overload sessions, several participants wrote of the need for time for more discussion, particularly in sessions led by outside presenters. Faculty also recognized the risks involved in participating in the seminar. One faculty member defined three manifestations of risk that participants incurred.

> First would be the risk of being seen as superfluous, or even silly, in an era which is rejoicing in its secularism. This Age of the Zen of Technology is embarrassed by spiritual considerations and is rapidly losing the ability to resolve difficulties and plan futures through spiritual means.

> Second . . . is the risk of being viewed as light or less than rigorous within academia. . . . Berea still falls prey to the demands of graduate schools, the workplace, the "real world . . ." The [desire] to be . . . regarded as viable academics . . . can wash away the strength for risk-taking.

> The most difficult form of risk-taking is that involved in encountering oneself and the constitution of one's inner being. Speaking in a group and waiting for responses is so very hard, but this pales in comparison to that small, quiet voice awakened by a search for the inner

landscape of teaching. It pales in comparison to the new reflections and hard changes we all know are inevitable.

A senior professor echoed her analysis. "I have seen how easy it is to escape from this more intimate approach by fleeing into the intellect, reveries, or cynical detachment," he wrote. "The right balance requires discernment and practice." He noted that he found this challenge "both exciting and daunting."

Participants' evaluations demonstrated that the seminar's benefits had justified their taking those risks and that the seminar experience had helped them begin to meet the resulting challenges. Participants expressed their hope that this group's dialogue could continue and that this work could be extended to involve other faculty.

CONCLUSIONS: FUTURE DIRECTIONS

The work of the Inner Landscape of Teaching Seminar has had several outcomes at Berea and beyond. Seminar participants agreed to continue meeting for a second year, to explore together topics led by members of the group. Seminar planners designed a new series for the next year as well, The Art and Soul of Teaching and Learning, facilitated by an Inner Landscape participant and involving 15 new faculty participants, including the college's new provost. During that year, the seminars gathered for two joint sessions, one on voice, led by Peter Elbow (1981; 1986), the other on soulful practices, led by Mary Rose O'Reilley (1993; 1998; 2000). Another outcome was a proposal for a mentoring program for new faculty, developed by seminar participants and others, which received funding from the Lilly Foundation. That successful program led to the development of a yearly seminar for new faculty held during our January short term, where new faculty are invited to become a learning community exploring multiple dimensions of teaching. Recent discussions of the nature of Berea's commitment to explore the Christian faith and its many expressions—within a community reflecting a wide range of religious beliefs, including no-belief—have been conducted in an open and thoughtful spirit stemming at least in part from the voices of seminar participants.

Reports on the seminar at several national conferences have been enthusiastically received, one manifestation of the growing interest in this work among a host of postsecondary institutions. Readings and resources, plus information on workshop and conference opportunities, are available now from several organizations: the Center for Teacher Formation and its Courage to Teach Program established by Parker Palmer (www.teacherformation.org/), the Education as Transformation Project (www.wellesley.edu/RelLife/transformation/), the Center for Contemplative Mind in Society (www.contemplativemind.org/), as well as from the Assembly for Expanded Perspectives on Learning (www.bsu .edu/web/aepl/Home.html).

Our hope is that faculty and administrators everywhere will recognize the benefit of this approach to faculty development and will devise ways to realize this work in their particular institutions. The fact that Berea is a small college with clearly stated commitments to undergraduate teaching, to faith exploration, and to community may have made it easier for us to engage faculty in dialogue about their vocation as educators. Yet despite this favorable context, we found that our faculty's need for such dialogue and awareness of the risks of engaging it were as strong as might be expected from faculty at larger institutions with different commitments. The positive response our program elicited from a diverse group of faculty confirms our sense that such faculty renewal is broadly needed in higher education today.

Meeting the challenge of finding resources—people as well as funds—to support our program turned out to be easier than we had anticipated, once we began looking. We accomplished much on a small budget; a fine program could be put together on an even smaller budget, by drawing more fully on local people (campus and community) who are engaged in inner work and are willing to share it, and by supporting participants in ways other than providing stipends.

What is important for faculty renewal programs—and indeed, for all good faculty development efforts—is to identify and empower planners who have a vision based on a deep understanding of faculty need, the creativity to find resources, and the commitment to make this journey in the company of others. Our seminar experience is one small piece of proof that many faculty members do believe that education involves whole people, and that many of us are willing to take on the hard work of living in community so that our inner selves, as well as those of our students, may be nurtured.

REFERENCES

Atkins, S. S., Brinko, K. T., Butts, J. A., Claxton, C. S., & Hubbard, G. T. (2001). Faculty quality of life. In D. Lieberman & C. Wehlburg (Eds.), *To improve the academy: Vol. 19. Resources for faculty, instructional, and organizational development* (pp. 323–345). Bolton, MA: Anker.

Austin, A. E., Brocato, J. J., & Rohrer, J. D. (1997). Institutional missions, multiple faculty roles: Implications for faculty development. In D. Dezure & M. Kaplan (Eds.), *To improve the academy: Vol. 16. Resources for faculty, instructional, and organizational development* (pp. 3–20). Stillwater, OK: New Forums Press.

Chitouras, J. (1993, Spring). Esoteric sound and color. *Gnosis, 27,* 36–40.

Cox, M. D. (2001). Faculty learning communities: Change agents for transforming institutions into learning organizations. In D. Lieberman & C. Wehlburg (Eds.), *To improve the academy: Vol. 19. Resources for faculty, instructional, and organizational development* (pp. 69–93). Bolton, MA: Anker.

Elbow, P. (1981). *Writing with power.* New York, NY: Oxford University Press.

Elbow, P. (1986). *Embracing contraries: Explorations in teaching and learning.* New York, NY: Oxford University Press.

Harris, M. (1987). *Teaching and religious imagination: An essay in the theology of teaching.* New York, NY: HarperCollins.

Leviton, R. (1994, January/February). Healing vibrations. *Yoga Journal, 1,* 59–64, 81–83.

Menges, R. J. (1996). Experiences of newly hired faculty. In L. Richlin & D. DeZure (Eds.), *To improve the academy: Vol. 15: Resources for faculty, instructional, and organizational development* (pp. 169–182). Stillwater, OK: New Forums Press.

Merton, T. (1965). *The way of Chuang Tzu.* New York, NY: New Directions.

O'Reilley, M. R. (1993). *The peaceable classroom.* Portsmouth, NH: Boynton/Cook-Heinemann.

O'Reilley, M. R. (1998). *Radical presence: Teaching as contemplative practice.* Portsmouth, NH: Boyton/Cook-Heinemann.

O'Reilley, M. R. (2000). *The barn at the end of the world: The apprenticeship of a Quaker, Buddhist shepherd.* Minneapolis, MN: Milkweed.

Palmer, P. J. (1983). *To know as we are known: Education as a spiritual journey.* San Francisco, CA: Harper.

Palmer, P. J. (1991). *The active life: Wisdom for creativity and caring.* San Francisco, CA: Harper.

Palmer, P. J. (1997). *The courage to teach: Exploring the inner landscape of a teacher's life.* San Francisco, CA: Jossey-Bass.

Palmer, P. J. (2000). *Let your life speak: Listening for the voice of vocation.* San Francisco, CA: Jossey-Bass.

Parks, S. (1986). *The critical years: Young adults and the search for meaning, faith, and commitment.* San Francisco, CA: Harper.

Robertson, D. L. (1999). Professors' perspectives on their teaching: A new construct and developmental model. *Innovative Higher Education, 23*(4), 271–294.

Smith, P. (1990). *Killing the spirit: Higher education in America.* New York, NY: Viking.

APPENDIX 8.1

TEACHING AS RELATIONSHIP: THREE CLASSROOM SCENARIOS

Robert J. Schneider, Berea College

Read carefully the assigned scenario below, then share with one another your immediate thoughts and feelings about the way you might handle the topic in the classroom in the light of the inventory of personal resources and strengths you began earlier.

I. Imagine that you have been asked to teach a course in one of the natural sciences or a course in western intellectual history. The paradigm of evolution either informs the subject matter of the course throughout or is covered as a specific topic. You expect that many students will be curious and open to learning about evolution, but you also expect that some may be troubled by this topic, since they have been taught that evolution is "just a theory," or contrary to the Bible, or atheistic. In fact, a colleague has informed you that one of your students told her that he had become physically ill when a biology teacher talked about evolution in another course. What thoughts come to mind about addressing this situation in your teaching about evolution?

II. Imagine that you are teaching a course in the Bible or a humanities course which includes texts from the Bible, such as the primaeval stories in Genesis, the Book of Isaiah, the Gospel of Luke, and other texts. You will approach them using historical and literary criticism. You expect that many students will be interested in and stimulated by this approach, but you also expect that some will be fundamentalist Christians who believe that the Bible is the literal and inerrant word of God, dictated by Him to the writers. Some of these students may respond with anxiety or hostility to this new and different approach. What thoughts come to mind about addressing this situation in your teaching of biblical texts?

III. Imagine that you are teaching a course in psychology or sociology or child and family studies or nursing. The syllabus includes the topic of homosexuality and/or homosexual behaviors and lifestyles. While you know that many students are open to learning about this topic, you also expect that there will be students who have been taught and believe that homosexuality is a sin and that homosexuals are condemned by God and are going to hell. You also assume, or may know, that the class includes one or more students who are uncertain about their own sexuality; gay but in the closet; lesbian and out; and a few who are contemptuous of men or women whom they perceive to be effeminate or "mannish." What thoughts come to mind about addressing this situation as you teach the subject matter?

9

Is the Thrill Gone?
An Investigation of Faculty
Vitality Within the Context
of the Community College

Cathie J. Peterson
Johnson County Community College

This single institutional case study investigated faculty vitality within the context of the community college by answering the following research questions: What are the characteristics of vital faculty within the community college? What effect does the environment have on faculty vitality? What do the vital faculty do to maintain their vitality? Qualitative research methods were employed to study the lives of the faculty within their naturalistic setting, thereby giving voice to the vital community college faculty.

INTRODUCTION

Community colleges have been members of the American higher education system since the early 20th century when society was changing and the need for educated workers in the nation's industries was expanding (Cohen & Brawer, 1996; Fields, 1962, London, 1978). This transition was accompanied by the pressure for upward social mobility that necessitated citizens' access to higher education (Cohen & Brawer, 1996; Fields, 1962; London, 1978; Lucas, 1994; Sarko, 1964). The public's demand for the opportunity to attend college was coupled with the belief in American institutions and their ability to lend authenticity, legitimacy, and credibility to an individual's pursuits and educational outcomes (Baker, 1994; Carnegie Commission on Higher Education, 1994; Cohen & Brawer, 1987, 1996; Diener, 1986; Fields, 1962; London, 1978).

Initially community colleges were founded on the notion of furnishing the first two years of an undergraduate education, thereby alleviating the tedious task of providing general education courses from the university's purview, hence the name junior college (Baker, 1994; Cohen & Brawer, 1987, 1996; Deegan, 1985; Diener, 1986; Fields, 1962; Kelley & Wilhun, 1970; London, 1978). During the past four decades, however the role of the community college and its faculty has evolved, changed, and matured, mirroring the evolution of the institutions themselves.

Researchers who examine faculty renewal at four-year colleges use the term "vitality" to investigate the manner by which faculty remain enthused and connected to their work in the higher education milieu. To date the investigation of faculty vitality has focused on vitality within the context of four-year colleges and universities, thereby ignoring one of the fastest growing segments of the higher education system—the community college. Scholars such as Baldwin (1990), Clark and Corcoran (1985) and Schuster (1985) argue that it is of utmost importance to consider and investigate how faculty within the community college environment remain energized, enthused, and renewed given the unique culture and mission of the community college.

Currently 200,000 faculty are teaching at 1,100 community colleges throughout the United States with a national enrollment of approximately 5,500,000 students (Carter & Ottinger, 1992; Cohen & Brawer, 1996; U.S. Department of Education, National Center for Education Statistics, 1998). These substantial numbers illustrate the significant influence community colleges wield in the realm of higher education.

How do community college faculty remain energized, connected, and revitalized? Some community college faculty report being disconnected from their peers, are afforded limited opportunities to conduct research, work with a student population composed primarily of academically challenged students, and teach five introductory courses a semester. Many researchers argue these conditions contribute to burnout and career dissatisfaction (Baker, 1994; Clark & Corcoran, 1985; Cohen & Brawer, 1996; Gleazer, 1967; Grubb & Associates, 1999; Sarko, 1964; Schuster, 1985).

There is without a doubt a paucity of research that illuminates the cultural milieu of community college faculty, who work within what some have referred to as higher education's teaching colleges (Baker, 1994; Cohen & Brawer, 1987, 1996; Fields, 1962; Grubb & Associates, 1999; London, 1978; Monroe, 1972; Outcalt, 2000). It is important to examine the vitality and renewal of community college faculty in lieu of the significant number of students these faculty educate, and the influential position the faculty possess, given that they work with students at the beginning of their college experience, a particularly vulnerable phase in many students' lives (Astin, 1984; Pascarella & Terenzini, 1991).

The purpose of this research is to explore the concept of faculty vitality within the context of the community college. The key concepts framing this exploration are taken from Baldwin (1990) and Clark and Corcoran's (1985) case studies that examined the vitality of faculty at various liberal arts institutions and the University of Minnesota. The genesis of their studies is embedded in their concern for the health and well-being of higher education given dropping enrollments, declining budgets, and the public's increasing criticism of public education in general.

Johnson County Community College (JCCC), a Midwestern community college, was chosen as an appropriate site to research the complicated and imprecise notion of vitality, thereby answering the following research questions.

- What are the characteristics of vital faculty within the context of a community college?

- What do the vital faculty do to maintain their vitality?

- What affect (role) does the environment have on faculty vitality?

The conceptual framework guiding this study is directly connected to the research conducted by Baldwin (1990), Clark and Corcoran (1985) and Schuster (1985), who investigated faculty vitality within the liberal arts college and university settings, respectively. Their explorations revealed that faculty vitality was influenced by environmental factors found within the milieu of higher education institutions as well as the personal characteristics of the individual faculty members.

Relevant themes disclosed by the research of Baldwin (1990), Clark and Corcoran (1985), and Schuster's (1985) case studies of faculty vitality provided structure to this exploration of faculty vitality within the context of the community college. The first of the germane themes is the importance of constructive environmental factors, which include positive administrative support, a clear definition of institutional purpose, recognition of faculty accomplishments, and the appreciation of a faculty member's worth as a member of the human race. The second theme refers to the prevalence of certain personal characteristics of the faculty, such as being highly motivated to conduct research, having aspirations to be more productive than their peers, possessing active personality types who publish, teach, and contribute service while never feeling "stuck" in their academic profession.

Numerous scholars have explored the concept of vitality and argue that it is a primitive notion used to describe a complex phenomenon (Clark & Corcoran, 1985), intimately associated with the social-psychological well-being of individuals within institutions of higher education (Ebben & Maher, 1979), closely coupled to the institution's culture and administrative support as well as relationships connecting students and faculty (Centra, 1985), a complicated term difficult to summarize while being closely associated to productivity (Baldwin, 1990), and dependent upon the cultural milieu of the institution, which in turn is influenced by administrators and students (Bevan, 1985; Bogen, 1978; Schuster, 1985).

Scholars argue that the context of the community college may present different notions of faculty vitality considering that vis-à-vis community college faculty report being disconnected from their colleagues and working with an academically challenged and diverse student population while teaching an inordinately high number of classes which affords little time to conduct research. Some scholars assert that the aforementioned factors contribute to burnout, frustration, and discontentment with one's academic career (Baker, 1994; Baldwin, 1990; Clark, 1985; Clark & Corcoran, 1985; Cohen & Brawer, 1996; Eaton, 1994; Gleazer, 1967; Grubb & Associates, 1999; Miller, Finley, & Shedd Vancko, 2000; Outcalt, 2000; Sarko, 1964; Schuster, 1985). It is important to explore faculty vitality within the community college environment to reveal the pedagogical activities and classroom endeavors of the community college faculty, giving voice to the faculty who some argue fulfill American higher education's teaching college niche (Clark, 1985; Cohen & Brawer, 1996; Eaton, 1994; Outcalt, 2000; Palmer & Vaughan, 1992).

RESEARCH DESIGN

The qualitative research method used to reveal the intricacies of the research site was a single institutional case study, affording access to the environmental factors which are essential to the investigation of faculty vitality. The case study also provided an avenue whereby the voices of the research participants were revealed, disclosing their educational beliefs, approaches to teaching, and personal characteristics that contribute to their enthusiasm and passion for their work in the classroom.

Research Site
Johnson County Community College was chosen as the site in which to conduct this study of faculty vitality. JCCC, a Midwestern single campus community college, founded in 1969, is a relative latecomer to the ranks of the American community college movement. Currently JCCC is housed on 285 acres in Johnson County, Kansas, serving a credit and noncredit student population of approximately 35,000 students. The institution prides itself on providing an academic environment where "learning comes first" (Johnson County Community College, 2001–2002, p. 3).

Accredited by North Central Association of Colleges, JCCC has more than 100 articulation agreements with regional colleges and universities (Johnson County Community College, 2001). The college's annual budget is $128,042,653 with an operating budget totaling $80,624,288. The college's membership in the League for Innovation in the Community College is predicated upon evidence of excellence, innovation, stability, access to superior resources, and quality leadership (Johnson County Community College and the League for Innovation in the Community College, 2000).

Employing 304 full-time faculty, whose primary responsibility is to teach the more than 50 one- and two-year degree and certificate programs, JCCC affords students access to numerous employment opportunities (Johnson County Community College, 2001). Of the full-time faculty, 51.06% are women and 48.94% are men (Johnson County Community College, FY03 staff profile, internal unpublished document).

According to the vice president of instruction, approximately 30% of the full-time faculty at JCCC hold terminal degrees, whereas all (100%) of the 304 full-time faculty have earned master's degrees.

JCCC was chosen as the institutional site most favorable for the investigation given the college's national ranking among community colleges, its membership in the prestigious League for Innovation in the Community College, and the fact that the institution affords access to over 300 full-time faculty, of which 30% hold doctorates. Finally JCCC's culture includes positive environmental conditions critical to the notion of faculty vitality. The researcher is on the staff at JCCC, making access to information easy.

Selection of Vital Faculty
Borrowing from Baldwin's (1990) research selection process, vital faculty were identified through the following research: Letters of introduction were sent to all full-time faculty. Attached to each letter of introduction was a nomination form, which included a clearly stated definition of vitality. To be included in

the study the faculty member had to receive at least two nominations from his or her colleagues.

The definition of vitality developed for this study reads as follows:

> Vital professors are inquisitive and engaged academically. They have earned the respect of their colleagues and take pleasure in being an active member of the academic profession. It is understood that vitality will exist in many different forms. Vital professors may be academic leaders, inspirational and inspiring teachers, productive scholars, engaged advisors, but they may *not* participate in these roles with equal amounts of enthusiasm and proficiency. A vital professor is interested in developing collegial relationships and is truly engaged in teaching in a community college environment.

A total of 304 letters and nomination forms, which included the aforementioned definition of vitality, were distributed through the Office of the Vice President of Instruction during the spring semester 2002. After the nomination forms were returned, each faculty member's name and the frequency of nomination were recorded on a grid. A total of 94 individuals returned their nomination forms. Of those nominated, 18 faculty received at least 2 nominations and 16 agreed to participate in the study.

Data Collection

Interviews with the 16 full-time faculty who agreed to participate were scheduled during the month following the distribution of the letter requesting nominations. The interviews, which lasted approximately one and one-half to two hours were conducted in locations throughout the JCCC campus. The interviews commenced after each participant agreed to the clearly defined research parameters, which were articulated in a consent form the participants signed and dated pursuant to the University of Kansas's Human Subject Committee Lawrence Campus investigation requirements. The semi-structured interview format was employed to elucidate and clarify themes. In addition to conducting face-to-face interviews with the 16 nominees, 10 interviews were conducted with various JCCC administrators.

The researcher ensured trustworthiness of the data collection by reviewing interview notes after each conversation was completed, listening to the tape recorded interviews at least four times, and returning to the interview partners to corroborate statements, asking the interview partners to clarify statements and comments made during each interview. The data were analyzed through the constant comparative method recommended by Merriam (1997) to develop categories and themes by "continuous comparison of incidents, respondents' remarks" (p. 179).

Limitations

JCCC is located in one of the country's wealthiest counties; therefore, the college has rarely been faced with budgetary concerns. This fact has afforded the faculty at JCCC the opportunity to develop any number of programs and activities to support their pedagogical activities in the most positive manner. The sample of faculty interviewed was not ethnically diverse. All of the faculty who participated in this study were Caucasians affording access to no ethnically diverse faculty members. Finally, because this study was conducted in the middle to latter part of the spring semester 2002, the responses to the request for nominations may have been limited due to faculty's very busy schedules.

RESEARCH FINDINGS

The three research questions identified at the beginning of this chapter were used to structure a discussion of the various themes that emerged during the interviews.

Who Are the Vital Faculty at JCCC?

The seven men and nine women nominated teach the following subjects: mathematics, art history, humanities, composition, accounting, nursing, and various computer programming areas. Minority populations were not represented in the sample of faculty whose ages range from early 30s to early 60s.

As illustrated in Table 9.1, nine of the participants were from the liberal arts division, two represented the computer instruction and media resources division, six taught in the science, health care and math division, and one taught in the business and technology division. Four participants began their college educations at a community college and earned their associate's degrees, 16 held both a bachelor's and master's degree, and 5 had earned terminal degrees. The average tenure teaching at JCCC was 14.5 years, the longest tenure teaching was 28 years, and the shortest tenure was 2 years.

Becoming a Community College Faculty Member

None of the 16 faculty who participated in this study indicated that they aspired to teach at a community college. After earning their undergraduate college degrees, 80% of the study participants said their career goals were to teach in the secondary schools. Anita's comments are typical, "I had no intention of

TABLE 9.1
Faculty Nomination Demographics

Subject	Pseudonym*	Highest Degree	Years Teaching	Department
#1	Evelyn	M.A.	22	English
#2	Maxine	M.A.	7	English
#3	Walter	Ph.D.	20	Humanities
#4	Connie	M.A.	26	Mathematics
#5	Sandra	M.A.	20	Business
#6	John	M.A.	13	Mathematics
#7	Christine	Ph.D.	19	Nursing
#8	Maria	M.A.	9	Nursing
#9	Rene	M.A.	3	English
#10	Victor	Ph.D.	19	Humanities
#11	William	M.A.	13	Business
#12	Curtis	Ph.D.	28	Humanities
#13	Jim	Ph.D.	2	Humanities
#14	Corrine	M.A.	6	Business
#15	Anita	M.A.	9	Humanities
#16	Bob	M.A.	9	Science

*All names are pseudonyms.

teaching at a community college. I thought I was going to teach at the secondary level . . . " Connie said, "I fell into teaching at the community college." Eight did, in fact, say that their career as a teacher began in the secondary schools; however, their family moved or they needed part-time employment and they "fell into" the job of their dreams.

It is interesting to note that the youngest members of this study disclosed that they went to graduate school with the expressed purpose of securing a teaching position in higher education, whether at a university or a four-year college. It did not occur to them to seek a teaching assignment at a community college. This fact is confirmed in research conducted by Cohen and Brawer (1996) and others who have found that currently many community college faculty are migrating into their teaching jobs directly from graduate school rather than from the secondary education classroom.

What Are the Characteristics of Vital Faculty?

It has been argued by Clark (1985) and others that the origins of vitality can be linked with the positive qualities individuals possess that encourage a high level of productivity. Baldwin (1990) and Schuster (1985) assert that the relationship between the individual and the institution inspire and promote vitality. So it is not surprising that the nominated faculty associated terms such as energy and enthusiasm with vitality.

Five of the faculty said vitality meant "energy and enthusiasm," "a passion and interest in the world" around them. Five faculty thought vitality meant "a sense of being alive, staying challenged, caring for self and others; being creative, active and constantly thinking about the nature of teaching and learning." Maxine likened vitality to being a "Tigger type person . . . they talk with their whole face—they have to try things."

The characteristics mentioned above and the personal traits of JCCC faculty are consistent with the findings of Baldwin (1990), Clark and Corcoran (1985), and Schuster (1985), who found that vitality resides in individuals who possess personal characteristics that inspire them to take their pedagogical accomplishments to a higher level. However, it is important to remember that the interaction with the institution's mission and goals enables faculty to be creative, productive, and enthused (Ebben & Maher, 1979). The environment and cultural milieu of the institution engages the faculty, which in turn encourages them to be energetic, challenged, and creative (Baldwin, 1990; Bevan, 1985; Centra, 1985; Clark & Corcoran, 1985; Maher, 1982; Schuster, 1985).

Passion for Teaching

Energy alone is insufficient to define vital faculty. According to Clark and Corcoran (1985) and Schuster (1985), the fundamental concepts of faculty vitality are grounded in the connection between the personal and professional goals of the faculty member and how tightly coupled faculty aspirations are aligned to institutional mission. The men and women who comprise this study are thoroughly committed to the community college's mission, and therefore find their pedagogical activities quite rewarding and stimulating. They love what they do; they feel "called" to teach within the community college environment. Their enthusiasm for teaching the community college student is all consuming.

Walter, one of the research participants, set the tone when he asserted, "I love what I am doing. Love is not too strong a word. It may not be strong enough. It's fun. This was my calling . . . college teaching." Evelyn, who teaches

English, said with a broad smile, "I love teaching. I have the best job on campus. I can't imagine doing anything else with my career." Bob said, "If you can see that light bulb go off in the student's eyes, it's great. Also, if you really like a subject, they pay you to learn about it and to talk about it."

High Academic Standards
Most of the faculty in this study reported setting high academic expectations for their students regardless of the fact that community college students are generally less academically prepared than their peers at universities or four-year colleges (Cohen & Brawer, 1996). Centra (1985) asserts that one of the fundamental elements of faculty vitality is "sound undergraduate instruction" (p. 143).

Connie, a participant in this study, stated in her book, *Opportunities for Excellence: Professionalism and the Two-Year College Mathematics Faculty*, that

> inherent in good teaching is the establishment of high standards. As we expect and demand quality student performance, students usually respond and rise to meet our expectations of excellence. We set high performance goals for all students, regardless of race, gender, socioeconomic class or disability . . . We want to set ambitious goals for ourselves and for students, but we also want to make those expectations reasonable and attainable. (Neptune, 2001, p. 21)

Several quotes heard during the interviews are listed below.

- I set high standards and expect them [students] to adhere to the standards. I feel strongly about setting high standards.

- My standards are very, very high. Anybody that has ever had me in clinical will tell you that I have really, really high standards. Years later they come back to thank me.

- I have high standards and I help the students develop skills that will help them later. I give hard tests and the classroom environment is difficult, as well.

Faculty Pride
Faculty who participated in this study were gratified by the academic success of their students. Several of the faculty expressed pride in the colleges their students chose after finishing at JCCC. In fact, most of the vital faculty actively

advised their students to look beyond the regional universities while encouraging them to consider transferring to elite Ivy League institutions.

This is an interesting topic to explore given the research conducted by Morphew, Twombly, and Wolf-Wendel (2001), who examined the formalized relationship developed between two urban community colleges and Smith College. The transfer agreements between Smith and Santa Monica and Miami-Dade "provide very bright community college students with an opportunity to attend an elite school as well as their potential to add to the richness and diversity of institutions like Smith College" (p. 1).

Victor indicated he was advising his brightest students to consider attending institutions such as Harvard, Yale, and Dartmouth for the very same reason, that is, "that community college students add diversity to the Ivy League institutions and benefit from an extraordinary education at an exceptional institution of higher education."

How Do Vital Faculty Maintain Their Vitality?

The JCCC faculty participate in a plethora of programs, which contribute to their vitality and enthusiasm for teaching in the community college system. They report conducting research, publishing textbooks and articles, and giving presentations at national professional conferences. Christine, a nursing instructor, says, "I have authored and written my own book on critical thinking. That was fun." Connie said, "The professor from Penn State was impressed with my work and asked me to supplement his text. I love to write." Schuster (1985) argues that purposeful production is an important component of faculty vitality, which reveals itself through the publication of textbooks and journal articles.

Learning exchange networks train faculty of the future in the pedagogical techniques of the community college. According to John, "Experienced faculty work closely with new faculty to ensure that the new faculty will get the expectations of what we think is the definition of a good teacher." John continues, "I have enjoyed working with new faculty and think the interaction has been energizing for me to think about what I am doing in the classroom."

Learning communities provide an avenue for faculty to co-teach a course with a colleague from another discipline. John's Algebra II course is combined with an English Composition II course. John's eyes light up when he describes the experience. "The [students] don't take any tests. They just write papers. I've taught this [math] class for nine years . . . to teach with someone else and have their input . . . It's been wonderful."

Teacher exchange/mentor programs connect advanced graduate students from regional universities with seasoned faculty at JCCC. This program prevents burnout and encourages senior faculty to become refreshed by "teaching new courses in one's discipline" (Bishop, 1997, p. 12). Both Curtis and Jim welcomed the opportunity to work with young scholars from area universities thereby sharing their expertise and knowledge with someone considering a teaching career at a community college. According to Curtis, "the faculty find a means to remain connected to the literature of their discipline while collaborating with advanced graduate students."

Peer review is a summative and formative evaluation process of new faculty in their third year of teaching prior to awarding tenure. As a member of a peer review panel tenured faculty observe new faculty in the classroom and provide opportunities for newly hired faculty and seasoned professionals to dialogue about the process of teaching and learning. Maxine appreciates the opportunity to participate as a peer reviewer because the activity "invites peer feedback and I can improve my own teaching when I am a panel member."

Service-learning. Many of the vital faculty at JCCC said that participation in the service-learning program was a productive endeavor that contributed to their renewal and enthusiasm. According to Maria, it "provides personal and professional growth opportunities, which is a nice way to connect with the community."

Parker Palmer Formation. This initiative is clearly committed to the belief that teaching and the pedagogical activities associated with teaching and learning are important. Maria said, "This program sustains me and is a part of my everyday life both professionally and personally. It's not about teaching techniques, it's about acknowledging who you are and bringing who you are into your classroom."

National Endowment of the Humanities. Several of the faculty from the liberal arts division mentioned that the program contributes to their renewal and enthusiasm because it is a program that affords community college faculty the occasion to travel abroad while studying an academic topic of particular interest. The chair of the liberal arts division shared these thoughts: "I believe that the content is important and it opens up new material, which leads to good things for students. We're comfortable with Western Culture but we're hesitant to bring in non–Western Culture because it's not our field."

The vital faculty state that participation in the aforementioned programs affords an occasion to stretch and grow intellectually, spiritually, and academically while continually seeking new ways to teach and learn.

What Affect Does the Environment Have on Faculty Vitality?
The following themes revealed in the literature are particularly salient issues with regard to environmental factors and their influence on faculty vitality.

- Decisive leadership and support

- A mutually acceptable mission

- Intellectually stimulating faculty development programs

- Positive interaction between students and faculty

- An atmosphere of collegiality and support for academic freedom

- Institutional recognition and rewards

- A cultural milieu that fosters open communication and a sharing of pedagogical practices (Baldwin, 1990; Bevan, 1985; Clark & Corcoran, 1985; Grubb & Associates, 1999; Maher, 1982; Schuster, 1985)

The 16 faculty who participated in this study stated that the support they received from the JCCC administration was crucial to their enthusiasm for teaching. They appreciated the spontaneous accolades they received from administrative staff.

The mission of the community college is unique to the landscape of higher education, and the success of its faculty is tightly coupled to the community college's mission. The faculty said they enjoyed working in the community college environment. Their enthusiasm contributes to the heart and soul of the community college and they are its most ardent supporters.

Faculty development programs. There is little doubt that programs associated with the Center for Teaching and Learning and the Parker Palmer Formation group play an important role in the vitality of most faculty. The faculty in this study report that the JCCC staff development office promotes communication while fostering an interchange of pedagogical ideas limiting the isolation of faculty. Jim said, "The staff development office has been very useful. I have been given the resources to do the things I want to do."

Students in the classroom. All 16 faculty in this study stated that the students in their classrooms contribute to their vitality and enthusiasm. Repeatedly the faculty said that the students were essential to their continued enthusiasm for teaching. Connie articulated her feelings this way: "I love the interaction with the students. I love watching the lights come on in people's eyes when something clicks with them for the first time." The faculty reported that the multiplicity of the students vis-à-vis ages, academic preparation, personal stories, and academic goals significantly enhanced their love of teaching and enthusiasm for their work as a member of the faculty.

Academic freedom. This notion is essential to the community college faculty member's vitality. Today's faculty assert that academic freedom is an influential concept crucial to their vitality. Connie shared these thoughts: "To me academic freedom is extremely important. If I felt confined that would be very wearing. It would deplete my energy. I feel energized by the freedom to design the learning activities and assessment tools in my classroom."

Grubb and Associates (1999) assert that community college faculty are quite isolated in their community college teaching endeavors, which he argues negatively influences the pedagogical activities of the classroom.

> The isolation of instructors is created by the lack of any activities that might draw them together *around teaching.* Opportunities for learning communities and collaborative teaching are rare . . . Without any central forum for discussion the status of teaching is almost invisible or inaudible. (p. 285)

Rarely did the faculty at JCCC say they felt isolated. Most faculty reported that their participation in JCCC's programs eliminated isolationism while encouraging a climate of collegiality.

It is important to note that those instructors who are heavily involved in online instruction and WebCT course development did report feeling out of touch with their colleagues. This fact may warrant further investigation into the potential stress distance education/online course development and instruction may produce.

Change. Whether faculty members change textbooks, their academic course assignment, the type of students they teach, the time of day they teach, and/or introduce technology into their classroom, half of the vital faculty agree that change is an important component of an environment that fosters and encourages vitality.

Recognition and rewards. The most contentious issue this study revealed was the system of institutional recognition and rewards. The research findings support rather ambivalent attitudes, even hostility and anger, toward the formalized nomination process for awards as well as the way in which awards are disseminated. The director of staff development said, "The notion of awards in higher education has been debated extensively. Are they motivational or not? There are two schools of thought—one that awards do motivate and the other that awards are very divisive." This debate will surely continue.

IMPLICATIONS FOR PRACTICE

This single institutional case study of faculty vitality at JCCC has investigated the personal characteristics of the faculty as well as the environmental factors that foster and encourage their enthusiasm, renewal, and passion for teaching within the community college. This research revealed that environmental characteristics such as decisive leadership and support, a mutually acceptable mission, intellectually stimulating faculty development programs, positive interaction between students and faculty, an atmosphere of collegiality, support for academic freedom, and institutional recognition and rewards contribute to the vitality of the faculty. The personal attributes, such as an interest in the world around them, a sense of humor, a passion for teaching, high academic standards, a pride in their students and where they transfer, a competitive spirit, and a commitment to the mission of the community college also augment and enhance faculty vitality.

The outcomes of this investigation present several implications for practice. Despite budget constraints affecting most community colleges, it is imperative that community colleges continue to maintain faculty training and staff development initiatives. Change and flexibility are key components of faculty vitality; therefore, it is important to support the change of textbooks, course schedules, and/or course topics throughout a faculty member's tenure. The faculty ought to be encouraged to discuss their pedagogical endeavors with their colleagues in order to foster collegiality, which is an essential component of vitality. There is no doubt that institutional awards are a notable aspect of faculty vitality; however, the nomination process and the rationale and criteria used to determine who receives institutional rewards should be clearly defined. Academic freedom positively influences faculty vitality, and community college administrators must foster an environment where academic freedom is celebrated and encouraged.

RECOMMENDATIONS FOR FUTURE RESEARCH

The notion of faculty vitality within the context of the community college is an important concept requiring further research. It is recommended that future research explore the notion of burnout to discern the ways in which it might be avoided. It would be helpful to investigate the vitality of administrators, which might reveal important environmental and personal characteristics that influence administrative vitality. The 16 faculty who participated in this study were not racially diverse; given this fact, the exploration of vitality among minority faculty might provide additional insights not revealed in this study. In light of the recent research by Morphew, Twombly, and Wolf-Wendel (2001), which explored the formalized transfer process between two urban community colleges, an investigation of the ways in which faculty establish similar links to elite institutions of higher education would prove interesting. Finally, studying the students who comprise the vital faculty members' classrooms might be beneficial to determine whether the pedagogical activities of vital faculty members enhance learning.

The community college faculty who participated in this study love teaching and are committed to their students. Without a doubt the vitality of these individuals is closely tied to the positive environmental factors of this institution, thereby creating a synergy between the institution and the individual.

REFERENCES

Astin, A. W. (1984, July). Student involvement: A developmental theory for higher education. *Journal of College Student Personnel, 25,* 297–308.

Baker, G. A., III. (Ed.). (1994). *A handbook on the community college in America: Its history, mission, and management.* Westport, CT: Greenwood Press.

Baldwin, R. G. (1990, March/April). Faculty vitality beyond the research university: Extending a contextual concept. *Journal of Higher Education, 61*(2), 160–180.

Bevan, J. (1985). Who has the role of building incentives? In R. G. Baldwin (Ed.), *New directions for higher education: No. 51. Incentives for faculty vitality* (pp. 45–58). San Francisco, CA: Jossey-Bass.

Bishop, C. (1997). *The community's college: A history of Johnson County Community College, 1969–1999.* Pittsburg, KS: Pittcraft Printing.

Bogen, G. (1978). Performance and vitality as a function of student-faculty fit. In W. C. Kirschling (Ed.), *New directions for institutional research, No. 20. Evaluating faculty performance and vitality* (pp. 51–67). San Francisco, CA: Jossey-Bass.

Carnegie Commission on Higher Education. (1994). *The open-door colleges: Policies for community colleges.* New York, NY: McGraw-Hill.

Carter, D. J., & Ottinger, C. A. (1992). *Community college faculty: A profile.* Washington, DC: American Council on Education, Division of Policy Analysis and Research.

Centra, J. A. (1985). Maintaining faculty vitality through faculty development. In S. M. Clark & D. R. Lewis (Eds.), *Faculty vitality and institutional productivity: Critical perspectives for higher education* (pp. 141–156). New York, NY: Teachers College Press.

Clark, B. (1985). *The academic life*. Princeton, NJ: Princeton University Press.

Clark, S., & Corcoran, M. (1985). Individual and organizational contributions to faculty vitality: An institutional case study. In S. M. Clark & D. R. Lewis (Eds.), *Faculty vitality and institutional productivity: Critical perspectives for higher education* (pp. 112–138). New York, NY: Teachers College Press.

Cohen, A. M., & Brawer, F. B. (1987). *The collegiate function of community colleges: Fostering higher learning through curriculum and student transfer*. San Francisco, CA: Jossey-Bass.

Cohen, A. M., & Brawer, F. B. (1996). *The American community college*. San Francisco, CA: Jossey-Bass.

Deegan, W. (1985). *Renewing the American community college: Priorities and strategies for effective leadership*. San Francisco, CA: Jossey-Bass.

Diener, T. (1986). *Growth of an American invention: A documentary history of the junior and community college movement*. Westport, CT: Greenwood Press.

Eaton, J. S. (1994). *Strengthening collegiate education in community colleges*. San Francisco, CA: Jossey-Bass.

Ebben, J., & Maher, T. (1979, May). *Capturing institutional vitality.* Paper presented at the annual forum of the Association for Institutional Research, San Diego, CA.

Fields, R. (1962). *The community college movement*. New York, NY: McGraw-Hill.

Gleazer, E. (1967). Preparation of junior college teachers. *Educational Record, 48*(2), 147–152.

Grubb, W. N., & Associates. (1999). *Honored but invisible: An inside look at teaching in community colleges*. New York, NY: Routledge.

Johnson County Community College. (2001). *Fact sheet*. Overland Park, KS: Author.

Johnson County Community College. (2001–2002). *College catalog*. Overland Park, KS: Author.

Johnson County Community College & The League for Innovation in the Community College. (2000). *Internal document*. Overland Park, KS: Author.

Kelley, W., & Wilhun, L. (1970). *Teaching in the community junior college*. New York, NY: Appleton-Century-Crofts.

London, H. (1978). *The culture of a community college*. New York, NY: Praeger.

Lucas, C. (1994). *American higher education: A history*. New York, NY: St. Martin's Press.

Maher, T. H. (1982, June). *Institutional vitality in higher education* (AAHE-ERIC Higher Education Research Currents). (ERIC Document Reproduction Service No. ED216668)

Merriam, S. B. (1997). *Qualitative research and case study applications in education.* San Francisco, CA: Jossey-Bass.

Miller, R. I., Finley, C., & Shedd Vancko, C. (2000). *Evaluating, improving, and judging faculty performance in two-year colleges.* Westport, CT: Bergin & Garvey.

Monroe, C. (1972). *Profile of the community college: A handbook.* San Francisco, CA: Jossey-Bass.

Morphew, C. C., Twombly, S. B., & Wolf-Wendel, L. E. (2001). Two urban community colleges and an elite private liberal arts college. *Community College Review, 29*(3), 1–21.

Neptune, C. (2001). *Opportunities for excellence: Professionalism and the two-year college mathematics faculty.* Memphis, TN: American Mathematical Association of Two-Year Colleges.

Outcalt, C. (2000). Community college teaching: Toward collegiality and community. *Community College Review, 28*(2), 57–70.

Palmer, J. C., & Vaughan, G. B. (1992). *Fostering a climate for faculty scholarship at community colleges.* Washington, DC: American Association of Community and Junior Colleges.

Pascarella, E. T., & Terenzini, P. T. (1991). *How college affects students: Findings and insights from twenty years of research.* San Francisco, CA: Jossey-Bass.

Sarko, L. (1964, October). The problem of teaching in community colleges. *Journal of Higher Education, 35*(7), 384–386.

Schuster, J. H. (1985). Faculty vitality: Observations from the field. In R. G. Baldwin (Ed.), *New directions for higher education: No. 51. Incentives for faculty vitality* (pp. 21–32). San Francisco, CA: Jossey-Bass.

U.S. Department of Education, National Center for Education Statistics. (1998). *Digest of education statistics.* Washington, DC: Author.

Section III

Best Practices for Faculty Development

10

Using Data to Enhance College Teaching: Course and Departmental Assessment Results as a Faculty Development Tool

Catherine M. Wehlburg
Texas Christian University

This chapter highlights the need for using assessment of student learning outcomes data to guide teaching-related faculty development decision-making. Literature on the topic suggests that using assessment results to inform faculty development discussions makes better use of both the assessment data and the time spent in faculty development. Feedback and consultations regarding feedback seem to be important variables in determining if changes in teaching will occur. Types of assessment data that may especially inform teaching-related conversations are discussed.

INTRODUCTION

Faculty development (Gillespie, Hilsen, & Wadsworth, 2002) and assessment (Huba & Freed, 2000; Hutchings & Marchese, 1990; Wehlburg, 2002) have been a part of education for a very long time. Faculty development is often considered to be the enhancement of teaching—thus improving student learning (Gillespie, Hilsen, & Wadsworth, 2002; Wilcox, 1997), while assessment has typically focused on determining academic quality (Banta & Associates, 1993). But not until recently have those in higher education seen the importance of connecting faculty development and assessment of student learning outcomes together to form an even more powerful way to enhance teaching and learning.

Gibbs (1999) identifies an interesting disparity between faculty acceptance of using data to modify research and grant-writing, but not teaching. "Imagine the impact on the quality of course design if no course would be funded to operate unless its plans had been through a competitive peer review exercise in which only one in six were approved" (p. 150). This scenario will, most likely, never occur, but it does highlight the differences in perception regarding use of data in teaching-related areas.

Since "teaching without learning is just talking" (Angelo & Cross, 1993, p. 3), we need to know what a student has learned in order to understand what can be modified or enhanced in terms of teaching. In other words, without knowing what a student has learned, it is impossible to know if teaching has occurred. If what Cross (1993) has stated is true, "the ultimate criterion of good teaching is effective learning" (p. 20), it becomes essential to have appropriate assessment results in order to undertake any type of faculty development work with a particular faculty member.

While there are different organizational structures, most institutions of higher education have an individual or a committee that oversees institutional assessment and one that oversees faculty development. On smaller campuses, the oversight might come at the departmental level rather than the institutional level, but it is still possible to tap into the information that is available. Regardless of structure, the individual faculty member is the key to improving teaching. The faculty member must first recognize a desire to modify her or his teaching methods and then must have access to assessment information at the course level. By looking at student outcomes and comparing them to course objectives, faculty can have a good idea about where their focus for change needs to be. While this may be done by the faculty member, many faculty may choose to seek a colleague or a staff member from the teaching/learning center to help interpret existing data (course evaluations, results from classroom assessments, for example) or to gather data directly (SGIDs or focus groups with students) and then to suggest teaching modifications. But there is another source of data that should be accessed: student learning outcomes.

While faculty at most institutions see assessment as, at best, a mandated hassle, the assessment process is actually a rich source of data that can (and should) be mined at the course and departmental level for the explicit purpose of improving teaching and learning. Unfortunately, some faculty members distrust the concept of assessment because of its dual purpose, what Ewell (2002) has called the dilemma of purpose. Ewell states, "it has become commonplace in discussions of assessment over the past two decades, for example, to make the distinction between 'accountability' and 'improvement'" (p. 6).

But using assessment data for improvement purposes is exactly what should be done in faculty development. In fact, according to Huba and Freed (2000), "the [assessment] process culminates when assessment results are used to improve subsequent learning" (p. 8). And, since in order to improve learning, a faculty member will, most likely, need to modify teaching methodologies, course design, or other instructional practices, assessment data must be used to inform the faculty development conversation. The types of data used for this conversation will, in part, be chosen based on individual faculty needs and the availability of resources. But many of these types of assessment results may already exist or be easily obtainable by the faculty member for use in modifying teaching.

TYPES OF ASSESSMENT DATA

Faculty should have access to a variety of outcomes measurements for student learning. While these may vary from department to department and institution to institution, the basic function is the same: information on how much and what type of learning students are gaining as a result of a course or program. Faculty can obtain these outcomes to see what areas of a course need specific attention.

Course-Specific Measures

Faculty may gain information regarding objectives and student learning in a specific course. This assessment data may or may not be used by the department to assess student learning, but it can give a great deal of information regarding a specific course to a faculty member and is necessary for understanding which parts of the course should be modified or retained. A faculty developer who is working with a faculty member with this type of data can help the faculty member better understand the areas of a course that need special attention. The advantage of these outcomes is that they are collected (in many cases) by the faculty member and give information about student learning (versus course evaluations or student satisfaction ratings). In some cases, the faculty developer may need to work with the faculty member to develop measures of student learning, but this can be done by taking already identified outcomes for a course or unit and then matching those with a student work product (answers on an exam or paper, or from another classroom assessment technique) through an analysis of course documents (Bers, Davis, & Taylor, 2000), or peer review of teaching (Chism, 1999).

When working with these student work products, the focus is not on an individual student. Rather, attention should be paid to overall findings, patterns within class, and, when available, changes over time. For example, by determining areas where many students are not achieving, a faculty member can better see where (and why) to modify teaching methodologies. This is not the same process that a faculty member would go through in terms of grading; however, the faculty member is looking at the data at the course level, not the student level. If possible, have the faculty member look across anonymous student work to see the patterns or the areas where many students are missing information.

Other course-specific measures include SGID results, course evaluations, or focus group outcomes. These can help a faculty member to gauge student perceptions to determine where the course needs to be modified, but without actually having specific student learning outcomes, student perceptions can only give part of the necessary picture.

Department-Level Outcome Measures

Many departments may have some type of an achievement test that is given to seniors or may collect departmental portfolio data. By determining which areas indicate lower levels of achievement, a faculty member can use that information for his or her course in the same manner as outlined in the section above. The advantage to looking at the broader departmental picture is that it becomes easier to see an individual course as a part of a program of study (the way a student sees it). In addition, by using departmental-level data to look at a particular course, a faculty member is demonstrating the need for using existing assessment data. This has great benefit to the individual faculty member and may benefit the department as a whole by "establish[ing] talking about teaching and documenting teaching practices as a normal part of the life of the department" (Gibbs, 1999, p. 152). Faculty developers can encourage this by asking about departmental data when working with an individual faculty member.

IMPORTANCE OF GATHERING AND USING EFFECTIVE FEEDBACK

Feedback is an essential part of the learning process, both for students and for faculty who are interested in enhancing their teaching. "Useful feedback lets you know not only how you are doing, but what you should do next to improve" (Huba & Freed, 2000, p. 122). Meaningful feedback should help point a faculty member in the right direction in terms of what parts of a course or a teaching methodology to focus on first. Without this assessment data, making changes in a course is just a shot in the dark.

Given the importance of feedback, it is surprising how often faculty have to be prompted to gather information or how often they dismiss the data that is collected. Chaffee (1997) has stated,

> compared with other kinds of enterprise, universities and colleges are systematically deprived of input from the people we serve . . . we typically have a weak system, with end-of-term surveys, if that—too late to improve a course while the student is still enrolled in it." (p. 46)

But it is this feedback (assessment data) that is required if faculty development is going to have meaningful and reliable impact on student learning. According to Brinko (1993), "among all instructional development efforts, the most promising way of fundamentally changing postsecondary teaching is to provide faculty with individualized formative feedback" (p. 574). She goes on to say that "this method . . . has not been consistently successful, possibly because many who feed back the information to the teacher are not trained in feedback-giving practice" (p. 474). Faculty developers should be adept at working with faculty to gather feedback, feeding back information to faculty and helping them to appropriately interpret the data and, when necessary, choosing a way to implement their interpretations in order to improve student learning. Evidence indicates that the use of appropriate types of consultations does positively affect the changes that a faculty member chooses to make (Cohen & Herr, 1982; McKeachie et al., 1980).

According to Brinko (1993), data should be gathered from multiple sources. This helps to ensure the validity of the data collected, but it also helps the faculty member to see that a particular issue is not just coming from angry student comments. In addition, one of the sources of data collection should be from the faculty member. There are a variety of ways of collecting self-reflection and self-assessment from the faculty member (teaching portfolios, self-assessments made after a specific course, or focusing on a specific course objective, etc.). This self-assessment part of the data collection can be especially powerful.

> Perhaps this positive attitude results in part from the stimulation of cognitive dissonance created by discrepancies between feedback recipients' self-ratings and feedback sources' assessments. In any case, if the cognitive dissonance is not too large or too small, it is likely to facilitate a change in behavior. (Brinko, 1993, p. 577)

Brinko also indicated that "feedback is more effective when mediated by a consultant" (p. 577), which points directly to the need for faculty developers to work with faculty in collecting and feeding back information regarding teaching issues.

THE RELATIONSHIP BETWEEN FACULTY DEVELOPMENT CENTERS AND ASSESSMENT OFFICES

While it is clear that using assessment results will benefit the work of the faculty member, students, and faculty developers, there are interesting findings that faculty who participate in faculty development activities are more likely to "assume ownership of institutional and departmental assessment programs" (Lopez, 1999, p. 17).

Lopez (1999) gathered information from institutional self-study and North Central Association accreditation reports and has indicated that one of the major problems at institutions regarding assessment is the lack of faculty support and participation. However, by working to educate faculty members about the uses and benefits of assessment, it has been possible to gain a "knowledgeable, enthusiastic cadre of faculty who are actively engaged in all aspects of the assessment program" (p. 17). Thus, she sees "faculty development as the primary solution to problems in faculty participation in assessment" (p. 17).

In a way, this highlights the strength of using data in faculty development conversations: Faculty may see the power of using data, first as a benchmark, but then as a regular part of the teaching and learning process. When decision-making about teaching issues becomes data-driven, there is a continuous need to gather meaningful information and to ask deeper and more meaningful questions about student learning. When questions are regularly asked and answered about student learning, "faculty members within the academic department can use the resulting data to make substantive and (relatively) immediate changes in course design, course sequencing, [and teaching methodologies]" (Wehlburg, 2000, p. 20).

CONCLUSIONS

By tapping into already existing assessment data and encouraging faculty to gather data on student learning outcomes, faculty developers can promote effective teaching changes leading to increased student learning outcomes. Assessment data can then become yet another tool to use in faculty development to continue to improve and enhance teaching and learning in higher education.

REFERENCES

Angelo, T. A., & Cross, P. K. (1993). *Classroom assessment techniques: A handbook for college teachers* (2nd ed.). San Francisco, CA: Jossey-Bass.

Banta, T. W., & Associates. (1993). *Making a difference: Outcomes of a decade of assessment in higher education.* San Francisco, CA: Jossey-Bass.

Bers, T. H., Davis, D., & Taylor, B. (2000). The use of syllabi in assessments: Unobtrusive indicators and tools for faculty development. *Assessment Update, 12,* 4–7.

Brinko, K. T. (1993). The practice of giving feedback to improving teaching: What is effective? *Journal of Higher Education, 64,* 575–593.

Chaffee, E. E. (1997). Listening to the people you serve. In B. L. Cambridge (Ed.), *Assessing impact: Evidence and action* (pp. 41–50). Washington, DC: American Association for Higher Education.

Chism, N. V. N. (1999). *Peer review of teaching: A sourcebook.* Bolton, MA: Anker.

Cohen, P. A., & Herr, G. (1982). Using an interactive feedback procedure to improve college teaching. *Teaching of Psychology, 9,* 138–140.

Cross, K. P. (1993, February/March). Involving faculty in TQU. *AACC Journal,* 15–20.

Ewell, P. (2002). *Perpetual movement: Assessment after twenty years.* Paper presented at the American Association for Higher Education Assessment Conference, Boston, MA. Retrieved May 6, 2004, from http://www.aahe.org/assessment/2002/PlenariesForFrames.htm

Gibbs, G. (1999). Improving teaching, learning, and assessment. *Journal of Geography in Higher Education, 23,* 147–155.

Gillespie, K. H., Hilsen, L. R., & Wadsworth, E.C. (Eds.). (2002). *A guide to faculty development: Practical advice, examples, and resources.* Bolton, MA: Anker.

Huba, M. E., & Freed, J. E. (2000). *Learner-centered assessment on college campuses: Shifting the focus from teaching to learning.* Needham Heights, MA: Allyn and Bacon.

Hutchings, P., & Marchese, T. (1990, September/October). Watching assessment questions, stories, prospects. *Change, 22*(5), 12–38.

Lopez, C. L. (1999). *A decade of assessing student learning: What have we learned; what's next?* Chicago, IL: North Central Association of Colleges and Schools Commission on Institutions of Higher Education.

McKeachie, W. J., Lin, Y-G, Daugherty, M., Moffett, M. M., Neigler, C., Nork, J., et al. (1980). Using student ratings and consultation to improve instruction. *British Journal of Educational Psychology, 50,* 168–174.

Wehlburg, C. M. (2000, Fall). Respecting students and faculty: The need for "intrusive" assessment. *The Department Chair, 11*(2), 20–22.

Wehlburg, C. M. (2002). More than a thermometer: Using assessment effectively. In G. S. Wheeler (Ed.), *Teaching and learning in college: A resource for educators* (4th ed., pp. 177–199). Elyria, OH: Info–Tec.

Wilcox, S. (1997). Becoming a faculty developer. In P. Cranton (Ed.), *New directions for adult and continuing education: No. 74. Transformative learning in action: Insights from practice* (pp. 23–32). San Francisco, CA: Jossey-Bass.

11

A Vision Beyond Measurement: Creating an Integrated Data System for Teaching Centers

Kathryn M. Plank
Alan Kalish
Stephanie V. Rohdieck
Kathleen A. Harper
The Ohio State University

Assessing the work of teaching and learning centers is crucial to maintain the support of our institutions; however, collecting and interpreting the right data can be a challenge. This chapter explores practical strategies for integrating assessment into daily work flow in order to generate information that accurately measures our impact, helps others understand and value our work, and enables us to improve what we do, without creating a major "add-on" task. We discuss ways to measure, track, and report work, and share means to use data for both summative and formative purposes that we hope will make the work of faculty developers easier, better, and appreciated.

INTRODUCTION

Documenting the impact of teaching and learning centers is more crucial today than ever. The very existence of centers may depend on it. Not surprisingly, we have seen a proliferation of sessions at recent Professional and Organizational Development Network in Higher Education (POD) conferences on assessment of faculty development, as well as several chapters in Volume 22 of *To Improve the Academy* (e.g., Bothell & Henderson, 2004; Milloy & Brooke, 2004). POD's Core Committee also emphasized the importance of assessment by making it the focus of the 2003–2004 POD grant competition.

However, while most faculty developers recognize the need for assessment, efforts to gather, organize, and make sense of the data can easily become overwhelming. This chapter explores practical strategies for designing an integrated data system that enables assessment, measures impact accurately, helps others understand and value the work of teaching and learning centers, and provides useful data for improving faculty development. We discuss a range of ideas about how best to measure, track, and report the work that centers do, and share our experiences and those of other centers with which we have been in contact on how best to use data for summative assessment and for formative purposes that we hope will make our work easier and better.

CONTEXT

There is not a large body of literature on the assessment of teaching and learning centers, yet this does not necessarily mean that centers do not assess their work. In their survey, Chism and Szabo (1997) concluded that "a substantial amount of evaluation activity occurs across programs" (p. 61). However, they also discovered that the assessment activities were not equally distributed across the services provided and often focused primarily on satisfaction surveys. They point out a number of obstacles that limit the depth and breadth of assessment done by centers.

Perhaps the most obvious obstacle is time. Just as some faculty fear that assessing instruction may crowd out the time needed to teach, teaching centers are also concerned "that the amount of time that would be needed to evaluate well would prevent staff members from serving their clients adequately" (Chism & Szabo, 1997, p. 60). How much assessment can we do and still do the work we are assessing?

In approaching these concerns about assessment, the staff of Faculty & TA Development (FTAD) at The Ohio State University realized that we could draw on the principles of assessment that we share with faculty. Although there is not much written about the assessment of our own work, our field has a rich collection of resources on the assessment of teaching and learning, much of which can be applied to the assessment of faculty development. For example, the American Association for Higher Education's (AAHE) *9 Principles of Good Practice for Assessing Student Learning* (1997) provides useful guidance for the process.

1) The assessment of student learning begins with educational values.

2) Assessment is most effective when it reflects an understanding of learning as multidimensional, integrated, and revealed in performance over time.

3) Assessment works best when the programs it seeks to improve have clear, explicitly stated purposes.

4) Assessment requires attention to outcomes but also and equally to the experiences that lead to those outcomes.

5) Assessment works best when it is ongoing, not episodic.

6) Assessment fosters wider improvement when representatives from across the educational community are involved.

7) Assessment makes a difference when it begins with issues of use and illuminates questions that people really care about.

8) Assessment is mostly likely to lead to improvement when it is part of a larger set of conditions that promote change.

9) Through assessment, educators meet responsibilities to students and to the public.

Allen, McMillin, Noel, and Rienzi (1999) and Banta, Lund, Black, and Oblander (1996) show how these principles can be applied in institutional assessment of learning. They provide useful models for teaching centers to consider as we make the connection from assessment of learning to assessment of our own practice.

In addressing the concern about the time necessary to assess our work, we realized it would be useful for us to listen to our own advice. When we talk with faculty about assessment of learning, we often quote Walvoord and Anderson's (1998) argument that we must integrate assessment into our teaching, that we can't "shove it to the periphery" (p. 13). If assessment is an additional task in the lives of already overburdened faculty, it will not receive the serious attention it needs to succeed. Likewise, assessment of the work of educational developers must be integrated into our daily work lives in order to be feasible, as well as useful and usable.

To achieve this integration, as suggested by Principles 2 and 5, we created a single data system that accomplishes as many of our office record-keeping functions and other administrative tasks as possible. We now use the same system to manage our work time, schedule appointments, track event registration, collect evaluation feedback, maintain our list of contacts, generate mailings, and produce monthly and annual reports. The goal is to have each piece of data entered only once, yet made readily available for a number of different outputs and purposes.

Improving the data collection system also enables us to collect the data that are most important, not just those that are easiest to collect. In applying the AAHE's first principle to institutional assessment, Banta et al. (1996) state that "institutional assessment efforts should not be concerned about valuing what can be measured but, instead, about measuring that which is valued" (p. 5). While it may once have been enough to count consultations and attendance, these methods do not reflect all that centers now do. We have added new procedures to assess the impact of what we do and to capture some of the work that often remains invisible and communicate it to others.

However, the most important element of this process is its collaborative nature. "There is, perhaps, no more important principle in the assessment literature than this: successful assessment requires collaborative efforts" (Banta et al., 1996, p. 35). To this end, the database system was made fully accessible from the start to all staff members through an office server that is accessible from each of their desktop computers. Consultants not only enter data from their own computers, but they also can search, sort, and print reports.

Discussions of how best to collect, categorize, and use data have become central to our staff development and strategic planning efforts. We have also been able to involve many stakeholders and users throughout the process. Active collaboration was and is crucial to aligning our goals with the goals of the university and assuring that the data system remains both useful and useable.

STATEMENT OF NEED

Chism and Szabo (1997) report that most centers do collect a substantial amount of evaluation data. Prior to this effort, our center was no different. We had a number of data collection processes in place for several years—each separately developed but not integrated with the others. However, like many centers, we have significantly changed the focus of our work over the past five years. Our old record-keeping system no longer fit our current activities and work style, and it was not efficient in gathering the data that it did capture. Add to that a major turnover in staff, and we were ready for change.

The first steps in our strategic planning process were to determine which data we were already collecting and locate the sources of these data. As is true of most of the centers in both the Chism and Szabo study (1997) and Chism's (2003) follow-up survey on the POD listserv, we were most complete in our tracking of information on events (workshops, seminars, etc.). Each term, faculty and teaching associates would register for our events on teaching, and our student assistants entered these registrations into a FileMaker Pro database, which was located on their computer only. This was a standard, flat-file database (i.e., a simple database in which all data are recorded in a single table), which kept records of attendance by each participant for each academic year. For example, Professor Smith would have one record in the 2001–2002 academic year database, with a list of any university-wide workshops or events she attended that year.

However, attendance lists from unit-based events (i.e., invited workshops done within a department or college) were stored in a separate document that was part of our staff members' individual monthly reports. Other information about individual events—such as materials, agendas, evaluations—was saved as hard copy in file folders, usually by the staff member who facilitated the event. So even though we collected a lot of data about events, making use of it involved searching in a number of different locations.

We also kept track of other activities via monthly reports. At the end of each month, staff members submitted reports of their consultations to the director in a word-processed document listing consultations, service, research, publications, and planning time for all work done that month. This system was useful in keeping track of staff time and clients served that month. These reports were summarized for the director (how many consultations we all did collectively each month and with which units on campus) and printed out for our files. Different aggregations were used monthly and at the end of the year to generate numbers (counting by hand) for both our performance reviews and for our reports to administration.

As indicated, our office has always done a good job of keeping track of consultations, events, and service. Like the centers in the Chism and Szabo (1997) study, we collected a lot of data. However, one of the concerns we had about the way we were collecting and reporting the data was the tremendous amount of time it took all of us at each level—for consultants to complete the monthly reports and for our student assistants to enter event information and generate monthly summaries. Because we kept annual rather than cumulative records, much of this work had to be repeated each year. Also, despite the time invested in entering data, they were not easily accessible for everyday use. Because records were not cumulative and because much information was kept in staff files, searching for a client's history with the unit or for attendance and evaluation data for an event was difficult. In our discussions at POD sessions and in consultations with other centers, we learned that others faced similar difficulties in making good use of their data.

Another dilemma we had with the system was that as we developed new programs and offered new services, the monthly reporting system became cumbersome. The system worked fairly well in the past, but as we grew and changed, we continually needed to add new fields, which made the database even more cumbersome. It grew by accretion without reorganization. One of the disadvantages of flat-file systems is that they can become very bulky when data only needed for some records must be attached to all records. The additional fields also required complicated and lengthy instructions for both the professional staff (to get agreement on how to report data) and for the student assistants trying to summarize data dispersed throughout individual staff reports and the event database.

More importantly, the system did not capture and communicate to others the full scope of our work. For example, like many centers, we did not keep robust data on all of the services we provided the university, such as serving on university committees, attending department committee meetings, or doing outreach both within the university and nationally. This work was a large part of what our office did, but was largely invisible in our reporting system.

Our annual report became even more of a challenge as the types of services grew and changed. Even without the new services, the program coordinator dedicated at least eight weeks every year to creating this annual report. It was a time-consuming process to go back to each individual staff person's monthly report and calculate by hand items such as how many consultations we did for faculty versus graduate teaching associates (GTAs) or the number of consultations versus the number of individual clients.

THE DATABASES

Relational Structure

Our solution was to create a system of relational databases (using FileMaker Pro) that would integrate all of our data collection into one easy system. Unlike a flat-file database, in which all data are stored in a single file, relational databases allow one to separate data among several files and to share between these files. Each file can focus on the data that are important for a specific category. For example, in our old flat-file database, each record was a person (e.g., Professor Smith), so all data had to be attached to a person. Information about a particular event (e.g., a list of the materials handed out) could not be stored efficiently in this database. With a relational system, we have one database organized around people and another organized around events. The appropriate data can be stored separately but shared between the files. Relational databases allow one to store more complete information in less space and with greater flexibility of use.

At the core of the system is our People database (see Figure 11.1). In this file, each record is a person our office has worked with. For example, Professor Smith will be entered as a record here, with her address, rank, department, etc. The key is that Professor Smith will only be entered into the system once. Once we have her record, her information can then be shared with the other databases, so it never needs to be reentered. If we need to update her information, changes are made in the People database and it is automatically updated everywhere the record is used. Through a variety of layouts, we can print letters, address labels, nametags, attendance sheets, address lists, and a number of other forms that can now be generated almost instantly for any given group of people in our system.

FIGURE 11.1
People Database

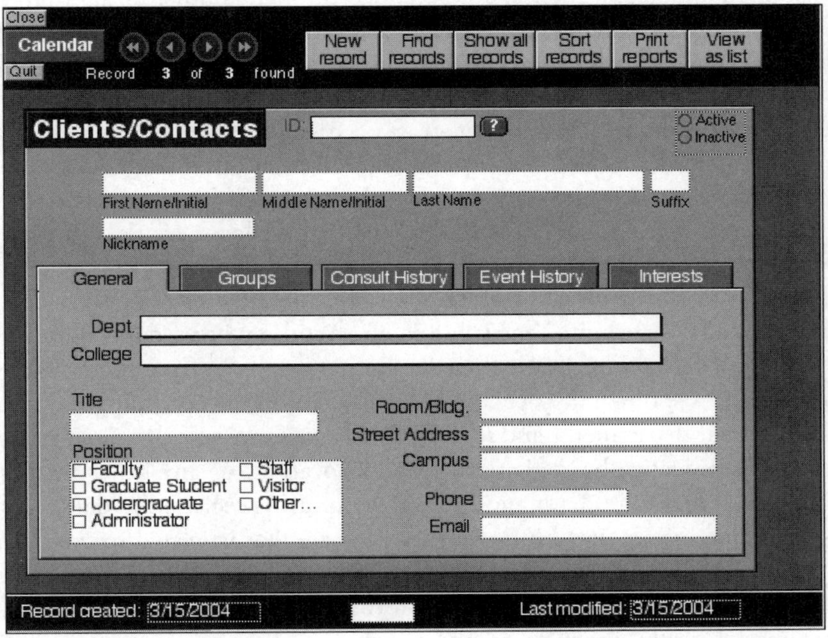

This screen shot shows the front page of the People database. Information entered here is shared with the other databases. Information about consultations is automatically imported from the consultation database onto the "consult history" card. A list of events attended is imported onto the "event history" card.

Not only can information from the People database be used by other databases, but data from those other files can also be displayed within the People database. For example, we have a Consultations database in which every record is an individual consultation. If we meet with Professor Smith five times during the year, we will have five records for her in the Consultations database. Each record will include information pertinent to that consultation, such as the consultant's name, type of consultation (classroom observation, office visit, etc.), date, time, time spent preparing, topics discussed, notes, and any materials provided.

These five consultation records for Professor Smith can be displayed in a portal in the People database. So when we call up her record, we see a listing of every consultation she's had with the office, even if with different consultants. A consultant can look up her record and access links to the actual consultation records in the Consultations database.

Similarly, from Professor Smith's record in the People database, we can see a list of all events that she has ever attended through another portal from the Events database. We replaced our old annual database with a cumulative Events database in which each record is an event, such as a workshop, seminar, or book group. This allows us to store information about events (e.g., topics, list of materials used) electronically so that it is easily accessible to everyone, which is particularly useful for those planning a subsequent event on similar topics.

The Events database has three other databases that feed into it (see Figure 11.2). The first, Registration, is used to register people for events, print attendance sheets, and so on. In our old system we were already registering people electronically, but with the relational system, the attendance information is automatically ported into the Events database and can be used in a number of ways. Now consultants can look at the Events database (from their desks) at any time to see how many people are registered for an upcoming event, including their departments and ranks. Likewise, we can quickly search for patterns of attendance by topic, time of day, location, or any other field (see Mullinix & Harr, 2003, for another system for using registration data).

Evaluations are typed into another database that is related to the Events database. It is easy for our student workers to enter them since the interface looks exactly like the paper evaluation forms. Averages of the quantitative responses are automatically calculated and displayed in the event record in the Events database, and the open-ended feedback can be printed out as well as viewed on screen. The time to input the evaluations is minimal, but the benefit is great. Whereas previously evaluations were kept by the staff member who facilitated the session, they are now easily accessible by all. It is useful, when planning an event, to be able to access quickly the feedback for previous, similar events. Having the feedback at hand makes it much more likely that we will actually use it in planning. We can also create summative reports quickly and easily for strategic planning purposes.

FIGURE 11.2
Events Database

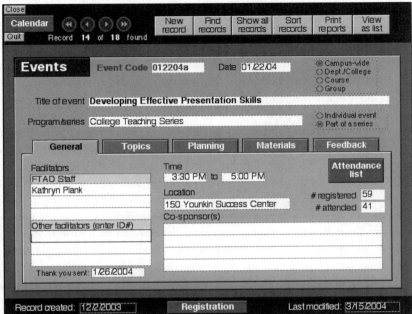

This screen shot shows the front page of the Events database. Clicking on the "planning" tab reveals records ported over from the planning time database. Clicking on the "feedback" tab shows summary data from the evaluations database. The "attendance list" button takes the user to the registration database. The registration numbers shown here are automatically calculated from the registration database.

The last of the three databases that feeds into the Events database is one that records the preparation time for planning an event. In our old system, staff members tracked their hours for their own staff evaluations. But in this system, the hours of all those involved are attached to the event. This practice has been very useful not only for accounting where our time goes, but more importantly, for what the cost of an event is. To do the kind of cost/benefit analysis recommended by Bothell and Henderson (2004), one must track the time investment in an event as well as the monetary investment. With these three databases feeding information about attendance, evaluation, and planning time into the Events database, we now have easily accessible data that we can use to make decisions for strategic planning.

Using the System

We now have much more data to use yet spend less time collecting them than we did previously. Clients are now added into our database system only once, not each year or each time they come for a consultation as they were before because the data were not carried over. The ability to generate summative reports automatically reduces greatly the time spent on both monthly reports and annual reports. In addition, the databases function as an integrated part of our daily work life. We no longer need to wait until the end of the month, week, or even day to enter information on an event we are planning or on a consultation. The database system is easily accessible and user-friendly enough that we enter data through a calendar interface as we plan and make appointments.

Another advantage of the current system over our old reports is the use of value lists, or predefined menus. For example, in many fields, such as "department," users choose from a menu, which not only saves them time typing but also ensures consistency. We also use a value list to record topics (e.g., "teaching portfolio" or "collaborative learning"). This list of check boxes allows us to quickly indicate in a consistent manner the topic of a consultation or an event. Not only is this a useful reminder of past consultations, but it also can be used in summative analyses and needs assessment. Tracking entries entered as "other" allows the value lists to grow as needed according to observed demand.

Integration in Workflow

The new database system created a paradigm shift within our office in the sense of information ownership. For example, because files on consultations, event materials, and event evaluations were previously being housed in individual staff offices, getting information to help design an event was challenging. Also, knowing if a client had come in to see someone else for a consultation, and if so, what was discussed was difficult without asking outright. The new databases allow each of us to see immediately what services a faculty member or GTA has used (consults and events), what the overall purpose or result of a consultation was, and the planning time and materials used for any past event.

Obviously, confidentiality is a concern in our work. The databases are password protected and available only within our office, and we are careful in what we say in the notes section. We feel that sharing within the office does not violate confidentiality since our clients are clients of the office, not of us individually. Records must be kept, and electronic files are no less confidential than paper files.

Making Work Visible

Finally, one of the driving forces behind the creation of a new database system was to create a space to better include and highlight our organizational development efforts. Many assessment systems highlight individual consultations and events often because these activities are the easiest things to count. However, they are not always where we have our greatest impact or where we spend the most time. Through our Service database, we can keep track of all meetings and consultations with colleges and units on campus. Each month, we can instantly generate a report of our service, automatically categorized under headings such as "national outreach" and "university service." Previously, work such as serving on the evaluation of teaching committee could be invisible, or at least marginalized as "committee work," even if there had been a way for our office to influence change at the university level. Now such work can be captured and highlighted.

CLOSING THE LOOP

As with any complete system of evaluation, this system strives to make data available for both formative and summative purposes. Each staff member has regular access to all of the data on her or his activities and the feedback received from clients. We have already begun to use these data to inform our revision of various programs and to improve our individual consulting efforts.

The database has also become central to our team planning processes. As we discuss topics for events each term and what books to buy, we have been able to base a judgment of faculty interest on data regarding topics of inquiries and consultations. When deciding on what new major projects we wish to focus, we can base our estimates of staff time and costs on data from prior activities.

Perhaps more interestingly, an unintended outcome of the process of designing a data system to meet our specific needs has been that the entire professional staff of our center has spent time thinking about what we all do. We are more aware of each other's projects, and we spend time discussing the nature of our work. Discussions of whether a particular activity might be better classified as "outreach" for the center or "community service within the university," or whether a meeting was an "organizational development consultation" or "service on a college committee," leads us to a better understanding of what we do, how it fits into the fabric of our institution, and how we can best describe its value to our clients.

Summary reports of activities and feedback have also made it easier for each of us to provide specific evidence for the claims we make in our self-assessments for individual performance reviews. Data can be sorted by staff members and provide a much fuller and more detailed picture of our work than had been possible previously. This has made and will continue to make performance management both more efficient and more accurate.

Having access to all of these data also means that our budget requests can be supported by a wealth of evidence to show that the programming we ask to have funded meets actual needs and addresses published institutional goals. For example, when asking for funding for an initiative to support departments in providing ongoing teaching assistance to GTAs, we were able to demonstrate that the programming would require an additional staff member to succeed. The data enabled us to get that position funded.

The integrated data system has made generating the reports needed to document our work to various stakeholders—deans, chairs, advisory committee, and central administration—almost automatic. As we decided what information to collect, we took into account what questions about our work we had been asked. Also, we were influenced by a then-current institutional move to use the performance scorecard model (Chang & Morgan, 2000), which seeks to reduce the size of regular reports by aggregating large amounts of data into a few indices of success. The monthly and annual reports that were generated with so much effort prior to this system have been transformed into much briefer documents, but much more information is almost immediately available on request. The bottom line, though, is that our services be effective at meeting the stated goals of enhancing teaching and learning.

ASSESSING OUR IMPACT

Having an integrated data system also helped us see what additional data we needed to collect to meet those goals. For example, like most centers, we regularly collected evaluations at the end of programs to assess participants' satisfaction. We were less systematic, however, in following up to find out if participants ever tried anything new in their teaching as a result of the program, or whether such attempts were successful or not.

To collect such information, which we hope will document some of the outcomes of our work, we developed a general services survey that asked about all of our services, including events, consultations, and service (Appendix 11.1). We opted for a single survey covering all services for two reasons. One is that those who use a variety of our services would then receive only one survey to fill out, rather than separate surveys for events, consultations, and so on.

Second, clients who were unaware of the variety of resources offered by our offices would see what other services are available.

The survey asks clients to indicate in what ways they have interacted with us within the past year. The list includes such things as workshops, individual consultations, and assistance on grant projects. The client also selects the topic(s) addressed during the interaction, using the same list of topics as is in the database system. Next we ask them to describe in what ways, if any, they have modified their teaching as a result of the interaction. We provide a list but also supply ample space for them to add other actions.

The survey is distributed annually to one-fourth of that year's clients. The database system makes it easy to select a sample of the year's clients at random, print out the mailing labels for the distribution, and to record which clients were surveyed within a particular year. This last record prevents the same person from getting surveyed every year.

As with the databases themselves, the survey is a living document that has the ability to change as we rethink the way we operate. The information we receive back from clients helps shape decisions about event planning, resource allotment, and public relations efforts.

CONCLUSION

Given the recent history of eroding support for long-standing teaching support centers and the move toward more program assessment in other aspects of higher education, a need clearly exists for structured, systematic collection and interpretation of evaluation data on the work we do. Likewise, as the specific activities and services demanded of teaching centers and our staff members have changed over time, even the best system of assessment requires revision. However, we need to be sure that we do not spend so much time doing assessment that we cannot do the work we wish to assess.

The staff of FTAD has sought to use the principles of good practice in assessment and the available technology in database management to build a system that better meets our current needs and has the flexibility to grow and change with us. While some of the specific details of our data system are idiosyncratic, many of the elements of our system are transferable, and the process we have used to devise our system could be useful to other centers. For example, developing an integrated system that prevents duplication of effort is crucial, as is finding ways to make the system fit within daily work activities rather than be an additional layer of effort.

If the system is to aggregate the work of multiple staff members, it should be created in a collaborative process. This builds buy-in and also assures that everyone will understand the categories of data so it will be collected consistently. More importantly, involving the entire team in the design process serves as staff development and strategic planning for the unit. A team approach also makes it much more likely that the evaluation will be used for formative purposes, both for improving individual performance and for connecting unit services to client and stakeholder needs. As with all evaluation, collecting data on teaching center activities and effectiveness should not be only for summative purposes; we must close the feedback loop and use the data to get better at what we do.

Finally, as we tell faculty all the time about evaluation of teaching, we can no longer (if we ever could) be excellent simply by assertion. The culture of evidence in higher education has spread to assessment of teaching quality, student outcomes, and academic programs. We should welcome it to the evaluation of the work of educational development programs, too. We know that teaching centers do outstanding work; we need to build the structures that let us prove it.

REFERENCES

Allen, M. J., McMillin, J. D., Noel, R. C., & Rienzi, B. M. (1999, June). *Outcomes assessment for program improvement.* Paper presented at the California State University Teacher-Scholar Summer Conference, San Jose, CA.

American Association for Higher Education. (1997). *9 principles of good practice for assessing student learning.* Washington, DC: Author. Retrieved May 6, 2004, from http://www.aahe.org/assessment/principl.htm

Banta, T. W., Lund, J. P., Black, K. E., & Oblander, F. W. (1996). *Assessment in practice: Putting principles to work on college campuses.* San Francisco, CA: Jossey-Bass.

Bothell, T. W., & Henderson, T. (2004). Evaluating the return on investment of faculty development. In C. M. Wehlburg & S. Chadwick-Blossey (Eds.), *To improve the academy: Vol. 22. Resources for faculty, instructional, and organizational development* (pp. 52–70). Bolton, MA: Anker.

Chang, R. Y., & Morgan, M. W. (2000). *Performance scorecards: Measuring the right things in the real world.* San Francisco, CA: Jossey-Bass.

Chism, N. V. N. (2003, March 14). Summary of responses on user records. Message posted to POD electronic mailing list, archived at http://listserv.nd.edu/cgi-bin/wa?A2=ind0303&L=pod&O=A&P=7509

Chism, N. V. N., & Szabo, B. (1997). How faculty development programs evaluate their services. *Journal of Staff, Program, and Organizational Development, 15*(2), 55–62.

Milloy, P. M., & Brooke, C. (2004). Beyond bean counting: Making faculty development needs assessment more meaningful. In C. M. Wehlburg & S. Chadwick-Blossey (Eds.), *To improve the academy: Vol. 22. Resources for faculty, instructional, and organizational development* (pp. 71–92). Bolton, MA: Anker.

Mullinix, B. B., & Harr, C. (2003). *Faculty-centered program development.* West Long Branch, NJ: Monmouth University, Faculty Resource Center. Retrieved December 11, 2003, from http://its.monmouth.edu/trainingGuest/POD-BIA/Mullinix-Harr%20BIA-FacCentrDev-HO.doc

Walvoord, B. E., & Anderson, V. J. (1998). *Effective grading: A tool for learning and assessment.* San Francisco, CA: Jossey-Bass.

APPENDIX 11.1

SERVICE EVALUATION

1) What was your primary goal in contacting FTAD?

2) What topic(s) was/were addressed? (Check all that apply.)
__ Modes of teaching (lecture, laboratory, cooperative learning, etc.)
__ Evaluation of learning (testing, grading)
__ Assessment of teaching (SEI, other)
__ Course preparation
__ Students (rapport, classroom management)
__ Diversity
__ Teaching with technology
__ Scholarship of teaching
__ Teaching portfolio/philosophy statement
__ Professional development
__ Other: _____

3) Please indicate and rate the service(s) provided.
   (Check all that apply.)

	Value				
	Not at all			Extremely	
_____ Face-to-face consultation	1	2	3	4	5
_____ Consultation by phone or email	1	2	3	4	5
_____ Administer mid-quarter feedback activity	1	2	3	4	5
_____ Review of student evaluations of instruction	1	2	3	4	5
_____ Classroom observation	1	2	3	4	5
_____ Classroom videotaping and consultation	1	2	3	4	5
_____ Used information resources (library, web site, etc.)	1	2	3	4	5
_____ Participation in Faculty Learning Community	1	2	3	4	5
_____ Committee meeting(s) attended by FTAD staff	1	2	3	4	5

_____ Departmental consultation
    with FTAD   1   2   3   4   5
_____ Grant preparation assistance   1   2   3   4   5
_____ Attended unit event where
    FTAD participated   1   2   3   4   5
_____ Attended FTAD-sponsored event   1   2   3   4   5
_____ Other_____   1   2   3   4   5

Comments:

4) **To what extent did you change your teaching as a result of your work with us?**

    Not at all   1   2   3   4   5   A great deal

5) **Using the (non-exhaustive!) list below, please indicate any changes you made as a result of your interaction with us. (Check all that apply.)**
_____ Tried a new teaching technique
_____ Modified presentation/delivery techniques
_____ Modified student discussion techniques
_____ Redesigned evaluation methods/materials
_____ Implemented/changed methods of collecting and using student feedback
_____ Redesigned course syllabus
_____ Revised class policies
_____ Implemented techniques to make classroom more inclusive
_____ Took steps to create a more civil classroom climate
_____ Used instructional technology a different amount or in a new way
_____ Became more scholarly about my teaching/designed and implemented a study of my teaching
_____ Modified materials in my teaching portfolio
_____ Devised a professional development plan
Other(s):

6) **Please give examples of the one or two most important changes indicated in Question 5.**

7) **How can we improve our service?**

8) **Please circle your academic rank:**
   Full professor   Assistant professor   Graduate student
   Associate professor   Lecturer   Other:_____

12

Achieving a Campus Consensus on Learning-Centered Teaching: Process and Outcomes

Phyllis Blumberg
Justin Everett
University of the Sciences at Philadelphia

Fifty faculty and staff members attended a consensus conference on learning-centered teaching. Within small groups, participants agreed that 1) this approach develops student responsibility for their learning; 2) a consistently implemented philosophy yields a culture of learning-centered teaching, and 3) graduates of such programs become lifelong learners, self-directing, self-initiating leaders. Not all participants agreed that they could fully implement this method. They emphasized that support by administrators is a prerequisite to making changes in teaching approaches. However, the conference effectively determined levels of agreement and stimulated discussion. Results were consistent with the literature on learning-centered teaching.

INTRODUCTION

During the 2001–2002 academic year, administrators at the University of the Sciences in Philadelphia (USP) conducted a yearlong strategic planning process and identified six strategic imperatives to direct aspects of the university's planning through 2010 (USP, 2002). One of the imperatives included the development of a culture of learning-centered teaching. According to Weimer (2002), learning-centered teaching (LCT) focuses on what students are learning, the conditions that foster learning, the students' ability to retain and apply their learning, and how well current learning facilitates future learning. When instruction is learning centered, the emphasis is on what the learners are doing and not what the teachers are doing. The first hurdle was to determine faculty perceptions of LCT.

To discover what the faculty thought of the concept, the director of the Teaching and Learning Center held a series of "town meetings" that all faculty were asked to attend. About half of the full-time faculty of about 150 attended at least one of these meetings. At the first forum in 2002, much confusion existed among the faculty members regarding the meaning of LCT. While some faculty members felt that they had already established a learning-centered environment in their classrooms, others felt that LCT could only occur in very small classes, and was therefore impossible at an institution where some classes are filled with several hundred students in a lecture hall. Some expressed the concern that LCT would negatively affect the content and rigor of their courses by requiring them to follow a prescribed method of delivery. They said that they did not want the content of their courses to be dumbed down because they had to utilize time-consuming teaching methods. Others simply resented LCT because they felt it interfered with their control over their own courses. It was clear that the faculty needed to be introduced to what LCT entails and how these methods could be applied in their classes without sacrificing content and rigor.

During the 2002–2003 academic year, USP began a two-pronged initiative toward creating an LCT culture. The first major initiative involved defining objectives, developing future action steps, and outlining outcome indicators. A tactical planning group (TPG) on LCT developed specific goals for this strategic imperative during the 2002 fall semester. The TPG identified the following goals for the LCT initiative.

- Faculty members, staff members, and administrators will know what LCT entails and how best to achieve it.

- The curricula will be consistent with LCT in terms of development, content, and delivery.

- Students will have the knowledge, ability, and resources to achieve responsibility and self-direction for their own learning.

- University policies, procedures, and practices will be compatible with a learning-centered philosophy.

At the same time, the Teaching and Learning Center (under the direction of the first author) focused on educating faculty and supporting their efforts to implement LCT. The Teaching and Learning Center hosted yearlong activities emphasizing LCT approaches, including 4 daylong workshops given by outside experts, 16 discussions on the topic, and a daylong event held for faculty and staff at the end of the year.

After a year of intensive work on educating and discussing LCT, the authors wanted to find out what the faculty and staff members' perceptions of LCT were, if they thought the strategies would be useful in their areas of responsibility, and how they thought the initiative could be implemented at USP. We decided to hold a consensus conference for all faculty and appropriate staff (appropriate staff members were determined to be those who worked in areas of high student interaction, such as student services).

Consensus conferences have been used in health care to help physicians and other medical personnel develop uniform practices within their various institutions and professions. Since our university has a science focus with a long history within the health sciences, it was decided that this would be a good platform for addressing LCT issues within our university. During a consensus conference, it is usual for a panel of experts to review current practices in the profession and/or institution and make recommendations to the staff, who would then attempt to arrive at a consensus regarding uniform procedures in the areas under discussion. At USP, our experts consisted of the people who interact with our students on a daily basis—the members of our faculty and staff. Therefore, all faculty and appropriate staff and administrators were the invited experts to help reach a consensus on LCT at our institution.

In this chapter, we share our experiences with the consensus conference and describe our processes for determining faculty and staff consensus. We will also share the faculty/staff response to the conference, and offer some insight into issues that must be considered from the perspectives of faculty, staff, and administration as a small university attempts to implement a holistic LCT approach. We believe that both administration and faculty/staff members at institutions of any size will benefit from our attempts to introduce our university community to LCT. Moreover, the literature review that follows demonstrates that our findings are consistent with the literature on LCT.

Setting

Approximately 2,500 undergraduate students and 300 graduate students attended USP, all majoring in the sciences and the health sciences. Most students enter immediately after high school graduation and matriculate for four to six years depending on the length of their educational program (e.g., four years to earn a B.S., six years to earn a PharmD., or five years to earn an MPT). Moreover, the student body is very ethnically diverse. Students range from developmental and traditional freshmen to doctoral-level students. There is an emphasis on covering much scientific material to prepare students for their respective licensure exams.

METHODS OF DATA COLLECTION AND ANALYSIS

Call to Participate
All faculty and appropriate staff and administrators were invited on multiple occasions to participate in a consensus conference. Invitations were extended in person at the faculty council meetings, through campus mail, and through email. Faculty and appropriate staff were informed of the goals of the consensus conference.

- To determine faculty and staff members' perceptions of LCT

- To discuss the usefulness of LCT in their areas of responsibility

- To discover how they thought LCT could be implemented at USP

The call to participate also stated that a position paper on LCT would be developed as a result of this conference.

Description of the Process
As the participants arrived for the half-day conference, they were asked to sit in groups of four that included others with whom they do not regularly work. Participants formed 11 groups (with a few groups of five since the exact number of participants was not divisible by four). In their groups, participants received a folder and directions for completing the summary sheets. One person in each group was asked to serve as the group facilitator and write the group's responses on their group's sheet.

Each group received a folder labeled with either a number or face card from an ordinary deck of cards. Inside the folder were several handouts describing learning-centered teaching to facilitate the discussion, including the statement from AAHE (2003) on key characteristics of learning-centered institutions, a one-page article on deep learning from the National Teaching and Learning Forum (Rhem, 1995), and two tables comparing the characteristics of LCT to traditional teaching and desirable outcome indicators that should occur with LCT compared to undesirable outcomes indicators (see Appendix 12.1); four cards each with a different suit of the number on the cover; and five copies of a summary sheet to be used for recording their consensus statements (one for each member of the group and a colored one to serve as the group summary sheet to be placed in the folder).

Groups were asked to reach a consensus, meaning that all participants of the small group could agree with the statements they composed. If they could not reach a consensus on a certain point, they were asked not to write it down. Total agreement within the small groups was critical because the goal of the conference was to discover how faculty and staff members understood LCT, whether they thought it was possible to implement it, and if so how they thought it should be implemented. The groups were given one hour to discuss six questions, and were told that each would report to others in the following hour. Their conversations were neither recorded nor analyzed. Instead, group members recorded the results of their discussions on summary sheets. The six questions discussed were:

- What are the key elements of a learning-centered philosophy?

- What is the relationship between active learning and learning-centered teaching?

- What are the characteristics of learning-centered teaching?

- What are the characteristics of graduates of learning-centered institutions?

- How can the above be achieved in a hypothetical college?

- How can we achieve the above?

These questions allowed the participants to achieve the three goals of our study. The first two questions allowed the participants to define LCT, the third and fourth questions allowed them to consider the pros and cons of LCT, and the final question allowed them to decide how to apply the ideas at USP. Moreover, each question is more specific than the one in front of it, which allowed the participants to move from general considerations of theory to realistic ideas for implementing LCT.

After the groups had finished discussing and answering the questions on the response sheet, new groups were formed using the playing cards in each group's folder. After each person had selected a card, participants holding clubs stayed where they were and held up folders, displaying the group's number. Hearts moved up one number, the spades moved up two numbers (i.e., 10 of spades went to the queen group), and the diamonds moved down one number. This game not only broke up the monotony of the activities, but also allowed the groups to be reformed in a random fashion quickly.

The statements individuals developed in the first groups were shared with their second groups. The goal of the second small-group discussions was to reach a consensus from among the statements agreed upon in the original small groups. During the second hour, the groups completed and turned in another colored summary sheet of their new groups' response to the six questions. It is these responses that were eventually analyzed. While this process did not move all participants to 100% agreement on all points, it allowed everyone to consider a wide spectrum of ideas from individuals who work in parts of the university where they might normally be isolated from one another. Moreover, it allowed them to write down what they could agree on.

Participants

Fifty people representing every academic department attended, as did individuals from academic administration, student affairs, student services, and institutional advancement. At the time of the conference, USP had 152 full-time members of the faculty, with 37% tenured, 13% tenure track, and 50% nontenure track. Participants ranged in level from instructors to deans, though most were teaching faculty (30% of the total full-time faculty attended).

Analyses of Summary Sheets

The summary sheets from the second groups were evaluated (independently) twice, first for general responses to the questions and second to begin conceiving broad categories for analysis. Each item noted by participants on the summary sheets was listed and counted, then broad categories were created so that the counted items could be placed in larger conceptual groups. The categories reflected common themes and concerns in higher education that were addressed by many, if not all, of the groups. The results reported here are taken directly from the data developed by these two analyses.

Item-by-item analysis. The director of the Teaching and Learning Center developed a master set of consensus statements by listing every response made by every group per question. Next she rearranged these lists to put all similar answers together and counted the similar statements. The end product of the item-by-item analysis was six response sets corresponding to the six questions with the most frequent responses noted, that is, broader inter-group consensus with the number of groups indicating such a statement, and also those that were only recorded once. The most frequent responses per question were the data that she considered further and are recorded in this chapter.

Category analysis. The second author, an English professor with a background in cooperative learning, conducted the second phase of the analysis by looking for common patterns or themes reflected in the different groups' answers. Each theme was reduced to a statement that, in the opinions of the researchers, reflected the spirit of each of the answers. The themes were listed underneath each of the five categories in the order of frequency. If a particular theme were mentioned in every response sheet, for example, it would appear close to the top of the list. If it was mentioned only once, it would appear closer to the bottom. This was not an attempt to list themes in order of importance, since minority opinions were considered equally important, but to reflect which items were spread across the greatest number of groups. The closer the items were to the top of the list, the more they represented a university-wide opinion.

External validation. Both analyses were shared with a committee of 10 faculty and 2 administrators to determine if they appeared to have face validity and that they emphasized the items that were actually discussed during the conference. These reviewers agreed that all of the themes listed in both data analyses fairly represented the discussion that took place at the conference. Following this, the authors summarizing the results of the consensus conference developed a position paper.

RESULTS

Item-by-Item Analysis

The following represents specific responses to each question that was recorded on the summary sheets by several groups, thus indicating broader inter-group consensus. Most of the words or phrases used here come directly from the summary sheets.

Question 1. What are the key elements of a learning-centered philosophy? All of the participants thought that LCT means helping students to develop responsibility for their own learning. Participants defined students who are learning-centered as inquisitive and self-motivating. Faculty and staff members acknowledged the roles they must play in helping students become responsible learners.

Further, participants agreed that the changes must be global. Everyone involved, from students to administrators, must understand and embrace the philosophy. All participants agreed that learning-centered approaches must be employed, with at least a portion of that dedicated to cooperative learning techniques. From a course designer's perspective, LCT requires clearly defined course goals, outcomes, and means of assessment. Most groups indicated that it was important to consider multiple modes of delivery in order to accommodate differences in student learning styles.

Question 2. What is the relationship between active learning and learning-centered teaching? Participants agreed that active learning is a necessary method for LCT, though some argued that this method involves presenting material in a way that captures a student's interest—including the use of traditional lectures. Responses indicated that faculty and staff members believed that LCT involves active learning, but active learning can exist on its own. Some groups summarized characteristics of either, without explaining their relationship. A few responses revealed misconceptions about the relationship between active learning and LCT as identified in the literature.

Question 3. What are the characteristics of learning-centered teaching? Responses stressed that effective instructional design is critical; the learning environment must accommodate different learning styles and various ways students learn; collaboration and teamwork are important; the instructor must spend time discussing the learning process with students; instructors must be responsive to student needs, what they know, and their level in school; instructor flexibility is important; teachers should help make students aware of their responsibilities and become actively involved in student learning; LCT can be very time-consuming; educators should serve as mentors and facilitators to their students in addition to providing information; faculty must foster academic risk-taking within safe boundaries; and there must be more extensive use of formative assessment.

Question 4. What are the characteristics of graduates of learning-centered institutions? The respondents described students/graduates of LCT programs as lifelong learners, problem-solvers, leaders, self-directing/initiating, confident, adaptive, analytical, team oriented, effective communicators, and aware of how they learn. Such graduates will be risk-takers, lifelong learners, inquisitive, and responsible members of their professions and society.

Question 5. How can the above be achieved in a hypothetical college? All respondents emphasized that an institutional commitment is essential, and that such commitment may require a significant investment in money, training, student services, and infrastructure redesign. Faculty incentives and rewards, it was noted, must be tied in to a learning-centered approach. This philosophy needs to be adopted at all levels (students, faculty, staff, administration), but a uniform commitment on the part of the faculty and administrators is most critical of all. The college must be willing to invest in real institutional changes that go beyond merely accepting the spirit of the philosophy.

Resources must be made available during the transition phase and beyond, and could pay for faculty release time from their teaching for transforming the university from its current status to a culture of LCT. Further, the participants identified necessary institutional characteristics, including having small classes; a redesigned physical environment that encourages interaction; the creation of more social space; and an investment in student services as central, rather than peripheral, elements of the learning experience. All classrooms need space that is flexible with movable chairs so that interactive environments can be more easily created.

The entire university community must be willing to approach LCT with an open mind and be flexible and committed to student learning. The curriculum needs to allow for a student orientation process every year to introduce learning-centered approaches to the new students so that they will understand that they have entered an active and involved learning environment. Further, the curriculum needs to introduce real-life situations early in the educational process (i.e., internships, co-op experiences in early years) so that students will better understand the relationship between their education, their work, and the communities in which they live.

Question 6. How can we achieve the above? Participants commented that USP needs to employ mechanisms for reward and recognition to encourage a buy-in at all levels. USP's community needs to review policies and syllabi in reference to this model. Infrastructure requirements such as money, resources, small classes, environmental changes, and curricular characteristics need to be in place. Faculty and staff members will need in-service training and workshops to learn how to best utilize the LCT approach. Additionally, there needs to be a transition period for both faculty and students as we move to implement learning-centered approaches. More internships or co-op experiences would be useful. The institution must be willing to take risks and try new things. Finally, some skeptical faculty members decided that LCT may require them to alter their methods of content delivery.

Category Analysis: Overall Themes

Five themes emerged from this data, listed here from broader concerns to concepts that are more specific.

First, conceptual or theoretical issues were identified.

- The entire university community must commit to the concept for us to develop a culture of LCT.

- Commitment implies that the entire university needs to become a community of collaborative learners.

- There must be an emphasis on student responsibility for learning.

- The classroom must also become a community of learners.

- To be adaptive to learners' varying needs, LCT must utilize different learning styles.

  Second, when teaching is truly learning centered, students or graduates:

- Will be self-motivated (willing to take responsibility for their learning)

- Will demonstrate academic integrity

- Will participate in cross-disciplinary learning experiences

- Will be team players, good cooperative learners, and leaders

- Will desire to become lifelong learners

- Will assess their own learning

- Will show appreciation of differences between individuals and cultures

- Will commit to global awareness, multiculturalism, cross-disciplinary learning, and social responsibility

  Third, certain curriculum or course design issues emerged. Instructors need clearly defined learning goals, objectives, and outcomes. Faculty need to:

- Recognize that the learning process is as important as the content

- Use alternative teaching methods in addition to lecture and labs

- Utilize cooperative learning experiences

- Develop critical thinking skills

- Realize that learning extends from the classroom to the community

- Accept that learning occurs in a variety of contexts, both in and out of the classroom

- Acknowledge that assessment serves multiple purposes by providing students, instructors, and administrators with valuable feedback

  Fourth, faculty roles must change. Among the initiatives the participants believed would benefit USP were:

- Prior to implementing changes, instructors need to be educated about and learn to use LCT models.

- New and existing faculty members need orientations to these approaches.

- Professors need to act as facilitators of learning.

- Teaching styles should accommodate student learning styles.

- Instructors and students need to participate in self-assessment and program assessment.

- Faculty members need to encourage learning for its own sake.

- Teachers need to support cross-disciplinary experiences.

Finally, to achieve the above, the following changes need to occur at this university.

- The university should sponsor faculty incentive awards for innovation and participation in learning-centered teaching.

- USP needs to provide workshop opportunities for students and faculty.

- The campus needs to be redesigned to function as an LCT environment.

For example, learning spaces must be created to facilitate learning through group interaction. We need to create more classroom, lab, and student services spaces for social interaction in addition to learning space. The physical space must be uncluttered, accessible, and inviting in order to create an engaging environment that encourages students, instructors, and administrators to interact as part of a community of learners. In addition to being housed in open, redesigned spaces, student support services should be supplied with adequate staff and resources. To allow this university to function at the highest level of professor-student interaction, lecture halls would have to be replaced with spaces that are more intimate.

Summary of Findings From Both Analyses
When additional people were asked to compare the results of these two analyses to see if they showed the same themes, agreement over themes was apparent. These themes appeared on most summary statements. The consensus statement themes are summarized in Table 12.1.

Dissemination of results. The authors developed a position paper on LCT based upon the information recorded in the summary sheets and described the process used to reach these consensus statements. The director of the Teaching and Learning Center met individually with all vice presidents, deans, and chairs and gave each a copy of the position paper. These meetings

TABLE 12.1
**Consistency of Faculty Consensus Statement Themes
With the Literature on Learning-Centered Teaching**

USP consensus statement theme	Is this statement consistent with the learning-centered literature? If yes, citation is given.	How the literature expands upon or clarifies the theme raised by the consensus conference participants
Learning-centered teaching means developing student responsibility for their own learning and meaning.	Yes: (Association of American Colleges and Universities [AAC&U], 2002; AAHE, 2003; Barr & Tagg, 1995; Coffman, 2002; Doherty, Riordan, & Roth, 2002; Fink, 2003; Tagg, 2003; Weimer, 2002)	This theme is consistently agreed upon as essential in all of the literature on learning-centered teaching.
This philosophy of an emphasis on learning must be accepted and implemented consistently across the entire university.	Yes: (AAC&U, 2002; AAHE, 2003; Doherty, et al., 2002; Tagg, 2003)	A consistency and alignment of philosophy, practices, and policies at all levels is needed.
The reward structure needs to be consistent with this value.	Yes: (AAC&U, 2002; AAHE, 2003; Barr & Tagg, 1995; Doherty et al., 2002; Tagg, 2003; Weimer, 2002)	Considerations for faculty and staff remuneration increases and promotions need to consider how the person demonstrated a focus on learning.
Instructional design and the learning environment should accommodate different learning styles.	Yes: (AAC&U, 2002; Doherty, et al., 2002; Fink, 2003)	In addition to accommodating learning styles, the overall goal of educational programs is to engage students in deep learning.
Being lifelong, self-directed, self-initiating learners and leaders, and possessing excellent problem-solving abilities characterize students/graduates of such learning-centered programs.	Yes: (AAC&U, 2002; Doherty et al., 2002; Fink, 2003; Tagg, 2003; Weimer, 2002)	This theme emphasizes the importance of going beyond the content of a course to articulate what students can do as a result of their learning.
It is necessary to have classrooms and a physical environment that is conducive to actively engaging students.	Yes: (Doherty et al., 2002; Tagg, 2003)	When classrooms have moveable furniture, faculty can make the environment meet their varied instructional needs better.

It is necessary to educate and orient all faculty and staff.	Yes: (AAC&U, 2002; Doherty, et al., 2002; Felder & Brent, 1996; Fink, 2003;Tagg, 2003; Weimer, 2002)	Transition to a culture of learning centeredness may involve different approaches to teaching and interacting with students. Faculty and staff need education and support to be able to make the necessary changes.
It is necessary to educate and orient all students as to why the university is using a learning-centered approach.	Yes: (AAHE, 2003; Felder and Brent, 1996)	A stronger statement of this theme would also explain and explicitly document the expected learning outcomes.
It is necessary to have an infrastructure and dedicated resources to foster a culture of learning-centered teaching.	Yes: (AAC&U, 2002; AAHE, 2003; Doherty, et. al., 2002)	Institutions that make the commitment to a culture of learning-centeredness need to direct resources to foster and support this culture.
It is necessary to have support and release time to encourage the transition to learning-centered teaching.	Yes: (AAC&U, 2002; AAHE, 2003; Doherty, et al., 2002)	Faculty and staff need assurance of the institution's serious commitment to this change as well as help in promoting it to help assure them that this is not a short-lived fad.

provided opportunities to further discuss ways for the center to promote LCT. Moreover, the results of the consensus conference were reviewed in open forums with faculty. The director also met with the departments of public relations, institutional advancement, and admissions to discuss how they might use these findings. The position paper from the consensus conference on LCT was placed on the university's web site (www.usip.edu/teaching/learner).

DISCUSSION

Usefulness of the Process

Good representation from all of the stakeholder constituencies is essential for the results to be valid. By helping almost one-third of our faculty work toward consensus on this issue, the conference allowed USP to establish validity and buy-in on our campus. More specifically, this process of discussion and development of a position paper was an efficient method for discovering many people's opinions and to summarize the findings on a current issue. This process also allowed for campus dialogue and learning to occur at the same time. The format of using two different small groups fostered much exchange of ideas.

Since we did not record what actually went on in the small groups, we cannot comment on the actual processes groups used. We do not know what points were contentious or why they failed to reach a consensus on other concepts. However, faculty commented that the discussion helped them to clarify their own thinking on learning-centered approaches. Because participants had invested in the discussion process, they looked forward to the results and attended sessions on the position paper that came from the conference. We believe that at other institutions faculty developers would find this process of conducting a consensus conference and developing a position paper useful for issues where the campus is striving to make changes.

Comparison With the Literature on Learning-Centered Teaching
As shown in Table 12.1, the consensus conference statements are very consistent with the literature on LCT. The participants correctly identified the key features of programs and of graduates. They also expressed the widely held view that there needs to be a great deal of alignment and consistency across all aspects of the university. Perhaps with greater knowledge as a result of the educational events held on campus, participants were asking for more administrative support and dedicated resources. Higher education associations and national panels (e.g., AAHE, AAC&U, & Doherty et al.) have also stressed the importance of infrastructure, resources, and rewards to achieve these broad changes in approach. Perhaps the only area that the participants did not express the views of the literature relates to the essential roles of assessment, both formative and summative, to determine the quality of learning. The literature stresses the role of assessment in the learning process, both as feedback to the learners and to help improve the educational programs.

Campus Validation
The position paper and the results discussed in this chapter represent a snapshot of the thinking about LCT by faculty, administrators, and staff at one university. The consensus conference validates the idea that the faculty, administrators, and staff at USP are at different points in their understanding and use of LCT. Some are very new to this type of teaching, while others have been doing it for a while. The themes identified more specific comments on how the institution can create such a culture (such as changing the physical environment) and less what the professors themselves need to do to make their own teaching more learning centered. Perhaps the faculty members believe that they cannot innovate in the classroom until the administrators put in place tangible support such as release time or changes in the class size or

environment. Others might need more assurance that this is indeed a new direction for this university and not just another academic trend. If the institution puts these supports in place, we believe that more faculty members will make changes in techniques and approaches in their own teaching. It is noteworthy that participants made fewer comments about how they will engage the students in the material in their own courses better, or how they will help them understand the purposes of learning more fully. Clearly, the Teaching and Learning Center can continue to focus on educating faculty and staff on ways of utilizing LCT in the classroom.

While this activity was not related to the TPG, and many more people participated in this consensus conference than the TPGs, the recommendations are consistent with and validate the recommended action steps of the TPG on LCT. Although not stated in these terms, participants affirmed the importance of the key results areas developed by the TPG. The statements made by the participants of the consensus conference indicate that these results need to be implemented to achieve a culture of LCT. Also, the list of the characteristics of learning-centered institutions and students or graduates of such programs developed by the participants of the consensus conference will be used to form a benchmark to assess our progress toward achieving these outcomes. The desired outcomes and characteristics will be used as a guide for reviewing this university's policies, procedures, and practices to see how compatible they are with a LCT philosophy. To help achieve this end, faculty can assess themselves to see if their own policies and practices are consistent with the consensus statements. Perhaps with the position paper reflecting the views of many people at USP, there will be greater impetus to work to achieve them.

CONCLUSION

The university administrators and the director of the Teaching and Learning Center should be very encouraged by how much this university agreed on the concepts of LCT after only one year of exposure to the concept. Many faculty and staff have a good understanding of what it is and the characteristics of graduates of such programs. Some of the concerns were similar to those raised a year earlier at the first faculty open forum (such as the perceived need for small classes and that LCT is time-consuming to develop and to implement). However, the statements made at the consensus conference also show greater insight and significant progress toward accepting this philosophy. The participants at the conference did not raise as many concerns (e.g., about reducing course content or rigor), as had been expressed previously on other occasions. Clearly, the faculty members have learned that there are alternatives to traditional lectures.

They now know that there are many different approaches to teaching and that the administration is not forcing them to radically change their methods overnight. It is our hope that because they are not being told how to teach as much as they feared there is now a greater willingness to consider learning-centered concepts.

All participants and the general university community should be very encouraged by the level of agreement generated by this conference. From an administrative perspective, perhaps the greatest benefit of this event was the ability to generate in an afternoon a degree of consensus that might otherwise have taken years to develop through emails, phone calls, and committee meetings. That, if nothing else, is an accomplishment.

REFERENCES

American Association for Higher Education. (2003). Resources for inquiry and action: The learning-centered institution. *Inquiry and Action, 1.* Retrieved December 11, 2003, from http://www.aahe.org/pubs/IASpring2003.pdf

Association of American Colleges and Universities. (2002). *Greater expectations: A new vision for learning as a nation goes to college.* Washington, DC: Author. Retrieved June 2, 2003, from http://www.greaterexpectations.org

Barr, R. B., & Tagg, J. (1995). From teaching to learning: A new paradigm for undergraduate education. *Change, 28*(2), 42–47.

Coffman, S. J. (2002). Ten strategies for getting students to take responsibility for their learning. *College Teaching, 51,* 2–4.

DeZure, D. (Ed.). (2000). *Learning from change: Landmarks in teaching and learning in higher education from* Change *magazine 1969–1999.* Sterling, VA: Stylus.

Doherty, A., Riordan, T., Roth, J. (Eds.). (2002). *Student learning: A central focus for institutions of higher education.* Milwaukee, WI: Alverno College Institute.

Felder, R. M., & Brent, R. (1996). Navigating the bumpy road to student-centered instruction. *College Teaching, 44,* 43–47. Retrieved December 3, 2003, from http://www.ncsu.edu/felder-public/Papers/Resist.html

Fink, L. D. (2003). *Creating significant learning experiences: An integrated approach to designing college courses.* San Francisco, CA: Jossey-Bass.

Graesser, A. C., Person, N. K., Hu, X. (2002). Improving comprehension through discourse processing. In D. F. Halpern & M. D. Hakel (Eds.), *New directions for teaching and learning: No. 89. Applying the science of learning to university teaching and beyond* (pp. 33–44). San Francisco, CA: Jossey-Bass.

Matlin, M. W. (2002). Cognitive psychology and college-level pedagogy: Two siblings that rarely communicate. In D. F. Halpern & M. D. Hakel (Eds.), *New directions for teaching and learning: No. 89. Applying the science of learning to university teaching and beyond* (pp. 87–103). San Francisco, CA: Jossey-Bass.

Rhem, J. (1995). Close Up Column: Going deep. *National Teaching and Learning Forum, 5*(1), 4.

Sternberg, R. J., & Grigorenko, E. L. (2002). The theory of successful intelligence as a basis for instruction and assessment in higher education. In D. F. Halpern & M. D. Hakel (Eds.), *New directions for teaching and learning: No. 89. Applying the science of learning to university teaching and beyond* (pp. 45–54). San Francisco, CA: Jossey-Bass.

Tagg, J. (2003). *The learning paradigm college.* Bolton, MA: Anker.

University of the Sciences in Philadelphia. (2002). *Tactical planning group report on creating a culture of student-centered learning and living.* Philadelphia, PA: Author.

Weimer, M. (2002). *Learner-centered teaching: Five key changes to practice.* San Francisco, CA: Jossey-Bass.

APPENDIX 12.1

CONSENSUS CONFERENCE MATERIALS

Characteristics of Learning-Centered Teaching and Traditional Teacher-Centered Instruction

How does each model address these questions?	Learning-centered teaching	Faculty-centered teaching
What drives the system?	*Student-learning-driven*	*Instructionally driven*
How are educational programs planned?	Educational objectives determine instructional format, varied modalities.	Traditional, instructor-driven modalities, that is, lecture, lab, recitation, and discussions predominate.
	Planned consistency among objectives, teaching/learning transactions, and assessments (Fink, 2003)	Arbitrary alignment among objectives, teaching/learning transactions, and assessments; possible inconsistencies
What are the major roles for faculty?	*Faculty become designers of learning environments for students (Barr & Tagg, 1995), facilitators of student active learning, and model expert thought processes.*	*Instructor, as content expert, conveys material.*
	Faculty enable students to learn effectively and efficiently in varied environments.	*Faculty transmit information, and may not provide enough assistance for students to master content.*
How is power distributed?	*Faculty control the content. Power is shared with students so that they can be involved in the conditions of learning. This balance of power leads to greater student responsibility (Weimer, 2002).*	*Faculty control the content, the learning process, the conditions for learning, and the assessments, all of which lead to dependent, unmotivated students (Weimer, 2002).*
What guides how students are taught?	Evidence-based research (Matlin, 2002; Sternberg & Grigorenko, 2002) guides the principles of the teaching/learning transactions and assessments.	Instructors teach largely based on how they were taught.
How are students taught?	Adaptation of teaching/learning transactions to accommodate students' learning styles, abilities, varied needs of diverse student population (DeZure, 2000)	Instruction tends to be a one-size-fits-all approach; students must adapt to the system to succeed.

How are students exposed to new material?	Students are directly involved in the discovery of knowledge, employ inquiry-based methods to understand and use the material (Graesser, Person, Hu, 2002); prior knowledge is considered to facilitate learning.	Faculty are concerned with coverage of a large amount of material, possibly at the expense of student understanding.
How do students spend their time?	*Students are actively engaged in their learning process.*	*Students often are passive receivers of information.*
How do students study?	Engaged students foster deep learning (material integrated, many associations made among concepts, allows for understanding and reflection) (Weimer, 2002).	Students often learn through memorization, and they may not create meaning from the material learned.
Why evaluate students?	*Evaluation promotes learning and improvement and provides feedback and results in competency decisions about students (Weimer, 2002).*	*Evaluation is separate from learning and is used to provide feedback and make grade distinctions among the students.*
Can all students succeed?	Faculty show concern for the well-being and success of all students and adapt teaching and learning transactions to accommodate for individual differences (Barr & Tagg, 1995).	Accepts idea that some students will fail or do not as well as others often because grading falls along a bell-shaped curve

Notes

- If a characteristic or indicator is not referenced it is because this idea can be found in most of this literature on learning-centered teaching.
- Key concepts are in italics.
- From: Blumberg, P. (2004). Beginning journey toward a culture of learning-centered teaching. *Journal of Student-Centered Learning, 2*(1), 69–80.

Key Outcome Indicators

Outcome domains	Desirable outcome indicators that should occur with learning-centered teaching	Unsatisfactory outcome indicators
Who is responsible for learning to occur?	*Students take responsibility for their own learning.*	*Faculty define what and how learning should occur.*
What roles do assessments play in courses?	*Assessment is part of the learning process with students engaged in self and peer assessment, faculty giving constructive feedback on how to improve (Weimer, 2002), and providing information to assign student grades.*	*Assessment provides information to assign student grades; may be seen as taking away time from teaching content.*
What is assessed?	Fundamental knowledge, skills, critical thinking, integration, values, learning how to learn (Fink, 2003)	May evaluate rote or surface learning of content at the expense of other objectives
What can students do with acquired knowledge?	Students are inquisitive explainers (Graesser et al., 2002).	Students are fact collectors (Graesser et al., 2002).
	Students are active users of knowledge (Graesser et al., 2002); knowledge is used to develop learning skills (Weimer, 2002).	Students are repositories of inert knowledge (Graesser et al., 2002).
How are students evaluated?	Multiple assessment methods should emphasize forward assessment (tests on ability to use what was covered in the class in a new way, career applications) (Fink, 2003).	Evaluation often emphasizes backward assessments (covers mostly what was covered in the class) (Fink, 2003).
Who should assess students?	*Self, peer, faculty, professional/practitioner assessments*	*Faculty*
Is there an end point to this learning?	*Students become self-directed, lifelong learners.*	*Learning about a discipline ends when the course is over*

Notes

- If a characteristic or indicator is not referenced it is because this idea can be found in most of this literature on learning-centered teaching.
- Key concepts are in italics.
- From: Blumberg, P. (2004). Beginning journey toward a culture of learning-centered teaching. *Journal of Student-Centered Learning, 2*(1), 69–80.

13

Teaching Partners: Improving Teaching and Learning by Cultivating a Community of Practice

Richard A. Holmgren
Allegheny College

The Teaching Partners Program and its follow-up activities demonstrate that a carefully designed faculty development program can shift a campus culture to derive significant, measurable benefits for faculty and students. The program seeks to transform the institutional culture from one in which teaching is sequestered behind closed doors to one that supports substantive conversations about both the learning-teaching process and the methods by which that process might best be facilitated. Following Shulman's (1993) lead, the program opens the doors of the classroom, reenvisions teaching as community property, and nurtures informed and sustaining discussion of teaching.

INTRODUCTION

The Teaching Partners Program responds to a faculty needs assessment with an integrated program that meets both faculty needs and enhances the learning experiences of students. Program components—an intensive workshop, class visits, and other events—are designed to reinforce one another and to provide faculty with the rewards necessary to sustain their participation. Our assessment of the program considers the impacts on the participants, their students, and the institution, and it demonstrates that the Teaching Partners Program has positive outcomes for the teaching experience of participants, the learning experiences of their students, and the larger college community.

DEFINING THE CAMPUS CULTURE: A NEEDS ASSESSMENT

In the spring of 1999, Professor of English Lloyd Michaels and Associate Professor of Mathematics Richard Holmgren were appointed as dean and associate dean of the college, respectively, at Allegheny College, a residential liberal arts college in northwestern Pennsylvania with approximately 130 faculty and 1,850 students. To prepare for their new administrative roles and to assess the needs of the faculty, Michaels and Holmgren interviewed individually over 90% of the full-time tenured or tenure-track faculty. Eighteen of the 24 tenure-track but not yet tenured faculty that we interviewed expressed a desire for more support for teaching, including workshops focused on teaching, formative observation and discussion of their teaching with colleagues, and structured opportunities to visit the classrooms of colleagues. Untenured faculty also indicated that in all but one department, informal discussion of issues and successes encountered in teaching was largely absent. These findings are consistent with views expressed by many tenured faculty who suggested that teaching is something that is done behind closed doors. One senior faculty member reported that he saw no need to assist new hires with developing their teaching, claiming that "we hired them because they are already good teachers and scholars." Like many faculty at institutions involved in the American Association for Higher Education Peer Review of Teaching Project, faculty at Allegheny readily sought and were offered assistance for their research, but many viewed teaching as a personal enterprise that does not benefit from being shared (Hutchings, 1996).

Teaching Partners was created to change this perception of teaching, and it draws on another need identified in faculty interviews—a need for community that values all facets of our work, including teaching. Faculty frequently reported a sense of isolation and a concomitant desire for connecting to a community of colleagues. A senior Teaching Partners participant illustrated this sense of isolation in an interview with an external consultant by describing a time when he would go to the dining hall and converse over lunch with colleagues; today he eats a yogurt at his desk because there is no time for a more leisurely break (Foster, 2000). On another occasion, a faculty member who has been a teaching innovator on campus was asked to consider preparing his work for publication or presentation at a conference on teaching and technology. He acknowledged that his findings were worth disseminating, but demurred, stating, "I don't want this kind of work to be what I'm known for on campus." Our needs assessment demonstrated that faculty desired but were not finding a community that supported their teaching. In fact, at least some faculty feared that they might lose the respect of their peers if they publicly joined such a community.

RESPONDING TO THE CHALLENGE:
CREATING A PROGRAM TO MEET THE NEEDS

Teaching Partners seeks to change the campus culture with respect to learning and teaching by providing faculty opportunities to learn about current research on learning and how it applies to their work, opportunities to share their teaching practice and explore new strategies in the company of colleagues, and opportunities to enhance their skills as supporters of one another's teaching. Faculty apply to the program, and 12 program participants are selected for the program each year. A representative cohort of the broader faculty is created in each program year by selecting from a range of disciplines and ranks. To facilitate institutional transformation and build credibility, faculty leaders, who Middendorf (2000) would call opinion leaders, are encouraged to participate each year. To date, 45 faculty have participated in the program, 22 of whom are women, 14 were tenured at the time they enrolled, and 22 were in their first three years of service when they enrolled in the program. Five faculty have left the college since participating in the program. Even so, nearly one-third of Allegheny's continuing full-time faculty are program participants.

In each program year, the 12 program participants engage in three activities: a weeklong summer workshop, exchanges of class visits during the academic year, and regular events for program participants to exchange ideas and build community. In the workshop, faculty refine their understanding of their students and human learning, learn and practice new teaching and course design strategies, and learn and practice techniques for providing helpful feedback about teaching to colleagues. Microteaching, in which participants present short teaching segments to one another and then receive feedback, is a primary component of the workshop and provides a laboratory in which faculty can test new teaching strategies, receive feedback on their teaching, and practice providing feedback about teaching to colleagues. During the academic year following the summer workshop, program participants exchange class visits and feedback with other members of the Teaching Partners Program. In these exchanges, participants further refine their teaching strategies and their ability to provide helpful feedback to colleagues. A series of discussions, lunches, and social events that are scheduled throughout the year and open to all program alumni provide participants venues to explore teaching related matters, to create the community infrastructure necessary to sustain a shift in the institutional culture.

The program design also recognizes that change in a campus culture cannot be mandated; it grows out of activities in which faculty willingly engage and which provide the intrinsic rewards necessary to sustain interest and commitment (Erickson & Erickson, 1979; Golin, 1990; Tiberius, Sacklin, Janzen, & Preece, 1993). Wergin (2003) asserts that faculty are motivated by four underlying desires: autonomy, community, efficacy, and recognition. Teaching Partners honors faculty autonomy: All participants are volunteers, and faculty have wide latitude in deciding how they fulfill the program requirements. The program builds community by incorporating common attendance at a workshop and shared classroom observations into the program structure and by regularly providing opportunities for substantive conversation about teaching. The increased teaching skill and confidence fostered by the program enhances participants' sense of efficacy. And regular positive references to the program and its success by the dean of the college and the college president recognizes the contributions of its participants.

DOCUMENTING CHANGE: ASSESSING PROGRAM IMPACT

Our assessment is intended to document the impact of the program on the teaching experiences of the participants, on the learning environment of their students, and on the culture of the institution. Before participating in the program, participants are interviewed individually by external evaluators with extensive experience in qualitative educational research. After participation, program faculty are interviewed annually in focus groups by the same evaluators. Interviews and focus groups are taped, transcribed, and coded by the evaluators and a report highlighting themes is sent to the director of the Teaching Partners Program.

Student experience is assessed by comparing the responses of students who have taken three or more courses from Teaching Partners participants on the National Survey of Student Engagement (NSSE) to the responses of students who have not taken courses from Teaching Partners participants. Since we do not have sufficient baseline data, we are unable to compare the response of students to participants' courses before they participated to the response of students to participants' courses after they participated, which is unfortunate. However, we have compared the response of students to participants' courses on a locally developed teaching evaluation form before participation in the program to the response of students to participants' courses after participation. Finally, we have compared the retention rates of first-year students who took courses from Teaching Partners participants in the fall semester of their first year to the retention rates of first-year students who did not take courses from program participants. The comparison of retention rates was done both before and after participation. To assess the impact on the campus culture, we have collected information through surveys, focus groups, interviews, and close observation of faculty behavior.

IMPACT ON FACULTY: IMPROVING AND RENEWING TEACHING

Now in its fourth year, the comments of participants in focus groups and meetings indicate that the Teaching Partners Program has fostered positive changes in participants' teaching and on-campus experiences. When asked about the program in focus groups with external evaluators, participants describe specific improvements in their teaching that are direct outgrowths of participating in Teaching Partners. For example, participants indicate that they are more aware of the different learning styles of students and as a result more likely to incorporate a mix of active learning strategies into their courses. They report increased use of collaborative learning strategies, class discussion, student designed projects and assignments, exams that are reflective or require higher order thinking skills, and classroom assessment tools such as minute papers. They also report that they are more likely to ask students to reflect on and search for improvements in their learning strategies.

Participants indicate that the workshop is particularly helpful, and that the follow-up activities sustain the momentum they gain at the workshop. Many untenured participants comment that involving faculty of all academic ranks and from many different divisions affirms for them that teaching is important to the institution and central to what we do. However, although the program has been helpful for untenured faculty and was designed with them in mind, its impact on faculty has been most dramatic for faculty with 10 or more years of teaching experience.

One faculty member who had been teaching at Allegheny for 12 years at the time she applied to the program indicated

> I like what I am doing more. I look forward to going to my classes and teaching in a way that I haven't for quite some time. . . . I think getting positive feedback with reassurance, both during the summer course and since, has made me feel like, yeah, I can do this and I can do this well. Thinking about my course more in advance and what I want to accomplish and how the pieces come together has made me more excited about going and putting it into practice. (Teaching Partners, 2000)

Another experienced colleague regularly goes out of his way to thank the program director for encouraging him to attend the summer course and to tell the director what new teaching strategies he is employing and how much more he is enjoying his teaching. Such renewed enthusiasm for teaching and learn-ing is typical of the response of tenured participants, and participants from all years continue to be active in campus discourse about teaching, at faculty meetings, in workshops for the general education faculty, and in committees focusing on curricular development and assessment.

IMPACT ON STUDENTS:
IMPROVING LEARNING EXPERIENCES AND SATISFACTION

Preliminary data on student response to the courses of Teaching Partners par-ticipants indicate that these changes are leading to improvements in students' experiences and the learning environment. An analysis of student responses on the 2001 NSSE indicates that students of Teaching Partners participants are engaging in more practices that correlate with increased student learning than are other students at Allegheny. For example, students who took three or more courses from a Teaching Partners participant are more likely to report that their courses emphasize applying theories and concepts, and less likely to em-phasize facts, ideas, or methods. Although the data set is small and not every observed shift is statistically significant, nearly all of the observed shifts are in the desired direction and in every case where the observed difference is statis-tically significant, it is in the desired direction. In particular on the 2001 NSSE, students who had taken three or more courses from a Teaching Part-ners participant in the past year were significantly more positive about the statement that that they would choose to attend Allegheny were they given the choice over again (p = .03).

The students' enthusiasm for attending Allegheny correlates with our finding that the retention rate of the 178 first-year students who took a course in the first semester of their first year from a faculty member who had partici-pated in Teaching Partners was better than the retention rate of the 383 first-year students who took no courses from Teaching Partners that semester, with rates of 90.0% and 87.0%, respectively. By contrast, the retention rate of the 187 first-year students who took a course in the first semester of their first year from a faculty member who would later participate in Teaching Partners was only slightly better than the retention rate of the 346 first-year students who took no courses from faculty who would be Teaching Partners that semester, with rates of 85.8% and 85.0%, respectively.

A comparison of student responses on Allegheny's locally developed course evaluations revealed that students in participants' courses after partici-pation in the program responded more favorably than students in partici-pants' courses before participation. In particular, students in the courses of

Teaching Partners after they had completed the workshop were significantly more likely to report that the instructor challenged them to actively engage the material than students in the courses of Teaching Partners before they participated in the program (p = .01). Students' overall rating of instructors also improved, although the improvement was not statistically significant in one of the two cohorts of Teaching Partners participants for which we have completed data analysis (p = .02 for the 2001 cohort). Students also reported that they learned more, the instructor was more available, assignments were more helpful, and the instructor's comments were more helpful in the courses of Teaching Partners participants after they participated in the program; but again, in most cases, these differences were not significant. Interestingly, the time and effort that students report applying to the courses of Teaching Partners participants remained essentially unchanged after program participation.

We continue to collect data on student experiences with Teaching Partners participants, and given current trends in the data, we expect to find more statistically significant positive shifts when data collection and analysis is completed.

IMPACT ON THE COLLEGE CULTURE:
EXPANDING A COMMUNITY OF PRACTICE

The experiences of participants and their students indicate that Teaching Partners is meeting its goal of improving teaching and learning at Allegheny College. However, the larger challenge is to parlay the faculty enthusiasm generated among program participants into a more sustaining and sustainable institutional culture that supports teaching and learning. As the proportion of Allegheny faculty who participate in Teaching Partners grows, efforts to institutionalize the culture being promoted by the program are increasing. In particular, a practice of shared classroom observations based on the Teaching Partners model is being promoted through workshops, conversations with department heads, and encouragement from the dean's office and the faculty review committee; a program of weekly lunch meetings focused on teaching has been successfully launched; and the dean and associate dean of the college seek to develop faculty mentoring networks in the coming year. Each of these initiatives involves collaborative work related to teaching and promotes faculty autonomy and community and faculty efficacy by enhancing faculty skills and self-confidence.

Response to the newly developed weekly lunch meetings, which we call Teaching Circles, suggests that faculty continue to seek opportunities to share their experiences in the classroom and to learn from one another. The circles are modeled on groups facilitated by Steve Golin at Bloomfield College (personal communication, October 12, 2001) and differ from more traditional teaching circles or brown-bag lunch discussions in several ways: The circles are agenda-less, and participants are asked to talk about whatever joys or challenges they are currently facing in their teaching. Participants commit to attending every week for an entire semester so that over the course of 12 or more meetings they can build the trust necessary to sustain a substantive and challenging dialogue. Participants are asked to focus on what they bring to the classroom as teachers (as opposed to complaining about the students), and they are asked to hold the contributions of other participants in confidence.

The pilot circle was extraordinarily successful. Participant attendance was near perfect, and all 12 of the original participants asked to continue with the group for a second semester. When the formation of a second circle was an-nounced via email, 10 faculty asked to join within 5 hours. Within 4 days, 16 faculty asked for one of the 12 places at the table. As a result, in the second se-mester of the program, nearly 20% of Allegheny's tenured and tenure-track faculty were engaged in an ongoing discussion of teaching that was independ-ent of Teaching Partners. The program continues to be fully subscribed with two circles of 12 faculty meeting each week.

The enthusiasm for these lunch meetings suggests that the college is suc-ceeding in creating a culture in which faculty appreciate the value of good talk about teaching. Over half of the college's tenured or tenure-track faculty have participated in either Teaching Partners or Teaching Circles, so we are reach-ing well beyond the cohort of "early adopters." By sustaining and institution-alizing these efforts and continually searching for new opportunities to pro-vide the supportive community sought by faculty, we are creating a responsive faculty culture that supports faculty, teaching, and student learning.

CONCLUSIONS

Transformational change in the academy requires focus, patience, and time, but Allegheny College's experiment demonstrates that it can be done. Struc-turing faculty development activities to foster organizational change can yield significant and sustainable benefits to faculty, students, and the institution. There is ample evidence to support our claim that Allegheny College's faculty development programs enhance the teaching experience for individual faculty and foster a sense of community and shared mission among program partici-pants. Analysis of student reports on national and locally developed assessment instruments, as well as retention data for first-year students, indicates that these changes have positive benefits for students. Sustained and widespread faculty involvement in ongoing teaching development programs demonstrates that these benefits are being extended to the larger college community. However, cultural change in the academy cannot be mandated. To be welcomed by the faculty, it must respond to their felt needs. To expand beyond a limited circle, it must include a representative cross-section that includes faculty leaders. To be sustainable, it must provide faculty the autonomy, community, efficacy, and recognition they seek.

NOTE

This work was supported by grants from the William and Flora Hewlett Foundation and the Andrew W. Mellon Foundation.

REFERENCES

Erickson, G. R., & Erickson, B. L. (1979). Improving college teaching: An evaluation of a teaching consultation procedure. *Journal of Higher Education, 50,* 670–683.

Foster, S. (2000). *Teaching partners program: Analysis of first interviews.* Unpublished report.

Golin, S. (1990). Peer collaboration and student interviewing: The master faculty program. *AAHE Bulletin, 43*(4), 9–10.

Hutchings, P. (1996). The peer review of teaching: Progress, issues, and prospects. *Innovative Higher Education, 20*(4), 221–234.

Middendorf, J. K. (2000). Finding key faculty to influence change. In M. Kaplan & D. Lieberman (Eds.), *To improve the academy: Vol. 18. Resources for faculty, instructional, and organizational development* (pp. 83–93). Bolton, MA: Anker.

Shulman, L. S. (1993, November/December). Teaching as community property: Putting an end to pedagogical solitude. *Change, 25*(6), 6–7.

Teaching Partners Lunch Discussion. (2000, October 13). Unpublished tape transcript.

Tiberius, R. G., Sacklin, H. D., Janzen, K. R., & Preece, M. (1993). Alliances for change: A procedure for improving teaching through conversations with learners and partnerships with colleagues. *Journal of Staff, Program, and Organizational Development, 11*(1), 11–22.

Wergin, J. F. (2003). *Departments that work: Building and sustaining cultures of excellence in academic programs.* Bolton, MA: Anker.

14

A Faculty Development Program to Promote Engaged Classroom Dialogue: The Oral Communication Institute

Kim M. Mooney
Traci Fordham
Valerie D. Lehr
St. Lawrence University

The St. Lawrence University faculty development program in oral communication promotes and enhances teaching strategies and philosophies for productive and civil classroom discourse. Started in January 2002, the Oral Communication Institute (OCI) provides a sustained forum in which faculty explore the relationship among oral communication, critical thinking, and deep learning. In addition to creating discourse communities, the OCI affords participants opportunities to develop strategies for interactive, reflective student learning. This chapter addresses the essential components for developing an oral communication institute: clear teaching and learning goals, a deliberate format and curriculum, experiential pedagogy, and opportunities for faculty dialogue and reflection.

INTRODUCTION

Among the majority of St. Lawrence University faculty, class discussions represent a preferred pedagogical strategy for enhancing students' critical reflections on readings, performances, and presentations. However, faculty freely acknowledge that creating and sustaining substantive classroom discussions present enduring challenges. On some days, a class may be highly interactive, but the next day students respond very little to a professor's questions and prompts. In other classes, a few students may dominate a conversation and silence other students, speaking not to learn per se, but to assert their deeply held convictions. In almost all classes, students stop taking notes as soon as the instructor stops speaking and a classmate starts. Sometimes this response seems to represent an effort to listen, but more often, it seems to be based on a belief that knowledge comes from instructors, not peers.

Research suggests that when students arrive at college, their preconceived understanding of what constitutes good discussion does not promote classroom interactions that result in productive learning encounters, particularly between people who initially disagree with each other (Shachtman, 1995; Tannen, 1998). Extensive survey data from our own students on the National Survey of Student Engagement (NSSE, 2001) support other research findings that students are inclined to view discussion as most attractive when those involved know that others agreed with them right at the conversation's outset (Trosset, 1998). On a small, residential campus like St. Lawrence, we know that to ask students to take classroom discussion seriously is to ask that they put themselves at risk: The peers with whom they live, study, and socially interact would know what they really think about issues even if their perspectives are not neatly aligned with those of their classmates or friends.

Historical and recent evidence from St. Lawrence faculty and student data indicated a pressing need for greater faculty development efforts focused on classroom discussion pedagogies. First, the development of students' writing and oral communication skills is stated as specific and mandatory teaching and learning objectives within our First-Year Program (FYP), a required, year-long residential living and learning community. Since its inception in the late 1980s, the FYP's faculty development efforts have focused far more on the student writing objectives even though the program's goals weigh the development of students' writing and oral communication skills equally. Second, the results from a 2001 faculty development and teaching committee survey indicated improving classroom discussions as the teaching issue of greatest interest to the faculty. Finally, results from the NSSE (2001) indicated "working with classmates on assignments outside of class" as the best single predictor for St. Lawrence students having conversations with others whom they define as different from themselves with respect to social and political backgrounds. This NSSE finding was a clear signal that the ways in which faculty organize and conceive of student discussion and dialogue can, in fact, have a significant impact on the likelihood of students engaging in productive conversations with each other both in and out of the classroom.

According to Mintz (1999), effective, holistic faculty development programs are those that are undertaken by both the institution and the faculty. Such programs acknowledge that teaching occurs within the context of values of the institution and are not only about improving the quality of teaching but about connecting classroom work to our understanding of the organization's faculty and student cultures. As a liberal arts institution, a central goal of St. Lawrence University is to foster the critical thinking skills that will prepare our students for life as responsible, contributing citizens. The university's goal statement includes as an aim that we encourage students to develop "a respect for differing opinions and for free discussion of these opinions; and an ability to use information logically and to evaluate alternative points of view." This aim echoes Baldwin's (1998) contention that college classrooms are critical places to promote civil and intellectually rigorous discussions to empower and prepare students for global citizenship.

In our then respective positions of associate dean for faculty affairs and associate dean for the first-year program, we (Kim and Val) began meeting with a small group of faculty from a number of disciplines including history, sociology, and speech and theater, who were interested in questions of civic engagement and classroom dialogue. Through our small group conversations and the support of the Center for Teaching and Learning, we submitted a proposal to the William and Flora Hewlett Foundation to support the development of a yearlong series of interconnected seminars and workshops, the Oral Communication Institute (OCI). The Hewlett Liberal Arts Program funding allowed us the time and opportunity necessary to think and talk collectively about the complex student communication and learning issues that we had identified. The primary objective of the OCI is not simply to convey the mechanics of developing strategies for good classroom discussions, but to promote a deeper understanding among faculty of the communication context in which those discussions will thrive.

To date, at the end of the second year of the OCI, 40 faculty members from 14 academic departments have participated. While the majority of participants have come from the ranks of assistant and associate professors, six full professors participated in this program.

THE GOALS OF THE ORAL COMMUNICATION INSTITUTE

Epistemology and the Teaching Process

Starting with an intensive three-day seminar during the annual January break and continuing with follow-up meetings in the spring and again in the fall of the next academic year, the OCI is intentionally structured to give faculty uninterrupted, quality time together. Because all participants prepare in advance for the institute by reading assigned texts, they arrive for the meetings with broad, and in many cases, new backgrounds in communication theories.

Generally, most educators believe that getting students to talk in class is a good thing but often cannot say why oral communication might be important to learning. Students themselves often view class or group discussions as evidence that the professor was not prepared to "teach" that day. Some of the problems we encounter in class, when students talk but do not seem to say much, or do not seem committed to communicating well with one another, come from *our* often hazy understandings of why we want them to talk in the first place. Why, indeed, does oral communication matter to the enterprise of learning? How we answer this question inevitably guides our pedagogies.

The most common faculty misconception prior to the start of the OCI is that it is designed to teach faculty how do design and grade students' speeches and oral presentations. While the formal and structured presentation is certainly a specific context of communication in the classroom and is addressed during the OCI, formal and informal assignment design is not the primary goal of the OCI. The goals for the institute focus on cultivating in faculty participants a deeper understanding of communication processes and the central roles oral communication plays in the creation and dissemination of knowledge. The underlying premise of the OCI is that both the articulation of one's thoughts and the careful listening to the ideas and opinions of others helps us to learn more profoundly.

Deepening faculty understanding of the complex process of communication. Effective speaking and listening increase the likelihood that what one comes to know during dialogue will be more sophisticated and multilayered, regardless of the conversation's content. Giving voice to knowledge, sharing that voice with others, listening to diverse perspectives, and modifying one's thinking are crucial learning processes and critical life skills. This philosophical assumption has shaped the ways in which we construct pedagogies for the OCI.

During the institute, faculty participants begin to develop a more holistic view of oral communication in their classes and reflect on what it means to be rhetorically sensitive, or more aware of the complexity of human communication (Hart & Burks, 1972). We, as leaders and facilitators, encourage faculty to talk about factors that are in play in college students' learning environments and how they as teachers might adapt their approaches to different classroom contexts and audiences. Once we begin discussion of how communication is essential to our classroom environments, and not simply a part of them, we are able to move beyond faculty's seeming need to learn how to "teach oral presentations" and onto more sophisticated discussions about oral communication in the classroom.

Educating faculty on the context of students' communication styles. Students come to our courses with myriad social positions and orientations and with many ways of thinking about and applying communication strategies. To be unaware or insensitive to the factors that influence students' communication styles and preferences is to risk not reaching them. If one of our objectives as teachers is to understand why students might be reticent to talk in class or why they do not communicate well (e.g., argue instead of listen and discuss), and to create more productive environments for learning, it behooves us to think more critically about students' roles in our classroom environment. To this end, OCI faculty participants discuss with each other the ways in which they would characterize their classrooms as communication environments. We ask them to think about the various subject positions that students have and how those social identities might influence the ways in which students communicate in the classroom.

OCI faculty also explore both the social and institutional obstacles that might impinge upon effective classroom dialogue. For this particular portion of the institute, faculty reflect on Tannen's (1998) *The Argument Culture* and talk about the many social, cultural, historical, and institutional challenges to effective dialogue and discussion.

Prompting faculty to be more self-reflective about their own communication. Through their interactions with students, faculty co-create classroom norms, expectations, and ways of thinking and behaving. An important goal in the OCI is to assist faculty in becoming more aware of their own communication styles and to begin evaluating how their communication in the classroom contributes to their students' learning and to the classroom environment as a whole. Time is allotted during early OCI meetings for faculty to analyze, write, and talk about their own classroom communication style.

Assisting faculty in the development and design of their course. Through their participation in the institute, OCI faculty are given numerous opportunities to collaborate with each other as they develop skills and design assignments that will help them create more interactive learning experiences for students. Faculty are encouraged to be mindful of providing environments that will encourage student confidence and competence in extemporaneous and deliberate discourse, especially when that discourse involves controversial or emotionally charged topics.

THE OCI FORMAT AND CURRICULUM

The OCI was designed to create opportunities for faculty to engage in meaningful dialogue and experiential learning with each other. As planning for the institute got underway, it became clear that initial contact about the OCI would best be presented to the faculty as a comprehensive course with a number of basic elements.

- The announcement of the institute provided a course description.

- An application process served as course registration.

- Stated regular meeting times established an institute schedule.

- A syllabus and common reading materials were included.

- Each seminar meeting was co-facilitated or team-taught.

- Each meeting entailed some individual, small group, and plenary work.

- A reflection paper was due at the end of the institute.

In its current format, the sequencing of the OCI work occurs in four distinct phases: the call for participation and preparation for the meetings; the January seminar; the spring workshops; and the fall follow-through and reflection work.

All documents mentioned in this chapter that do not appear in an appendix can be found at the St. Lawrence University Center for Teaching and Learning web site at http://www.stlawu.edu/ctl/oci.htm.

Soliciting Faculty Participation

In the early fall, all faculty receive a letter describing the OCI goals and format. An application form is attached to the letter and interested faculty are asked to submit the form so that as facilitators, we gain a sense of faculty teaching goals and the types of courses in which faculty hope to incorporate oral communication pedagogies. With only 20 available seats each year, priority is given to continuing faculty members.

In order to expect faculty members to commit to a yearlong series of meetings and readings, a stipend equivalent to a course overload is offered. Five weeks in advance of the meetings, participants receive reading materials (see Appendix 14.1) and a syllabus (see Appendix 14.2).

The January Seminar

The first phase of the yearlong OCI commitment begins with an intensive, three-day seminar during the winter break before spring semester classes begin. Each morning and afternoon is conceptualized as a distinct session, with guiding questions and relevant readings assigned for each day.

Day one. Our primary goal the first day is to ask faculty to consider why they wish to make dialogue and discussion central to their courses and how this desire may be related to the epistemological goals they have for their classes. That is, if a primary course goal is to lead students to definitive conclusions, how will the use of dialogue enhance the course? Alternatively, if a primary course goal is to encourage students to explore values and beliefs, how will dialogue contribute? In what ways do different forms of dialogue contribute to these epistemological objectives? We then ask faculty to discuss inquiry-based pedagogies and how they might extend their perspectives on the role of dialogue.

Day two. On the second day, we begin to discuss some of the obstacles to engaged dialogue that we see in our classrooms. This discussion covers issues ranging from how the limited racial and ethnic diversity of St. Lawrence affects student dialogue in the classroom to how the argument culture (Tannen, 1998) is apparent in the ways in which students interact with one another. We consider how our pedagogies can take such influences into account and discuss the necessity of working with students to help them to become more attentive listeners.

Day three. On the third day, we ask faculty to consider the connections between their goals for oral communication and their goals for writing assignments. The purpose is to address the ways that the speaking and writing can be reinforcing learning tools, even while recognizing the differences between the two forms of expression.

As a final opportunity to talk with one another in some detail about a particular course, we ask faculty to bring a copy of the syllabus for the course(s) they intend to modify as a result of their OCI work. They are grouped with a few other participants to work through a series of questions asking how they might try to create a different environment in the classroom to encourage student communication, how they might build dialogue into their courses, and how, or if, they might need to modify some content coverage in order to use dialogue and discussion to foster deeper understanding.

January Pedagogy

Throughout the January seminar, we use pedagogies that illustrate and suggest what faculty might want to do in their classrooms. Thus, each seminar session combines paired, triadic, or small-group conversations, and also includes large-group discussions. When in smaller groups, the participants are given carefully designed questions intended to help the group connect its own experiences with the readings. Examples of the types of questions asked of participants appear throughout this section and in Appendix 14.2. As facilitators, we use the small-group time to convene ourselves and modify the day's plans in order to best respond to emerging issues and requests. A final, important goal of the January seminar pedagogy is to build a discourse community. That is, this community of faculty has begun to develop a shared understanding of student communication issues. We believe this mutual knowledge contributes to the success of the OCI because it illustrates so powerfully the extent to which collaborative, engaged dialogue contributes to learning. At the end of the January seminar, an OCI listserv is created to further facilitate OCI faculty communication between meetings.

Spring Workshops

As announced in advance of the institute, OCI participants are scheduled to meet four times during the spring semester. These meetings afford opportunities to expand the sense of community created in January and to address specific classroom issues that emerge from the January conversations. The four spring meetings draw on various local experts from either the OCI group or the St. Lawrence faculty at large to lead discussion or hands-on workshops on issues that all participants have agreed at the end of January would be helpful and interesting.

After both January seminars in 2002 and 2003, it was clear that faculty were interested in exploring the role of technology in classroom discussions. They wanted to talk more about the ways in which technology may be used both in and out of class to create richer dialogues in the classroom. In both years, OCI participants agreed to demonstrate for the group how they utilize online discussion assignments to initiate and enrich student-to-student conversations both inside and out of the classroom. The group then discussed the merits and drawbacks of online dialogue as an impetus for more fruitful in-class dialogue. The other post-January workshop suggestions were similar for each year and covered the design and grading of formal student oral presentations, the use of creative role-play and other theater exercises to engage even the most reticent students, and a panel of OCI participants reporting on the efficacy of their pedagogical attempts.

Fall Reflection

Throughout the January and spring meetings, the substance of the OCI sessions is focused on specific classroom dialogue and discussion issues as identified by the participating OCI faculty and as presented in the assigned readings. The pedagogy of the January and spring meetings is experiential in nature so the OCI faculty can apply and practice both new and familiar approaches to generating and sustaining classroom discussions. In the fall, the number of plenary meetings is substantially reduced and faculty are asked instead to begin to work more directly with one another in dyads or in small groups rather than as a larger collective.

The reasons behind the pedagogical shift are both logistical and philosophical. We are concerned that to continue the expectation of regular group meetings after changing to a fall schedule would create numerous conflicts that would cause us to lose participants along the way to committee and other standing obligations. The second, more strongly held conviction had to do with the underlying premise of the OCI. Ongoing faculty-to-faculty interaction is a crucial and desirable learning tool for all OCI participants. If we believe fostering more engaged communication between students will develop an understanding of how much they can learn from each other, the same conviction must hold true for faculty.

Once the fall semester is underway, the OCI group meets in a plenary session, which has two primary functions: to review and refresh the themes from the spring meetings and to disseminate the two primary assignments for the fall, both of which are described below.

Peer partner program. Each OCI participant is paired with another OCI faculty member outside of his or her discipline or department. The partnerships are envisioned on a number of potential levels but never on an evaluative one. At a minimum, the partners complete reflective conversation worksheets that pose questions to encourage them to engage in conversations that contextualize their respective teaching and learning philosophies. The questions also promote clarification of their goals around the role of oral communication strategies and assignments in a designated course. When introducing the peer partner program to the OCI faculty, the exchange of classroom visits is discussed as an ideal follow-through to the reflective conversation worksheets and feedback conversations. Although the class visits are optional, there is a clear expectation that if peer partners decide to take this route, they will review best practices in collegial classroom visits as described in Chism's (1999) resource book on peer review. The circumstances under which partners meet and the frequency of the meetings are determined by each partnership.

Reflective writing assignment. The final OCI assignment involves submitting a paper at the end of the fall semester. The writing assignment attempts to connect the peer partner dialogue work and OCI participants' own teaching and learning philosophy and practices. In their writing, faculty reflect on the substance and process through which they worked when completing the reflective conversation worksheet on their own and to explain how conversations with a peer partner crystallized their thinking and influenced their decisions about using oral communication strategies in class. Finally, the writing assignment asks the faculty to reflect on their participation in the OCI, and to comment on how critically engaged conversations with colleagues about pedagogy affected their own teaching and learning experiences.

A final OCI plenary meeting is held in mid-December, after submitting their papers. The group comes back together to talk about their responses and perhaps draw parallels between the usefulness of their dialogues with their colleagues and the powerful potential for student learning through dialogues with their peers.

FACULTY RESPONSE TO THE OCI

The formal survey instrument discussed below offers affirmative documentation of faculty members' reasons for why they want to create more oral communication opportunities for their students, but our observations of and interactions with OCI participants also informed us of the program's success. At the end of each seminar day in January, faculty members would leave the Center for Teaching and Learning to go to their offices to work on a new assignment or to revise a syllabus based on an activity or conversation from that day's OCI session. The faculty participants did not wait a semester as originally planned to implement their new goals; they were revising their syllabi for courses that were scheduled to start in three days. Nor did the OCI participants limit their efforts to the one course they had identified as their "OCI course"; their oral communication goals for students were integrated into their other spring semester courses as well. The faculty engagement and excitement throughout the January meetings continued throughout the semester and generated tremendous faculty interest across campus.

After 20 St. Lawrence faculty members participated in the inaugural OCI, the Center for Teaching and Learning sponsored a panel presentation for members in this first group to talk about their perspectives on the institute and the impact on their classroom teaching. Over 25 colleagues from all over campus who had not participated in the OCI attended the presentation. This faculty development program had captured the faculty's interest; the following week we received over 20 applications for the second year.

The OCI faculty response has been powerful and positive, though not without helpful criticisms. The selective comments below capture the general consensus expressed through email correspondence with OCI participants after the first January seminar in 2002. Because there was consensus on what strategies worked and what strategies needed work, as facilitators, we were provided with a strong sense of the format, curricular, and pedagogical elements to maintain or retool for the next year.

Favorable OCI Elements Expressed in the Survey

- What I learned at the OCI was to ask what I expected out of class discussions. Why was it useful to have them? I came away from the OCI with an understanding that much like writing, talking something out is a process by which we think through an issue or an idea.

- Before the three-day workshop began, the readings began to reshape my thoughts about how we listen and engage in dialogue as well as how we speak.

- I found lots of great, pragmatic ideas for some useful transformations in my classes and was given the time and context for serious, critical reflecting about my pedagogy and teaching philosophy.

- The most valuable thing for me was simply the conversations with colleagues (both small groups or pairs) and hearing about the kinds of classroom situations they encounter and things they have tried and whether they worked well.

OCI Elements Requiring Improvement

- The amount of theoretical reading was too great and did not provide enough discussion to warrant the quantity.

- The use of jargon and references to unfamiliar authors by some participants confused faculty from different disciplines.

Faculty Reflections on their Goals and Rationales

On the first and last days of the 2003 January seminar, OCI faculty completed a questionnaire which included the item, "What are your rationales and goals for incorporating oral communication by students into your course(s)?" On the pre-institute survey, the most frequently cited rationale for incorporating oral communication opportunities in classes was the general belief that students learn better when they are actively engaged with the material. Faculty listed a variety of goals for incorporating oral communication in their course(s), most often citing the desire to get students to take responsibility for their own learning, to enhance oral communication skills, and to help students "engage over differences" (i.e., to be more respectful of each other and think to about diverse viewpoints).

In the post-institute survey, OCI faculty generated more goals per person than they did for the pre-institute one. Many themes carried over from pre-institute to post-institute assessment, but in the post-institute survey, many OCI participants made greater connections between using more dialogue-centered pedagogies in their courses and improving students' critical thinking. The post-institute commentary confirms the level of engagement with and commitment to the numerous ideas and teaching applications shared over the course of the three-day seminar.

THE FUTURE OF THE OCI

In January 2004, we arrived at the end of the Hewlett Foundation funding and our capacity to offer hefty stipends to OCI participants for a full-year institute. We did use the remaining grant funds to offer a modified institute for interested OCI faculty alumni. The two-day agenda was designed to help faculty participants renew their thinking and share their best practices related to oral communication in teaching and learning. We also introduced the group to deliberative and sustained dialogue techniques to foster conversations about possible applications for these types of group dialogues in the broader campus community. Through our work with the OCI, we have become involved with the St. Lawrence University Journey Towards Democracy dialogue project sponsored by the Association of American Colleges and Universities (http://www.aacu-edu.org/civic_engagement/projects.cfm) and are beginning to design ways in which the two programs may combine efforts to create a whole new set of workshops on dialogue-centered pedagogies for interested faculty.

Based on the success of the OCI, we believe that we have cultivated the foundation for an institutional commitment to oral communication across the curriculum. The three of us are involved in a newly formed working group established to address the need for academic and peer-mentoring support for student oral communication skills, and to think about how this effort should be connected to already existing support for student research and writing skill development. Such a program would complement the progress that faculty are making through the increased integration of dialogue and discussion-centered pedagogies in their classroom teaching.

ACKNOWLEDGMENTS

The authors wish to acknowledge the generous support of the William and Flora Hewlett Foundation Liberal Arts Program without which this faculty development project would not have been fully realized. We also thank Michael Reder for his helpful suggestions on an earlier version of this manuscript.

REFERENCES

Baldwin, R. G. (1998). Academic civility begins in the classroom. *Essays on Teaching Excellence, 9*. Retrieved May 9, 2004, from http://www.unm.edu/~castl/ Castl_Docs/Packet9/Academic%20Civility%20Begins%20in%20the%20Class room.html

Chism, N. V. N. (1999). *Peer review of teaching: A sourcebook*. Bolton, MA: Anker.

Hart, R. P., & Burks, D. M. (1972). Rhetorical sensitivity and social interaction. *Speech Monographs, 39*, 75–91.

Mintz, J. (1999, Spring). Faculty development and teaching: A holistic approach. *Liberal Education, 85*, 32–37.

National Survey of Student Engagement. (2001). *Results from St. Lawrence University.* Bloomington, IN: Indiana University. Retrieved December 1, 2003, from http://www.indiana.edu/~nsse/

Shachtman, T. (1995). *The inarticulate society: Eloquence and culture in America.* New York, NY: Free Press.

Tannen, D. (1998). *The argument culture: Stopping America's war of words.* New York, NY: Ballantine.

Trosset, C. (1998, September/October). Obstacles to open discussion and critical thinking: The Grinnell College study. *Change, 30*(5), 44–49.

APPENDIX 14.1

St. Lawrence University Oral Communication Institute

Reading List for Year II

Burbules, N. C. (1993). *Dialogue in teaching: Theory and practice.* New York, NY: Teacher's College Press.

Burbules, N. C., & Rice, S. (1991). Dialogue across differences: Continuing the conversation. *Harvard Educational Review, 61,* 393–416.

Cary, L. (1991). *Black ice.* New York, NY: Vintage.

Finkel, D. (2000). *Teaching with your mouth shut.* Portsmouth, NH: Boynton & Cook.

Garrison, J. W., & Kimball, S. L. (1993). Dialoguing across differences: Three hidden barriers. Retrieved May 9, 2004, from http://www.ed.uiuc.edu/EPS/PES-Yearbook/93_docs/GAR_KIMB.htm

Tannen, D. (1998). *The argument culture: Stopping America's war of words.* New York, NY: Ballantine.

Tatum, B. (1992). Talking about race, learning about racism: The application of racial identity development theory in the classroom. *Harvard Educational Review, 62,* 1–24.

Trenholm, S. (1999). *Thinking through communication: An introduction to the study of human communication* (Chapter 3., 3rd ed.). Boston, MA: Allyn and Bacon.

Appendix 14.2

St. Lawrence University OCI Annotated January Syllabus

Monday January 13, 2003: Morning

Question: What are our goals in cultivating productive dialogue in our classes?

- We ask participants to think about how they currently conceptualize and use oral communication in their classrooms.

- In small groups, OCI faculty discuss classrooms as communication environments by talking about the identities that people bring to the classroom and how these factors influence learning.

Monday, January 13, 2003: Afternoon

Question: How are different discourse strategies useful in relation to different epistemological assumptions?

- Participants talk in small groups about the readings to consider how different authors conceptualize dialogic-centered pedagogies and whether these ideas make sense given the particular realities on our campus.

- Participants then discuss the epistemological foundation of their courses and this affects their use of dialogue.

Relevant readings: Finkel; Burbules, Chapters 5 & 6, *Dialogue in Education*

Tuesday, January 14, 2002: Morning

Question: What factors make communication and dialogue more complex?

- We talk in small groups and as a large group about how issues of diversity/marginality affect discourse at St. Lawrence.

Relevant readings: Cary

Tuesday, January 14, 2003: Afternoon

Question: What are obstacles to engaged dialogue in the classroom?

- In plenary, the group discusses the readings in order to identify factors that interfere with engaged dialogue, including the limitations to effective listening. The discussion is then directed to how we might overcome some of these obstacles.

Relevant readings: Garrison & Kimball; Tannen; Tatum; Trenholm

Wednesday, January 15, 2003: Morning (with the writing program director)
Question: How might writing and oral communication complement one another in our courses?

- The group discusses the ways in which writing and speaking have similar and different expressive properties and how we might design pedagogies that use writing and speaking in complementary ways.

Wednesday, January 15, 2003: Afternoon
Question: What changes might we make to syllabi in order to better foster our communication goals? All participants bring syllabi to this session.

- In pairs, faculty talk about the specific course each plans to modify as a result of their OCI work.

15

Whispers and Sighs: The Unwritten Challenges of Service-Learning

Rona J. Karasik
St. Cloud State University

Documentation of the benefits of service-learning abound, and published case studies of successful service-learning programs may be found for a variety of disciplines. Faculty new to service-learning, however, are likely to find themselves facing a variety of unexpected challenges. While these challenges are neither insurmountable nor unknown to experienced service-learning practitioners, they can make starting a service-learning program remarkably time-consuming and unnecessarily frustrating. Unfortunately, pitfalls and program flops are rarely published. This chapter forewarns some of the challenges associated with service-learning and offers realistic approaches to dealing with them successfully.

INTRODUCTION

While service-learning has been around since the 1960s and perhaps even earlier (Stanton, Giles, & Cruz, 1999), this unique form of experiential education is now rapidly taking center stage on many campuses (Colby, Ehrlich, Beaumont & Stephens, 2003). Numerous studies have documented service-learning benefits for students, ranging from personal and interpersonal development, to civic engagement and enhanced critical thinking skills (Eyler & Giles, 1999). In turn, communities can gain needed assistance and a renewed appreciation of the skills and talents of local students (Westacott & Hegeman, 1996). Similarly, service-learning has the potential to enhance a faculty member's service and teaching, as well as research (Ward, 1998).

Harvesting the many benefits of service-learning requires careful planning, however, and faculty new to service-learning may find themselves facing a variety of unexpected challenges. While these challenges are neither insurmountable nor unknown to experienced service-learning practitioners, they can make starting a service-learning program remarkably time-consuming and unnecessarily frustrating. Unfortunately, pitfalls and program flops are rarely published. Rather, they are heard as whispers and sighs among faculty in between classes, on the way to meetings, and over lunch at professional conferences. This chapter will document some of these challenges and offer realistic coping strategies. As the old saying goes, "forewarned is forearmed."

WHAT IS SERVICE-LEARNING?

One of the first backroom whispers to be heard is *"What really is service-learning?"* Often service-learning is confused with other community-based experiential endeavors, such as volunteer work, community service, field work, and internships. Like these other forms of experiential learning, service-learning seeks to engage students in hands-on activities designed to provide opportunities for learning and development (Flannery & Ward, 1999; Howard, 1993; 1998). Service-learning is, however, a unique pedagogical approach which seeks to balance equally the learning needs of students with the service needs of the community (Furco, 1996). Designed with different goals in mind, other forms of community-based experiential learning tends to be focused more substantially on either student learning (e.g., internships and field work) or on community outcomes (e.g., volunteerism and community service) (Furco, 1996; Jacoby, 1996; Karasik & Berke, 2001).

While many sources are available for a more complete discussion of the principles of service-learning (Furco, 1996; Heffernan, 2001; Howard, 1993, 1998; Rhoads & Howard, 1998; Stanton, Giles & Cruz, 1999), it is helpful to outline some of the essential elements. This includes, on the service side, having students provide meaningful service that meets a need or goal that has been identified by the community. On the learning side, it is necessary to have students complete assignments designed to help them reflect on their service work as it relates to the learning objectives of the course (Weigert, 1998).

Service-learning is a practice that can take many forms, depending upon the learning goals of the students and the current needs of the community. For example, students in a class studying youth literacy might serve as elementary school reading tutors (Rice & Pollack, 2000), while classes in gerontology might find themselves learning about aging and older adults as they participate in intergenerational recreational and chore activities (e.g., grocery shopping)

(Karasik & Berke, 2001; Westacott & Hegeman, 1996). Matching the appropriate community need with the pedagogical objectives of a particular course is one of the first challenges of service-learning.

CHALLENGE 1: PEDAGOGY

Discussions of the pedagogical challenges of service-learning can fill many volumes in their own right (Heffernan, 2001; Jacoby & Associates, 1996; Rhoads & Howard, 1998). What follows is a brief overview of the key pedagogical concerns faculty face in implementing a new service-learning program.

Getting Started

Because service-learning can take so many forms, it is easy to become overwhelmed (or underwhelmed) with ideas for how to get started. Several good resources exist that can help. For example, Heffernan's (2001) *Fundamentals of Service-Learning Course Construction* describes the six basic models for service-learning ranging from "pure" service-learning to discipline and problem-based models to ways of incorporating service-learning into specialized capstone courses, service internships, and community-based action research. The text also includes information on the basics of service-learning implementation, including sample syllabi. Heffernan's text is produced by Campus Compact, "a national coalition of . . . college and university presidents devoted to the civic purposes of higher education" (Campus Compact, 2000, p.1). Additional Campus Compact resources are available in their *Introduction to Service-Learning Toolkit* (Campus Compact, 2000), and on their web site: www.compact.org

Best practice articles from within one's own field are another good place to start, since approaches to service-learning vary by discipline (Howard, 1993; Karasik, Maddox, & Wallingford, in press). The American Association for Higher Education's *Series on Service-Learning in the Disciplines* is an excellent source in this regard (Zlotkowski, 1996). It is important to keep in mind, however, that best practice articles tend to focus on what works rather than on what does not. Colleagues experimenting with service-learning in your discipline, as well as faculty from other fields, are another excellent resource. They are the most likely to give an accounting not only of what worked but also of what did not.

Meeting Course Objectives

By definition, the work students perform in service-learning must be linked to the objectives of the course. Like any other course assignment, careful consideration must be given to the question *"What do I want students to learn from this?"* While this question may seem fairly straightforward, it does require that the objectives of the course be made explicit. Rather than trying to fit a particular activity to an objective, far more productive is to start with the objectives, then envision ways of accomplishing them. Remembering that service-learning may or may not be the best pedagogical approach to a particular goal is important. Pressure to "do" service-learning should not be the primary reason for trying it.

On the other hand, there is a great deal of learning that can be accomplished through service-learning (Eyler & Giles, 1999; McEwen, 1996). This learning may be primarily content based (Morton, 1996), or more likely, it will incorporate higher-order outcomes such as critical thinking, personal and interpersonal development, and perspective transformation (Eyler & Giles, 1999). An important challenge here stems from our limited ability to control the types of experiences from which our students are learning. Clearly, not all experiences are likely to produce positive learning outcomes. For example, Erickson and O'Conner (2000) raised the concern that some service contact experiences may be more likely to promote rather than reduce student prejudices. Similarly, Paul Loeb, author of *Soul of a Citizen* (1999) and *Generations at the Crossroads* (1994), recounted a story of a student who missed the forest for the trees when, while raving about his experience at a homeless shelter, expressed hope that the shelter would still be around for his grandchildren to work in. While few have publicly documented these negative outcomes, careful integration of students' service experiences into the course content is clearly vital. Critical reflection is a key component to achieving such integration.

Reflection
An underlying premise of service-learning is that having students "do" service is not enough to cultivate effective learning. Rather, students must be helped to integrate their experiences with theory (Bringle & Hatcher, 1999). There are many ways to help students reflect on what they are learning, ranging from group discussions (large and small) and journals (including weekly reflection questions and e-journals), to directed readings and analytic papers (Bringle & Hatcher, 1999; Cooper, 1998; Dunlap, 1998; Kottkamp, 1990).

The challenge for many faculty is selecting reflection formats that match their teaching style. In-class discussions require faculty flexibility to seize upon the elusive teachable moment. While the concept of reciprocity may not have been on the class schedule for that day, a student's complaint about being overwhelmed by cookies from her elderly community shopping partner requires a shift in plans. Discussions of this kind can be highly satisfying and effective for students, although constant shifts of this nature can play havoc with class schedules.

Written journals can provide faculty with more time for reflecting on the reflection, but may lose the immediacy of the moment. Lengthy journals may also be less practical for faculty with heavy grading loads. Many faculty find hybrid approaches of reflection to be satisfactory, perhaps by scheduling regular in-class discussions along with weekly open-ended written reflection questions to be completed outside of class (Karasik & Berke, 2001).

How to Cover Everything

Another unwritten but often whispered challenge for faculty is that it is almost impossible to cover everything—whether you include service-learning or not. This reality can make anyone skittish about adding to an already overloaded course. With this mind-set, service-learning could never happen. Rather, service-learning must be seen as integral to the course (Howard, 1998).

Designing a service-learning component requires rethinking a course and prioritizing important elements. Service-learning opportunities may then be used, where appropriate, to illustrate key concepts and ideas. Service-learning should be seen, thus, as a core educational tool in the same way that textbooks, lectures, and class discussions are viewed. Use of a particular approach will depend upon the outcomes desired. In many cases, service-learning is an effective way to convey course information (e.g., about diverse populations, civic responsibility, and real-world practice).

Designing a Service-Learning Component

Once one decides on service-learning as an approach, the ever-present challenges of defining the details remain. The answer to many questions such as *"Where will students be placed?"* and *"What exactly will they be doing?"* will depend upon both the learning goals of the class and the needs of the community. Other basic considerations include *"How many hours must students complete?"* and *"Will the service-learning assignment be optional or mandatory?"* These questions are solved often by trial and error. Some faculty find that a one-time project (e.g., a day-long community event) is sufficient to engage students in community concerns, while many others opt for semester-long service placements requiring 20 to 30 hours or more on site in the community.

Similarly, practitioners do not agree as to whether service-learning should be optional or mandatory (Karasik, in press). Arguments for mandatory participation include having all students gain the potential benefits of service-learning. A mandatory approach is not, however, without risks. For example, one must consider the responsibility of the university to a community partner for possible negative outcomes if an unwilling student feels forced into participating. Potential problems may range from students not showing up to being unprepared, uncooperative, or even disruptive when they do. Such negative behavior can mar the service-learning experience for all involved and place student-community partnerships at risk. While empirical data on negative outcomes for community partners are limited, anecdotal data on individual "bad apple" problems may be found (Karasik, in press).

Alternative approaches to requiring service-learning of all students is to offer service-learning as an optional assignment. Several optional models are available, including making service-learning available for an additional course credit (a fourth credit option) or offering service-learning as part of a part-nered course such as a related internship (Heffernan, 2001). A third approach is to offer alternative nonservice assignments within the class—such as term papers or other intensive assignments. The challenge is, of course, to create and evaluate assignments of equivalent scale and benefit.

Assessment and Evaluation of Student Learning

Measuring the outcomes of service-learning poses yet another series of challenges. In many ways, the problem is no different than measuring outcomes of other pedagogical approaches—which is to say that it is a significant challenge (Driscoll, Holland, Gelmon, & Kerrigan, 1996; Gelmon, Holland, Driscoll, Spring, & Kerrigan, 2001). Studies suggest that students like service-learning and believe they get more out of it than traditional classes, although gains in factual knowledge are fairly equivalent (Eyler & Giles, 1999). Two important questions to consider are thus *"Do students gain in other areas beyond factual knowledge"* and *"How do you measure such gains?"* While traditional evaluation modes such as examinations are helpful in measuring factual knowledge, they are rarely adequate in getting at touted service-learning benefits such as inter-personal development, civic engagement, and enhanced critical thinking. Other evaluative approaches that have been suggested include using pre/post assessments of learning goals (e.g., to determine students' perceptions), formal written evaluations by students, data regarding if and for how long students continue service beyond course requirements, and data on students' selection of majors and occupations following service-learning.

While the above measures can help in gauging the impact of service-learning on overall student learning, the question remains of how one can best measure individual student performance. For example, *"Should service-learning be graded, and if so, how?"* Howard (1993) stressed the importance of grading the learning and not the service, using the example that in a traditional history class you would test students on the knowledge they had gained from an assigned reading, not on their ability to read the assignment. If participating in service-learning is equivalent to doing the assigned reading, then assignments such as final papers where students reflect on their service experience and integrate it with course concepts might be the basis for a grade. Students do not always appreciate, however, this approach to evaluation. It is not uncommon for a student to reflect on a less than exemplary grade by saying *"but I really liked the service-learning"* or *"but I completed my required hours"* or *"I worked really hard at the service part."* These comments reflect the increased commitment students feel to classes with service-learning, as well as the importance of making grading procedures clear from the outset.

Assessment and Evaluation: Impact on the Community

Assessing the impact of service-learning on the community is no less important, nor less challenging. Many components require evaluation, ranging from each constituencies' satisfaction with the university-community partnership to the actual impact of the service on the community. With regard to satisfaction with the partnership, Gelmon et al. (2001) suggested using indicators such as partners' "perception of mutuality and reciprocity," "responsiveness to concerns," and "willingness to provide feedback" (p. 92) via interviews, surveys, and focus groups. While such formal measures are helpful, it is important to be sensitive to informal indicators of satisfaction (e.g., praise) or lack thereof (e.g., frustration or lack of communication) as well.

The ease with which one can measure the impact of students' service on the community depends upon how the goals of service-learning have been identified. While the task of defining mutually beneficial goals will be discussed more fully in the following section, Gelmon et al. (2001) offers several broad indicators of community impact such as the "types of services provided," "number of clients served," "number of students involved," "variety of activities offered," "impact on resource utilization through services provided by faculty/students," and "impact on community issues" (p. 92), which are useful to consider here.

CHALLENGE 2: THE COMMUNITY

Community is a key component of service-learning. Without community support, service-learning could not exist. Gaining community support, however, can be a complex task. While many community groups welcome student participation, others do not. More than one faculty member has been taken by surprise by a potential community partner's resistance to their advances. Some have even given up their aspirations for service-learning because they have been unable to gain entry into the community. To increase the ease with which access is granted, one needs to consider the overall relation between universities and the surrounding community.

The Ivory Tower

Despite efforts to the contrary, the ivory tower image of universities is very much alive. Similarly, while some communities view local universities as economic and educational resources, many also see universities as conspicuous consumers of land, parking, and law enforcement. Post-homecoming images of drunken, out-of-control college students do little to diminish this unfortunate stereotype. Remarkably, positive stories describing student and faculty contributions to the community (e.g., as employees, volunteers, taxpayers, and supporters of the local economy) do not make for interesting news. While service-learning and other forms of community interaction could be a way to repair a university's image problem, one must address the essential questions of *"How and where does one begin?"*

Reaching Out

A first step in gaining community support is to identify potential community partners (local agencies, community groups, etc.) that may have an interest in working jointly on a service-learning project. More often than not this will require some fact finding to know who does what in a particular community. Becoming informed suggests you have a genuine interest in the local community. It does not, however, guarantee that the community will have an interest in you.

The next step is to make a connection—networking is not just for the business world. Personal interaction builds trust. As simple as it may sound, meeting someone off campus can go a long way to dispelling the aloof faculty stereotype. Similarly, inviting a potential partner to class as a guest speaker might help to create a connection both to faculty and students, while also acknowledging that the community member has valuable expertise.

Communication is also a key component. Open discussion of potential concerns is important. In some cases, building trust might be an issue. In other cases, concerns may exist about limited resources, liability, staffing, time constraints, exploitation of clients, or poor interactions with the university, faculty, or students in the past. Many such issues may be resolved by examining alternative approaches. For example, if an agency is concerned about being able to handle too many students at one time, perhaps additional community sites may be added to ease the burden. This solution may be easier to do in larger areas where the concentration of appropriate community opportunities is greater. In some cases, community concerns may be so great that developing a service-learning partnership elsewhere may be necessary, leaving the possibility of collaboration with the initial partner open for the future.

Building a Partnership

By definition, communities need to be collaborative partners in service-learning. Hence, it is necessary to approach a community agency or organization by asking what it is that *they* see as a need students could fulfill. All too often, the temptation is to approach potential community partners with notions of how students and the university can *fix* the community. While the desire to help is commendable, unwanted help is likely to widen the town–gown divide. Gugerty and Swezey (1996) warned educators against perpetuating the notions that "there exists superior and deficient cultures" (p. 95) and "that faculty know better how to solve local problems than . . . those who live in [the] communities" (p. 96). For service-learning to work, educators and communities must work together as equal partners to develop projects that serve the needs of the students and the greater community (Karasik & Berke, 2001).

Mutually Beneficial Tasks

In order to identify mutually beneficial tasks, each constituency first must understand their own needs. For faculty, this step means carefully reviewing the curriculum to define concretely the objectives of the course. While this task may seem too simple to mention, more than one faculty member has been hard pressed to articulate the exact knowledge and skills they expect their students to take away from the course. Faculty must then be able to express clearly these course objectives and their goals for service-learning to their community partners.

Community partners, on the other hand, need to be realistic about what services students can provide for them and what they can provide for students. Students are apprentices rather than experts. Good communication between the partners as to what students will (and will not) do is important. Other considerations (e.g., expectations, supervision, orientation, liability, background checks, timelines, division of labor, and evaluation) should be discussed and perhaps even put into writing before presenting the service-learning project to the students. Even then, a means for ongoing communication throughout the service-learning process is necessary to maintain a viable, mutually beneficial relationship.

CHALLENGE 3: THE STUDENTS

Like the community, students are a key component of service-learning. With-out the students, service-learning would not exist. In fact, enhancing student learning is one of the primary reasons many faculty get involved in service-learning. In turn, students like service-learning—at least they say they do after it is over. Several studies have reported that the vast majority of students par-ticipating in service-learning perceived significant benefits from doing so (Chapman & Morley, 1999; Hessmiller & Brown, 1995; Karasik et al., in press; McKenna & Rizzo, 1999). Of course, the challenge for faculty is getting students to participate in service-learning so that they may experience its many benefits.

"You Want Me to What?"

While many students welcome service-learning opportunities with enthusi-asm, other students greet the prospect of service-learning with more reticence. As one student so aptly put it during a service-learning introduction: *"You want me to what? You have got to be kidding!"* Even if students do not openly voice this concern, one would be wise to be prepared for such a reaction. Un-derstanding the source of a student's resistance is the first step to countering it.

For some students, resistance comes from being asked to do something new or different. The unknown can spark numerous questions, such as *"What will be expected of me?" "Who are the people I will be working with?" "Is this some-thing I can do well?"* and the ever popular *"How much time and effort will I have to put into this?"* It is helpful to be ready for such concerns by preparing a de-tailed introduction to the service-learning project. This may be done in a vari-ety of ways, including in-class discussions, instructions in the course syllabus, and through various handouts that students can refer to after the initial shock is over. In fact, a multi-pronged approach spread out over the first week of class is probably best—beginning with a brief discussion of what service-learning is, who will be served by the work, what types of tasks the class will be doing, and what the instructor's expectations for the students are. By spreading out the discussions, students have time to think about the project and to formu-late their questions.

It is also helpful to make the unknown known by having students who have previously done service-learning (either from the current class or a previ-ous class) give "testimony" to the benefits of service-learning. Having service-learning "survivors" promote the experience is amazingly effective in getting new students on board. Introducing the community partners in class can also help to alleviate some of the fear that comes with exploring new territory.

However, not all of the student resistance comes from encountering a new learning opportunity. A more challenging problem stems from student concerns about the amount of time service-learning requires. Karasik (in press) found that while a majority of students elected to participate in an optional service-learning program, of those who did not, time was their main concern, with students citing other school, family, and work commitments as insurmountable barriers to putting in service-learning hours. Transportation and distance to community sites emerged as related concerns. Suggested strategies for helping students make time for service-learning included:

- Requiring service-learning as a mandatory part of the course (an approach with a number of pros and cons)

- Offering a wide range of service opportunities to meet individual scheduling and transportation needs

- Offering "behind the scenes" type positions (e.g., project manager, project historian)

- Considering offering alternative, non-service-learning assignment options (Karasik, in press)

One Size Does Not Fit All

In addition to the possibility of student resistance to service-learning, it is important to remember that different types of service-learning approaches will work better with different groups of students. While tailoring programs to individual students can be difficult, it is helpful to consider differences in students' learning styles, backgrounds, and developmental stages (McEwen, 1996). Students who are new to higher education, for example, and those without any experience in the field may be less confident about approaching individual community agencies. Bringing community partners into the class as part of the project introduction is thus particularly important for this group. Introductory students may also require more supervision of their service-learning experiences both by the faculty and community partners (Karasik et al., in press).

On the other hand, upper-level and graduate students, as well as students with significant background in the field, may require a less hands-on approach. Experienced students may prefer to seek out their own service experiences which complement or possibly contrast their current or future employment areas. These students may also be more inclined to select service projects requiring greater initiative and preparation such as working with an agency to design a new service or to lead a new community program (Karasik et al., in press).

Follow-Through

Once students are suitably enticed to do service-learning, follow-through becomes an additional challenge. While ensuring that students complete their assignments satisfactorily is not a new concern of faculty, the stakes are raised when there are others relying on the students' work. As part of the collaborative process described earlier, faculty and community partners need to discuss contingencies ahead of time. If attainable, students will tend to rise to the expectations set out for them. Students failing to show up when expected or not completing promised tasks can, however, damage the collaborative relationship. Thus, preventative measures such as spelling out expectations and consequences during the orientation phase are essential, as is regular communication with community partners to gauge their satisfaction and concerns.

Similarly, checking in regularly with the students via the reflection process is necessary to make sure they are actively engaged and satisfied with their experiences. In addition to helping students make connections between their service work and course content, faculty must also ensure that the students are being provided with tasks that afford them good learning opportunities. Finding at mid-semester or later that students are either overwhelmed by their placements or discouraged at being relegated to the sidelines can be quite disheartening. Worse yet is finding students who have failed even to begin their service experiences because of procrastination or an inability to connect with the community partners.

Even when things are going smoothly, faculty should be prepared to handle the inevitable sticky assessment issues, such as what to do when a student wants to "drop out" of a service experience or how to grade a student who has not completed the requisite hours by the end of the semester. A stickier issue comes from the unfortunate fact that service-learning is not immune to cheating, with more than one student having "fudged" hours on their timesheets. While such eventualities are an unfortunate part of academia, here again prevention is the best policy.

CHALLENGE 4: THE UNIVERSITY

Colleges and universities play an interesting role in service-learning. Service is prominent in many institutions' mission statements, although there is considerable variability in exactly what is meant by this term (Ward, 1998). Certainly, universities stand to benefit when service-learning enhances both student learning and community relations. Alternatively, institutions incur some risk of reputation and possible liability should a university-community collaboration go awry. Thus it would seem that universities have a vested interest in the success of local service-learning endeavors. To that end, there are many ways a university can support service-learning. Not surprisingly, there are also many ways for it to impede the process.

Campus Resources

The first challenge of finding institutional support for service-learning is knowing where to look. Many campuses have service-learning coordinators, and perhaps even offices devoted to service-learning, volunteer services, faculty development, or other similar endeavors. While the function of such offices will vary from institution to institution, they are typically a good place to begin to gather resources and ideas. They may also be a good place to network with other faculty doing service-learning. For campuses without such services, seeking out other service-learning faculty via more informal avenues such as email and word of mouth can be helpful.

University grant assistance offices are another potential resource, particularly if you are interested in securing financial support for developing or expanding a service-learning program. While money has been tight in the past, service-learning is currently one of the hot funding buzz words, along with civic engagement and other service-related teaching approaches. A challenge with securing outside resources, however, is being careful to develop programs that are sustainable after the initial funding period. Programs that require ongoing external monetary support are going to be much more difficult to maintain over the long run.

In addition to financial support, there may also be opportunities to secure additional time to develop and administer service-learning. Such opportunities (which often come under the guise of names such as "scholarship," "reassignment time," and "course buyout") typically are best pursued through one's immediate supervisor. As with financial support, it is helpful to consider the sustainability of a particular service-learning program should such additional time become unavailable in the future.

Faculty Development

Another way an institution can support service-learning is by recognizing it as a valuable tool. Many institutions of higher education view research as their most important priority, leaving faculty with little time to prepare unique classroom experiences. Similarly, service-learning faculty may encounter peers unfamiliar with the approach who view service-learning as lacking in academic rigor. In a rare volume directed at explaining service-learning to university administrators, Jacoby and Associates (1996) offered suggestions for how institutions can enhance the sustainability of service-learning programs by accounting for the needs of the university, faculty, and community as well as the students. For example, Rue (1996) highlighted the importance of having administration take service-learning "seriously in tenure and promotion decisions" (p. 261). Faculty wishing to initiate or strengthen support for service-learning at their institution might consider finding a way for this book to reach the hands of their administrators.

The Brick Wall

Despite the good intentions of many institutions, there may be times when faculty wonder whose side the university is on. As is the nature of most institutions, change (and the spread of new ideas) happens slowly. While service-learning is currently a hot topic around many campuses, one should note that less than 10 years ago getting funding or support for such endeavors was difficult. Persistence does pay off. Even so, be prepared for the inevitable "*you can't do that here*" from offices where one might have expected support. For instance, while local academic administrators may be enamored with students' efforts to build a community playground for children of all abilities, the institution's business office may be less than receptive to helping these students find a way to accept donations for a playground that will not be sited directly on the university campus.

Similarly frustrating challenges have been experienced by faculty attempting to schedule service-learning classes outside of traditional time slots, as well as those seeking to have students access campus resources typically reserved for faculty and administration (e.g., the services of university grant offices). While the specific nature of the challenges will vary by institution and service-learning project, the resulting experience of exasperation is universal. Perseverance, persistence, and creativity are key elements to survival when you run up against a brick wall. Of course, a little spin never hurts either with such experiences providing teachable moment material for faculty and students alike.

CHALLENGE 5: THE FACULTY ROLE

The final set of service-learning challenges stems from within the faculty members themselves. Faculty are the essential element in designing and implementing service-learning programs. Ultimately, faculty must decide if service-learning is the right approach for their courses. They are also in charge of seeing that the challenges of designing and implementing a sound service-learning program are addressed.

What Am I Getting Myself Into?

There are many self-evaluative aspects faculty should consider before beginning service-learning. For example, taking on a new teaching approach requires both time and energy—commodities that are in short supply for many faculty. The good news is that service-learning does become easier with experience. The reality is, however, that maintaining an effective service-learning program requires the same continued vigilance as other teaching approaches.

Working collaboratively with the community can also pose unique challenges for faculty, as it places them outside their traditional university roles. Community meetings may become a way of life for faculty sponsoring service-learning programs, and many a lesson plan has been scrapped at the last minute when a unique service experience is brought to the classroom. On the other hand, class discussions may never be so lively or well informed.

JUST REWARDS

With good reason, the majority of literature touts the benefits of service-learning. Despite the many challenges of service-learning, the rewards are significant. For students, it is a way to learn by doing. For the community, it is a way to tap into the many talents students can provide. For the university, it is a way to improve community relations. For faculty, it is a way to connect on different levels with students, the community, teaching, and their chosen field. While those who do service-learning may grumble in the hallways and over lunch about the problems they face, most practitioners stay on the front lines. Their dedication speaks volumes. For all its challenges, when done properly, service-learning works.

REFERENCES

Bringle, R., & Hatcher, J. (1999). Reflection in service learning: Making meaning of experience. *Educational Horizons, 77*(4), 179–185.

Campus Compact. (2000). *Introduction to service-learning toolkit: Readings and resources for faculty.* Providence, RI: Author.

Chapman, J., & Morley, R. (1999). Collegiate service-learning: Motives underlying volunteerism and satisfaction with volunteer service. *Journal of Prevention and Intervention in the Community, 18*(1/2), 19–33.

Colby, A., Ehrlich, T., Beaumont, E., & Stephens, J. (2003). *Educating citizens: Preparing America's undergraduates for lives of moral and civic responsibility.* San Francisco, CA: Jossey-Bass.

Cooper, D. (1998). Reading, writing, and reflection. In R. A. Rhoads & J. Howard (Eds.), *Academic service learning: A pedagogy of action and reflection* (pp. 47–56). San Francisco, CA: JosseyBass.

Driscoll, A., Holland, B., Gelmon, S., & Kerrigan, S. (1996). An assessment model for service-learning: Comprehensive case studies of impact on faculty, students, community, and institution. *Michigan Journal of Community Service Learning, 3,* 66–71.

Dunlap, M. (1998). Methods of supporting students' critical reflection in courses incorporating service-learning. *Teaching of Psychology, 25*(3), 208–210.

Erickson, J., & O'Conner, S. (2000). Service-learning: Does it promote or reduce prejudice? In C. O'Grady (Ed.), *Integrating service learning and multicultural education in colleges and universities* (pp. 59–70). Mahwah, NJ: Lawrence Erlbaum.

Eyler, J., & Giles, D. (1999). *Where's the learning in service-learning?* San Francisco, CA: Jossey-Bass.

Flannery, D., & Ward, K. (1999). Service learning: A vehicle for developing cultural competence in health education. *American Journal of Health Behavior, 23*(5), 323–331.

Furco, A. (1996). Service-learning: A balanced approach to experiential education. *Expanding boundaries: Serving and learning.* Washington, DC: Corporation for National Service.

Gelmon, S., Holland, B., Driscoll, A., Spring, A., & Kerrigan, S. (2001). *Assessing service-learning and civic engagement: Principles and techniques.* Providence, RI: Campus Compact.

Gugerty, C., & Swezey, E. (1996). Developing campus-community relationships. In B. Jacoby & Associates (Eds.), *Service-learning in higher education: Concepts and practices* (pp. 92–108). San Francisco, CA: Jossey-Bass.

Heffernan, K. (2001). *Fundamentals of service-learning course construction.* Providence, RI: Campus Compact.

Hessmiller, J., & Brown, K. (1995). Learning to act: Service-learning integrates theory and practice. In J. Eby (Ed.), *Service-learning: Linking academics and the community* (pp. 213–220). Grantham, PA: Pennsylvania Campus Compact.

Howard, J. (1998). Academic service learning: A counternormative pedagogy. In R. A. Rhoads & J. Howard (Eds.), *Academic service learning: A pedagogy of action and reflection* (pp. 21–29). San Francisco, CA: Jossey-Bass.

Howard, J. (Ed.). (1993). *Praxis I: A faculty casebook on community service learning.* Ann Arbor, MI: OCSL Press.

Jacoby, B. (1996). Service-learning in today's higher education. In B. Jacoby & Associates (Eds.), *Service-learning in higher education: Concepts and practices* (pp. 3–25). San Francisco, CA: Jossey-Bass.

Jacoby, B., & Associates. (Eds.). (1996). *Service-learning in higher education: Concepts and practices.* San Francisco, CA: Jossey-Bass.

Karasik, R. (in press). Breaking the time barrier: Helping students "find the time" to do intergenerational service-learning. *Gerontology & Geriatrics Education.*

Karasik, R., & Berke, D. (2001). Classroom and community: Experiential education in family studies and gerontology. *Journal of Teaching in Marriage and Family: Innovations in Family Science Education, 1*(4), 13–38.

Karasik, R., Maddox, M., & Wallingford, M. (in press). Intergenerational service-learning across levels and disciplines: "One size (does not) fit all." *Gerontology & Geriatrics Education.*

Kottkamp, R. (1990). Means for facilitating reflection. *Education and Urban Society, 22,* 182–203.

Loeb, P. (1994). *Generations at the crossroads: Apathy and action on the American campus.* New Brunswick, NJ: Rutgers University.

Loeb, P. (1999). *Soul of a citizen: Living with conviction in a cynical time.* New York, NY: St. Martin's Griffin.

McEwen, M. (1996). Enhancing student learning and development through service-learning. In B. Jacoby & Associates (Eds.), *Service-learning in higher education: Concepts and practices* (pp. 53–91). San Francisco, CA: Jossey-Bass.

McKenna, M., & Rizzo, E. (1999). Student's perceptions of the "learning" in service-learning courses. *Journal of Prevention & Intervention in the Community, 18*(1/2), 111–123.

Morton, K. (1996). Issues related to integrating service-learning into the curriculum. In B. Jacoby & Associates (Eds.), *Service-learning in higher education: Concepts and practices* (pp. 276–296). San Francisco, CA: Jossey-Bass.

Rhoads, R. A., & Howard, J. (Eds.). (1998). *Academic service learning: A pedagogy of action and reflection.* San Francisco, CA: JosseyBass.

Rice, K., & Pollack, S. (2000). Developing a critical pedagogy of service learning: Preparing self-reflective, culturally aware, and responsive community participants. In C. O'Grady (Ed.), *Integrating service learning and multicultural education in colleges and universities* (pp. 115–134). Mahwah, NJ: Lawrence Erlbaum.

Rue, P. (1996). Administering successful service-learning programs. In B. Jacoby & Associates (Eds.), *Service-learning in higher education: Concepts and practices* (pp. 246–275). San Francisco, CA: Jossey-Bass.

Stanton, T., Giles, D., & Cruz, N. (1999). *Service-learning: A movement's pioneers reflect on its origins, practice and future.* San Francisco, CA: Jossey-Bass.

Ward, K. (1998). Addressing academic culture: Service learning, organizations, and faculty work. In R. A. Rhoads & J. Howard (Eds.), *Academic service learning: A pedagogy of action and reflection* (pp. 73–80). San Francisco, CA: Jossey-Bass.

Weigert, K. (1998). Academic service learning: Its meaning and relevance. In R. A. Rhoads & J. Howard (Eds.), *Academic service learning: A pedagogy of action and reflection* (pp. 3–10). San Francisco, CA: Jossey-Bass.

Westacott, B., & Hegeman, C. (Eds.). (1996). *Service learning in elder care: A resource manual.* Albany, NY: Foundation for Long Term Care.

Zlotkowski, E. (1996). Foreword. In L. Adler-Kassner, R. Crooks, & A. Watters (Eds.), *Composition—Writing the community: Concepts and models for service-learning in composition* (pp. v–vii). Washington, DC: American Association for Higher Education.

16

Junior Faculty Participation in Curricular Change

Judi Hetrick
Miami University, Oxford, Ohio

Participation in curriculum change can be both a necessity and a professional landmine for junior faculty members. They do not, however, have to choose between sitting on the sidelines or sacrificing young careers by working for large-scale change. This chapter presents the elements of successful curriculum change, roles junior faculty can play, and roles they should avoid—or accept with caution.

INTRODUCTION

During my second year as a tenure-track faculty member, I was asked to serve on an interdepartmental group exploring how to change the journalism curriculum for my university. While the challenge was exciting, I had seen professors denied tenure when their focus wavered from the twin goals of classroom excellence and publication. Is it possible for junior faculty to participate successfully in curricular change? This chapter summarizes information in the literature on the process of curricular change, then defines roles that junior faculty can successfully adopt—or avoid.

Of course, many professors at all stages of their careers relish making changes to keep classes up to date, especially when their own research uncovers new information and insights they can pass along to students. As Ratcliff (1996) points out, about 5% of the university curriculum nationwide is officially changed every year as individual professors introduce new courses or one-time offerings. The actual percentage of change, though not recorded, is much higher, as instructors work within the space provided by brief and general catalog course descriptions to introduce new topics and techniques into their classrooms.

Deeper, more systematic curricular change—change that goes beyond the individual course—is also a collegiate tradition as a power uniquely vested in the faculty. But as Levine (1978) noted 25 years ago, a Carnegie Council survey found that

> not all faculty are equally involved in educational policy. Forty-three percent of the faculty indicate that a small group of senior professors has disproportionate power in decision-making, and 77% feel that junior faculty have too little say in the running of their departments. (pp. 424–425)

More recently, in their overview report on general education curricular reform at 71 New England colleges and universities, Arnold and Civian (1997) noted,

> We are especially mindful of the differences arising from the competition between junior and senior cohorts within faculties. On one hand, there are professors and experienced associate professors whose futures with their institutions are for the most part assured and who have grown accustomed to influence and prestige on campus. On the other hand, there are assistant professors yet to achieve full acceptance, who often must struggle for the right to participate in decision-making at their institutions. . . . Even at institutions that were otherwise successful in bringing about change, cohort competition sometimes alienated segments of the faculty from each other and the newly created curriculum. (pp. 21–22)

Is it any wonder that, as Ratcliff (1996) noted, "Folk wisdom says that reforming undergraduate education is a troublesome, tumultuous, and difficult assignment" (p. 5). One reason the process may seem difficult is that much knowledge about curricular change is transmitted as an informal or folk process, one whose assumptions and techniques are not systematically articulated. The way curricular change occurs in any given field and at any given institution may be largely learned informally. The information that senior faculty know by virtue of their longer tenure is unpublished and often unexamined.

Junior faculty also have a myriad of other issues and stresses in their work lives. Research has shown that junior faculty work at least 48 hours a week and are more likely to experience severe time constraints than their senior colleagues. They also sense a lack of collegiality and feel isolated (Finkelstein &

LaCelle-Peterson, 1992). These factors can prevent all but the most exceptional quick-starters from plugging into the informal faculty network early in their university careers.

Can junior faculty members learn to become a successful, vital part of a curricular reform effort, without jeopardizing their young careers? Their promotion and tenure depends heavily on both the work they do during their first few years in any faculty position, and on how that work is received by their senior colleagues. Participation in curricular reform efforts can drain time and energy away from research, writing, and classroom teaching—even without its capacity to alienate the very people who will decide the future of the junior faculty members.

Some go so far as to counsel junior faculty to be seen and not heard. In a first-person advice column for *The Chronicle of Higher Education's Career Network*, an assistant professor writing under a pseudonym gave a two-part answer to the question:

> What is the best strategy for tenure?... Complete the specified requirements... and remain silent.... By remaining "silent," I don't mean not speaking; I mean not saying anything of substance that draws attention to one's thinking, and thereby lessening the possibility of petty conflicts entering into the tenure process. (Adso, 2002)

Such advice is obviously unrealistic and extreme, but the sentiment behind it is not unfamiliar to many junior faculty. Yet, despite some danger that may reside in speaking one's mind, work in broader curricular reform can also build bridges to senior colleagues and allow junior faculty to enter into a conversation with them that is vitally important for the faculty itself as a whole as well as for our students. Junior faculty share responsibility for the curriculum not just as it is taught in their own classrooms but also as it is offered by programs, departments, schools, and entire universities. Engaging in this process is a unique opportunity to serve both the academic institution and the larger society and to contribute to the broader conversation about the fundamental issues of higher education. Some junior faculty have no choice but to take part in the curricular change process, so learning more about it can help them manage the work and dodge some potential dangers.

DEFINING CURRICULAR CHANGE

Different authors use the terms "curriculum," "curricular reform," and "curriculum change" to describe a gamut of meta-instructional activities that range from fashioning an individual course syllabus to overhauling an entire university's core course of instruction. In this chapter, curricular change refers to the cooperative effort by a group of faculty, often with input from administrators and students, to bring institutionalized change to a key class, set of classes, or course of study at the program, departmental, divisional, college, or university level. A key attribute of successful curricular change, as opposed to instructional change, is that it does not rely on the teaching efforts of one individual. Rather, it is embedded in course descriptions, sequences of study, degree requirements, or other institutional requirements.

This type of change is foundational and can be transformational. As Keller (1982) noted in her study of Harvard University's influential revamping of its core curriculum,

> Curriculum change is the most visible way in which that the institution [American higher education] adapts to changing conditions in our society. College faculties invest so much of their time and energy in debate over curricular structure because it provides a useful framework for discussing issues of a more complex, fundamental, and elusive sort. (pp. viii–ix)

Conceptualizing Curricular Change

Regardless of whether a change embraces a university-wide core set of classes or only one or a few offerings within a small program, participants can conceptualize these efforts in several different ways. And while any conceptualizations may be shaped by disciplinary worldviews, diverse approaches to theorizing, or even idiosyncratic local history, exploring them can be an important first step toward effectively taking part in the process.

Lindquist (1996), in an excellent introduction to the theories underlying the curricular change process, summarized four major approaches:

- Rational Planning. This is the research and development center model that believes successful change is based on reason and evidence.

- Social Interaction. This is the agricultural extension agent model that believes personal networks and communication are the keys to change. It looks at how groups of people—ranging from innovators and early adopters to laggards—react to new ideas and to each other.

- Human Problem-Solving. This is a modified group therapy model that looks at psychological resistance to change and offers techniques ranging from leadership training to focus groups to help people work through their problems and accept transitions.

- Political. As with any model that looks at vying factions, the political model sees people building coalitions with powerful individuals and with groups, and then leveraging authoritative decisions mandating change. (pp. 635–642)

Likewise, in discussing the desirability of team or collaborative leadership in an entire college or university, Bensimon and Neumann (1993) sketch conceptions of organizations that roughly parallel Lindquist's models: bureaucracies, where the rational prevails; collegiums, where human communication and consensus is at the fore; political systems; and symbolic systems, where change occurs through the manipulation of symbols.

Curricular change also can be conceptualized as a dichotomous process. Keller (1982) saw Harvard's as process entailing "the interplay between academic thought and politics" (pp. viii–ix). Cuban (1999) worried that at Stanford, broad subject matter change was sometimes used to avoid innovation in instructional techniques. He pointed out that the two often cannot be separated: "Professors seeking student understanding see the close intersection between subject matter and pedagogy. The two are entangled and need to be worked on simultaneously" (p. 170).

Not only are subject matter and ways of teaching entangled, but so are the approaches Lindquist (1996) outlines. After sketching the four different conceptualizations, he concluded that no one model is adequate to describe what happens in curricular change; a combination of theories is needed to understand the entire process. For example, the mere presentation of objective information, which should be adequate for a rational planning model, does not take social interaction into account. Simply looking at change as an exercise involving factions pro and con, as a political analysis might do, does not take into account the more subtle interpersonal interactions that shape our working lives.

A theoretical model that borrows from multiple approaches allows the different individuals involved in curricular change to fashion various roles and activities according to their strengths. This chapter follows that eclectic paradigm and assumes that any change process should be team-based and that those teams will be influenced by their members' participation in diverse disciplines and disciplinary cultures. Work by Kekale (1999), who compared the departments of sociology, ecology, physics, and history at two different Finnish universities, indicated links between disciplinary cultures and department leadership styles. He discovered that sociology professors, for example, have "the strong expectation that all the (important) decisions should be made collectively and democratically" (p. 226), while experimental physicists showed little interest in the topic at all, taking much leadership for granted and suggesting that any type of "leadership is good as long as it works" (p. 232).

Couple such differences in disciplinary worldviews with varied individual strengths and idiosyncrasies, and the suggestion of any general understandings about the change process may seem a gross oversimplification. But such an analysis can offer helpful guidance even if it cannot account for every local variation. Kekale's work warns that, depending on how disciplinarily diverse the group is, it is important to articulate different expectations of how the process will work and be led. Early awareness about these process issues may lessen problems further into the discussion. Acknowledging that more than one type of group and human interaction will come into play may ease frustrations with the process. It is easy to imagine how a physical scientist invested in a rational planning model may not at first understand a sociologist's devotion to democratic interaction.

But just as different assumptions can endanger the communication process, an understanding of different roles can enhance the way a group works. And knowing that the interactions will not follow one neat academic model can help junior faculty tailor their roles to their strengths.

Determinants of Successful Curricular Change

Researchers in the area of curricular change vary in some details, but they broadly agree that successful curricular change depends on good leadership, adequate resources, and rewards for participants; excellent planning and realistic goals; good information, particularly in planning and implementation; and good communication.

ROLES FOR JUNIOR FACULTY THAT MAY FACILITATE THE CURRICULAR CHANGE PROCESS

On the issues of leadership, resources, and rewards, all faculty, and especially junior faculty, may have limited influence, depending on their college or university's administrative and bureaucratic structure.

While planning and goal-setting may also be outside the realm of total faculty control, even junior faculty can advocate forcefully for their importance and begin to develop roles in the critical areas involving information and communication. Planning, including how to initially structure a process, will influence the success of any curricular change effort. Arnold and Civian (1997) stress the importance of structure.

> The point cannot be overemphasized. Mundane as the matter seems, there is a payoff in attending to such simple matters as the way in which committees are appointed, who is consulted (or not) in the design process, and the effect of proposals on the status quo, as well as in hammering out the details of implementation in advance. This may all seem obvious, but our inquiry [into change at 71 schools] found that the obvious is often ignored, forgotten, or given short shrift. (p. 20)

Olguin and Schmitz (1996) additionally advise that a change process follow accepted procedures. In looking at initiatives that successfully transform curricula to add diversity, they found that successful change leaders "presented their plans as they would have any other plan in the campus governance process" (p. 454).

Effective curricular change needs to be thought of as ongoing and not as a one-time problem. The cost of reaching too far, and then failing, can be high.

> Virtually all of the campuses in our study that attempted major change failed to accomplish it in the face of enormous political and financial pressures. Embittered visionaries involved in the failed change frequently retreated from active campus participation, so great was their disappointment in the compromises reached... Where dramatic change is desirable, it is best accomplished in modest stages. (Civian, Arnold, Gamson, Kanter, & London, 1996, p. 653)

Change on a smaller scale, such as the departmental level, is more likely to be successful than broad, sweeping change. Civian et al. suggest that faculty feel most comfortable within their departments and so are more comfortable dealing with change based there: "Faculty even in small colleges view their departments as home, and they are likely to accept change emanating from their departments... Faculty are most resistant to college or institution-wide curricular change (p. 648)." One reason for this comfort may be that their voices are louder, and their influence is therefore greater at home (Levine, 1978).

Roles Junior Faculty Can Play

Whether they are working within the department or the larger institution, many junior faculty are just as qualified as senior colleagues to work with information and communication. Tasks in these areas are likely to be numerous and varied enough that junior faculty members can tailor how much they do to match both their expertise and the amount of time they wish to invest in the process.

Planning stage data-gatherer. While change is being planned, the need for information is great, whether or not you subscribe to the rational planning model. The types of information that can be gathered and shared include both benchmarking data and information from professional organizations and out-side disciplinary colleagues. This can help answer many critical questions. What are other institutions doing in the area you are trying to change? What are the current best teaching practices in your field, both nationally and inter-nationally? How might the changes you are considering affect accreditation in your field? What do experts among the broader community of your colleagues say about contemporary curricula? What studies or pilot programs have been tried or are in process? What articles have been written that address the issues you also are addressing?

Constituent and special-interest advocate. Junior faculty can advocate for constituencies not represented on the curricular change team, seeking repre-sentation or other ways to have their voices heard throughout the process. These constituencies could range from students and faculty groups (including junior faculty) to outside interests, such as alumni, employers, or graduate schools. They could also include academic concerns. How does the new cur-riculum deal with diversity? With international issues? With problem-solving or team-building skills? One way to advocate for these constituencies is by polling them. What do your alumni, students, or outside interests think of the current curriculum? What suggestions do they have for change? If your disci-plinary background includes training in scientific surveys, this type of research could be an ideal avenue for junior faculty participation. But even without this background, if scientific generalizability is not a goal, anyone can gather help-ful information for relatively low cost through the use of online survey instru-ments such as Flashlight or surveymonkey.com. Focus groups can also be con-vened to give qualitative data about the current curriculum and ideas for change.

As members of content specialty/instructor teams. One of the earliest proj-ects that aimed to transform curricula with feminist theory, at the University of Arizona in the 1980s, employed interdisciplinary weekly seminars for fac-ulty. Many of the seminar leaders, especially early in the program, were junior feminist faculty (Aiken, Anderson, Dinnerstein, Lensink, & MacCorquodale, 1988). While the seminars were in large part considered a part of a successful curricular transformation project, the issue of who best teaches whom is also a complicated one. The down side of junior faculty instructing senior faculty is touched on in the next section.

Pilots. Once a new curriculum is designed, it will need to be tested with small groups of students before being implemented across the board. Because junior faculty are frequently involved in developing courses as a part of their new jobs, the development and teaching of pilot courses that meet the goals of the new curriculum may be a natural area for their involvement in the larger process.

Assessment-stage data-gatherer. Once new courses are introduced and tried, they must be assessed. As Ferren and McCafferty (1992) have noted, "Without thoughtful attention to the implementation of new requirements, curricular reform will not bring the desired results" (p. 90). Again, junior faculty expertise may come into play here, or becoming part of the assessment team may help junior faculty learn techniques that they can apply to their own work as their careers develop.

Communicators. The good communication that is so important to the success of a curricular change effort can be formal or informal, person-to-person or mediated, part of an ongoing process or carefully orchestrated for special occasions. Within the array of communication tools and techniques, most junior faculty can find jobs that play to their strengths, be it designing a web page or moderating a listserv email discussion, talking to colleagues one-on-one, or moderating a "town meeting" with a special constituency.

Persuaders and peacemakers. Because of the high stakes involved in the curricular change process, such efforts are likely to encounter strife and resistance to change. Middendorf (1998) advocates gathering information from those who will be affected by the change in order to understand any resistance. "To understand general concerns, you need only to know what makes all people resist change. These include time, motivation, experience, control, expertise, effort, fear, and rewards" (p. 206). Resistance can then be mitigated as concerns are addressed. But because political as well as personal forces will be at work, the process will also need peacemakers to broker comprises (Cuban, 1999).

Roles for Junior Faculty to Approach Warily

As any change is planned and strategized, the literature points to a few key roles that most junior faculty may not be established enough to take, that may endanger their other work, or that may inhibit their long-term effectiveness.

Primary team-builder. This leadership role is key to any group effort but is "highly demanding. Doing it well requires a high level of commitment and a steep investment of time" (Bensimon & Neumann, 1993, p. 12). Unless junior faculty workloads are carefully structured to allow for the time and effort required, accepting an assignment as team leader may be overwhelming.

Sole or main content specialists/instructors. While junior faculty may have important new content specializations, successful teaching, even of other teachers, is a complicated dynamic linked to more than knowledge. Despite the successes of the University of Arizona's early feminist curricular transformation process, its leaders also chronicled resistance linked in part to faculty status. As described in Aiken et al. (1988), a group of "relatively young, less privileged feminist women (the majority of them untenured) [taught] relatively older, generally powerful men" (p. 139). This experience led to advice that future teaching teams include more senior faculty and that the seminar participants be more diverse in status: "It is only realistic to recognize that the power of the individuals presenting the material has much to do with its acceptance. We would also suggest a balance of junior and senior, tenured and untenured participants" (p. 156).

Opinion leader. Not all leaders are officially designated, and anyone working for change should not underestimate the importance of having informal opinion leaders on their side. Middendorf (2000), who recommends identifying opinion leaders through interviews with faculty, has written,

> They are the most important faculty in facilitating a change regarding teaching because, even though they usually have no official position of power, they do have considerable influence on others' attitudes and behaviors. They serve as the hub of the faculty communication network. They make careful judgments and good decisions, and they decrease uncertainty because their peers trust their evaluation. (p. 85)

While junior faculty could be opinion leaders under some circumstances, this role is generally an informal one that evolves through time. Junior faculty should consider trying to learn who are the established opinion leaders and be wary of trying to force themselves into that role.

Mavericks. Because the goal of curricular change is to implement lasting change that goes beyond one instructor's efforts, working outside the group process generally is not effective. Specifically, Keller (1982) reports on changes at Harvard in 1968–1969: "Two new courses, Social Change in America (Social Relations 148) and Radical Perspectives on Social Change (Social Relations 149) were organized by Students for a Democratic Society, headed (or fronted) by two junior faculty members" (p. 30). While the courses were taught to up to 1,000 students, the institution never adopted them. In looking at less radical change, Middendorf (1998) has discovered that those faculty who gain reputations as cutting-edge classroom innovators rarely are effective at single-handedly bringing about lasting change. These innovators are "useful as testers or demonstrators of change, but usually not as opinion leaders" (p. 210).

CONCLUSION

When the process begins to change a curriculum, every faculty member, including those just hired or only a few years into their jobs, has the choice of becoming a change agent, a resister, or someone who tries to sit on the sidelines while others participate. I share the assumption found in most of the literature that working for change is usually a positive activity that can and should improve what and how we teach and what and how our students learn. Advice published for people working in K–12 education applies to college and university curriculum work as well.

> A change facilitator can be anyone . . . It's not important where on the organizational chart the person falls; what is important is that facilitators support, help, assist, and nurture. Sometimes their task is to encourage, persuade, or push people to change, to adopt an innovation and use it in their daily schooling work. (Hord, Rutherford, Huling-Austin, & Hall, 1987, p. 3)

Not every change should be made, and not every change should be made at every institution. Levine (1978) noted that "successful curriculum change is most likely when an innovation is consistent with the norms, values, and traditions of the environment in which it is being introduced" (p. 432). Without such consistency, not only may reform fail, but it can exact a heavy personal toll. Civian et al. (1996) state, "Faculty members or administrators who choose to crusade for programs that dramatically alter the status quo are not only unlikely to succeed, but may end up bitter and disillusioned" (p. 654). Junior faculty who have staked too much may also end up being denied tenure or feel the need to leave.

However, if junior faculty choose to participate in the change process, or if their participation is not optional, an understanding of how it has worked and how it can be conceptualized, planned, and customized can be a key to effective and efficient participation in the process. That participation is not without risks, but it also promises rewards.

Civian et al. (1996) have shown one clear benefit of working for curricular change. "By and large, faculty members who have been involved in curricular change report that they find the process of designing and implementing new curricula to be intellectually stimulating and professionally satisfying" (p. 653). Participation with a curricular change committee can lessen feelings of isolation and lack of collegiality commonly reported by new faculty. It also can acquaint those who will step into senior roles in a few short years with traditions, history, and folk wisdom of their institutions, while at the same time they begin to make their marks on them.

What at first glance may seem to be a simple practical decision about where a junior faculty member can best invest limited energy, a decision to participate in curricular change can also lead to personal and spiritual growth. In *The Courage to Teach,* Palmer (1997) advocates for a holism that calls people to teach as fully integrated individuals and members of communities. Instead of playing games—remaining silent for fear of retribution—by joining with others for appropriate change we can begin to see how our work as individuals and in individual classrooms fits into a larger curriculum and how we as individuals fit into and help maintain the larger academic community.

REFERENCES

Adso, J. (2002, February 27). Figuring out what counts in the tenure game. *Chronicle of Higher Education Career Network.* Retrieved November 9, 2002, from http://chronicle.com/jobs/2002/02/2002022701c.htm

Aiken, S., Anderson, K., Dinnerstein, M., Lensink, J. N., & MacCorquodale, P. (1988). Changing our minds: The problematics of curriculum integration. In S. H. Aiken (Ed.), *Changing our minds: feminist transformations of knowledge* (pp. 134–163). Albany, NY: State University of New York Press.

Arnold, G., & Civian, J. T. (1997, July/August). The ecology of general education reform. *Change, 29*(4), 19–23.

Bensimon, E. M., & Neumann, A. (1993). *Redesigning collegiate leadership: Teams and teamwork in higher education.* Baltimore, MD: Johns Hopkins University Press.

Civian, J. T., Arnold, G., Gamson, Z. F., Kanter, S., & London, H. B. (1996). Implementing change. In J. G. Gaff, J. L. Ratcliff, & Associates (Eds.), *Handbook of the undergraduate curriculum: A comprehensive guide to purposes, structures, practices, and change* (pp. 647–660). San Francisco, CA: Jossey-Bass.

Cuban, L. (1999). *How scholars trumped teachers: Change without reform in university curriculum, teaching, and research, 1890–1990.* New York, NY: Teachers College Press.

Ferren, A. S., & McCafferty, J. K. (1992). Reforming college mathematics. *College teaching, 40*(3), 87–90.

Finkelstein, M. J., & LaCelle-Peterson, M. W. (1992). New and junior faculty: A review of the literature. In M. D. Sorcinelli & A. E. Austin (Eds.), *Developing new and junior faculty* (pp. 5–14). San Francisco, CA: Jossey-Bass.

Hord, S. M., Rutherford, W. L., Huling-Austin, L., & Hall, G. E. (1987). *Taking charge of change.* Alexandria, VA: Association for Supervision and Curriculum Development.

Kekale, J. (1999). "Preferred" patterns of academic leadership in different disciplinary (sub)cultures. *Higher Education, 37,* 217–238.

Keller, P. (1982). *Getting at the core: Curricular reform at Harvard.* Cambridge, MA: Harvard University Press.

Levine, A. (1978). *Handbook on undergraduate curriculum: A report for the Carnegie Council on Policy Studies in Higher Education.* San Francisco, CA: Jossey-Bass.

Lindquist, J. (1996). Strategies for change. In J. G. Gaff, J. L. Ratcliff, & Associates (Eds.), *Handbook of the undergraduate curriculum: A comprehensive guide to purposes, structures, practices, and change* (pp. 633–660). San Francisco, CA: Jossey-Bass.

Middendorf, J. K. (1998). A case study in getting faculty to change. In M. Kaplan & D. Lieberman (Eds.), *To improve the academy: Vol. 17. Resources for faculty, instructional, and organizational development* (pp. 203–224). Stillwater: OK: New Forums Press.

Middendorf, J. K. (2000). Finding key faculty to influence change. In M. Kaplan & D. Lieberman (Eds.), *To improve the academy: Vol. 18. Resources for faculty, instructional, and organizational development* (pp. 83–93). Bolton, MA: Anker.

Olguin, E., & Schmitz, B. (1996). Transforming the curriculum through diversity. In J. G. Gaff, J. L. Ratcliff, & Associates (Eds.), *Handbook of the undergraduate curriculum: A comprehensive guide to purposes, structures, practices, and change* (pp. 436–456). San Francisco, CA: Jossey-Bass.

Palmer, P. J. (1997). *The courage to teach: Exploring the inner landscape of a teacher's life.* San Francisco, CA: Jossey-Bass.

Ratcliff, J. L. (1996). What is a curriculum and what should it be? In J. G. Gaff, J. L. Ratcliff, & Associates (Eds.), *Handbook of the undergraduate curriculum: A comprehensive guide to purposes, structures, practices, and change* (pp. 5–29). San Francisco, CA: Jossey-Bass.

17

Assessing the Academic and Professional Development Needs of Graduate Students

Laurie Bellows
Ellen Weissinger
University of Nebraska–Lincoln

This chapter will describe the results of a survey that assessed the self-perceived career goals and academic and professional development needs of master's and doctoral-level graduate students at the University of Nebraska–Lincoln. Both graduate students (n = 440) and graduate program coordinators (n = 23) were surveyed to provide an empirical basis for developing a strategic plan for graduate student academic and professional development activities. Results suggested that doctoral and master's students express different developmental needs, and that doctoral students' needs differed at different stages of their academic career. Implications for practice inherent in the survey findings are discussed, and the benefits of broadening the definition of graduate student training and development are examined.

INTRODUCTION

Recent research on the preparation of graduate students suggests that many feel unprepared for the full range of academic and professional roles that they will face during their careers (Golde & Dore, 2001; National Research Council, 1992). Although teaching and research assistantships provide one form of training for future scholars, Austin (2002) found a general lack of systematic professional development opportunities available for graduate students, and Montell (1999) reported that a majority (68%) of science doctoral students in an online survey were dissatisfied with the career preparation they received in their graduate programs. The notion that graduate education inadequately prepares students for their future career roles and responsibilities has prompted calls for an expanded understanding of the full spectrum of professional development needs of graduate students (Association of American Universities, 1998; Austin, 2002; Committee on Science, Engineering, and Public Policy, 1995; Golde & Dore, 2001; National Association of Graduate-Professional Students [NAGPS], 2001).

This chapter will describe the results of a survey that assessed the professional development needs of master's and doctoral-level graduate students at the University of Nebraska–Lincoln (UNL). Both graduate students and graduate program coordinators were surveyed in this project, which was designed to provide an empirical basis for developing a strategic plan for graduate student academic and professional development activities. Also discussed are the implications for practice inherent in the survey findings and the benefits of broadening the definition of graduate student training and development.

RELATED LITERATURE ON GRADUATE STUDENT DEVELOPMENT

A number of recent studies have revealed what some investigators call a mismatch between the training doctoral students receive and the jobs they take (Golde & Dore, 2001; NAGPS, 2001; Nerad & Cerny, 1999, 2000). In 2001, NAGPS conducted a national survey in which a sample of graduate students was asked to report on their experiences in graduate school. Although an overwhelming majority of those responding to the survey reported high satisfaction with their doctoral programs and their advisors, survey participants reported inadequate preparation for both nonacademic and academic careers and a lack of appropriate preparation for teaching. Also, the authors noted that few students reported receiving training in the ethical standards and issues in their field despite increased attention at the national level to research ethics. Similarly, in a survey of Ph.D. alumni 10 years after receiving their degrees, respondents indicated that they needed help preparing for academic job interviews, writing a curriculum vita and cover letters, and suggestions on where to find job openings (Nerad & Cerny, 1999, 2000). Respondents also reported that training in teamwork, collaboration, and interdisciplinary work would have helped them be more prepared for their current job responsibilities.

In their national survey of advanced Ph.D. students, Golde and Dore (2001) found that while the majority of respondents expressed a strong interest in a faculty career, there was a "three-way mismatch between students goals, training and actual careers" (p. 5). In their report, the authors recommended major changes in graduate education to better prepare graduate students for their future careers, including a greater emphasis on teaching, more information about the job market, and support for those interested in nonacademic careers. Smith, Pedersen-Gallegos, and Riegle-Crumb (2002) examined relationships between graduate training, job satisfaction, and work of Ph.D. physical scientists and found that many of the graduates arrived on the job market ill-equipped to meet the challenges their new positions required. Only one-third of the respondents reported high levels of training in teaching and working in an interdisciplinary context, although the majority of respondents indicated that these two skills were important in their current work.

New visions of graduate education that involve broader definitions of graduate training and development have emerged. The new agenda includes preparing graduate students for future faculty roles, professional practice, or for careers in business, government, and industry. Graduate education that integrates a broad range of academic and professional development opportunities—from preparing students to teach to creating a forum for exploring ethical issues to providing a better understanding of the variety of institutions and organizations in which Ph.D.s work—can close the gap between traditional doctoral training and the work expected of those who obtain Ph.D.s.

Graduate student professional development begins the day students enroll in graduate studies and continues until they graduate. From learning how to be a successful graduate student (e.g., choosing an advisor, developing a plan of study) to developing advanced professional skills (e.g., supervising and mentoring undergraduate students, acquiring grant-writing skills), professional development encompasses a wide range of experiences beyond traditional disciplinary training. The ultimate goal of these activities is to help graduate students be more effective—and more marketable—in academia, business, government, or industry. However, an effective professional development program is more than career counseling or job placement services; it should focus on helping the graduate student develop a professional sense of self (Darwin, 2000). Professional development activities that include a process of reflection—for example, learning how to construct an academic portfolio—provide a context for exploring what it means to be a professional and helps graduate students articulate their own scholarly strengths and interests. Professional development experiences also can expand graduate students' thinking beyond the discipline, helping them develop a broader definition of what it means to be a professional in their field (Darwin, 2000).

Since 1988, the UNL has had a strong instructional development program to meet the training and development needs of graduate teaching assistants and their departments (e.g., campus-wide TA workshops, the Institute for International Teaching Assistants, and individual instructional consultation). More recently, the Office of Graduate Studies recognized the need to provide a broader and more complex array of development activities (LaPidus, 1997). In 2002, the Office of Graduate Studies at UNL set out to develop a strategic plan for expanding graduate student academic and professional development programming. Before we took the first step in designing the new initiatives, however, we surveyed graduate students and the faculty members who serve as graduate program coordinators about the perceived academic and professional development needs of graduate students.

AN ASSESSMENT OF GRADUATE STUDENTS' ACADEMIC AND PROFESSIONAL DEVELOPMENT NEEDS

Developing the Student Survey

The purpose of the student survey was to learn more about UNL graduate students' self-perceived career goals and their academic and professional development needs. Both paper-and-pencil and web-based versions of the student survey were developed.

In order to create closed-ended survey items, we first developed a comprehensive list of future career goals and possible academic and professional development topics. To accomplish this, we drew from the literature on graduate student professional development and we searched web sites to identify a range of topics (e.g., cover letters, conference presentations, poster sessions, and grant writing). The final version of the student survey included 14 items related to future career goals, 16 items related to academic and professional development, and 9 items related to program delivery options. The survey's look and layout were modeled after a graduate student survey developed by the Center for Teaching Excellence at the University of California–Santa Cruz.

The student survey was organized into two sections: About You and About Your Future (Appendix 17.1). The first section—About You—asked about the student's department, degree sought, number of years in graduate school, plans to pursue an academic career, and whether the respondent was currently teaching. The second section—About Your Future—included three parts: 1) respondents' future career goals, 2) possible academic and professional development topics that would help prepare them for the future, and 3) their preferred modes of delivery for development activities. For each area (future career goals, professional development topics, and delivery options) respondents were given a list of choices and were asked to mark all that applied to their situation.

Procedures for the Student Survey

In September 2002, the Office of Graduate Studies emailed department graduate program coordinators asking for their help in distributing the survey to UNL graduate students. We distributed 1,133 hard copies of the survey to departments via campus mail; at the request of several departments, we made the survey available via the web as well.

Results

Useable data were obtained from 438 respondents (230 hard copies; another 208 surveys were completed online). Because we were not able to determine the exact number of online surveys distributed, it is not possible to calculate a response rate for the survey. As a broad comparison, 438 students represent 12.5% of the degree-seeking graduate students at UNL. Fifty percent of the respondents were currently seeking a master's degree (n = 220), while the other half indicated they were doctoral students (n = 218). This represents 11.5% of the master's students and 13.8% of the doctoral students at UNL. In addition, 48.2% of the students responding to the survey indicated that they were planning a career in academia; 33% of the respondents were currently teaching; and 48.3% of those not teaching indicated they planned to teach before they graduate.

Student's Career Goals

We listed 14 possible career paths and asked students to indicate their future career goals. Master's and doctoral student respondents most often selected "professor (Research I institution)" (32.7%), "professor (Comprehensive Liberal Arts institution)" (31.3%), and "research in a university" (27.7%) as their future career goals. Table 17.1 shows a comparison of the top three career choices by Ph.D. and master's-level respondents.

TABLE 17.1
Top Three Career Goals

Ph.D. Respondents (n = 218)	%	Master's Respondents (n = 220)	%
Professor (Research I institution)	42.7	Industrial career	22.9
Professor (Comprehensive/ Liberal Arts institution)	34.4	Consultant	22.9
Research in a university	31.3	Start own business	22.9

These findings are consistent with the results of the Golde and Dore (2001) survey of advanced Ph.D. students that suggested most doctoral students are primarily interested in a faculty career. In contrast, many masters' students in our sample aspired to nonacademic careers.

Academic and Professional Development Needs
Respondents were asked to choose the development topics that best fit their unique needs. A list of 16 possible academic and professional development topics was provided. Respondents most often selected "job market and interview strategies" (54.5%), "curriculum vitae and cover letters" (48.4%), "publishing in graduate school" (47.7%), "writing a dissertation" (46.4%), and "conference presentations" (44.8%). Table 17.2 shows a comparison of the 16 topics by Ph.D. and master's-level respondents.

TABLE 17.2
Academic/Professional Development Topics

Ph.D. Respondents (n = 218)	%	Master's Respondents (n = 220)	%
Postdoctoral fellowships	63.9	Job market and interview strategies	57.8
Writing a dissertation	57.9	Curriculum vitae and cover letters	47.2
Job market and interview strategies	52.8	Publishing in graduate school	45.4
Publishing in graduate school	51.4	Conference presentations	43.1
Curriculum vitae and cover letters	50.9	Alternative career opportunities	40.4
Conference presentations	47.2	Writing a dissertation	35.8
Grantsmanship	45.8	Preparing for industrial career	33.5
Teaching portfolio	41.2	Grantsmanship	33.0
Teaching/instructional strategies	36.6	Interdisciplinary research	30.7
Interdisciplinary research	35.2	Teaching/instructional strategies	28.4
Faculty roles/responsibilities	31.0	Professional ethics	25.7
Alternative career opportunities	30.1	Teaching portfolio	22.5
Preparing for industrial career	28.7	Faculty roles and responsibilities	20.2
Professional ethics	23.1	Postdoctoral fellowships	19.7
Academic citizenship	17.6	Academic citizenship	18.3
Other	10.2	Other	10.6

We took a closer look at the needs of doctoral students at different stages of their graduate program (first year, second year, third year, or fourth year or more). The top three topics most often selected by students at different stages were:

- First year: "writing a dissertation" (61.1%), "conference presentations" (55.6%) and "publishing in graduate school" 55.6%, and "postdoctoral fellowships" (55.6%)

- Second year: "writing a dissertation" (72%), "postdoctoral fellowships" (60%), and "curriculum vitae" (56%)

- Third year: "postdoctoral fellowships" (60%), "job market and interview skills" (57.5%), "publishing in graduate school" (57.5%), and "writing a dissertation" (57.5%)

- Fourth year or more: "postdoctoral fellowships" (76.8%), "job market and interview skills" (59.4%), and "writing a dissertation" (44.9%)

FIGURE 17.1
Professional Development Topic by Program Stage for Ph.D. Students (n = 218)

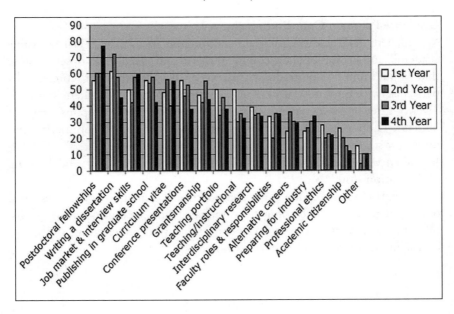

Delivery Options for Development Activities

We listed nine possible delivery methods and asked respondents about their preferences for experiencing development activities. Respondents most often chose "Internet resources" (40.5%), "professional development seminars" (29.8%), and "campus-wide workshops (interdisciplinary)" (28.9%). Table 17.3 presents a comparison of the most frequently selected delivery methods by Ph.D. and master's respondents.

TABLE 17.3
Preferred Method of Delivery

Ph.D. Respondents (n = 218)	%	Master's Respondents (n = 220)	%
Internet resources (web page)	56.0	Internet resources (web page)	62.6
Campus-wide workshops (interdisciplinary)	47.8	Online workshops	46.0
Professional development seminar(s)	44.0	Professional development seminar(s)	43.2

Graduate Program Coordinators Survey

We emailed UNL graduate program coordinators (n = 77) a list of 14 possible academic and professional development topics and asked them to select those that would interest their graduate students or that they thought represented a particularly important training or development need for their students. Twenty-three graduate chairs responded to the survey (response rate of 29.9%). The topics that were most often selected included "job market and interview strategies" (91.3%), "curriculum vitae and cover letters" (73.9%), "conference presentations" (69.6%), "grantsmanship" (65.2%), and "writing a dissertation" (60.9%).

Several graduate chairs suggested additional academic and professional development topics, including time management, technical writing skills, planning an academic career, basic communication/presentation skills, and balancing the demands of graduate school.

USING GRADUATE STUDENT NEEDS ASSESSMENT RESULTS
TO DESIGN AN ACADEMIC AND PROFESSIONAL
DEVELOPMENT PROGRAM

The graduate student survey and the graduate chairs' survey both provided important information about UNL graduate students' academic and professional development interests. We interpreted the results of our needs assessment in the context of recent studies that suggest different models for organizing graduate student preparation activities (Austin, 2002; Nyquist, 2002; Poock, 2001). From the national discussions on doctoral education, Nyquist compiled a set of core competencies that all Ph.D.s should be able to demonstrate: disciplinary knowledge; a commitment to an informed career choice; teaching competency; an understanding of diversity of students and workplaces; an understanding of the mentoring process; an ability to connect one's work to others; a global perspective; the ability to see oneself as a scholar-citizen; the ability to communicate and work in teams; and an understanding of ethical responsibilities as researchers, teachers, and professionals. Poock identified a similar set of five competency themes: communication, leadership, teaching and instruction, professional adaptability, and self-awareness. Austin suggested that graduate student development involves several dimensions which include various understandings, abilities, and skills. According to Austin, graduate students develop professional responsibilities as researchers, teachers, engaged scholars, and institutional/organizational citizens, and they develop professional identities in terms of being a faculty member, a professional, a member of the discipline, and a balanced and integrated individual.

Clearly, some of the understandings, skills, and abilities set forth by Austin, Nyquist, and Poock fall under the realm of departmental or discipline-specific training, while others can be effectively nurtured by a campus-wide effort. For example, specific research processes and procedures are often developed at the department level, yet many graduate students would benefit from a general session on grant writing and grant management strategies. Similarly, pedagogical content knowledge—the understanding of pedagogical approaches to discipline or subject matter (Shulman, 1986)—is best developed at the department level while more general teaching practices (understanding how students learn, assessment of student learning, teaching with technology, undergraduate advising) can be addressed at the campus level. Departments are in a better position to help graduate students understand the range of opportunities in which disciplinary expertise can be used while discussions at the campus level can help students understand the nature of academic appointments, the characteristics of students, and the different types of higher education institutions.

Based on the literature review and the results of the needs assessment, the Office of Graduate Studies developed a new initiative, the Graduate Student Academic and Professional Development Program. The goal of our program is to provide graduate students a diverse set of professional development activities to enhance the preparation they receive in their home departments. It is a centralized, integrated approach to professional development designed to supplement the good work being done at the department level, thereby strengthening graduate education at UNL. The program includes three major areas of emphasis: academic, career, and instructional development.

We learned from the survey that graduate students want additional opportunities to develop communication skills in areas such as grant writing and conference presentations. The academic development component includes workshops and resources on topics such as time management, how to publish in graduate school, and navigating the Ph.D. Departments interested in strengthening the research component of their graduate capstone courses can look to the Graduate Student Academic and Professional Development Program to help facilitate sessions on grant writing, technical report writing, and the ethical conduct of research.

The career development component helps graduate students explore the various academic and nonacademic career paths available to them. Workshops are offered in collaboration with other UNL units such as career services and the counseling and psychological services office. The career development component also includes the Preparing Future Faculty (PFF) program, a national initiative designed to better prepare those graduate students interested in an academic career.

Because the majority of the respondents indicated an interest in careers that include teaching, we believe it is important to supplement departmental teaching assistant training efforts. The instructional development component provides support services for graduate teaching assistants, including our annual campus-wide TA orientation, the Institute for International Teaching Assistants, and collaboration with academic departments to provide discipline-specific training programs. Our graduate teaching assistants receive additional support through classroom observation and assistance with gathering student feedback for the purposes of documenting their teaching. Also, we are available to help departments provide systematic training and supervised experiences in teaching.

Because students told us that they prefer some development activities to be delivered electronically, the Graduate Student Academic and Professional Development Program created additional support through online resources. We are currently preparing an online version of our *Instructional Guide for University of Nebraska–Lincoln Teaching Assistants,* and additional web resource materials, including online workshop modules, are being developed. A graduate student electronic list is another vehicle for delivering useful information and suggestions for how to navigate through graduate school, and we are using Blackboard to encourage cross-disciplinary discussions on professional development topics.

Our program also provides support to departments applying for federal training grants, both at the development and delivery stages. We help departments develop their training and teaching grant proposals and assist departments with the supervised instructional training support that many training grants require. By preparing students for diverse career opportunities, these training grants are another vehicle for broadening graduate education.

The results of this needs assessment have helped us think developmentally about graduate student professional development (Nyquist & Sprague, 1998). For example, 72% of the doctoral students in their second year indicated an interest in the topic "writing a dissertation" while 77% of the doctoral students in their fourth year were more interested in learning about postdoctoral fellowships. From these findings, we can develop workshops for graduate students that are tailored to each stage of their careers.

Ongoing Evaluation of the Graduate Student Academic and Professional Development Program

Because many aspects of our program are still relatively new, we collect varied forms of ongoing evaluation data that can be used to refine our offerings. Program evaluation currently involves data collected at the end of each workshop. These are self-reported satisfaction indicators with open-ended comments that ask participants what new ideas, information, and/or approaches were learned during the workshop and "how likely" or "how prepared" they are to implement the strategies or processes discussed in the workshop.

Attendance data is another means of evaluating the extent to which a program is meeting its goals. We designed a database to track the number of graduate students and faculty mentors who currently use our program services. We record the following data: 1) general domain of consultation (academic, career, or instructional development), 2) consultation activity (e.g., provided resources, gave feedback, videotaped class), and 3) when appropriate, specific consultation topic (e.g., teaching portfolio, diversity, instructional technology, vitae). Also, we keep registration records of workshop participants to track the specific kinds of students who participated in our programs and the departments we are serving. These records will be sorted at the end of the year and reports generated to help us track the resources expended for each activity and to help us plan more effectively (Chism, 1998).

Future program assessment will include follow-up surveys and possibly focus groups to measure the effectiveness in meeting the needs of graduate students and the impact on their graduate student experience at UNL.

PROFESSIONAL DEVELOPMENT FOR GRADUATE STUDENTS: IMPLICATIONS FOR PRACTICE

Increasingly, universities are restructuring their graduate programs to include a broader and more sophisticated menu of professional development opportunities (Gaff, 2002). Excellent examples of these innovative student development programs can be found at the University of California, Arizona State University, North Carolina State University, Northwestern University, University of Michigan, University of Texas–Austin, University of Colorado–Boulder, and University of Wisconsin–Madison. The PFF program is another example of a national professional development initiative that many universities have integrated into their training programs for advanced graduate students. Some universities, such as the University of Texas–Austin, have used their PFF program as a foundation for a more comprehensive professional development program (Cherwitz & Sullivan, 2002).

While many of these programs are located in the graduate school, program administrators often rely on collaborative relationships between the graduate school and other campus programs to provide graduate students a range of professional development experiences. For example, Northwestern University's Beyond Books series—workshops that feature tips and advice to help graduate students navigate successfully through graduate school—is sponsored by the graduate school, the PFF program, the Searle Center for Teaching Excellence, university career services, and the student affairs division. Sharing resources in this way eliminates a major obstacle in providing professional development programs: increased resources (money and personnel) in a time of reduced budgets.

Another significant concern expressed by faculty and administrators is the fear that professional development activities will lengthen students' time to graduation. How can additional experiences be incorporated into doctoral training without taking time away from research and scholarship and without increasing time to degree? The answer will be different depending on the program and the institution. At UNL, participation in most of our workshops is voluntary, and we are considerate of both our graduate students' time and departmental concerns. We plan our program activities with a goal of optimizing the amount of time we ask of students while maximizing the benefits for our graduate students.

The benefits of offering a carefully designed comprehensive professional development program for graduate students far outweigh the drawbacks. Research indicates that graduate students who are integrated academically into their programs and into the campus community are more likely to complete their degrees than students who feel isolated and disconnected from the campus (Lovitts & Nelson, 2000). And, recent reports on graduate education suggest that professional development programs will lead to increased student satisfaction with both their graduate experience and with their future careers (Golde & Dore, 2001; Lovitts & Nelson, 2000).

The nature of graduate education is changing. Greater emphasis is being placed on professional development of graduate students by professional organizations such as the Council of Graduate Schools, National Science Foundation, and the American Association of Colleges and Universities. The Professional and Organization Development Network in Higher Education (POD) has a storied history in offering instructional and professional development for faculty; more recently, the instructional development needs of teaching assistants have been emphasized in POD's strategic plan (i.e., the development of a TA developers committee). Perhaps the time has come for POD to adopt a broader definition of professional development to include graduate students, especially Ph.D.s and post-doctorates, and provide national leadership in developing programs and services to meet the specific needs of our future professionals.

REFERENCES

Association of American Universities. (1998). *Committee on graduate education: Report and recommendations.* Washington, DC: Author. Retrieved August 13, 2002, from http://www.aau.edu/reports/GradEdRpt.html

Austin, A. E. (2002). Preparing the next generation of faculty: Graduate school as socialization to the academic career. *Journal of Higher Education, 73*(1), 94–122.

Cherwitz, R. A., & Sullivan, C. A. (2002, November/December). Intellectual entrepreneurship: A vision for graduate education. *Change, 34*(6), 23–27.

Chism, N. V. N. (1998). Evaluating TA programs. In M. Marincovich, J. Prostko, & F. Stout (Eds.), *The professional development of graduate teaching assistants* (pp. 249–262). Bolton, MA: Anker.

Committee on Science, Engineering, and Public Policy. (1995). *Reshaping the graduate education of scientists and engineers.* Washington, DC: National Academy Press.

Darwin, T. J. (2000). *Professional development as intellectual opportunity.* Paper presented at the National Communication Association Conference, Seattle, WA. Retrieved November 5, 2003, from https://webspace.utexas.edu/cherwitz/www/ie/td.html

Gaff, J. G. (2002, November/December). Preparing future faculty and doctoral education. *Change, 34*(6), 63–66.

Golde, C. M., & Dore, T. M. (2001). *At cross purposes: What the experiences of today's graduate students reveal about doctoral education.* Philadelphia, PA: Pew Charitable Trusts. Retrieved April 19, 2002 from http://www.phd-survey.org

LaPidus, J. B. (1997). *Doctoral education: Preparing for the future.* Washington, DC: Council of Graduate Schools. Retrieved September 10, 2002, from http://www.cgsnet.org/pdf/doctoraledpreparing.pdf

Lovitts, B. E., & Nelson, C. (2000, November/December). The hidden crisis in graduate education: Attrition from Ph.D. programs. *Academe, 86*(6). Retrieved May 9, 2004, from http://www.aaup.org/publications/Academe/2000/00nd/ND00LOVI.HTM

Montell, G. (1999). In on-line survey, graduate students in science rate their doctoral programs. *Chronicle of Higher Education,* p. A16.

National Association of Graduate-Professional Students. (2001). *The 2000 national doctoral program survey.* Washington, DC: Author. Retrieved September 10, 2002, from http://survey.nagps.org

National Research Council. (1992). *Educating mathematical scientists: Doctoral study and the postdoctoral experience in the United States.* Washington, DC: National Academy Press.

Nerad, M., & Cerny, J. (1999, Fall). From rumors to facts: Career outcomes of English Ph.D.s. *Council of Graduate Schools Communicator, 32*(7), 1-11. Retrieved May 9, 2004, from http://www.grad.washington.edu/envision/PDF/TenYears Later.pdf

Nerad, M., & Cerny, J. (2000). Improving doctoral education: Recommendations from the "Ph.D.s 10 years later study." *Council of Graduate Schools Communicator, 33*(2), 6. Retrieved May 9, 2004, from snet.org/PublicationsPolicyRes/communicatorpdfs/2000/march2000.pdf

Nyquist, J. D. (2002, November/December). The Ph.D.: A tapestry of change for the 21st century. *Change, 34*(6), 12-20.

Nyquist, J. D., & Sprague, J. (1998). Thinking developmentally about TAs. In M. Marincovich, J. Prostko, & F. Stout (Eds.), *The professional development of graduate teaching assistants* (pp. 61–88). Bolton, MA: Anker.

Poock, M. C. (2001). A model for integrating professional development in graduate education. *College Student Journal, 35*(3), 345–353. Retrieved May 9, 2004, from http://articles.findarticles.com/p/articles/mi_m0FCR/is_3_35/ai_80744646

Shulman, L. S. (1986). Those who understand: Knowledge growth in teaching. *Educational Researcher, 15,* 4–14.

Smith, S. J., Pedersen-Gallegos, L., & Riegle-Crumb, C. (2002). The training, careers, and work of Ph.D. physical scientists: Not simply academic. *American Journal of Physics, 70*(11), 1081–1092.

APPENDIX 17.1

GRADUATE STUDENT SURVEY

The Office of Graduate Studies Wants to Know: How Can We Help?

We'd like to offer you a range of professional development activities that will help you prepare for your future—whether you're planning a career in academia or industry. Please take a few minutes to respond to this survey. When you're finished, just fold it into thirds, staple it, and drop it in the campus mail!

I. About You:

A. Department:_____

B. Citizenship: (e.g., U.S., Japan)_____

C. Degree(s) sought: _____Master's   _____Ph.D.   _____Other

D. Your level: _____1st Year   _____3rd Year
              _____2nd Year   _____4th or More

E. Do you plan to pursue an academic career upon completion of your degree?

   _____Yes   _____No   _____Unsure

F. Are you currently teaching?   If no, do you plan to teach before you graduate?

   _____Yes   _____No   _____Yes   _____No

II. About Your Future

G. Please indicate your future career goals. Mark all that apply.

   ☐ Professor (Research I institution)   ☐ Professor (Community College)
   ☐ Professor (Comprehensive, Liberal   ☐ Research in private sector
     Arts institution)   ☐ Research in a university
   ☐ Non-college teaching   ☐ Start own business
   ☐ Research in non-profit or government   ☐ College administrator
   ☐ Manager in non-profit or government   ☐ Industrial career
   ☐ Self-employment   ☐ Consultant
   ☐ Other (please indicate):_____

H. Here are some possible academic and professional development topics that we could explore. Check all those that interest you.

   ☐ Job market and interview strategies   ☐ Grantmanship
   ☐ Professional ethics   ☐ Interdisciplinary research and training
   ☐ Developing a teaching portfolio   opportunities
   ☐ Publishing in graduate school   ☐ Conference presentations
   ☐ Postdoctoral fellowships   ☐ Curriculum vitae and cover letters
   ☐ Teaching/instructional strategies   ☐ Writing a dissertation
   ☐ Faculty roles and responsibilities   ☐ Preparing for industrial careers
   ☐ Alternative career opportunities   ☐ Academic citizenship (service to community)

[MORE ON BACK]

I. What **other** topics would you like to explore in the context of workshops, seminars, or pedagogy courses?

J. How would you like to receive this assistance/information? Please check all that apply.

☐ Campus-wide workshop (interdisciplinary)   ☐ Graduate Studies' pedagogy course
☐ Professional development seminar(s)   ☐ Online workshop(s)
☐ Department colloquium(s)   ☐ Internet resources (web page)
☐ Individual mentoring by department   ☐ Individual mentoring by senior
   faculty   graduate student(s)

☐ Other? Please list._____

_____

_____

K. Do you have any additional comments or suggestions?

Office of Graduate Studies
1100 Seaton Hall
CC 0619

18

Faculty Development in Community Colleges: A Model for Part-Time Faculty

Mary Rose Grant
Saint Louis University

Historically, part-time faculty have not received the same development opportunities as full-time faculty. This study surveyed current practices in faculty development for both full-time and part-time faculty in 232 public two-year colleges throughout the United States. Over 90% reported that they had a formal faculty development program for both faculty cohorts, funded with 1%–5% of their operating budgets. About one half of the colleges designated a faculty development coordinator, used needs assessment to determine program content, and evaluated program outcomes. Results of this study were used to design a generic model for part-time faculty development.

FACULTY DEVELOPMENT IN COMMUNITY COLLEGES

Faculty are the core of any institution of higher education. They are one human resource that is vital to the institution's mission. Community colleges rely on full-time and part-time faculty to meet standards of quality in their teaching mission. The increasing number and reliance on part-time faculty warrants serious consideration in terms of academic quality and institutional integrity (Banachowski, 1996; Gappa & Leslie, 1993; Roueche, Roueche, & Milliron, 1995). Faculty development is an institutional commitment to academic integrity (O'Banion, 1994). Faculty development programs serve as vehicles for professional growth and renewal and should be open to all part-time as well as full-time faculty (Murray, 2002; Schuster, 1995). According to national statistics, 64% of the faculty at community colleges was part-time in 1997, an increase of 22% in five years (American Association of State Colleges and Universities [AASCU], 1999; National Center for Education Statistics, 2002; National Education Association [NEA], 2001). This shift in the demographics of faculty in the community college is not an episodic or short-term trend but a permanent feature in higher education (AASCU, 1999). For community college administrators, assessing the roles and responsibilities of part-time faculty becomes more critical. An investment in support structures for part-time faculty, including integration into the learning community, strengthens the institutional mission (Gappa & Leslie, 1993, 1997).

This study investigates current practices in faculty development of both full- and part-time faculty in public community colleges of different sizes and accreditation regions. A formal, comprehensive model for part-time faculty development emerges from this study, which identifies elements of planning, implementation, funding, and evaluation.

Historically, before the late 1960s, faculty development programs were essentially nonexistent (Schuster, 1990). Faculty development efforts prior to the mid-1960s were limited to orientation of new faculty, sabbatical leaves, reduced teaching loads, and visiting professorships (Bergquist & Phillips, 1975).

Faculty development expanded in the 1970s, especially in the area of teaching improvement. The momentum continued to build, providing opportunities to enhance teaching effectiveness, to improve student learning, and to revitalize existing faculty (Gaff, 1975; Hammons, 1983; Richardson & Moore, 1987).

As the faculty development movement progressed, models were developed that stressed the interrelationship and overlap of all aspects of faculty development: personal, professional, instructional, and organizational (Schuster, 1990). A number of studies in the 1980s recommended the inclusion of part-time faculty in faculty development programs (Miller & Ratcliff, 1986; Richardson & Moore, 1987; Williams, 1986).

This study may provide basic information and insights that can be used to initiate, plan, and implement comprehensive faculty development programs in any type of institution of higher education that routinely depends upon the expertise and employment of part-time faculty. The results of this research may also provide demographically different institutions a foundation on which to build formal full-time and part-time faculty development programs and add to the strategies they use to successfully institutionalize these programs. The information garnered from this study was used to inform, plan, develop, and implement a comprehensive model of professional development for part-time faculty in Saint Louis University's School for Continuing Education, whose demographics and ratio of full- to part-time faculty is similar to that found in most community colleges.

In addition, a literature search revealed that no studies had compared faculty development programs or practices among accreditation regions. By sampling faculty development programs nationwide, the sub-elements of faculty development programs among accreditation regions were categorized and compared in this study. National data categorized in this way could become a departure point for further investigation into how meeting accreditation performance standards promotes inclusive faculty development as a critical factor in improving teaching and learning.

METHOD

A random sample of 300 community colleges was selected from an address database provided by the American Association of Community Colleges (AACC) to participate in this nationwide study. A 30-item survey was mailed to the president at each of the colleges to be forwarded to the administrator or faculty member responsible for faculty development. A total of 232 institutions returned completed surveys (77%). The survey was divided into six sections to assess program practices, content, coordination, participation, funding, and evaluation associated with faculty development. Responding schools were categorized into six accreditation regions: Middle States Association of Colleges and Schools (MSACS), North Central Association of Colleges and Schools (NCACS), New England Association of Schools and Colleges (NEASC), Northwest Association of Schools and Colleges (NWASC), Southern Association of Colleges and Schools (SACS), and Western Association of Schools and Colleges (WASC). The responding community colleges were also divided into size subcategories: small, full-time equivalent (FTE) students less than 1,500; medium, FTE students between 1,500 and 4,000; and large, FTE students greater than 4,000. Besides descriptive statistics, chi-square and one-way analysis of variance (ANOVA) were performed to analyze data.

RESULTS

Demographics

Of the 232 responding community colleges, over one-half represented single-campus institutions (n = 133; 57%) and many were located in rural communities (n = 79; 34%). The response rates by accreditation region were SACS (n = 76; 83%), NCACS (n = 80; 82%), MSACS (n = 25; 78%), NWASC (n = 23; 74%), WASC (n = 24; 67%), and NEASC (n =4 ; 33%). The mean FTE number of students at the responding colleges was 3,757, while the ratio of the means of part-time (n = 264) to full-time (n = 121) faculty was 2 to 1. Based on the FTE number of students enrolled, more medium sized (n = 92) schools were included in the survey than larger (n = 76) or smaller schools (n = 64).

The mean number of full-time faculty in small colleges was 57; in medium colleges, 95; and in large colleges, 208. A one-way ANOVA of these means was significant, $F(2, 229) = 38.008$, $p = .0001$. Small and medium schools had fewer full-time faculty than large schools. The ANOVA for mean number of full-time faculty among accreditation regions was not significant. The mean number of part-time faculty reported by campus and community setting ranged from 197 for single campuses to 355 for multiple campuses and from 120 for schools in rural communities to 421 for schools in urban communities. The ANOVA was significant by college size, $F(2, 228) = 31.270$, $p = .0001$, campus setting, $F(1,229) = 12.373$, $p = .001$, and community setting, $F(3,227) = 13.160$, $p = .0001$. Small and medium colleges had fewer part-time faculty than large colleges. Single-campus colleges located in small towns and rural communities had fewer part-time faculty than those with multiple campuses in suburban or urban settings.

Generally, the person who responded to the survey was an administrator (n = 206; 89%). Vice presidents for instruction (n = 65; 28%) or academic deans (n = 55; 24%) most often completed the survey.

Ninety percent (n = 209) of colleges reported that they had a formal faculty development program. The mean number of years a formal faculty development program was reported to be in place was 13. With regard to faculty development program practices, all institutions reported that they provided activities in four areas: professional, personal, curricular, and organizational. Results for the professional subcategory are reported in Table 18.1.

TABLE 18.1
Number and Percentage of Community Colleges That Provide Professional Development Practices

Practice	Faculty Full-Time		Part-Time		Both		Neither		Total
	n	%	n	%	n	%	n	%	n
Travel funds	108	46.6	2	0.9	122	52.6	0	0.0	232
Released time									
On campus	97	42.2	1	0.4	113	49.1	19	8.3	230
Off campus	112	48.9	1	0.4	98	42.8	18	7.9	229
Tuition-free courses									
On campus	117	50.4	0	0.0	73	31.5	42	18.1	232
Learning grant	81	35.7	0	0.0	66	29.1	80	35.2	227
Tuition-free courses									
Off campus	90	39.3	0	0.0	37	16.2	102	44.5	229
Return to industry	94	41.0	0	0.0	27	11.8	108	47.2	229
Tuition-free courses									
Other colleges	50	22.2	0	0.0	16	7.1	159	70.7	225
Exchange program	61	27.1	0	0.0	10	4.4	154	68.4	225
Sabbatical leave	168	74.3	0	0.0	2	0.9	56	24.8	226
Other	6	54.5	0	0.0	5	45.5	0	0.0	11

All responding institutions (100%) provided travel funds for either full-time faculty only (47%) or both full-time and part-time faculty (53%), followed by released time for full-time faculty only (49%) or both faculty cohorts (43%). Travel funds were more often reported in large schools than medium or small schools for both faculty cohorts. Chi-square was significant, $X^2(4, N = 232) = 12.037$, p =. 017, for travel funds. Sabbatical leave (n = 168; 74%) was only offered to full-time faculty. Several significant differences were found among accreditation regions for full-time and part-time faculty for learning grants, $X^2(5, N = 232) = 24.398$, p =. 0001, released time on campus, $X^2(10, N = 232) = 21.945$, p =. 015, released time off campus, $X^2(10, N = 232) = 21.352$, $p = .019$, tuition-free courses on campus, $X^2(5, N = 232) = 23.229$, p

= .0001, and tuition free courses off campus, $X^2(5, N = 232) = 25.358$, $p = .0001$. Professional development practices for both faculty groups were reported more often in the NWASC and WASC accreditation regions than in the other regions, where professional development practices were reported most often for full-time faculty only. The results of personal development practices are presented in Table 18.2.

TABLE 18.2

Number and Percentage of Community Colleges That Provide Personal Development Practices

Practice	Faculty								
	Full-Time		Part-Time		Both		Neither		Total
	n	%	n	%	n	%	n	%	n
Interpersonal skills	41	17.8	0	0.0	100	43.5	89	38.7	230
Stress management	38	16.5	0	0.0	99	43.0	93	40.4	230
Time management	36	15.7	0	0.0	83	36.2	110	48.0	229
Retirement planning	89	38.7	0	0.0	76	33.0	65	28.3	230
Other	3	30.0	0	0.0	6	60.0	1	10.0	10

Personal development practices were either offered for both full- and part-time faculty (33%–44%) or not offered at all (28%–48%). The most often reported personal development practice for full-time faculty only was retirement planning (n = 89; 37%). The three most reported personal development practices for both faculty cohorts were interpersonal skills (n = 100; 44%), stress management (n = 99; 43%), and time management (n = 83; 36%). No significant differences were found for full-time and part-time faculty for personal development practices by college size or accreditation region.

Curricular Development Practices

Regarding curricular development practices, as represented in Table 18.3, most institutions (n = 162, 70%) reported the availability of curricular practices for both full- and part-time faculties, followed by departmental instructional practices for both (n = 157, 68%).

TABLE 18.3

Number and Percentage of Community Colleges That Provide Curricular Development Practices

Practice	Faculty								Total
	Full-Time		Part-Time		Both		Neither		
	n	%	n	%	n	%	n	%	n
Instructional practices	36	15.7	1	0.4	162	70.7	30	13.1	229
Departmental	35	15.2	0	0.0	157	68.0	39	16.9	231
Outside consultant	38	16.9	0	0.0	98	43.6	89	39.6	225
Teaching networks	32	14.0	0	0.0	46	20.1	151	65.9	229
Other	3	42.9	0	0.0	4	57.1	0	0.0	7

Two-thirds of the institutions (n = 151; 66%) reported that teaching networks (forums for sharing experiences, instructional tools, and advice among teachers within similar learning environments) were not available to either full- or part-time faculty. No significant differences were reported for full- or part-time faculty for curricular development practices by college size or accreditation region.

Organizational Development Practices

The results of organizational development are seen in Table 18.4. Orientation of new faculty was reported by most of the responding institutions (n = 182; 78%) for both full and part-time faculty, followed by the provision of faculty handbooks (n = 177; 76%) for both faculty groups. No significant differences were reported for full-time or part-time faculty for organizational development activities by college size or accreditation region.

Faculty Development Program Content

In the area of faculty development program content, more than one-half (n = 133; 58%) of the reporting institutions used a formal needs assessment to determine program content. The most common assessment method used was a survey (n = 76, 61.3%) done once a year or more (n = 118, 91%). Full-time faculty (96%) were more often included in the assessment process than part-time faculty (69%).

TABLE 18.4

Number and Percentage of Community Colleges That Provide Organizational Development Practices

Practice	Full-Time		Part-Time		Both		Neither		Total
	n	%	n	%	n	%	n	%	n
Orient new faculty	36	15.5	3	1.3	182	78.4	11	4.7	232
Faculty handbook	20	8.6	10	4.3	177	76.3	25	10.8	232
Policy updates	37	15.9	0	0.0	169	72.8	26	11.2	232
Management techniques	34	15.0	1	0.4	60	26.4	132	58.1	227
Other	1	50.0	0	0.0	1	50.0	0	0.0	2

Faculty Development Coordinator

A designated faculty development coordinator was reported in one-half (52%) of responding institutions. Released time (45%) rather than salary (37%) was allotted to the faculty development coordinator. Colleges in the WASC region reported that they had a designated faculty development coordinator more often than other regions, $X^2(5, N = 232) = 21.000, p = .001$; however, the WASC colleges provided less compensation in the form of salary than the other regions, $X^2(5, N = 232) = 11.314, p = .045$. Chi-square for faculty development coordination along college size was also significant, $X^2(2, N = 232) = 9.201, p = .01$. The larger schools had more faculty development coordinators, more procedures for selection, and more criteria for qualification than medium or small schools. Responding institutions with no designated faculty development coordinator (48%) reported that faculty development was the responsibility of the vice president for instruction (53%) or a faculty development committee (39%). Chi-square for faculty development coordination by a vice-president for instruction was significant among accreditation regions, $X^2(5, N = 232) = 11.154, p = .048$. The WASC and NEASC regions reported less vice president responsibility for faculty development coordination than other regions.

Faculty Development Program Participation

With regard to faculty development participation, most responding colleges offered development activities to full-time faculty (79%) and part-time faculty (85%). Chi-square was significant for full-time faculty participation by

college size, $X^2(2, N = 232) = 24.073, p =. 0001$, and for part-time faculty participation, $X^2(2, N = 232) = 9.532, p = . 009$. The larger the college, the more
likely it was that either full-time or part-time faculty were eligible to participate. Over one-half the responding colleges (53%) reported no compensation
was available for participation in faculty development activities. The factor
most influencing participation was released time (50%), followed by personal
and professional growth (47%).

The accreditation regions were divided over compensation for faculty development participation. Most colleges in the NWASC (59%), SACS (53%),
and WASC (71%) provided compensation while most in the MSACS (76%),
NCACS (61%), and NEASC (75%) did not.

Faculty Development Program Funding
Nearly all responding colleges (n = 214; 93%) received funding for faculty development programs. The sources for funding most often reported were state
funds (76%), followed by grants (43%). Some institutions (35%) reported the
use of institutional funds and local operating budgets to support faculty development. The distribution of faculty development program funds was reported to be the responsibility of the vice president for instruction (50%) or
the faculty development committee (38%). How funds were distributed was
reported to be through the faculty development committee (58%) and individual departments (36%), followed by allotments directly to faculty (32%).
The percentage of college budget typically (97%) allotted to faculty development was under 5%.

Among accreditation regions, there were some significant standouts in the
area of funding, $X^2(5, N = 232) = 24.662, p =. 0001$.Fewer than half (48%) of
the colleges in the MSACS reported state funding for faculty development programs. How funds were distributed was significant, $X^2(5, N = 232) = 16.765,$
$p = .0005$. MSACS tended (50%) to allocate funds directly to faculty more
than in other regions. Colleges in WASC rarely allocated funds directly to faculty. Chi-square for funds allocated to part-time faculty was significant, $X^2(5,$
$N = 232) = 18.056, p = .003$. In NWASC a larger number of colleges (35%) target funds specifically for part-time faculty than all other regions (< 11%).

Faculty Development Program Evaluation
Less than one-half (47%) of the community colleges reported that they had
a formal evaluation process. Based on college size, chi-square was significant,
$X^2(2, N = 232) = 6.507$, p = .039, more medium than large or small schools
reported formal evaluation procedures. However, most (58%) of those who

reported an evaluation process did not have established criteria for evaluation. Chi-square by accreditation region for program evaluation was significant, $X^2(5, N = 232) = 13.192, p =. 022$. The WASC region had formal evaluation procedures more often than other regions. Chi-square for established criteria for program evaluation was also significant, $X^2(5, N=232) = 14.361, p = .013$. The WASC was more likely to provide established criteria than other accreditation regions. Faculty (76%) and administrators (64%) were most often reported to participate in the evaluation process. Colleges in the WASC region were less likely to have administrators participate in the evaluation process, $X^2(5, N = 232) = 13.835, p = .017$. The evaluation process was used in most institutions (78%) to determine new program direction, followed by outcome verification (63%) in regard to program goals.

DISCUSSION

Unlike previous research that reported a lack of comprehensive faculty development programs in community colleges (Hoerner, Clowes, & Impara, 1991; Murray, 1995, 1999, 2002; Richardson & Moore, 1987), this study concluded that the availability of faculty development in the four subcategories of professional, personal, organizational, and curricular was institution-wide across community colleges and accreditation regions and seemed to be well planned, coordinated, and supported and included part-time faculty.

Faculty development, as a formalized, structured, and comprehensive program for full- and part-time faculty in United States public community colleges, has grown in depth, breadth, and scope over the past 5 to 10 years. Community colleges are reexamining the role of part-time faculty in their institutions and making efforts to integrate professional, personal, curricular, and organizational goals into their faculty development program practices. The increasing ratio of part-time to full-time faculty (NEA, 2001) may have prompted the increase in practices for faculty development in both cohorts.

Community colleges seem to be more focused on institutional mission, that is, teaching and learning, than on enhancement of faculty knowledge alone. Hence, the frequency of occurrence of curricular and organizational practices was reported more often than more traditional practices, such as sabbatical leaves and conference attendance. The increase in curricular practices may also indicate that, with changing enrollment patterns, increased requirements for accountability, performance standards, student retention, and learning outcomes, faculty development must include practices to increase faculty knowledge about the teaching and learning process itself.

Orientation and enculturation of both full-time and part-time faculty is critical to institutional mission. Increased utilization of and reliance on part-time faculty necessitates the increase in efforts to integrate part-time faculty into the mainstream of the campus (Balch, 1999; Banachowski, 1996; Brewster, 2000). This change in faculty demographics changes the way education is delivered. Institutions, in this study, seemed to recognize that organizational fit, job satisfaction, and retention of qualified teaching staff is essential and cost effective.

Many institutions (40%) reported that personal development practices were not available, and, if they were, the most common was in the area of interpersonal skills. Schuster (1990) predicted an increase in this type of development practice, which could not be documented in this report. In accordance with O'Banion (1994), though, when faculty development for the purpose of personal growth leads to professional growth with improved organizational communication and student interaction and is linked to institutional goals, the result can be better institutions and better education.

With regard to faculty development content, it appears that more institutions are making efforts to meet the needs of individual faculty by developing programs that are cohesive and relevant to faculty interests and demographics and based on assessed needs. This confirmed the findings of Murray (1995, 1999, 2002) and Schuster, Wheeler, and Associates (1990) about faculty ownership of development programs. Also, according to Sandford and McCaslin (2003), community colleges should continually update professional development activities to meet changing faculty needs.

In this study, many vice presidents for instruction or academic deans completed the study survey, suggesting that these positions are most often recognized to be responsible for faculty development, even when a faculty development coordinator was in place. It appears that administrators remain responsible and accountable for implementation of and funding for faculty development programs.

With regard to faculty participation in development activities, it seems that most faculty are eligible. This may be due to several factors: 1) the need for a more technologically oriented and proficient faculty; 2) the recognition that a learning institution must promote individual learning for organizational development; and 3) the lifelong learning and continuing education philosophy of the community college dictates inclusion of all. In accord with Balch (1999), as community college leadership recognizes the strategic role all stakeholders play in institutional mission, professional development policies and procedures will be enhanced and better defined.

Compensation for participation in faculty development is a matter of extrinsic versus intrinsic incentives. Previous researchers reported that community colleges relied on intrinsic rewards based on faculty commitment and individual professionalism as appropriate incentives (Hoerner et al., 1991; Impara, Hoerner, Clowes, & Allkins, 1991). Sandford and McCaslin (2003) reported that both intrinsic and extrinsic rewards were perceived to be important in influencing part-time faculty participation. From the results of this study, faculty participation was voluntary and more influenced by intrinsic rather than extrinsic incentives or monetary awards.

Most community colleges (93%) received financial support for faculty development from multiple funding sources and spend 1%–5% of their total budget on faculty development. The cost effectiveness of hiring part-time faculty cannot diminish the need to fund professional development. As the number of part-time faculty increases, hiring rationale must be reexamined. Educational quality rather than economic pressures should weight hiring procedures and influence funding for faculty development.

Confirming the findings by Burnstad (1994), Maxwell and Kazlauskas (1992), and Murray (1999, 2002), most institutions have no formal evaluation process in place or established criteria to evaluate their programs. Evaluation procedures must be planned from the outset and implemented as an integral part of a comprehensive faculty development program in order to be effective.

CONCLUSIONS

Crucial to the academic integrity of the institution and consistent with the teaching and learning mission, community colleges must emphasize the importance of professional development of all faculty. To recruit and retain quality faculty, a formal, comprehensive program to orient, enculturate, renew, and develop all faculty is essential. Faculty development must be an integral part of the institution's strategic plan. Only a systemic approach to faculty development, with high-level administrative support and permanent funding sources, will effect institutional as well as individual change. In creating development programs that are relevant and focused on individual needs, institutions can address the growing diversity of faculty demographics, as well as incorporate processes that promote continuous institutional learning and innovation. Formal program evaluation, with established criteria, is critical to program integrity and viability. Differences in faculty development programs and practices along accreditation regions dictate further investigation of faculty development as tied to assessment, student retention, and learning outcomes.

Based on these conclusions a formal, systematic, and comprehensive model for faculty development is proposed. The generic nature of the model makes it applicable for either full- or part-time faculty and provides a framework in which the institution can structure an evolutionary faculty development program, which is specific to its culture and faculty demographics.

The components of this model are focused on the organizational, curricular, professional, and personal needs of the faculty and operationalized in five areas: administration, planning, program content, implementation, and evaluation. Administrative support, commitment of time, personnel, and financial resources are vital to program planning and practice. Planning begins with identification of institutional goals and assessment of faculty needs. Given that faculty ownership is imperative to the success of the model, a faculty development coordinator is designated and a council of full-time and part-time faculty selected. This group determines specific competencies, informed by needs analysis, to be achieved by relevant program activities. Measurable objectives are generated and linked to expected outcomes. Program implementation and participation demands program awareness and promotion. Formal criteria for program evaluation are established, which allow for continuous reassessment of program effectiveness.

As community colleges expand efforts to maximize professional development for part-time faculty, a model of development, tailored to achieve identified competencies and linked to institutional mission, can enhance and improve organizational, as well as, individual performance.

REFERENCES

American Association of State Colleges and Universities. (1999). *Facing change: Building the faculty of the future.* Washington, DC: Author.

Balch, P. (1999). Part-time faculty are here to stay. *Planning for Higher Education, 27*(3), 32–40.

Banachowski, G. (1996). Perspectives and perceptions: The use of part-time faculty in community colleges. *Community College Review, 24*(2), 49–62.

Bergquist, W. H., & Phillips, S. R. (1975). Components of an effective faculty development program. *Journal of Higher Education, 46*(2), 177–211.

Brewster, D. (2000). The use of part-time faculty in the community college. *Inquiry, 5*(1), 66–76.

Burnstad, H. M. (1994). Management of human resources in the community college. In G. A. Baker, III (Ed.), *A handbook on the community college in America: Its history, mission, and management* (pp. 386–395). Westport, CT: Greenwood Press.

Eble, K. E., & McKeachie, W. J. (1985). *Improving undergraduate education through faculty development.* San Francisco, CA: Jossey-Bass.

Gaff, J. G. (1975). *Toward faculty renewal: Advances in faculty, instructional, and organization development.* San Francisco, CA: Jossey-Bass.

Gappa, J. M., & Leslie, D. W. (1993). *The invisible faculty: Improving the status of part-timers in higher education.* San Francisco, CA: Jossey-Bass.

Gappa, J. M., & Leslie, D. W. (1997). *Two faculties or one? The conundrum of part-timers in a bifurcated workforce* (Inquiry No. 6). Washington, DC: American Association for Higher Education.

Hammons, J. (1983). Faculty development: A necessary corollary to faculty evaluation. In A. M. Cohen & F. B. Brawer (Eds.), *New directions for community colleges: No. 41. Evaluating faculty and staff* (pp. 75–82). San Francisco, CA: Jossey-Bass.

Hoerner, J., Clowes, D., & Impara, J. (1991). Professional development programs in community and technical colleges: Are occupational-technical faculty needs well served? *Journal of Studies in Technical Careers, 13*(4), 351–360.

Impara, J., Hoerner, J., Clowes, D., & Allkins, M. (1991). Professional development programs: A comparison of full-time and part-time occupational faculty. *Community Services Catalyst, 21*(2), 8–12.

Maxwell, W. E., & Kazlauskas, E. J. (1992). Which faculty development methods really work in community colleges? A review of research. *Community/Junior College Quarterly, 16,* 351–360.

Miller, D. J., & Ratcliff, J. L. (1986). Analysis of professional activities of Iowa Community College faculty. *Community/Junior College Journal, 10,* 317–343.

Murray, J. P. (1995). Faculty (mis)development in Ohio two-year colleges. *Community College Journal of Research and Practice, 19,* 549–593.

Murray, J. P. (1999). Faculty development in a national sample of community colleges. *Community College Review, 27*(3), 47–64.

Murray, J. P. (2002). Faculty development in SACS-accredited community colleges. *Community College Review, 29*(4), 50–67.

National Center for Education Statistics. (2002). *A profile of part-time faculty: Fall 1998.* Washington, DC: U.S. Department of Education.

National Education Association Higher Education Research Center. (2001). Part-time faculty. *Update, 7*(4), 1–4.

O'Banion, T. (1994a). Teaching and learning: A mandate for the nineties. *Community College Journal, 64*(4), 21–25.

Richardson, R., & Moore, W. (1987). Faculty development and evaluation in Texas community colleges. *Community/Junior College Quarterly, 11,* 19–32.

Roueche, J. E., Roueche, S. D., & Milliron, M. D. (1995). *Strangers in their own land: Part-time faculty in American community colleges.* Washington, DC: Community College Press.

Sandford, B., & McCaslin, N. L. (2003, October). *Assessment of professional development activities, instructional needs, and methods of delivery for part-time technical and occupational faculty in U.S. community colleges.* Paper presented at the Midwest Research to Practice Conference in Adult, Continuing, and Community Education, Columbus, OH. Retrieved May 9, 2004, from http://www.alumni-osu .org/midwest/midwest%20papers/Sandford%20&%20McCaslin--Done.pdf

Schuster, J. H. (1990). The need for fresh approaches to faculty renewal. In J. H. Schuster, D. W. Wheeler, & Associates (Eds.), *Enhancing faculty careers: Strategies for development and renewal* (pp. 3–19). San Francisco, CA: Jossey-Bass.

Schuster, J. H. (1995). Whither the faculty? The changing academic labor market. *Educational Record, 76*(4), 28–33.

Schuster, J. H., Wheeler, D. W., & Associates. (Eds.). (1990). *Enhancing faculty careers: Strategies for development and renewal.* San Francisco, CA: Jossey-Bass.

Williams, J. (1986). *A study of professional development practices of part-time instructors at selected League for Innovation community colleges.* Los Angeles, CA: League for Innovation in the Community College.

19

Entertaining Strangers: Providing for the Development Needs of Part-Time Faculty

Patricia Hanrahan Valley
Embry-Riddle Aeronautical University

For institutions of higher education that have increasingly relied upon part-time faculty members to meet the needs of a rapidly changing society, the challenge has been to provide adequate preparation and development opportunities for these instructors, many of whom have never taught before. This study investigated the characteristics of the part-time faculty, the extent to which they believed they had been oriented by the institution to assume their teaching roles, and their reported need for selected professional development activities at Embry-Riddle Aeronautical University's Extended Campus, an institution employing more than 2,800 adjuncts. The data provided by the needs assessment were instrumental in developing programs for part-time faculty development.

THE USE OF PART-TIME FACULTY IN HIGHER EDUCATION

The dawn of the 21st century has brought increasing concerns to higher education. Breneman (2002) noted that the recession in the early 2000s posed threats to an under-funded system and challenged the nation's commitment to accessibility for all qualified students as college tuition costs rose and student debt increased. Change, adaptation, and caution have characterized many institutions of higher education's approaches to these challenges. The continued call for educational reform and increased accountability has stimulated renewed emphasis on the quality of teaching at the undergraduate level while resources were dwindling.

Within this shifting context, institutions of higher education have continued to employ a large number of part-time faculty to teach primarily undergraduate courses. As the number of nontraditional students has continued to increase and institutions have adapted their missions and programs to meet the demands of the market, changing patterns in academic employment have been redefining faculty roles. The demand for new degree programs has created more need for specialized faculty, and at the same time budgets have been leaner and faculty have been called upon to bring more varied qualifications and preparation to the academy. The primary reasons for the growing numbers of part-time faculty have been increases in student enrollment and in the number of programs offered, along with static revenue.

Colleges and universities have continued to employ a large number of part-time faculty to teach primarily undergraduate courses. Roueche, Roueche, and Milliron (1995) reported that part-time faculty did approximately 45% of all teaching in higher education. Institutions with large extension programs, such as Nova Southeastern University, University of Phoenix, University of Maryland's University College, and Embry-Riddle Aeronautical University employ primarily part-time faculty (Haeger, 1998). Roueche et al. (1995) observed that part-time faculty brought expertise from the real world to technical and vocational programs, and Fulton (2000) suggested that appropriate uses for part-time faculty within colleges and universities exist that "enhance program quality and . . . provide a variety of experiences for students" (p. 39). Fulton maintained that hiring practicing experts in specific fields (e.g., hiring a dynamic marketing executive to teach a marketing seminar) makes sense, and Jacobs (1998) noted that part-time faculty who are practitioners in their field often have access to resources and other experts that benefit the institution. They provide a link between instruction and the practices in industry.

THE NEEDS OF PART-TIME FACULTY

The Need for Integration Into the Academic Community
With the increasing changes in mission, programs, and personnel, a number of academic and institutional issues have surfaced that have to be addressed if colleges and universities are to effectively meet their missions. Roueche, Roueche, and Milliron (1996a) indicated that colleges and universities would have to improve the integration of the part-time faculty into the academic community as well as develop systemic plans for change that would clarify the purpose, mission, and major goals of adjunct employment and development.

Gappa and Leslie (1993) reported that part-time faculty members were often regarded as consumable resources rather than as contributors to the health and integrity of the organization. They suggested that if part-time faculty were incorporated into the institution, they would bring greater commitment and continuity to their roles. Leslie (1998), Lyons, Kysilka, & Pawlas (1999) and Roueche et al. (1995) stated that part-time faculty must be regarded as a vital part of the academic community, as the extent to which the institution integrates these faculty members into their organizations determines to a large degree the extent to which the institution will meet its mission.

The Need for Improved Working Conditions

Some part-time faculty members have experienced what they believe to be less than satisfactory working conditions. Leslie (1998) reported that "... the global picture of part-time faculty attitudes is one of competence, high morale, and a healthy level of professional engagement. But pockets of discontent exist" (p. 4). Leslie concluded that the general sources of dissatisfaction for part-time faculty were working conditions and institutional culture. Conditions such as low pay, no benefits, lack of office space, and little job security coupled with minimal status within the department or college separate the part-time instructor from the full-time faculty, create inequity, and damage the institution.

The American Federation of Teachers (2002) recommended standards that would equitably adjust pay scales, provide for adjunct evaluation, establish an adjunct promotion system, and compensate part-timers for office hours and committee service. Leslie (1998) relayed that

> ... the effectiveness and validity of the whole higher education enterprise is entangled in the question of what faculty do, how their work and careers are constructed, and whether they can achieve the ends that society wants from its colleges and universities. (p. 6)

The Need for Faculty Development

The development of the part-time faculty is essential if the institutions that employ them are to foster effective teaching and learning. As part-time faculty have become an integral part of teaching and learning at many institutions, supplying students with a wealth of knowledge from industry and permitting greater flexibility in class scheduling, the challenge of providing support and development that enhances faculty effectiveness has increased.

Eble and McKeachie (1985) defined faculty development as "programs to promote faculty growth, to help faculty members acquire knowledge, skills, and sensitivities" (p. 11). Gaff (1975) described faculty development as activities that further the instructional, professional, and personal growth of faculty members. Faculty development programs vary in mission, although the majority of programs for part-time faculty emphasize instructional development as a means of improving teaching and learning. Instructional development has been defined as "programs that facilitate student learning, prepare learning materials, and redesign courses" (Eble & McKeachie, 1985, p. 11). According to Bensimon, Ward, and Sanders (2000) and Wunsch (1994), the specific goals for faculty development programs generally include orienting faculty to the culture of the university, developing a collegial atmosphere, and exposing faculty to best teaching practices.

Gappa (1984) observed that most part-time faculty members are not hired for their pedagogical knowledge, but rather for their professional competence; thus, many of them have no familiarity with college practices and procedures. Nor do they necessarily understand students' educational needs. Wyles (1998) has maintained that colleges and universities must take these factors into consideration when planning orientation and development programs, as the adjuncts' needs may be quite different from those of the full-time faculty.

Over half of new adjuncts arrive at universities having never been fully responsible for teaching a course. Their first preparation needs are securing class materials, designing course syllabi, and setting class expectations. They need to develop a sound plan for teaching their courses. Unfortunately, the degree to which institutions meet these course preparation needs varies. Lyons et al. (1999) observed that sometimes institutions provide a course outline, sample syllabus, textbook, and other course materials to the instructor, while in other instances the adjunct is expected to develop a new course with little support or direction. Regardless of the degree of course preparation needed, Lyons et al. and Stone (1996) maintained that part-time faculty members should understand how to set course goals and design clear course objectives based on Bloom's taxonomy of cognitive learning.

Lankard (1993) reported that orientation is crucial in developing faculty loyalty and commitment. O'Banion (1994) noted that part-time faculty need to understand the mission of the institution, and Boice (1992) suggested that they also need to understand the expectations the institution has of them, realize how to acclimate to the institution, and grasp the policies and other technical aspects of the institution that affect them. New faculty members also need to understand the learner and how to use a variety of instructional strategies. Keim and Biletzky (1999) found in their study of part-time faculty teaching at four community colleges that faculty who participate in development activities are more likely to use a variety of teaching strategies, such as small-group discussions, demonstrations, and activities that promote critical thinking.

Four approaches to faculty support and development have been commonly used for part-time faculty (Approaches to Staff Development, 1986).

- Curriculum development approach: provides for workshops and other courses that help part-timers improve their teaching

- Peer support network approach: enables instructors to turn to each other for help and support

- Personnel management approach: structures policies for effective recruitment, orientation, and staff development

- Adult education: recognizes that as adults, faculty members learn best when their needs are recognized

More vehicles for program delivery exist than ever before. Steinert (2000) noted that faculty development programs can utilize computer-based delivery methods to target the specific needs of individual faculty members, and Gillespie (1998) considered computer-based programs to be appropriate methods for teaching faculty, especially if faculty are to be encouraged to use technology in their classrooms. Killion (2000) noted that a variety of online learning options exist for the delivery of information via the Internet or CD-ROM, ranging from simple email to more sophisticated means such as streaming video, chat rooms, bulletin boards, and online course platforms that provide many functions in one package. Branzburg and Kennedy (2001) found that the best online learning experiences for teachers' professional development employ web-based communication tools such as course email, bulletin boards, and teacher training courses.

THE SETTING OF THE STUDY

Embry-Riddle Aeronautical University (ERAU) is committed to promoting teaching effectiveness through faculty development, the use of current technologies and methodologies, and the production of scholarship that tangibly improves teaching. The university seeks to provide all faculty, including its over 2,800 part-time faculty members, with a working environment that fosters professional development and that encourages the use of innovative techniques and methodologies, realizing the valuable role that faculty have played in molding the lives of the future leaders of the aviation and aerospace community.

The Extended Campus's mission has been to educate adult students, and the campus has targeted its programs to meet the educational needs of nontraditional undergraduate and graduate students who are usually involved in either the military or industry and seeking education that relates directly to the workplace. The best-qualified individuals to teach these working adults are credentialed professionals involved full-time in industry or the military.

The employment of part-time faculty has provided a number of benefits to Embry-Riddle's Extended Campus. Of paramount significance has been the up-to-date information and relevant, real-life illustrations of textbook concepts that these experts from industry bring to their adult students, and the flexibility in course scheduling. Although most new faculty members have never taught before coming to ERAU, their energy and enthusiasm for their subjects has resulted in generally high teaching evaluations from their students.

At the time of the study in fall 2002, ERAU was a multicampus institution with three distinct campus divisions: two residential campuses and an extended campus. The university served 6,156 undergraduate and 318 graduate students, for a total of 6,474 students on its two residential campuses. ERAU's Extended Campus offered both classroom and online courses and degrees via a network of over 130 teaching centers located throughout the United States and Europe, as well as a large distance learning department. The Extended Campus served an unduplicated annual headcount of 25,801 adult students from fall 2001 to summer 2002. Of the 4,202 degrees granted to students from all three campuses from June 2001 to July 2002, 2,812 were undergraduate and 1,008 were graduate students.

DESIGN OF THE STUDY

The study was conducted as a part of ERAU's Extended Campus's ongoing efforts toward enhancing teaching effectiveness through faculty development. The population of the study was composed of 1,212 part-time faculty members who had taught at least one course for ERAU's Extended Campus from August 15, 2001, to August 15, 2002. A total of 500 part-time faculty members were selected by simple random sample and were mailed surveys. A total of 406 completed surveys (81.2% response rate) were returned. The survey instrument was based on the following dimensions of faculty development: orientation, knowledge of the institution, faculty meetings, content delivery preferences, and the elements of effective teaching.

FINDINGS OF THE STUDY

Characteristics of the Institution's Part-Time Faculty

As ERAU educates students for careers primarily in aviation and aerospace, it was not unexpected to learn that 83.5% (338) of the part-time faculty members who responded were male. The majority of the respondents were between 40 to 64 years old. Two-thirds of the faculty possessed a master's degree, and almost one-third possessed a doctoral degree. Total years of teaching experience varied, with 18.4% of the faculty having a total of one to two years of college or university teaching experience, and 15.6% having 15 or more years of experience. The majority of the part-time faculty (44.6%) had taught one to two years at ERAU; however, a total of 29.4% reported teaching for six or more years. A majority of the faculty indicated that they taught for the satisfaction of teaching (56.3%), while another 17% taught for the professional experience. An additional 13.5% reported that their primary motivation was to earn extra income.

Faculty's Orientation to Their Teaching Roles

The respondents reported that during orientation they were most concerned with understanding the university's academic policies, writing the course syllabus, and gaining access to course materials, and that they were least concerned with how they would teach and the preparation of lesson plans. These findings fit with the needs of new part-time faculty as reported by Roueche et al. (1996b) who stated that providing new part-time faculty with information about the course to be taught and how the course fits into the broader curriculum was very important. The focus of new part-time faculty and those who oriented them to ERAU centered on the immediate concerns of understanding institutional academic policies and the preparation of course materials, while how they would actually teach the course was of less immediate concern.

Part-Time Faculty's Knowledge of the Institution

Respondents rated the level of importance and their level of understanding of each of the variables that constituted knowledge of the institution: understanding the institution's mission, knowledge of academic programs, knowledge of new events, and knowledge of new policies. The respondents considered understanding the mission of the institution to be most important. Next in importance to the respondents was the need to understand the institutions' academic programs; understanding new policies was also considered somewhat important; and of least importance to the respondents was receiving knowledge of new institutional events.

A small but statistically significant difference was found between the faculty's level of understanding and ascribed level of importance for each of the following: the institution's mission, the knowledge of academic programs, the knowledge of new events, and the knowledge of new policies. Thus, it was concluded that the part-time faculty valued possessing knowledge of the institution's mission, academic programs, new events, and new policies, and that the faculty would benefit from receiving more information in these areas. It was also concluded that means of communication with the faculty would have to improve to address this need.

Part-Time Faculty's Participation in Faculty Meetings

The majority of the respondents reported that the benefits of collegial relationships and obtaining current information about ERAU they received from attendance at local faculty meetings was somewhat high or high. The faculty members' perceptions regarding the benefit of attending faculty meetings in improving their teaching was more varied. One-fourth indicated that the benefit was high; over one-fourth reported that the benefit was somewhat high; and one-fourth reported the benefit was somewhat low. The top three benefits of attending local faculty meetings reported by the participants were forming collegial relationships, obtaining current information about ERAU, and improving their teaching.

Significant differences were found between the benefit of obtaining current information about ERAU at faculty meetings and its importance and between the benefit of improving teaching and its importance. Thus, it was concluded that part-time faculty would benefit from receiving more current information and help in improving teaching at faculty meetings.

Both collegiality and obtaining new information were significant predictors of attendance at faculty meetings, which indicated that these factors were most likely important elements of faculty meetings. Most faculty attended two or three of the four faculty meetings scheduled annually. The most frequently reported hindrance from attending faculty meetings was work responsibilities, with 48.3% listing this as a factor that prevented attendance. A little over one-fourth indicated that they were never hindered from attending faculty meetings; 8.9% missed meetings for reasons other than those listed in the survey; 8.6% missed meetings because of family obligations; 6.9% reported missing due to a long drive to faculty meetings; and only 1.7% reported that faculty meetings were not beneficial.

Expressed Interest in Specific Areas of Professional Development

Course organization. Almost three-quarters of the respondents reported their level of understanding regarding course organization to be high, while over three-quarters reported their perception of the importance of course organization to be high. Thus, no significant difference between the level of understanding and the level of importance of course organization was found.

Improving student writing. Respondents' understanding of improving student writing was lower than their understanding of course organization. Two-thirds of the faculty rated the importance of improving student writing as high, and one-quarter listed the importance of this area as somewhat high. A significant difference between the level of understanding and the level of importance of improving student writing was found.

Use of technology. Over half of the respondents reported their understanding of using technology in the classroom as high, and one-third considered their understanding to be somewhat high. Over half reported their perception of the importance of using technology in the classroom as high, and over one-third considered their perception to be somewhat high. No significant difference between the level of understanding and the level of importance of using technology in the classroom was found.

Assessment of student progress. The respondents appeared confident in their understanding of assessing student progress, with over one-half rating their understanding as high, and one-third indicating their understanding to be somewhat high. Almost three-quarters of the faculty rated their perception of the importance of assessing student progress as high, and the rest indicated their perception to be somewhat high. Thus, a significant difference between the level of understanding and the level of importance in assessing student progress was found.

Accessing library services. The part-time faculty seemed less sure of their understanding of helping students gain access to library services. Only 35.9% rated their understanding as high in this area, and 41.1% indicated their understanding as somewhat high. Half rated their perception of the importance of helping students gain access to library services as high, and another 37% indicated its importance as somewhat high. A significant difference between the level of understanding and the level of importance of helping students gain access to library services was found.

Expressed Interest in and Use of Teaching Strategies

The faculty were interested in and used class discussion, with two-thirds of the faculty reporting high use and high interest. The next item to receive a large number of high ratings was the use of lecture, with almost everyone reporting their use of lecture as either high or somewhat high. The majority indicated a high interest in critical thinking. Simulations, in-class quizzes, and demonstrations were used least and were also less frequently used. Significant differences were found between the levels of use and the levels of interest in class discussion, lecture, critical thinking, writing activities, written feedback, small group discussion, group projects, hands-on activities, simulations, and demonstrations.

The findings indicated that part-time faculty members were interested in learning how to use written feedback in their teaching. They were also interested in learning more about using the teaching strategies of critical thinking, writing activities, group projects, hands-on activities, simulations, and demonstrations. The large number of faculty who did not employ a wide range of teaching strategies also suggested that the part-time faculty would benefit from faculty development activities related to teaching strategies, as Keim and Biletzky (1999) found that faculty who participate in development activities are more likely to use a variety of teaching strategies.

Conclusions and Improvement to Practice

Orientation to the Teaching Role

The results of the study indicated that new part-time faculty members' first orientation need is to obtain information on the course to be taught, with help in writing the course syllabus and accessing course resources. The new faculty members needed to understand academic policies, and they needed information on how to organize lesson plans and how to teach.

Interestingly, the faculty reported their need of information on how to teach as lower than the amount of information that they received. However, the faculty's reported use of only a few teaching strategies indicates that they do need more teaching information. Two factors may have influenced the reported low need of teaching information: 1) Concern for the immediate need of preparation as opposed to the more distant need for teaching information, and 2) over-confidence stemming from the common belief, especially of novices, that teaching is a natural ability for which one does not need special instruction. Quite possibly, the new faculty did not realize the benefits of learning how to teach.

As a result of the study, the Center for Teaching and Learning Effectiveness (CTLE) produced a series of online, customizable orientation modules that every new faculty member was required to complete before teaching for ERAU. Four modules were developed: 1) Introduction to Embry-Riddle, 2)

Preparing to Teach, 3) How to Teach, and 4) and Introduction to Aviation. The appropriate modules were assigned to new adjuncts by their chairs, and the chairs monitored the new instructors' successful completion of the orientation modules.

The Faculty Orientation Manual was also updated to provide the new adjuncts with a hardcopy source of current academic information relevant to their teaching.

Identification With the Institution

The part-time faculty needed more knowledge of the institution, which would help them to feel more a part of the university. Specifically, the faculty wanted more communication of information in all four areas mentioned in the survey: institutional mission, knowledge of academic programs, knowledge of new events, and knowledge of new programs. As a result of the study, all 3,000 part-time faculty members were given university email accounts and access to the university intranet. This greatly improved the institution's ability to communicate with the part-time faculty members.

Faculty meetings were viewed as beneficial by a majority of the part-time faculty, and the meetings helped the faculty form and maintain collegial relationships. The respondents also reported that obtaining current information about the university and improving teaching were important at faculty meetings. As a result, the CTLE began producing workshops on teaching. A train-the-trainer approach was used to ensure that all faculty had the opportunity to benefit from the workshop material. The director of CTLE presented the workshops and also provided support materials at the annual regional meetings attended by the center faculty chairs (CFCs), so that the CFCs could tailor the workshop material and present it to their part-time faculty at local faculty meetings.

Both collegiality and obtaining new information were significant predictors of meeting attendance. The most frequently reported hindrance from attending faculty meetings was work responsibilities, and over 25% indicated that they were never hindered from attending faculty meetings. Thus, it appeared that the majority of part-time faculty members perceived the meetings as beneficial, and their reasons for not being able to attend were not related to the quality of the meetings. The addition of the workshop support materials and videos produced by CTLE further enhanced the instructional benefit of attending the meetings.

Preferred Delivery Methods for Professional Development

The most preferred delivery methods for professional development were as follows: 1) attending conferences, 2) workshops at faculty meetings, 3) access to course-specific teaching advice on the web, 4) completing teacher training courses online, and (5) receiving email bulletins. The respondents reported needing information to help in improving student writing, assessing student progress, helping students access library services, and using a variety of teaching strategies. Faculty were interested in learning how to use written feedback in their teaching, incorporating critical thinking into their lessons, developing writing activities, directing group projects, providing hands-on activities, creating simulations, and conducting demonstrations. Accordingly, these topics were slated for future workshops.

Implementation of Programs

As a result of this study, programs to promote the development of the part-time faculty were implemented. Initiatives included producing a video on teaching with technology, providing partial funding for part-time faculty members to present at conferences, and promoting the scholarship of teaching and learning as an activity in which part-time faculty can participate (conducting action research in the classroom and sharing with colleagues at faculty meetings).

An online orientation was developed and became mandatory for all new faculty. Responsibility for the oversight of the orientation was delegated to the center faculty chairs, and the program was very successful in preparing new faculty to teach. Regional faculty meeting agendas were expanded to included at least one teaching and learning presentation or activity that the center faculty chairs could take back to use with the part-time faculty at their centers. Faculty meetings were used to promote part-time faculty members' professional development.

A committee was formed to further investigate ways of meeting the development needs of the adjuncts and to conduct a comparative review of part-time faculty pay. The practice of electing two representatives from the part-time faculty in each of the institution's regions to the faculty senate continued, as the practice was invaluable in providing the institution with the perspective of the adjuncts.

ERAU has made significant progress toward addressing the needs of its adjuncts and remains committed to providing students with well-prepared instructors possessing both academic credentials and industry experience. An institution like ERAU, whose reputation depends on the quality of its adjuncts, must adequately provide for their orientation and development, and meeting their stated needs was instrumental in the successful implementation of the faculty development programs.

References

American Federation of Teachers. (2002). *Standards of good practice in the employment of part-time/adjunct faculty: Fairness and equity.* Washington, DC: Author. Retrieved May 9, 2004 from http://www.aft.org/higher_ed/images/Booklet.pdf

Approaches to staff development for part-time faculty. (1986, July 1). *ERIC Digest.* (ERIC Document Reproduction Service No. ED270180). Retrieved May 9, 2004, from http://www.ericfacility.net/databases/ERIC_Digests/ed270180.html

Bensimon, E. M., Ward, K., & Sanders, K. (2000). *The department chair's role in developing new faculty into teachers and scholars.* Bolton, MA: Anker.

Boice, R. (1992). *The new faculty member.* San Francisco, CA: Jossey-Bass.

Branzburg, J., & Kennedy, K. (2001, September). Online professional development. *Technology and Learning, 22*(2), 18–27.

Breneman, D. W. (2002, July 14). For colleges, this is not just another recession. *Chronicle of Higher Education,* p. B7.

Eble, K. E., & McKeachie, W. J. (1985). *Improving undergraduate education through faculty development.* San Francisco, CA: Jossey-Bass.

Fulton, R. D. (2000, May). The plight of part-timers in higher education. *Change, 32*(3), 38–42.

Gaff, J. G. (1975). *Toward faculty renewal: Advances in faculty, instructional, and organization development.* San Francisco, CA: Jossey-Bass.

Gappa, J. M. (1984). *Part-time faculty: Higher education at a crossroads* (ASHE-ERIC Higher Education Research Report No. 3). Washington, DC: Association for the Study of Higher Education.

Gappa, J. M., & Leslie, D. W. (1993). *The invisible faculty: Improving the status of part-timers in higher education.* San Francisco, CA: Jossey-Bass.

Gillespie, K. H. (Ed.). (1998). The impact of technology on faculty development, life, and work. *New directions for teaching and learning: No. 76. The impact of technology on faculty development, life, and work.* San Francisco, CA: Jossey-Bass.

Haeger, J. D. (1998). Part-time faculty, quality programs, and economic realities. In D. W. Leslie (Ed.), *New directions for higher education: No. 104. The growing use of part-time faculty: Understanding causes and effects* (pp. 81–88). San Francisco, CA: Jossey-Bass.

Jacobs, F. (1998). Using part-time faculty more effectively. In D. W. Leslie (Ed.), *New directions for higher education: No. 104. The growing use of part-time faculty: Understanding causes and effects* (pp. 9–17). San Francisco, CA: Jossey-Bass.

Keim, M. C., & Biletzky, P. (1999, December). Teaching methods used by part-time community college faculty. *Community College Journal of Research & Practice, 23,* 727–737.

Killion, J. P. (2000, Summer). Log on to learn. *Journal of Staff Development, 21*(3), 48–53.

Lankard, B. A. (1993). *Part-time instructors in adult and vocational education.* Columbus, OH: ERIC Clearinghouse on Adult, Career, and Vocational Education. (ERIC Reproduction Service No ED363797)

Leslie, D. W. (1998). New directions for research, policy development, and practice. In D. W. Leslie (Ed.), *New directions for higher education: No. 104. The growing use of part-time faculty: Understanding causes and effects* (pp. 95–100). San Francisco, CA: Jossey-Bass.

Lyons, R. E., Kysilka, M. L., & Pawlas, G. E. (1999). *The adjunct professor's guide to success.* Boston, MA: Allyn and Bacon.

O'Banion, T. (1994). *Teaching and learning in the community college.* Washington, DC: Community College Press.

Roueche, J. E., Roueche, S. D., & Milliron, M. D. (1995). *Strangers in their own land: Part-time faculty in American community colleges.* Washington, DC: Community College Press.

Roueche, J. E., Roueche, S. D., & Milliron, M. D. (1996a, Spring). Identifying the strangers: Exploring part-time faculty integration in American community colleges. *Community College Review, 23*(4), 33–48.

Roueche, J. E., Roueche, S. D., & Milliron, M. D. (1996b, March). In the company of strangers: Addressing the utilization and integration of part-time faculty in American community colleges. *Community College Journal of Research and Practice, 20*(2), 105–117.

Steinert, Y. (2000, January). Faculty development in the new millennium: Key challenges and future directions. *Medical Teacher, 22,* 44–50.

Stone, T. E. (1996). Developing instructional objectives, lesson plans, and syllabi. In V. Bianco-Mathis & N. Chalofsky (Eds.), *The adjunct faculty handbook* (pp. 28–39). Thousand Oaks, CA: Sage.

Wunsch, M. A. (1994). New directions for mentoring: An organizational development perspective. In M. A. Wunsch, R. J. Menges, & M. D. Svinicki (Eds.), *New directions for teaching and learning: No. 57. Mentoring revisited: Making an impact on individuals and institutions* (pp. 9–13). San Francisco, CA: Jossey-Bass.

Wyles, B. (1998). Adjunct faculty in the community college: Realities and challenges. In D. W. Leslie (Ed.), *New directions for higher education: No. 104. The growing use of part-time faculty: Understanding causes and effects* (pp. 89–93). San Francisco, CA: Jossey-Bass.

20

Promoting a Sound Process for Teaching Awards Programs: Appropriate Work for Faculty Development Centers

Nancy Van Note Chism
Indiana University–Purdue University Indianapolis

Examination of a sample of teaching awards programs at colleges and universities in the United States shows that the selection process for most is not based on explicit criteria, evidence that matches the criteria, and announced standards for making judgments about the candidates. If teaching awards programs are to be effective on any level, whether serving as a symbol of institutional commitment, affirming good teachers, or inspiring others to teach well, the quality of their selection process must be credible. This chapter provides recommendations for how faculty development centers can help their institutions to craft a selection process that will enhance their existing programs or help shape new ones.

INTRODUCTION

Nestled within a department structure or highly visible at the campus level, teaching awards programs are part of the landscape at many colleges and universities. Some programs are carefully planned and thoughtfully enacted, but others are fraught with problems. As part of their organizational development mission to support and enhance the conditions within which teaching takes place, faculty development centers can make an important contribution by helping to ensure that teaching awards programs on their campuses are intentional and effective.

314

This chapter reports findings from a study of teaching awards at colleges and universities in the United States and focuses on ways in which faculty development centers can help to improve awards programs on their campuses.

TEACHING AWARDS LITERATURE

The body of literature on teaching awards programs is small and often directed to purposes other than assessing the quality of the programs. For example, Lowman (1994) examined the nomination letters submitted for an awards program to arrive at characteristics commonly associated with excellent teaching, rather than to draw implications about the programs themselves. Often, the work that has been published on teaching awards is solely descriptive, with national or multicampus systems surveying the programs in operation within their purview or locale and summarizing the program features (Adams, 1977; Francis, 1976; McNaught & Anwyl, 1993; Warren & Plumb, 1999).

Some work has been done on the impact of awards programs (Chism & Szabo, 1997; Francis, 1976; McNaught & Anwyl, 1993), finding that awards programs reinforce and support good teaching and are important for publicly affirming the importance that the institution places on teaching but have little documented direct impact on teaching improvement through motivating other faculty to earn awards by teaching better.

Carusetta (2001) uses a framework proposed by Menges (1996) for evaluating the soundness of an awards program in assessing a program at her campus. Yet studies do not seem to exist that analyze the type of criteria, evidence, and standards in use by teaching awards programs.

The study addressed the following research questions:

- What criteria are teaching awards programs based on?

- In order to make judgments, what kinds of evidence do teaching awards programs collect?

- What standards do awards programs use to judge the evidence?

- Is there a match between the criteria and the evidence sought?

METHODS

The study began with a survey of teaching awards programs that were described on the World Wide Web. The list of teaching centers on the web site of the Center for Teaching Excellence at the University of Kansas was used as part of a purposeful sampling strategy (Patton, 2002) that focuses on sources that are most likely to be information-rich, based on the reasoning that campuses with teaching centers were also more likely to have awards programs. If teaching awards programs were not described on the site of the teaching center, the academic affairs page of the institution or the campus web site were examined, using search engines. The decision rules for inclusion allowed only those programs for which complete information was available on the web (programs for which a packet of information had to be picked up or a telephone call made were excluded) and only those awards programs that were explicitly for teaching. This search produced usable information on 118 awards programs at 66 institutions.

In this first sample, two-year institutions and liberal arts colleges were underrepresented. This result may be due either to the fact that there are fewer awards programs at these institutions or that they use the World Wide Web less frequently to post information. To obtain more information from two-year and liberal arts colleges, a special email survey for information was sent to the chief academic officer at a random sample of 100 of these institutions, using lists from the Carnegie Classification of Institutions of Higher Education web site (http://www.carnegiefoundation.org/Classification/index.htm). This search produced usable information on 26 programs at 19 institutions, bringing the total sample to 144 programs at 85 institutions located in 33 states. Of these, 45 are classified as Doctoral/Research Universities-Extensive; 10 as Doctoral/Research Universities-Intensive; 13 as Master's Colleges and Universities I or II; 12 as Baccalaureate Colleges-General; and 5 as Community Colleges.

The information that was extracted from the program descriptions pertained to the criteria the programs list, the evidence that they seek, and the standards that they use in making the decisions on teaching award winners. Three coders worked with the data, differences were reconciled in meetings, and the codes and data excerpts were entered into a database for sorting and display.

Findings

In exploring the criteria, evidence, and standards and the match between these within a given awards program, the study relied on Angelo's (1996) definition of these factors of interest: "In the jargon of assessment and evaluation, the criteria of exemplary teaching will tell us *what* to look for; the indicators *where;* and the standards *how"* (p. 58).

No program in the sample explicitly listed standards for judging award winners. Perhaps judges in some programs use rating sheets that may indicate some level of excellence or procedures that call for them to rank candidates against each other using some scale that may or may not have reference points, but these were not publicly available.

With respect to criteria and evidence, more data were found. Table 20.1 displays the categories that were developed to accommodate the information on criteria.

TABLE 20.1
Criteria Used in Teaching Awards Programs in Study

%	#	Criteria Category Name Sample	Size: n = 144
52	73	Global (excellent teacher) as the only criterion, or no criteria specified at all	
38	55	Specific characteristics of teaching performance listed	
29	42	Impact on student learning, promotion of learning outside classroom	
27	39	Student-centered approach, shows concern for growth and development	
24	35	Content knowledge, mastery of subject	
20	29	Leadership in promoting teaching on campus	
16	23	Range of teaching activities undertaken during career or current practice	
16	23	Curriculum development efforts, innovation in teaching	
13	18	Other	
8	12	Scholarship of teaching activities	
6	8	Professional development efforts	
5	7	Rigor of standards for student performance	

Note: With the exception of the first factor, percentages reflect the use of multiple criteria and thus do not total 100%.

Additional data that add to the information in the table include:

- When programs listed specific characteristics of teaching, these clustered into the following categories: communication skills, organization, high standards, clear goals, enthusiasm, strategies for student engagement, and focus on higher order thinking skills.

- Within the "Other" category are the following: 1) listed by six programs (4% of the sample)—appreciation for diversity; 2) mentioned by two programs—citizenship, openness to new ideas, resourcefulness, and interdisciplinary teaching; and 3) mentioned by only one program each—

record of obtaining grants for teaching, participation in recruiting efforts, and visibility outside campus.

Table 20.2 displays findings on the evidence of teaching excellence specified by the 144 programs in the sample.

TABLE 20.2
Evidence Requested by Teaching Awards Programs in Study

%	#	Evidence Category Name	Sample Size: n = 144
92	133	Letters	
		• Nomination letters (29%; 38% = with letters of support)	
		• Letters of support (63%; 62% = more than one kind)	
		⁓ from current or former students (44%)	
		⁓ from peers/other faculty (41%)	
		⁓ from administrators (deans, chairs) (20%)	
		⁓ from unspecified writers (6%)	
61	88	Student ratings of instruction	
49	70	Curriculum vitae	
37	53	Philosophy of teaching statement	
28	40	List of teaching responsibilities	
25	36	Other	
20	29	Syllabi or other course materials	
20	29	Peer review summary or summary of classroom observation	
14	20	Teaching portfolio (3% = specific contents; 11% = unspecified contents)	
13	19	List of professional contributions in teaching (papers, presentations)	
12	17	List of contributions to promotion of teaching on campus	
10	15	List of previous rewards or recognitions for teaching	
8	12	Unspecified "additional documentation," coupled with other evidence	
8	12	Documentation of involvement with students outside classroom	
7	10	Description of growth in teaching and self-learning over time	
7	10	List of professional development activities in teaching	
6	9	Descriptions of innovations in teaching	
5	7	No evidence specified at all (send "documentation")	

Note: Percentages reflect the use of multiple types of evidence and thus do not total 100%.

With respect to the letter as the most popular form of evidence, some additional data include:

- 33% of the programs rely on nomination letters or letters of support alone and require no other source of evidence.

- 41% of the programs that ask for letters call for multiple letters of support.

- In 74% of the cases calling for letters of nomination or support, the letter writers are not given any instructions about what their letter should address.

- Only one program asks that the letter writers have specific evidence (the candidate's teaching portfolio) before them when they write their letters.

- Four of the 144 programs state that the letter writer should have first-hand knowledge of the candidate's teaching, one of which requires that the person have team-taught, been part of a teaching circle, or participated in curriculum development with the candidate.

The "No evidence specified" category, coded in the case of seven programs, includes directions to nominators or candidates to send appropriate documentation, with no more specific details on this. In 12 cases, requests were made for an appendix or "supporting documentation" to be submitted in addition to other evidence.

Evidence requirements that were not frequently mentioned across the sample were coded as "Other." These included grade distribution charts, votes of students, a list of favorite web sites, a record of outreach teaching to local high schools, videotapes, and telephone interviews with the committee.

One additional observation that can be made about the findings in general is that several awards programs are constructed around a two-stage process, whereby votes or letters are solicited during the first phase, and then selected candidates are invited to submit additional materials during the second phase.

DISCUSSION

The most striking observation on the criteria employed by teaching awards programs at U.S. colleges and universities is that for over half of the programs in this study's sample, no criteria more specific than "teaching excellence" are mentioned. The most common source of evidence is the letter, for which the writer is typically not given any instruction on what to address nor has any standard information about the candidate from which to write the letter.

Clearly, most teaching awards programs operate under the assumption that we do not need to be explicit about what we are awarding and that we know it when we see it.

Moreover, by failing to match criteria to evidence, these programs are collecting evidence that may not address their criteria (when they have them) or give them irrelevant materials. The reliance by most awards programs on secondary forms of evidence (such as appraisals by others) rather than primary evidence (such as course materials, teaching philosophy statements, or samples of student work) indicates reluctance on the part of many committees to actually engage the evidence firsthand.

The process of having two phases to an awards competition is another issue that influences the process in potentially undesirable ways. While it is advantageous to screen candidates, both for the efficiency of the selection process and the faculty who are preparing nomination materials, it is no less important at this stage to do so in a systematic way, since the results of the first phase necessarily influence the final selection.

Although the findings from this study indicate a range of problems inherent in the design of awards programs generally, it must also be pointed out that many programs have exemplary qualities, some in identifying criteria and aligning these with campus statements on teaching excellence, others in the careful specification of evidence. These components can be held forth as models for good practice. (See Appendix 20.1 for some examples.)

When teaching awards are unsystematic, however, several possible reasons may exist. First, the teaching awards may be more symbolic than substantive. In other words, as long as some people are chosen and elevated, the awards program has served its goal by making support for teaching visible. Second, awards program committees may feel that they have to take shortcuts in making judgments since it would be too time-consuming to do a thorough job. Many awards programs are low-stakes activities that involve a plaque or small monetary award. So investing a lot of time in making the awards decision might not seem worthwhile to the committee. Third, not much thought may go into the development of awards programs, or fourth, their framers may not have much knowledge of teaching and learning.

The mixture of findings in the literature on the impacts of teaching awards programs noted at the start of this chapter might cause institutions to avoid implementing or continuing such programs. However, when a program is pursued as a desirable activity compatible with the goals of a given institution, conceptualizing this award to meet its purpose seems important. Helping with this task lies well within the province and expertise of faculty development centers.

RECOMMENDATIONS

Potential ways in which faculty development centers can help reframe or develop teaching awards programs on their campuses include the following:

- Promoting reflection about the purposes of the award

- Fostering the identification of criteria for teaching awards

- Helping programs to identify categories of evidence to be submitted by candidates

- Assisting with identifying standards

Promoting Reflection About the Purposes of the Award

If the purpose of a program is largely symbolic, that is, the award is being created to show that the campus values teaching, the need for a systematic process is no less important than if the program is to address the goals of affirming individuals or inspiring others (Menges, 1996; Middleton, 1987). An awards program that has vague criteria, relies on little evidence, and has no standards will quickly be revealed as meaningless and consequently will undermine its symbolic value. It will be labeled a "popularity contest," and rightly so. If the purpose is to affirm individuals, it is important to communicate what values are being promoted and to set in place mechanisms for identifying which faculty exemplify these values. If the purpose is to inspire others, the open communication of the values and standards is important for outlining the goals that faculty will have to pursue in their quest for excellence as well as what evidence they should be collecting to support their case.

Fostering the Identification of Criteria for Teaching Awards

This task is central to faculty appraisal activities on all campuses. It is at the heart of peer review systems, promotion and tenure or annual review procedures, student ratings instrument construction, and even faculty development planning. If a campus has not identified those characteristics of teaching that are important in its context, all of these activities are without an anchor. While a beginning point is the literature on teaching effectiveness (summarized in Chism, 2004), which faculty development centers can bring to the table, campus-specific goals will influence the articulation of which characteristics are most salient in the particular context. For example, on campuses where remote learners are a big part of the population, excellence in the use of instructional technologies needed for distance education may be important, whereas at a small, residential school, in-person accessibility through office hours or faculty participation in student events may be more important. The work of listing these criteria for teaching excellence is not easy, yet it is a fascinating discussion that can be developmental in itself for all those who participate. While even on a small campus, disciplinary differences exist in the ways in which teaching is approached, the identification of a broad list of characteristics is not impossible and is essential to all faculty appraisal activities (some examples can be found in Appendix A).

Helping Programs to Identify Categories of Evidence to Be Submitted by Candidates

The discussion will revolve around ways to gather good information on whether the teaching of a given candidate exhibits the criteria and to what degree. In much of the evaluation literature (e.g., Centra, 1993), charts exist that indicate where one might find evidence for judging certain aspects of teaching. Another example from the general literature is McAlpine and Harris (2002), who list seven areas of teaching, sample criteria for performance, and evidence that may indicate acceptable, good/excellent, and exemplary performance. Constructing such a grid around the criteria that have been identified for the campus and having those framing the award think logically about what forms of evidence would inform them about each is a task that a faculty development center can facilitate. Such an exercise is akin to the normal way in which developers help faculty to develop student assessment plans. If the use of active learning methods is a criterion, for example, would the syllabus be a good indicator? Would sample course materials? Would a student rating item on active learning? All of the above?

Since most awards programs rely on letters of nomination or support, one simple thing that faculty development centers can do to enhance the value of these as evidence is to direct the letter writers to the set of criteria for the award. If even more standardization is desired, the request for letters can be replaced by the use of forms, either in print or electronic, that ask people to speak to each criterion and give them space for comment, along with a space at the end for additional comments that the nominator/supporter wishes to make. Asking letter writers to review documents or have some other source of direct knowledge of the candidate's performance can help to make the letters more substantive. For example, in one competition, candidates must prepare a teaching portfolio, which is then reviewed by those who are to write letters (see FACET example in Appendix 20.1 for details).

It is important in the specification of evidence for teaching awards to adhere to the same recommendations on good evaluation of teaching that are promoted throughout the literature on faculty evaluation by calling for evidence to be collected from multiple sources, using multiple methods, over multiple points in time (Braskamp & Ory, 1994; Centra, 1993).

Assisting With Identifying Standards

Perhaps the most problematical part of the task is the development of standards. Because no awards program in the sample studied listed standards, those developing programs must find it hard to define and articulate levels of accomplishment. An example of the articulation of standards, in addition to the McAlpine and Harris (2002) paper mentioned above, is a guide to evaluating philosophy of teaching statements (Schonwetter, Sokal, Friesen, & Taylor, 2002) that lists categories of superior, average, and poor. At first, it may be possible to develop tentative standards, such as the following for the example of the scholarship in teaching.

- Acceptable: Participation in campus events on teaching, presence of reflective comments and references to the literature on teaching and learning in philosophy of teaching statement

- Good/excellent: Above, plus participation in inquiry on teaching, presentation of teaching work at conferences or workshops

- Exemplary: Above, plus at least one publication on the scholarship of teaching and learning

Both sources above use other schemes, which serve as good models.

These standards may then be tested during a first year of use and refined, progressively arriving at the articulation of standards for excellence that may be useful for other faculty appraisal purposes in addition to the awards program. Making these standards explicit is similar to using grading rubrics to provide students with guidelines and goals. They shape behaviors as well as enable constructive feedback and consistent judgments. Articulation of standards early on can also be useful in reframing the initial stage of two-stage awards processes by deterring frivolous nominations as well as providing a straightforward screening mechanism.

Stimulating Continual Inquiry as the Program Unfolds

New circumstances, changing values in teaching, and new actors all will necessarily influence the effectiveness of teaching awards programs. In keeping with the reflective practice values promoted by faculty developers, centers can help existing awards programs to develop a system for examining their process at key intervals. Whether this be scholarship on the impact of the program or formative evaluation for ongoing improvement, this activity is important to the health of the program. Menges (1996) offers a useful list of questions for assessing teaching awards programs that may be used for self-assessment (see Appendix 20.2).

SUMMARY

Teaching awards programs that are not well conceived and implemented fall into the category of those unexamined practices that ultimately undermine the work of teaching development. Helping institutions to revise or develop new programs is thus an important arena for faculty developers. The issues that are involved are ideal for the convening of a community of inquiry, an effective organizational development tool (Wenger, 1998; Wenger, McDermott, & Snyder, 2002). Such communities begin with a problem relevant to their work and engage in dialogue and information collection to explore the issue and generate alternative courses of action. The role of the developer is to serve as a resource, helping the faculty to locate insightful work that bears on the issue, as well as to facilitate the discussion by helping to schedule meetings, communicate between meetings, and keep the discussion on track and inclusive during meetings.

Ultimately, the work of helping faculty to identify criteria, evidence, and standards for teaching awards can be useful to the campus in additional ways. These criteria and evidence may inform annual review or promotion and tenure procedures. They may be used by faculty in formulating their teaching development plans. If a standard set of criteria and evidence is judged to be useful for several purposes, it might form the basis for an electronic teaching portfolio that faculty can use in the storage of information on their teaching. Such a portfolio would enable quick retrieval of information in a standard format for several purposes, thus enhancing the efficiency of these processes.

The developer who wishes to foster a community of inquiry on teaching awards is not starting from scratch. As indicated above, many lists of the characteristics of teaching effectiveness are in the literature, as are suggestions in the evaluation literature on evidence that speaks to certain areas of teaching. It is also likely that somewhere in the documentation of teaching appraisal processes on one's campus, there is language that speaks to criteria, evidence, or standards that can be used as a start. Many campuses have listed these on the World Wide Web. These lists can be retrieved and used as discussion starters (see Appendix 20.1 for examples).

The work of faculty development thrives within a climate where the many dimensions of excellence in teaching are appreciated and articulated, where excellence in teaching is pursued and rewarded, and where unexamined practices influencing growth and recognition of teaching are unearthed and critiqued. Engaging in the exploration of teaching awards programs is thus an important faculty development task, for the organization as well as for the individuals involved.

NOTE

The author wishes to acknowledge the help of Brian King and Melody Coryell in the data collection and coding process.

REFERENCES

Adams, C. C. (1977). *Faculty awards programs: Campus-based and systemwide.* Long Beach, CA: California State University and Colleges, Center for Professional Development. (ERIC Document Reproduction Service No. ED136725)

Angelo, T. A. (1996). Relating exemplary teaching to student learning. In M. D. Svinicki & R. J. Menges (Eds.), *New directions in teaching and learning: No. 65. Honoring exemplary teaching* (pp. 57–64). San Francisco, CA: Jossey-Bass.

Braskamp, L. A., & Ory, J. C. (1994). *Assessing faculty work: Enhancing individual and institutional performance.* San Francisco, CA: Jossey-Bass.

Carusetta, E. (2001). Evaluating teaching through teaching awards. In C. Knapper & P. Cranton (Eds.), *New directions in teaching and learning: No. 88. Fresh approaches to the evaluation of teaching* (pp. 31–40). San Francisco, CA: Jossey-Bass.

Centra, J. A. (1993). *Reflective faculty evaluation: Enhancing teaching and determining faculty effectiveness.* San Francisco, CA: Jossey-Bass.

Chism, N. V. N. (2004). *Characteristics of effective teaching in higher education: Between definitional despair and certainty.* Manuscript submitted for publication.

Chism, N. V. N., & Szabo, B. (1997). Teaching awards: The problem of assessing their impact. In D. DeZure & M. Kaplan (Eds.), *To improve the academy: Vol. 16. Resources for faculty, instructional, and organizational development* (pp. 181–200). Stillwater, OK: New Forums Press.

Francis, J. B. (1976). *An evaluation of programs to recognize and reward teaching excellence.* Buffalo, NY: State University of New York at Buffalo, Department of Higher Education. (ERIC Document Reproduction Service No. ED156723)

Lowman, J. (1994). Professors as performers and motivators. *College Teaching, 42,* 137–141.

McAlpine, L., & Harris, R. (2002). Evaluating teaching effectiveness and teaching improvement: A language for institutional policies and academic development practices. *International Journal of Academic Development, 7*(1), 7–17.

McNaught, C., & Anwyl, J. (1993). *Awards for teaching at Australian universities* (Centre for the Study of Higher Education Research Working Papers No. 93.1). Victoria, Australia: University of Melbourne. (ERIC Document Reproduction Service No. ED368291)

Menges, R. J. (1996). Awards to individuals. In M. D. Svinicki & R. J. Menges (Eds.), *New directions in teaching and learning: No. 65. Honoring exemplary teaching* (pp. 3–9). San Francisco, CA: Jossey-Bass.

Middleton, A. (1987, October). Teaching awards and tokenism. *Teaching Professor, 1*(8), 3–4.

Patton, M. Q. (2002). *Qualitative evaluation and research methods* (3rd ed.). Thousand Oaks, CA: Sage.

Schonwetter, D. T., Sokal, L., Friesen, M., & Taylor, K. L. (2002). Teaching philosophies reconsidered: A conceptual model for the development and evaluation of teaching philosophy statements. *International Journal of Academic Development, 7*(1), 83–97.

Warren, R., & Plumb, E. (1999). Survey of distinguished teacher award schemes in higher education. *Journal of Further and Higher Education, 23*(2), 245–255.

Wenger, E. (1998). *Communities of practice: Learning, meaning and identity.* New York, NY: Cambridge University Press.

Wenger, E., McDermott, R., & Snyder, W. M. (2002). *Cultivating communities of practice: A guide to managing knowledge.* Boston, MA: Harvard Business School Press.

APPENDIX 20.1

A SELECTION OF EXEMPLARY AWARDS PROGRAMS

Distinguished Faculty Teaching Award, California State University–Long Beach
http://www.csulb.edu/~senate/Awards/DFTA/guidelinedfta.html

> Criteria are defined in some detail and evidence includes secondary
> evaluations, but also syllabi, course materials, and reflective statement
> from the candidate.

Distinguished Teaching Award, University of California–Berkeley
http://teaching.berkeley.edu/dta-guidelines.html

> This award uses criteria that have been defined in the handbook for
> faculty as indicators of teaching excellence. A two-stage judging
> process exists. Required evidence for the first stage includes general
> information and evaluations from others and the second stage evi-
> dence entails statements of goals and experience as well as supporting
> course materials along with the other evidence.

Bender Teaching Awards, The George Washington University
http://www.cidd.gwu.edu/excellence/bender.html

> This program is an example of an award with clear criteria, some of
> which indicate how the criteria might be measured. The award re-
> quests teaching materials as well as letters, student evaluations, and
> other secondary measures.

Teaching Recognition Program, University of Illinois–Chicago
http://www.uic.edu/depts/oaa/cetl/TRP/index.html

> This award is very thorough in its discussion of both criteria and evi-
> dence. It refers candidates to a table developed by the Teaching Doc-
> umentation Task Force that matches criteria to evidence in the evalu-
> ation of teaching.

Alumni Teaching Excellence and Board of Governors' Teaching Excellence
Awards, University of North Carolina–Greensboro
http://www.uncg.edu/tlc/ateacri.htm

These awards both follow the same two-stage process. Criteria are spelled out clearly. A statement of teaching philosophy, goals, and methods as well as a teaching curriculum vitae are required during the first phase, and teaching portfolio during the second. The awards information provides an itemized list of what the portfolio should contain, which includes reflective statements as well as course materials and materials submitted by others.

Faculty Colloquium on Excellence in Teaching (FACET) Award, Indiana University
http://www.iupui.edu/~facet/03callweb3.htm

Candidates seeking membership to this teaching academy must complete a course portfolio, which is then reviewed by two peers. The guidelines speak to the importance of documenting teaching and call for reflective and full information. FACET uses a web-based form that prompts both candidates and peer reviewers to provide consistent information.

APPENDIX 20.2

QUESTIONS TO ASK IN EVALUATING TEACHING AWARD PROGRAMS

From: Menges, R. J. (1996). Awards to individuals. In M. D. Svinicki & R. J. Menges (Eds.), *New directions in teaching and learning: No. 65. Honoring exemplary teaching* (pp. 3–9). San Francisco, CA: Jossey-Bass. This material is used by permission of John Wiley & Sons, Inc.

Selection Validity Test

The selection validity test asks to what extent the program does what it claims to do, that is, how well does it select from all the eligible teachers those who are truly exemplary. This test has two dimensions: accuracy and representativeness.

Accurate selection

Does the program reflect core values of the institution? For example, if setting high expectations for students is a core value, how is that value reflected in the program? If collaboration among faculty is valued at the institution, how is that value reconciled with a program that is inherently competitive?

Are selection criteria and procedures generally known by faculty? Is there consensus that they are "correct"?

Does selection utilize information of various types (both qualitative and quantitative) and information from several sources?

Are nominees considered not only in light of their past accomplishments but also in light of their teaching plans for the future?

How confident are those who make selections that recipients are demonstrably superior in terms of program criteria?

Representativeness

Do recipients fairly represent the variety of fields (disciplines and other programs of study) and instructional situations (seminar, lab, studio, clinic, lecture hall)?

Do recipients fairly represent the variety of instructional activities that faculty perform (both in class and out)?

Is the program free of gender and ethnic biases?

Faculty Motivation Test

A successful program to honor exemplary teaching will energize faculty, making them more attentive to their teaching and its impact. This should be apparent to students and colleagues, and it should be evident more generally in the climate of the institution. The first four questions below deal with ways that programs can ensure the incentive value of awards, and the remainder suggest evidence for increased faculty motivation.

Ensuring Incentive Value

Are awards sufficiently numerous to encourage qualified faculty to apply?

Can each recipient choose from a menu of awards what is personally most valuable?

Is the value of the award at least as great as the effort required to obtain it?

Do unsuccessful applicants receive information about how their applications could be strengthened?

Evidence of Increasing Motivation

Are application rates increasing? Is there clamor for expansion of the program?

Do recipients report positive experiences in the wake of receiving the award?

Is there evidence that informal conversation about teaching has increased and become more thoughtful?

Do more teaching-related items appear on agendas of departmental and committee meetings?

Are instructional experiments and innovations more common?

Have student course and teacher evaluations become more positive?

Test of Public Perceptions

This test seeks evidence that external audiences have increased appreciation that teaching is valued and rewarded at the institution and that the quality of teaching and learning has improved.

Is media coverage about teaching more extensive and more positive?

When prospective students and their parents ask about teaching and programs of study, are their questions answered more readily?

When legislators ask about such matters as faculty workload, are their questions better informed?

Has external funding for the support of instructional innovation increased?

Bibliography

Adams, C. C. (1977). *Faculty awards programs: Campus-based and systemwide*. Long Beach, CA: California State University and Colleges, Center for Professional Development. (ERIC Document Reproduction Service No. ED136725)

Adso, J. (2002, February 27). Figuring out what counts in the tenure game. *Chronicle of Higher Education Career Network*. Retrieved November 9, 2002, from http://chronicle.com/jobs/2002/02/2002022701c.htm

Aguirre, A., Jr. (2000). *Women and minority faculty in the academic workplace: Recruitment, retention and academic culture* (ASHE-ERIC Higher Education Report, 27[6]). San Francisco, CA: Jossey-Bass.

Aiken, S., Anderson, K., Dinnerstein, M., Lensink, J. N., & MacCorquodale, P. (1988). Changing our minds: The problematics of curriculum integration. In S. H. Aiken (Ed.), *Changing our minds: feminist transformations of knowledge* (pp. 134–163). Albany, NY: State University of New York Press.

Allen, M. J., McMillin, J. D., Noel, R. C., & Rienzi, B. M. (1999, June). *Outcomes assessment for program improvement*. Paper presented at the California State University Teacher-Scholar Summer Conference, San Jose, CA.

Altemeyer, B. (1988). *Enemies of freedom: Understanding right-wing authoritarianism*. San Francisco, CA: Jossey-Bass.

American Association of State Colleges and Universities. (1999). *Facing change: Building the faculty of the future*. Washington, DC: Author.

American Association for Higher Education. (1997). *9 principles of good practice for assessing student learning*. Washington, DC: Author. Retrieved May 6, 2004, from http://www.aahe.org/assessment/principl.htm

American Association for Higher Education. (2003). Resources for inquiry and action: The learning-centered institution. *Inquiry and Action, 1*. Retrieved December 11, 2003, from http://www.aahe.org/pubs/IASpring2003.pdf

American Federation of Teachers. (2002). *Standards of good practice in the employment of part-time/adjunct faculty: Fairness and equity*. Washington, DC: Author. Retrieved May 9, 2004, from http://www.aft.org/higher_ed/images/ Booklet.pdf

Angelo, T. A. (1996). Relating exemplary teaching to student learning. In M. D. Svinicki & R. J. Menges (Eds.), *New directions in teaching and learning: No. 65. Honoring exemplary teaching* (pp. 57–64). San Francisco, CA: Jossey-Bass.

Angelo, T. A., & Cross, P. K. (1993). *Classroom assessment techniques: A handbook for college teachers* (2nd ed.). San Francisco, CA: Jossey-Bass.

Antonio, A. L. (2002). Faculty of color reconsidered. Retaining scholars for the future. *Journal of Higher Education, 73*(5), 582–602.

Approaches to staff development for part-time faculty. (1986, July 1). *ERIC Digest.* (ERIC Document Reproduction Service No. ED270180). Retrieved May 9, 2004, from http://www.ericfacility.net/databases/ERIC_Digests/ed270180.html

Argyris, C., & Schon, D. (1978). *Organizational learning: A theory of action perspective.* Reading, MA: Addison-Wesley.

Arnold, G., & Civian, J. T. (1997, July/August). The ecology of general education reform. *Change, 29*(4), 19–23.

Association of American Colleges. (1985). *Integrity in the college curriculum: A report to the academic community.* Washington, DC: Author.

Association of American Colleges and Universities. (2002). *Greater expectations: A new vision for learning as a nation goes to college.* Washington, DC: Author. Retrieved June 2, 2003, from http://www.greaterexpectations.org

Association of American Universities. (1998). *Committee on graduate education: Report and recommendations.* Washington, DC: Author. Retrieved August 13, 2002, from http://www.aau.edu/reports/GradEdRpt.html

Astin, A. W. (1984, July). Student involvement: A developmental theory for higher education. *Journal of College Student Personnel, 25,* 297–308.

Astin, A. W. (1993). *What matters in college? Four critical years revisited.* San Francisco, CA: Jossey-Bass.

Astin, H. S., Antonio, L. S., Cress, C. M., & Astin, A. W. (1997). *Race and ethnicity in the American professoriate, 1995–96.* Los Angeles, CA: Higher Education Research Institute, University of California Los Angles.

Astin, H. S., & Cress, C. M. (1998). *A national profile of women faculty in research universities.* Invitational Conference at Harvard University, Committee for Gender Equity, Cambridge, MA.

Astin, H. S., & Cress, C. M. (2002). Women faculty transforming research universities. In L. S. Hornig (Ed.), *Equal rites, unequal outcomes: Women in American research universities* (pp. 53–88). New York, NY: Kluwer.

Atkins, S. S., Brinko, K. T., Butts, J. A., Claxton, C. S., & Hubbard, G. T. (2001). Faculty quality of life. In D. Lieberman & C. Wehlburg (Eds.), *To improve the academy: Vol. 19. Resources for faculty, instructional, and organizational development* (pp. 323–345). Bolton, MA: Anker.

Atkins, S. S., & Hageseth, J. A. (1991). The academic chairperson: Leading faculty is like herding cats. *Journal of Staff, Program, and Organizational Development, 9*(1), 29–35.

Austin, A. E. (2002). Preparing the next generation of faculty: Graduate school as socialization to the academic career. *Journal of Higher Education, 73*(1), 94–122.

Austin, A. E., Brocato, J. J., & Rohrer, J. D. (1997). Institutional missions, multiple faculty roles: Implications for faculty development. In D. Dezure & M. Kaplan (Eds.), *To improve the academy: Vol. 16. Resources for faculty, instructional, and organizational development* (pp. 3–20). Stillwater, OK: New Forums Press.

Aycock, A. (2003). Serendipity and SoTL: An ethnographic narrative. In C. Schroeder & A. Ciccone (Eds.), *Learning more about learning* (pp. 26–37). Milwaukee, WI: University of Wisconsin–Milwaukee, Center for Instructional and Professional Development.

Baker, G. A., III. (Ed.). (1994). *A handbook on the community college in America: Its history, mission, and management.* Westport, CT: Greenwood Press.

Balch, P. (1999). Part-time faculty are here to stay. *Planning for Higher Education, 27*(3), 32–40.

Baldwin, R. G. (1990, March/April). Faculty vitality beyond the research university: Extending a contextual concept. *Journal of Higher Education, 61*(2), 160–180.

Baldwin, R. G. (1998). Academic civility begins in the classroom. *Essays on Teaching Excellence, 9.* Retrieved May 9, 2004, from http://www.unm.edu/~castl/Castl_Docs/Packet9/Academic%20Civility%20Begins%20in%20the%20Classroom.html

Banachowski, G. (1996). Perspectives and perceptions: The use of part-time faculty in community colleges. *Community College Review, 24*(2), 49–62.

Banta, T. W., & Associates. (1993). *Making a difference: Outcomes of a decade of assessment in higher education.* San Francisco, CA: Jossey-Bass.

Banta, T. W., Lund, J. P., Black, K. E., & Oblander, F. W. (1996). *Assessment in practice: Putting principles to work on college campuses.* San Francisco, CA: Jossey-Bass.

Barr, R. B., & Tagg, J. (1995). From teaching to learning: A new paradigm for undergraduate education. *Change, 28*(2), 42–47.

Bartlett, T. (2002, March 22). The unkindest cut. *Chronicle of Higher Education,* p. A10.

Bass, R. (1999, February). The scholarship of teaching: What's the problem? *Inventio: Creative thinking about learning and teaching, 1*(1). Retrieved April 29, 2004, from http://www.doit.gmu.edu/Archives/feb98/randybass.htm

Baumgartner, L. M. (2001). An update on transformational learning. In S. B. Merriam (Ed.), *New directions for adult and continuing education: No. 89. The new update on adult learning theory* (pp. 15–24). San Francisco, CA: Jossey-Bass.

Bensimon, E. M., & Neumann, A. (1993). *Redesigning collegiate leadership: Teams and teamwork in higher education.* Baltimore, MD: Johns Hopkins University Press.

Bensimon, E. M., Ward, K., & Sanders, K. (2000). *The department chair's role in developing new faculty into teachers and scholars.* Bolton, MA: Anker.

Berquist, W. H., Greenberg, E. M., & Klaum, G. A. (1993). *In our fifties: Voices of men and women reinventing their lives.* San Francisco, CA: Jossey-Bass.

Bergquist, W. H., & Phillips, S. R. (1975). Components of an effective faculty development program. *Journal of Higher Education, 46*(2), 177–211.

Bers, T. H., Davis, D., & Taylor, B. (2000). The use of syllabi in assessments: Unobtrusive indicators and tools for faculty development. *Assessment Update, 12,* 4–7.

Bevan, J. (1985). Who has the role of building incentives? In R. G. Baldwin (Ed.), *New directions for higher education: No. 51. Incentives for faculty vitality* (pp. 45–58). San Francisco, CA: Jossey-Bass.

Bishop, C. (1997). *The community's college: A history of Johnson County Community College, 1969–1999.* Pittsburg, KS: Pittcraft Printing.

Bogdan, R. C., & Biklen, S. K. (1992). *Qualitative research for education: An introduction to theory and methods.* Needham Heights, MA: Allyn and Bacon.

Bogen, G. (1978). Performance and vitality as a function of student-faculty fit. In W. C. Kirschling (Ed.), *New directions for institutional research, No. 20. Evaluating faculty performance and vitality* (pp. 51–67). San Francisco, CA: Jossey-Bass.

Boice, R. (1992). *The new faculty member.* San Francisco, CA: Jossey-Bass.

Boice, R. (1993). Primal origins and later correctives for midcareer disillusionment. In M. J. Finkelstein & M. W. LaCelle-Peterson (Eds.), *New directions for teaching and learning: No. 55. Developing senior faculty as teachers* (pp. 33–41). San Francisco, CA: Jossey-Bass.

Bonwell, C. C., & Eison, J. A. (1991). *Active learning: Creating excitement in the classroom* (ASHE-ERIC Higher Education Report No. 1). Washington, DC: George Washington University, Graduate School of Education and Human Services.

Bothell, T. W., & Henderson, T. (2004). Evaluating the return on investment of faculty development. In C. M. Wehlburg & S. Chadwick-Blossey (Eds.), *To improve the academy: Vol. 22. Resources for faculty, instructional, and organizational development* (pp. 52–70). Bolton, MA: Anker.

Bowden, J. (1989). *Curriculum development for conceptual change learning: A phenomenographic pedagogy.* Paper presented at the sixth annual (international) Conference of the Hong Kong Educational Research Association, Hong Kong.

Boyd, R. D. (1989). Facilitating personal transformation in small groups, Part I. *Small Group Behavior, 20*(4), 459–474.

Boyd, R. D. (1991). *Personal transformation in small groups: A Jungian perspective.* London, England: Routledge.

Boyer, E. L. (1989). *The condition of the professoriate: Attitudes and trends, 1989.* Princeton, NJ: Carnegie Foundation for the Advancement of Teaching.

Bradley, A. (1999, January 11). Zeroing in on teachers: Quality Counts '99 [Special issue]. *Education Week, 18*(17), 46–47, 49–52.

Branch, V. (1995). Teaching is "job number one": New faculty at a comprehensive university. *Journal of Staff, Program, and Organizational Development, 12*(4), 209–218.

Branzburg, J., & Kennedy, K. (2001, September). Online professional development. *Technology and Learning, 22*(2), 18–27.

Braskamp, L. A., & Ory, J. C. (1994). *Assessing faculty work: Enhancing individual and institutional performance.* San Francisco, CA: Jossey-Bass.

Breneman, D. W. (2002, July 14). For colleges, this is not just another recession. *Chronicle of Higher Education,* p. B7.

Brewster, D. (2000). The use of part-time faculty in the community college. *Inquiry, 5*(1), 66–76.

Bringle, R., & Hatcher, J. (1999). Reflection in service learning: Making meaning of experience. *Educational Horizons, 77*(4), 179–185.

Brinko, K. T. (1993). The practice of giving feedback to improving teaching: What is effective? *Journal of Higher Education, 64,* 575–593.

Brown, M. C. (2000). Involvement with students: How much can I give? In M. Garcia (Ed.), *Succeeding in an academic career: A guide for faculty of color* (pp. 71–88). Westport, CT: Greenwood Press.

Buchanan, E. (2002). Examining and promoting student learning through a hybrid course environment. In C. Schroeder & A. Ciccone (Eds.), *Models in our midst* (pp. 9–19). Milwaukee, WI: University of Wisconsin–Milwaukee, Center for Instructional and Professional Development.

Burnstad, H. M. (1994). Management of human resources in the community college. In G. A. Baker, III (Ed.), *A handbook on the community college in America: Its history, mission, and management* (pp. 386–395). Westport, CT: Greenwood Press.

Campus Compact. (2000). *Introduction to service-learning toolkit: Readings and resources for faculty.* Providence, RI: Author.

Carnegie Commission on Higher Education. (1994). *The open-door colleges: Policies for community colleges.* New York, NY: McGraw-Hill.

Carnevale, A. P., Gainer, L. J., & Meltzer, A. S. (1990). *Workplace basics: The essential skills employers want.* San Francisco, CA: Jossey-Bass.

Carter, D. J., & Ottinger, C. A. (1992). *Community college faculty: A profile.* Washington, DC: American Council on Education, Division of Policy Analysis and Research.

Carusetta, E. (2001). Evaluating teaching through teaching awards. In C. Knapper & P. Cranton (Eds.), *New directions in teaching and learning: No. 88. Fresh approaches to the evaluation of teaching* (pp. 31–40). San Francisco, CA: Jossey-Bass.

Centra, J. A. (1976). *Faculty development practices in US colleges and universities.* Princeton, NJ: Educational Testing Service.

Centra, J. A. (1985). Maintaining faculty vitality through faculty development. In S. M. Clark & D. R. Lewis (Eds.), *Faculty vitality and institutional productivity: Critical perspectives for higher education.* New York, NY: Teachers College Press.

Centra, J. A. (1993). *Reflective faculty evaluation: Enhancing teaching and determining faculty effectiveness.* San Francisco, CA: Jossey-Bass.

Cerbin, W. (1996). Inventing a new genre: The course portfolio at the University of Wisconsin–La Crosse. In P. Hutchings (Ed.), *Making teaching community property: A menu for peer collaboration and peer review* (pp. 52–56). Washington, DC: American Association for Higher Education.

Chaffee, E. E. (1997). Listening to the people you serve. In B. L. Cambridge (Ed.), *Assessing impact: Evidence and action* (pp. 41–50). Washington, DC: American Association for Higher Education.

Chambers, J. (1998). *Teaching and learning centers in US higher education: Current and projected roles and services.* Unpublished report, Florida Community College, Jacksonville, FL.

Chang, R. Y., & Morgan, M. W. (2000). *Performance scorecards: Measuring the right things in the real world.* San Francisco, CA: Jossey-Bass.

Chapman, J., & Morley, R. (1999). Collegiate service-learning: Motives underlying volunteerism and satisfaction with volunteer service. *Journal of Prevention and Intervention in the Community, 18*(1/2), 19–33.

Cherwitz, R. A., & Sullivan, C. A. (2002, November/December). Intellectual entrepreneurship: A vision for graduate education. *Change, 34*(6), 23–27.

Chism, N. V. N. (1998). Evaluating TA programs. In M. Marincovich, J. Prostko, & F. Stout (Eds.), *The professional development of graduate teaching assistants* (pp. 249–262). Bolton, MA: Anker.

Chism, N. V. N. (1999). *Peer review of teaching: A sourcebook.* Bolton, MA: Anker.

Chism, N. V. N. (2003, March 14). Summary of responses on user records. Message posted to POD electronic mailing list, archived at http://listserv.nd.edu/cgi-bin/wa?A2=ind0303&L=pod&O=A&P=7509

Chism, N. V. N. (2004). *Characteristics of effective teaching in higher education: Between definitional despair and certainty.* Manuscript submitted for publication.

Chism, N. V. N., & Szabo, B. (1997). How faculty development programs evaluate their services. *Journal of Staff, Program, and Organizational Development, 15*(2), 55–62.

Chism, N. V. N., & Szabo, B. (1997). Teaching awards: The problem of assessing their impact. In D. DeZure & M. Kaplan (Eds.), *To improve the academy: Vol. 16. Resources for faculty, instructional, and organizational development* (pp. 181–200). Stillwater, OK: New Forums Press.

Chitouras, J. (1993, Spring). Esoteric sound and color. *Gnosis, 27,* 36–40.

Civian, J. T., Arnold, G., Gamson, Z. F., Kanter, S., & London, H. B. (1996). Implementing change. In J. G. Gaff, J. L. Ratcliff, & Associates (Eds.), *Handbook of the undergraduate curriculum: A comprehensive guide to purposes, structures, practices, and change* (pp. 647–660). San Francisco, CA: Jossey-Bass.

Clark, B. (1985). *The academic life.* Princeton, NJ: Princeton University Press.

Clark, S., & Corcoran, M. (1985). Individual and organizational contributions to faculty vitality: An institutional case study. In S. M. Clark & D. R. Lewis (Eds.), *Faculty vitality and institutional productivity: Critical perspectives for higher education* (pp. 112–138). New York, NY: Teachers College Press.

Coffman, S. J. (2002). Ten strategies for getting students to take responsibility for their learning. *College Teaching, 51,* 2–4.

Cohen, A. M., & Brawer, F. B. (1987). *The collegiate function of community colleges: Fostering higher learning through curriculum and student transfer.* San Francisco, CA: Jossey-Bass.

Cohen, A. M., & Brawer, F. B. (1996). *The American community college.* San Francisco, CA: Jossey-Bass.

Cohen, P. A., & Herr, G. (1982). Using an interactive feedback procedure to improve college teaching. *Teaching of Psychology, 9,* 138–140.

Colby, A., Ehrlich, T., Beaumont, E., & Stephens, J. (2003). *Educating citizens: Preparing America's undergraduates for lives of moral and civic responsibility.* San Francisco, CA: Jossey-Bass.

Committee on Science, Engineering, and Public Policy. (1995). *Reshaping the graduate education of scientists and engineers.* Washington, DC: National Academy Press.

Cooper, D. (1998). Reading, writing, and reflection. In R. A. Rhoads & J. Howard (Eds.), *Academic service learning: A pedagogy of action and reflection* (pp. 47–56). San Francisco, CA: JosseyBass.

Cox, M. D. (2001). Faculty learning communities: Change agents for transforming institutions into learning organizations. In D. Lieberman & C. Wehlburg (Eds.), *To improve the academy: Vol. 19. Resources for faculty, instructional, and organizational development* (pp. 69–93). Bolton, MA: Anker.

Cranton, P. (1992). *Working with adult learners.* Toronto, Ontario: Wall & Emerson.

Cranton, P. (1994, November/December). Self-directed and transformative instructional development. *Journal of Higher Education, 65*(6), 726–744.

Cranton, P. (1996). Professional development as transformative learning: New perspectives for teachers of adults. *Journal of Higher Education, 65,* 726–744.

Cranton, P. (1997). *New directions for adult and continuing education: No. 74: Transformative learning in actions: Insights from practice.* San Francisco, CA: Jossey-Bass.

Cranton, P. (2002, Spring). Teaching for transformation. In J. M. Ross-Gordon (Ed.), *New directions for adult and continuing education: No. 93. Contemporary viewpoints on teaching adults effectively* (pp. 63–71). San Francisco, CA: Jossey-Bass.

Crawley, A. (1995). Faculty development programs at research universities: Implications for senior faculty renewal. In E. Neal & L. Richlin (Eds.), *To improve the academy: Vol. 14. Resources for faculty, instructional, and organizational development* (pp. 65–90). Stillwater, OK: New Forums Press.

Creamer, E. G. (1998). *Assessing faculty publication productivity: Issues of equity* (ASHE-ERIC Higher Education Report, 26[2]). Washington, DC: George Washington University, Graduate School of Education and Human Development.

Cross, K. P. (1993, February/March). Involving faculty in TQU. *AACC Journal,* 15–20.

Cross, K. P., & Steadman, M. H. (1996). *Classroom research: Implementing the scholarship of teaching.* San Francisco, CA: Jossey Bass.

Cuban, L. (1999). *How scholars trumped teachers: Change without reform in university curriculum, teaching, and research, 1890–1990.* New York, NY: Teachers College Press.

Daley, B. (2002). Facilitating adult learning in higher education. In C. Schroeder & A. Ciccone (Eds.), *Models in our midst* (pp. 21–31). Milwaukee, WI: University of Wisconsin–Milwaukee, Center for Instructional and Professional Development.

Darwin, T. J. (2000). *Professional development as intellectual opportunity.* Paper presented at the National Communication Association Conference, Seattle, WA. Retrieved November 5, 2003, from https://webspace.utexas.edu/cherwitz/www/ie/td.html

Deci, E., Kasser, T., & Ryan, R. (1997). Self-determined teaching: Opportunities and obstacles. In J. Bess (Ed.), *Teaching well and liking it: Motivating faculty to teach effectively* (pp. 57–71). Baltimore, MD: Johns Hopkins University Press.

Deegan, W. (1985). *Renewing the American community college: Priorities and strategies for effective leadership.* San Francisco, CA: Jossey-Bass.

DeZure, D. (Ed.). (2000). *Learning from change: Landmarks in teaching and learning in higher education from* Change *magazine 1969–1999.* Sterling, VA: Stylus.

Diamond, R. M. (2002). Faculty, instructional, and organizational development: Options and choices. In K. H. Gillespie, L. R. Hilsen, & E. C. Wadsworth (Eds.), *A guide to faculty development: Practical advice, examples, and resources* (pp 2–8). Bolton, MA: Anker.

Dieker, L. (2002). Inquiry into video streaming. In C. Schroeder & A. Ciccone (Eds.), *Models in our midst* (pp. 35–39). Milwaukee, WI: University of Wisconsin–Milwaukee, Center for Instructional and Professional Development.

Diener, T. (1986). *Growth of an American invention: A documentary history of the junior and community college movement.* Westport, CT: Greenwood Press.

Dirkx, J. M. (1998). Transformative learning theory in the practice of adult education: An overview. *PAACE Journal of Lifelong Learning, 7,* 1–14.

Doherty, A., Riordan, T., Roth, J. (Eds.). (2002). *Student learning: A central focus for institutions of higher education.* Milwaukee, WI: Alverno College Institute.

Driscoll, A., Holland, B., Gelmon, S., & Kerrigan, S. (1996). An assessment model for service-learning: Comprehensive case studies of impact on faculty, students, community, and institution. *Michigan Journal of Community Service Learning, 3,* 66–71.

Dunlap, M. (1998). Methods of supporting students' critical reflection in courses incorporating service-learning. *Teaching of Psychology, 25*(3), 208–210.

Eaton, J. S. (1994). *Strengthening collegiate education in community colleges.* San Francisco, CA: Jossey-Bass.

Ebben, J., & Maher, T. (1979, May). *Capturing institutional vitality.* Paper presented at the annual forum of the Association for Institutional Research, San Diego, CA.

Eble, K. E., & McKeachie, W. J. (1985). *Improving undergraduate education through faculty development.* San Francisco, CA: Jossey-Bass.

Elbow, P. (1981). *Writing with power.* New York, NY: Oxford University Press.

Elbow, P. (1986). *Embracing contraries: Explorations in teaching and learning.* New York, NY: Oxford University Press.

Eliot, T. S. (1964). *Selected essays.* New York, NY: Harcourt, Brace, & World.

Ellner, C. L., & Barnes, C. P. (Eds.). (1983). *Studies of college teaching: Experimental results, theoretical interpretations, and new perspectives.* Lexington, MA: D.C. Heath.

Epper, R., & Bates, A. (2001). *Teaching faculty how to use technology: Best practices from leading institutions.* Phoenix, AZ: Oryx Press/American Council on Education.

Erickson, G. (1986). A survey of faculty development practices. In M. Svinicki, J. Kurfiss, & J. Stone (Eds.), *To improve the academy: Vol. 5. Resources for student, faculty, and institutional development* (pp. 182–196). Stillwater, OK: New Forums Press.

Erickson, G. R., & Erickson, B. L. (1979). Improving college teaching: An evaluation of a teaching consultation procedure. *Journal of Higher Education, 50,* 670–683.

Erickson, J., & O'Conner, S. (2000). Service-learning: Does it promote or reduce prejudice? In C. O'Grady (Ed.), *Integrating service learning and multicultural education in colleges and universities* (pp. 59–70). Mahwah, NJ: Lawrence Erlbaum.

Ewell, P. (2002). *Perpetual movement: Assessment after twenty years.* Paper presented at the American Association for Higher Education Assessment Conference, Boston, MA. Retrieved May 6, 2004, from http://www.aahe.org/assessment/2002/PlenariesForFrames.htm

Eyler, J., & Giles, D. (1999). *Where's the learning in service-learning?* San Francisco, CA: Jossey-Bass.

Fassel, D. (1990). *Working ourselves to death: And the rewards of recovery.* New York, NY: HarperCollins.

Felder, R. M., & Brent, R. (1996). Navigating the bumpy road to student-centered instruction. *College Teaching, 44,* 43–47. Retrieved December 3, 2003, from http://www.ncsu.edu/felder-public/Papers/Resist.html

Ferren, A. S., & McCafferty, J. K. (1992). Reforming college mathematics. *College teaching, 40*(3), 87–90.

Fields, R. (1962). *The community college movement.* New York, NY: McGraw-Hill.

Fife, J. (1991). Foreword. In W. Toombs & W. Tierney, *Meeting the mandate: Renewing the college and departmental curriculum* (p. xiii). Washington, DC: George Washington University, School of Education and Human Development.

Fink, D. L. (2003). *Creating significant learning experiences: An integrated approach to designing college courses.* San Francisco, CA: Jossey-Bass.

Finkelstein, M. J., & LaCelle-Peterson, M. W. (1992). New and junior faculty: A review of the literature. In M. D. Sorcinelli & A. E. Austin (Eds.), *Developing new and junior faculty* (pp. 5–14). San Francisco, CA: Jossey-Bass.

Finkelstein, M. J., Seal, R. K., & Schuster, J. H. (1998). *The new academic generation: A profession in transformation.* Baltimore, MD: Johns Hopkins University Press.

Flannery, D., & Ward, K. (1999). Service learning: A vehicle for developing cultural competence in health education. *American Journal of Health Behavior, 23*(5), 323–331.

Foster, S. (2000). *Teaching partners program: Analysis of first interviews.* Unpublished report.

Foster, W. (1989). Toward a critical practice of leadership. In J. Smyth (Ed.), *Critical perspectives on educational leadership* (pp. 39–63). London, England: Falmer Press.

Francis, J. B. (1976). *An evaluation of programs to recognize and reward teaching excellence.* Buffalo, NY: State University of New York at Buffalo, Department of Higher Education. (ERIC Document Reproduction Service No. ED156723)

Fuerst, P. A. (1984). University student understanding of evolutionary biology's place in the creation/evolution controversy. *Ohio Journal of Science, 84*(5), 218–228.

Fulton, R. D. (2000, May). The plight of part-timers in higher education. *Change, 32*(3), 38–42.

Furco, A. (1996). Service-learning: A balanced approach to experiential education. *Expanding boundaries: Serving and learning.* Washington, DC: Corporation for National Service.

Gaff, J. G. (1975). *Toward faculty renewal: Advances in faculty, instructional, and organization development.* San Francisco, CA: Jossey-Bass.

Gaff, J. G. (2002, November/December). Preparing future faculty and doctoral education. *Change, 34*(6), 63–66.

Gappa, J. M. (1984). *Part-time faculty: Higher education at a crossroads* (ASHE-ERIC Higher Education Research Report No. 3). Washington, DC: Association for the Study of Higher Education.

Gappa, J. M., & Leslie, D. W. (1993). *The invisible faculty: Improving the status of part-timers in higher education.* San Francisco, CA: Jossey-Bass.

Gappa, J. M., & Leslie, D. W. (1997). *Two faculties or one? The conundrum of part-timers in a bifurcated workforce* (Inquiry No. 6). Washington, DC: American Association for Higher Education.

Garcia, M. (2000). *Succeeding in an academic career: A guide for faculty of color.* Westport, CT: Greenwood Press.

Gardiner, L. F. (1996). *Redesigning higher education: Producing dramatic gains in student learning* (ASHE-ERIC Higher Education Report, 23[7]). San Francisco, CA: Jossey-Bass.

Geisel, T. (1990). *Oh, the places you'll go!* New York, NY: Random House.

Gelmon, S., Holland, B., Driscoll, A., Spring, A., & Kerrigan, S. (2001). *Assessing service-learning and civic engagement: Principles and techniques.* Providence, RI: Campus Compact.

Gibbs, G. (1999). Improving teaching, learning, and assessment. *Journal of Geography in Higher Education, 23,* 147–155.

Giddens, A. (1984). *The constitution of society.* Los Angeles, CA: University of California Press.

Gillespie, K. H. (Ed.). (1998). *New directions for teaching and learning: No. 76. The impact of technology on faculty development, life, and work.* San Francisco, CA: Jossey-Bass.

Gillespie, K. H., Hilsen, L. R., & Wadsworth, E.C. (Eds.). (2002). *A guide to faculty development: Practical advice, examples, and resources.* Bolton, MA: Anker.

Gleazer, E. (1967). Preparation of junior college teachers. *Educational Record, 48*(2), 147–152.

Golde, C. M., & Dore, T. M. (2001). *At cross purposes: What the experiences of today's graduate students reveal about doctoral education.* Philadelphia, PA: Pew Charitable Trusts. Retrieved April 19, 2002 from http://www.phd-survey.org

Golin, S. (1990). Peer collaboration and student interviewing: The master faculty program. *AAHE Bulletin, 43*(4), 9–10.

Gordon, V. N., Habley, W. R., & Associates. (2000). *Academic advising: A comprehensive handbook.* San Francisco, CA: Jossey-Bass.

Grabove, V. (1997, Summer). The many facets of transformative learning theory and practice. In P. Cranton (Ed.), *New directions for adult and continuing education: No. 74. Transformative learning in action: Insights from practice* (pp. 89–95). San Francisco, CA: Jossey-Bass.

Graesser, A. C., Person, N. K., Hu, X. (2002). Improving comprehension through discourse processing. In D. F. Halpern & M. D. Hakel (Eds.), *New directions for teaching and learning: No. 89. Applying the science of learning to university teaching and beyond* (pp. 33–44). San Francisco, CA: Jossey-Bass.

Graf, D., & Wheeler, D. (1996). *Defining the membership: The POD membership survey.* Ames, IA: Professional and Organizational Development Network in Higher Education.

Gravett, S. (1996). Conceptual change regarding instruction: The professional enhancement of faculty. *Journal of Staff, Program, and Organizational Development, 13*(3), 207–214.

Grubb, W. N., & Associates. (1999). *Honored but invisible: An inside look at teaching in community colleges.* New York, NY: Routledge.

Gugerty, C., & Swezey, E. (1996). Developing campus-community relationships. In B. Jacoby & Associates (Eds.), *Service-learning in higher education: Concepts and practices* (pp. 92–108). San Francisco, CA: Jossey-Bass.

Gullatt, D., & Weaver, S. (1997, October). *Use of faculty development activities to improve the effectiveness of U.S. institutions of higher education.* Paper presented at the meeting of the Professional and Organizational Development Network in Higher Education, Nines City, FL.

Habley, W. R., & Crockett, D. S. (1988). The third ACT national survey of academic advising. In W. H. Habley (Ed.), *The status and future of academic advising: Problems and promise* (pp. 11–76). Iowa City, IA: ACT National Center for the Advancement of Educational Priorities.

Haeger, J. D. (1998). Part-time faculty, quality programs, and economic realities. In D. W. Leslie (Ed.), *New directions for higher education: No. 104. The growing use of part-time faculty: Understanding causes and effects* (pp. 81–88). San Francisco, CA: Jossey-Bass.

Hageseth, J. A., & Atkins, S. S. (1988). Assessing faculty quality of life. In J. G. Kurfiss (Ed.), *To improve the academy: Vol. 7. Resources for student, faculty, and institutional development* (pp. 109–120). Stillwater, OK: New Forums Press.

Hageseth, J. A., & Atkins, S. S. (1989). Building university community: Where's the staff? *Journal of Staff, Program, and Organizational Development, 7*(4), 173–180.

Hake, R. R. (1998). Interactive-engagement versus traditional methods: A six-thousand-student survey of mechanics test data for introductory physics courses. *American Journal of Physics, 66*(1), 64–74.

Hammons, J. (1983). Faculty development: A necessary corollary to faculty evaluation. In A. M. Cohen & F. B. Brawer (Eds.), *New directions for community colleges: No. 41. Evaluating faculty and staff* (pp. 75–82). San Francisco, CA: Jossey-Bass.

Harris, M. (1987). *Teaching and religious imagination: An essay in the theology of teaching.* New York, NY: HarperCollins.

Hart, R. P., & Burks, D. M. (1972). Rhetorical sensitivity and social interaction. *Speech Monographs, 39,* 75–91.

Heffernan, K. (2001). *Fundamentals of service-learning course construction.* Providence, RI: Campus Compact.

Heifetz, R. A. (1994). *Leadership without easy answers.* Cambridge, MA: Harvard University Press.

Hessmiller, J., & Brown, K. (1995). Learning to act: Service-learning integrates theory and practice. In J. Eby (Ed.), *Service-learning: Linking academics and the community* (pp. 213–220). Grantham, PA: Pennsylvania Campus Compact.

Higher Education Research Institute. (1999). *The American college teacher: National norms for 1998–99 HERI faculty survey.* Los Angeles, CA: University of California.

Ho, A. S. P. (1998). A conceptual change staff development programme: Effects as perceived by the participants. *International Journal for Academic Development, 3*(1), 25–38.

Hoerner, J., Clowes, D., & Impara, J. (1991). Professional development programs in community and technical colleges: Are occupational-technical faculty needs well served? *Journal of Studies in Technical Careers, 13*(4), 351–360.

Hord, S. M., Rutherford, W. L., Huling-Austin, L., & Hall, G. E. (1987). *Taking charge of change.* Alexandria, VA: Association for Supervision and Curriculum Development.

Howard, J. (1998). Academic service learning: A counternormative pedagogy. In R. A. Rhoads & J. Howard (Eds.), *Academic service learning: A pedagogy of action and reflection* (pp. 21–29). San Francisco, CA: Jossey-Bass.

Howard, J. (Ed.). (1993). *Praxis I: A faculty casebook on community service learning.* Ann Arbor, MI: OCSL Press.

Huba, M. E., & Freed, J. E. (2000). *Learner-centered assessment on college campuses: Shifting the focus from teaching to learning.* Needham Heights, MA: Allyn and Bacon.

Hubbard, G. T., & Atkins, S. S. (1995). The professor as a person: The role of faculty well-being in faculty development. *Innovative Higher Education, 20,* 117–128.

Hubbard, G. T., Atkins, S. S., & Brinko, K. T. (1998). Holistic faculty development: Supporting personal, professional, and organizational well-being. In M. Kaplan (Ed.), *To improve the academy: Vol. 17. Resources for faculty, instructional, and organizational development* (pp. 35–49). Stillwater, OK: New Forums Press.

Huber, M. T., & Morreale, S. P. (Eds.). (2002). *Disciplinary styles in the scholarship of teaching and learning: Exploring common ground.* Washington DC: American Association for Higher Education and the Carnegie Foundation for the Advancement of Teaching.

Hurtado, S., Milem, J. F., Clayton-Pedersen, A. R., & Allen, W. R. (1998). Enhancing campus climates for racial/ethnic diversity: Educational policy and practice. *Review of Higher Education, 21*(3), 279–302.

Hutchings, P. (1996). The peer review of teaching: Progress, issues, and prospects. *Innovative Higher Education, 20*(4), 221–234.

Hutchings, P. (2000). *Opening lines: Approaches to the scholarship of teaching and learning.* Menlo Park, CA: The Carnegie Foundation for the Advancement of Teaching.

Hutchings, P., & Marchese, T. (1990, September/October). Watching assessment questions, stories, prospects. *Change, 22*(5), 12–38.

Imel, S. (1998). *Transformative learning in adulthood*. Washington, DC: Office of Educational Research and Improvement. (ERIC Document Reproduction Service No. ED42326). Retrieved April 29, 2004, from http://www.cete.org/acve/docgen.asp?tbl=digests&ID=53

Impara, J., Hoerner, J., Clowes, D., & Allkins, M. (1991). Professional development programs: A comparison of full-time and part-time occupational faculty. *Community Services Catalyst, 21*(2), 8–12.

Jacobs, F. (1998). Using part-time faculty more effectively. In D. W. Leslie (Ed.), *New directions for higher education: No. 104. The growing use of part-time faculty: Understanding causes and effects* (pp. 9–17). San Francisco, CA: Jossey-Bass.

Jacoby, B. (1996). Service-learning in today's higher education. In B. Jacoby & Associates (Eds.), *Service-learning in higher education: Concepts and practices* (pp. 3–25). San Francisco, CA: Jossey-Bass.

Jacoby, B., & Associates. (Eds.). (1996). *Service-learning in higher education: Concepts and practices*. San Francisco, CA: Jossey-Bass.

Johnson County Community College. (2001). *Fact sheet*. Overland Park, KS: Author.

Johnson County Community College. (2001–2002). *College catalog*. Overland Park, KS: Author.

Johnson County Community College & The League for Innovation in the Community College. (2000). *Internal document*. Overland Park, KS: Author.

Jones, E. A., & Ratcliff, J. R. (1990, April). *Is a core curriculum best for everybody? The effect of different patterns of coursework on the general education of high- and low-ability students*. Paper presented at the annual meeting of the American Educational Research Association, Boston, MA.

Kalivoda, P., Broder, J., & Jackson, W. K. (2003). Establishing a teaching academy: Cultivation of teaching at a research university campus. In C. M. Wehlburg & S. Chadwick-Blossey (Eds.), *To improve the academy: Vol. 21. Resources for faculty, instructional, and organizational development* (pp. 79–92). Bolton, MA: Anker.

Karasik, R. (in press). Breaking the time barrier: Helping students "find the time" to do intergenerational service-learning. *Gerontology & Geriatrics Education*.

Karasik, R., & Berke, D. (2001). Classroom and community: Experiential education in family studies and gerontology. *Journal of Teaching in Marriage and Family: Innovations in Family Science Education, 1*(4), 13–38.

Karasik, R., Maddox, M., & Wallingford, M. (in press). Intergenerational service-learning across levels and disciplines: "One size (does not) fit all." *Gerontology & Geriatrics Education.*

Karpiak, I. (2000). The "second call": Faculty renewal and recommitment at midlife. *Quality in Higher Education, 6*(2), 125–134.

Keim, M. C., & Biletzky, P. (1999, December). Teaching methods used by part-time community college faculty. *Community College Journal of Research & Practice, 23,* 727–737.

Kekale, J. (1999). "Preferred" patterns of academic leadership in different disciplinary (sub)cultures. *Higher Education, 37,* 217–238.

Keller, P. (1982). *Getting at the core: Curricular reform at Harvard.* Cambridge, MA: Harvard University Press.

Kelley, W., & Wilhun, L. (1970). *Teaching in the community junior college.* New York, NY: Appleton-Century-Crofts.

Killion, J. P. (2000, Summer). Log on to learn. *Journal of Staff Development, 21*(3), 48–53.

Kotter, J. P. (1996). *Leading change.* Boston, MA: Harvard Business School Press.

Kottkamp, R. (1990). Means for facilitating reflection. *Education and Urban Society, 22,* 182–203.

Kozma, R. (1985, May/June). A grounded theory of instructional innovation in higher education. *Journal of Higher Education, 56*(3), 300–319.

Laden, B. V., & Hagedorn, L. S. (2000). Job satisfaction among faculty of color in academe: Individual survivors or institutional transformers? In L. S. Hagedorn (Ed.), *New directions for institutional research: No. 105. What contributes to job satisfaction among faculty and staff* (pp. 57–66). San Francisco, CA: Jossey-Bass.

Langley, D. J., O'Connor, T. W., & Welkener, M. M. (2004). A transformative model for designing professional development activities. In C. M. Wehlburg & S. Chadwick-Blossey (Eds.), *To improve the academy: Vol. 22. Resources for faculty, instructional, and organizational development* (pp. 145–155). Bolton, MA: Anker.

Lankard, B. A. (1993). *Part-time instructors in adult and vocational education.* Columbus, OH: ERIC Clearinghouse on Adult, Career, and Vocational Education. (ERIC Reproduction Service No ED363797)

LaPidus, J. B. (1997). *Doctoral education: Preparing for the future.* Washington, DC: Council of Graduate Schools. Retrieved September 10, 2002, from http://www.cgsnet.org/pdf/doctoraledpreparing.pdf

Lazerson, M., Wagener, U., & Shumanis, N. (2000, May/June). Teaching and learning in higher education, 1980–2000. *Change, 32*(3), 13–19.

Leslie, D. W. (1998). New directions for research, policy development, and practice. In D. W. Leslie (Ed.), *New directions for higher education: No. 104. The growing use of part-time faculty: Understanding causes and effects* (pp. 95–100). San Francisco, CA: Jossey-Bass.

Levine, A. (1978). *Handbook on undergraduate curriculum: A report for the Carnegie Council on Policy Studies in Higher Education.* San Francisco, CA: Jossey-Bass.

Levinson-Rose, J., & Menges, R. (1981). Improving college teaching: A critical review of research. *Review of Educational Research, 51,* 403–434.

Leviton, R. (1994, January/February). Healing vibrations. *Yoga Journal, 1,* 59–64, 81–83.

Lewis, K. G. (1996). Faculty development in the US: A brief history. *International Journal of Academic Development, 1*(2), 26–33.

Lick, D. W. (2002). Leadership and change. In R. M. Diamond (Ed.), *Field guide to academic leadership* (pp. 27–47). San Francisco, CA: Jossey-Bass.

Lieberman, D. A., & Guskin, A. E. (2003). The essential role of faculty development in new higher education models. In C. M. Wehlburg & S. Chadwick-Blossey (Eds.), *To improve the academy: Vol. 21. Resources for faculty, instructional, and organizational development* (pp. 257–272). Bolton, MA: Anker.

Lindquist, J. (1996). Strategies for change. In J. G. Gaff, J. L. Ratcliff, & Associates (Eds.), *Handbook of the undergraduate curriculum: A comprehensive guide to purposes, structures, practices, and change* (pp. 633–660). San Francisco, CA: Jossey-Bass.

Loacker, G., & Mentkowski, M. (1993). Creating a culture where assessment improves learning. In T. W. Banta (Ed.), *Making a difference: Outcomes of a decade of assessment in higher education* (pp. 5–24). San Francisco, CA: Jossey-Bass.

Loeb, P. (1994). *Generations at the crossroads: Apathy and action on the American campus.* New Brunswick, NJ: Rutgers University.

Loeb, P. (1999). *Soul of a citizen: Living with conviction in a cynical time.* New York, NY: St. Martin's Griffin.

London, H. (1978). *The culture of a community college.* New York, NY: Praeger.

Lopez, C. L. (1999). *A decade of assessing student learning: What have we learned; what's next?* Chicago, IL: North Central Association of Colleges and Schools Commission on Institutions of Higher Education.

Lovitts, B. E., & Nelson, C. (2000, November/December). The hidden crisis in graduate education: Attrition from Ph.D. programs. *Academe, 86*(6). Retrieved May 9, 2004, from http://www.aaup.org/publications/Academe/2000/00nd/ND00LOVI.HTM

Lowman, J. (1994). Professors as performers and motivators. *College Teaching, 42,* 137–141.

Lucas, C. (1994). *American higher education: A history.* New York, NY: St. Martin's Press.

Lyons, R. E., Kysilka, M. L., & Pawlas, G. E. (1999). *The adjunct professor's guide to success.* Boston, MA: Allyn and Bacon.

Maher, T. H. (1982, June). *Institutional vitality in higher education* (AAHE-ERIC Higher Education Research Currents). (ERIC Document Reproduction Service No. ED216668)

Matlin, M. W. (2002). Cognitive psychology and college-level pedagogy: Two siblings that rarely communicate. In D. F. Halpern & M. D. Hakel (Eds.), *New directions for teaching and learning: No. 89. Applying the science of learning to university teaching and beyond* (pp. 87–103). San Francisco, CA: Jossey-Bass.

Maxwell, W. E., & Kazlauskas, E. J. (1992). Which faculty development methods really work in community colleges? A review of research. *Community/Junior College Quarterly, 16,* 351–360.

Mazur, E. (1997). *Peer instruction: A user's manual.* Upper Saddle River, NJ: Prentice-Hall.

McAlpine, L., & Harris, R. (2002). Evaluating teaching effectiveness and teaching improvement: A language for institutional policies and academic development practices. *International Journal of Academic Development, 7*(1), 7–17.

McCall, G., & Simmons, J. (1969). *Issues in participant observation: A text and reader.* Reading, MA: Addison-Wesley.

McEwen, M. (1996). Enhancing student learning and development through service-learning. In B. Jacoby & Associates (Eds.), *Service-learning in higher education: Concepts and practices* (pp. 53–91). San Francisco, CA: Jossey-Bass.

McKeachie, W. J., Lin, Y-G, Daugherty, M., Moffett, M. M., Neigler, C., Nork, J., et al. (1980). Using student ratings and consultation to improve instruction. *British Journal of Educational Psychology, 50,* 168–174.

McKenna, M., & Rizzo, E. (1999). Student's perceptions of the "learning" in service-learning courses. *Journal of Prevention & Intervention in the Community, 18*(1/2), 111–123.

McLeish, J. (1968). *The lecture method.* Cambridge, England: Cambridge Institute of Education.

McNaught, C., & Anwyl, J. (1993). *Awards for teaching at Australian universities* (Centre for the Study of Higher Education Research Working Papers No. 93.1). Victoria, Australia: University of Melbourne. (ERIC Document Reproduction Service No. ED368291)

McNeel, S. P. (1994). College teaching and student moral development. In J. R. Rest & D. Narváez (Eds.), *Moral development in the professions: Psychology and applied ethics* (pp. 27–49). Mahwah, NJ: Lawrence Erlbaum.

Menges, R. J. (1996). Awards to individuals. In M. D. Svinicki & R. J. Menges (Eds.), *New directions in teaching and learning: No. 65. Honoring exemplary teaching* (pp. 3–9). San Francisco, CA: Jossey-Bass.

Menges, R. J. (1996). Experiences of newly hired faculty. In L. Richlin & D. DeZure (Eds.), *To improve the academy: Vol. 15: Resources for faculty, instructional, and organizational development* (pp. 169–182). Stillwater, OK: New Forums Press.

Merriam, S. B. (1997). *Qualitative research and case study applications in education.* San Francisco, CA: Jossey-Bass.

Merton, T. (1965). *The way of Chuang Tzu.* New York, NY: New Directions.

Meyers, R. (2003). An examination of students' use of evidence in group quiz discussions. In C. Schroeder & A. Ciccone (Eds.), *Learning more about learning* (pp. 15–23). Milwaukee, WI: University of Wisconsin-Milwaukee, Center for Instructional and Professional Development.

Mezirow, J. (1990). *Fostering critical reflection in adulthood: A guide to transformative and emancipatory learning.* San Francisco, CA: Jossey-Bass.

Mezirow, J. (1991). *Transformative dimensions of adult learning.* San Francisco: Jossey-Bass.

Mezirow, J. (1997, Summer). Transformative learning: Theory to practice. In P. Cranton (Ed.), *New directions for adult and continuing education: No. 74. Transformative learning in action: Insights from practice* (pp. 5–12). San Francisco, CA: Jossey-Bass.

Mezirow, J. (2000). Learning to think like an adult: Core concepts of transformation theory. In J. Mezirow & Associates (Eds.), *Learning as transformation: Critical perspectives on a theory in progress* (pp. 3–34). San Francisco, CA: Jossey-Bass.

Middendorf, J. K. (1998). A case study in getting faculty to change. In M. Kaplan & D. Lieberman (Eds.), *To improve the academy: Vol. 17. Resources for faculty, instructional, and organizational development* (pp. 203–224). Stillwater: OK: New Forums Press.

Middendorf, J. K. (2000). Finding key faculty to influence change. In M. Kaplan & D. Lieberman (Eds.), *To improve the academy: Vol. 18. Resources for faculty, instructional, and organizational development* (pp. 83–93). Bolton, MA: Anker.

Middleton, A. (1987, October). Teaching awards and tokenism. *Teaching Professor, 1*(8), 3–4.

Miles, M., & Fullan, M. (1992, June). Getting reforms right: What works and what doesn't. *Phi Delta Kappa, 73*(10), 745–752.

Miles, M., & Huberman, A. (1984). *Qualitative data analysis: A sourcebook of new methods.* Beverly Hills, CA: Sage.

Miller, D. J., & Ratcliff, J. L. (1986). Analysis of professional activities of Iowa Community College faculty. *Community/Junior College Journal, 10,* 317–343.

Miller, R. I., Finley, C., & Shedd Vancko, C. (2000). *Evaluating, improving, and judging faculty performance in two-year colleges.* Westport, CT: Bergin & Garvey.

Milloy, P. M., & Brooke, C. (2004). Beyond bean counting: Making faculty development needs assessment more meaningful. In C. M. Wehlburg & S. Chadwick-Blossey (Eds.), *To improve the academy: Vol. 22. Resources for faculty, instructional, and organizational development* (pp. 71–92). Bolton, MA: Anker.

Mintz, J. (1999, Spring). Faculty development and teaching: A holistic approach. *Liberal Education, 85,* 32–37.

Monroe, C. (1972). *Profile of the community college: A handbook.* San Francisco, CA: Jossey-Bass.

Montell, G. (1999). In on-line survey, graduate students in science rate their doctoral programs. *Chronicle of Higher Education,* p. A16.

Morphew, C. C., Twombly, S. B., & Wolf-Wendel, L. E. (2001). Two urban community colleges and an elite private liberal arts college. *Community College Review, 29*(3), 1–21.

Morton, K. (1996). Issues related to integrating service-learning into the curriculum. In B. Jacoby & Associates (Eds.), *Service-learning in higher education: Concepts and practices* (pp. 276–296). San Francisco, CA: Jossey-Bass.

Mullinix, B. B., & Harr, C. (2003). *Faculty-centered program development.* West Long Branch, NJ: Monmouth University, Faculty Resource Center. Retrieved December 11, 2003, from http://its.monmouth.edu/trainingGuest/POD-BIA/Mullinix-Harr%20BIA-FacCentrDev-HO.doc

Murray, J. P. (1995). Faculty (mis)development in Ohio two-year colleges. *Community College Journal of Research and Practice, 19,* 549–593.

Murray, J. P. (1999). Faculty development in a national sample of community colleges. *Community College Review, 27*(3), 47–64.

Murray, J. P. (2002). Faculty development in SACS-accredited community colleges. *Community College Review, 29*(4), 50–67.

National Association of Graduate-Professional Students. (2001). *The 2000 national doctoral program survey.* Washington, DC: Author. Retrieved September 10, 2002, from http://survey.nagps.org

National Center for Education Statistics. (2002). *A profile of part-time faculty: Fall 1998.* Washington, DC: U.S. Department of Education.

National Education Association Higher Education Research Center. (2001). Part-time faculty. *Update, 7*(4), 1–4.

National Research Council. (1992). *Educating mathematical scientists: Doctoral study and the postdoctoral experience in the United States.* Washington, DC: National Academy Press.

National Survey of Student Engagement. (2001). *Results from St. Lawrence University.* Bloomington, IN: Indiana University. Retrieved December 1, 2003, from http://www.indiana.edu/~nsse/

Neptune, C. (2001). *Opportunities for excellence: Professionalism and the two-year college mathematics faculty.* Memphis, TN: American Mathematical Association of Two-Year Colleges.

Nerad, M., & Cerny, J. (1999, Fall). From rumors to facts: Career outcomes of English Ph.D.s. *Council of Graduate Schools Communicator, 32*(7), 1-11. Retrieved May 9, 2004, from http://www.grad.washington.edu/envision/PDF/TenYears Later.pdf

Nerad, M., & Cerny, J. (2000). Improving doctoral education: Recommendations from the "Ph.D.s 10 years later study." *Council of Graduate Schools Communicator, 33*(2), 6. Retrieved May 9, 2004, from snet.org/PublicationsPolicyRes/communicatorpdfs/2000/march2000.pdf

Nyquist, J. D. (2002, November/December). The Ph.D.: A tapestry of change for the 21st century. *Change, 34*(6), 12–20.

Nyquist, J. D., & Sprague, J. (1998). Thinking developmentally about TAs. In M. Marincovich, J. Prostko, & F. Stout (Eds.), *The professional development of graduate teaching assistants* (pp. 61–88). Bolton, MA: Anker.

O'Banion, T. (1994). Teaching and learning: A mandate for the nineties. *Community College Journal, 64*(4), 21–25.

O'Banion, T. (1994). *Teaching and learning in the community college.* Washington, DC: Community College Press.

Olguin, E., & Schmitz, B. (1996). Transforming the curriculum through diversity. In J. G. Gaff, J. L. Ratcliff, & Associates (Eds.), *Handbook of the undergraduate curriculum: A comprehensive guide to purposes, structures, practices, and change* (pp. 436–456). San Francisco, CA: Jossey-Bass.

Olson, K. (2003). Using comparative practice to test the veracity of learning theories designed to promote "deep understanding." In C. Schroeder & A. Ciccone (Eds.), *Learning more about learning* (pp. 38–49). Milwaukee, WI: University of Wisconsin–Milwaukee, Center for Instructional and Professional Development.

O'Malley, R. (2002). SoTL reflections on efforts to find appropriate technology on pedagogy to stimulate student participation in the learning process. *Models in our midst* (pp. 41–47). Milwaukee, WI: University of Wisconsin–Milwaukee, Center for Instructional and Professional Development.

O'Meara, K. (2002). Uncovering the values in faculty evaluation of service as scholarship. *Review of Higher Education, 26*(1), 57–80.

O'Reilley, M. R. (1993). *The peaceable classroom.* Portsmouth, NH: Boynton/Cook-Heinemann.

O'Reilley, M. R. (1998). *Radical presence: Teaching as contemplative practice.* Portsmouth, NH: Boynton/Cook-Heinemann.

O'Reilley, M. R. (2000). *The barn at the end of the world: The apprenticeship of a Quaker, Buddhist shepherd.* Minneapolis, MN: Milkweed.

Outcalt, C. (2000). Community college teaching: Toward collegiality and community. *Community College Review, 28*(2), 57–70.

Padilla, A. M. (1994). Ethnic minority scholars, research, and mentoring: Current and future issues. *Educational Researcher, 23*(4), 24–27.

Palmer, J. C., & Vaughan, G. B. (1992). *Fostering a climate for faculty scholarship at community colleges.* Washington, DC: American Association of Community and Junior Colleges.

Palmer, P. J. (1983). *To know as we are known: Education as a spiritual journey.* San Francisco, CA: Harper.

Palmer, P. J. (1991). *The active life: Wisdom for creativity and caring.* San Francisco, CA: Harper.

Palmer, P. J. (1997). *The courage to teach: Exploring the inner landscape of a teacher's life.* San Francisco, CA: Jossey-Bass.

Palmer, P. J. (2000). *Let your life speak: Listening for the voice of vocation.* San Francisco, CA: Jossey-Bass.

Parks, S. (1986). *The critical years: Young adults and the search for meaning, faith, and commitment.* San Francisco, CA: Harper.

Pascarella, E. T., & Terenzini, P. T. (1991). *How college affects students: Findings and insights from twenty years of research.* San Francisco, CA: Jossey-Bass.

Patton, M. Q. (2002). *Qualitative evaluation and research methods* (3rd ed.). Thousand Oaks, CA: Sage.

Paul, R. W., Elder, L., & Bartell, T. (1997). *California teacher preparation for instruction in critical thinking: Research findings and policy recommendations.* Sacramento, CA: California Commission on Teacher Credentialing.

Pintrich, P. R., Marx, R. W., & Boyle, R. A. (1993). Beyond cold conceptual change: The role of motivational beliefs and classroom contextual factors in the process of conceptual change. *Review of Educational Research, 63*(2), 167–199.

Pohland, P., & Bova, B. (2000). Professional development as transformational learning. *International Journal of Leadership in Education, 3*(2), 137–150.

Poock, M. C. (2001). A model for integrating professional development in graduate education. *College Student Journal, 35*(3), 345–353. Retrieved May 9, 2004, from http://articles.findarticles.com/p/articles/mi_m0FCR/is_3_35/ai_80744646

Prawat, R. (1992, May). Teachers' belief about teaching and learning: A constructivist perspective. *American Journal of Education, 100*(3), 354–395.

Professional and Organizational Development Network in Higher Education. (2001). *Membership directory and networking guide.* Miami Beach, FL: Author.

Proust, M. (1948). *La prisonniere.* (J. O'Brien, Ed. & Trans.). New York, NY: Columbia University Press. (Original work published 1924)

Ramsden, P. (1992). *Learning to teach in higher education.* London, England: Routledge.

Ratcliff, J. L. (1996). What is a curriculum and what should it be? In J. G. Gaff, J. L. Ratcliff, & Associates (Eds.), *Handbook of the undergraduate curriculum: A comprehensive guide to purposes, structures, practices, and change* (pp. 5–29). San Francisco, CA: Jossey-Bass.

Rathburn, J. (2002). Using technology to enhance learning and understanding. In C. Schroeder & A. Ciccone (Eds.), *Models in our midst* (pp. 49–58). Milwaukee, WI: University of Wisconsin–Milwaukee, Center for Instructional and Professional Development.

Rhem, J. (1995). Close Up Column: Going deep. *National Teaching and Learning Forum, 5*(1), 4.

Rhoads, R. A., & Howard, J. (Eds.). (1998). *Academic service learning: A pedagogy of action and reflection.* San Francisco, CA: JosseyBass.

Rice, K., & Pollack, S. (2000). Developing a critical pedagogy of service learning: Preparing self-reflective, culturally aware, and responsive community participants. In C. O'Grady (Ed.), *Integrating service learning and multicultural education in colleges and universities* (pp. 115–134). Mahwah, NJ: Lawrence Erlbaum.

Richardson, R., & Moore, W. (1987). Faculty development and evaluation in Texas community colleges. *Community/Junior College Quarterly, 11,* 19–32.

Robertson, D. L. (1997). Transformative learning and transition theory: Toward developing the ability to facilitate insight. *Journal on Excellence in College Teaching, 8*(1), 105–125.

Robertson, D. L. (1999). Professors' perspectives on their teaching: A new construct and developmental model. *Innovative Higher Education, 23*(4), 271–294.

Roueche, J. E., Roueche, S. D., & Milliron, M. D. (1995). *Strangers in their own land: Part-time faculty in American community colleges.* Washington, DC: Community College Press.

Roueche, J. E., Roueche, S. D., & Milliron, M. D. (1996a, Spring). Identifying the strangers: Exploring part-time faculty integration in American community colleges. *Community College Review, 23*(4), 33–48.

Roueche, J. E., Roueche, S. D., & Milliron, M. D. (1996b, March). In the company of strangers: Addressing the utilization and integration of part-time faculty in American community colleges. *Community College Journal of Research and Practice, 20*(2), 105–117.

Rue, P. (1996). Administering successful service-learning programs. In B. Jacoby & Associates (Eds.), *Service-learning in higher education: Concepts and practices* (pp. 246–275). San Francisco, CA: Jossey-Bass.

Sandford, B., & McCaslin, N. L. (2003, October). *Assessment of professional development activities, instructional needs, and methods of delivery for part-time technical and occupational faculty in U.S. community colleges.* Paper presented at the Midwest Research to Practice Conference in Adult, Continuing, and Community Education, Columbus, OH. Retrieved May 9, 2004, from http://www.alumni-osu.org/midwest/midwest%20papers/Sandford%20&%20McCaslin--Done.pdf

Sarko, L. (1964, October). The problem of teaching in community colleges. *Journal of Higher Education, 35*(7), 384–386.

Saunders, S. A., & Ervin, L. (1984). Meeting the special advising needs of students. In R. B. Winston, T. K. Miller, S. C. Ender, T. J. Grites, & Associates (Eds.), *Developmental academic advising: Addressing students' educational, career, and personal needs* (pp. 250–286). San Francisco, CA: Jossey-Bass.

Schonwetter, D. T., Sokal, L., Friesen, M., & Taylor, K. L. (2002). Teaching philosophies reconsidered: A conceptual model for the development and evaluation of teaching philosophy statements. *International Journal of Academic Development, 7*(1), 83–97.

Schroeder, C. (2001). Faculty change agents: Individual and organizational factors that enable or impede faculty involvement in organizational change (Doctoral dissertation, University of Wisconsin–Madison, 2001). *Dissertation Abstracts International,* No. 0262.

Schroeder, C., & Ciccone, A. (Eds.). (2002). *Models in our midst.* Milwaukee, WI: University of Wisconsin–Milwaukee, Center for Instructional and Professional Development.

Schroeder, C., & Ciccone, A. (Eds.). (2003). *Learning more about learning.* Milwaukee, WI: University of Wisconsin–Milwaukee, Center for Instructional and Professional Development.

Schuster, J. H. (1985, September). Faculty vitality: Observations from the field. *New Directions for Higher Education: No. 51.* (pp. 21–32).

Schuster, J. H. (1990). The need for fresh approaches to faculty renewal. In J. H. Schuster, D. W. Wheeler, & Associates (Eds.), *Enhancing faculty careers: Strategies for development and renewal* (pp. 3–19). San Francisco, CA: Jossey-Bass.

Schuster, J. H. (1995). Whither the faculty? The changing academic labor market. *Educational Record, 76*(4), 28–33.

Schuster, J. H., Wheeler, D. W., & Associates. (Eds.). (1990). *Enhancing faculty careers: Strategies for development and renewal.* San Francisco, CA: Jossey-Bass.

Self, D. J., & Baldwin, D. C., Jr. (1994). Moral reasoning in medicine. In J. R. Rest & D. Narváez (Eds.), *Moral development in the professions: Psychology and applied ethics* (pp.147-162). Mahwah, NJ: Lawrence Erlbaum.

Self, D. J., Olivarez, M., & Baldwin, D. C., Jr. (1994). Moral reasoning in veterinary medicine. In J. R. Rest & D. Narváez (Eds.), *Moral development in the professions: Psychology and applied ethics* (pp. 163–171). Mahwah, NJ: Lawrence Erlbaum.

Senge, P., Kleiner, A., Roberts, C., Ross, R., Roth, G., & Smith, B. (1999). *The dance of change: The challenges to sustaining momentum in learning organizations.* New York, NY: Currency Doubleday.

Senge, P. M. (1990). *The fifth discipline: The art & practice of the learning organization.* New York, NY: Currency Doubleday.

Shachtman, T. (1995). *The inarticulate society: Eloquence and culture in America.* New York, NY: Free Press.

Shulman, L. S. (1986). Those who understand: Knowledge growth in teaching. *Educational Researcher, 15,* 4–14.

Shulman, L. S. (1993, November/December). Teaching as community property: Putting an end to pedagogical solitude. *Change, 25*(6), 6–7.

Shulman, L. S. (1999, July/August). Taking learning seriously. *Change, 31*(4), 11–17.

Smith, P. (1990). *Killing the spirit: Higher education in America.* New York, NY: Viking.

Smith, S. J., Pedersen-Gallegos, L., & Riegle-Crumb, C. (2002). The training, careers, and work of Ph.D. physical scientists: Not simply academic. *American Journal of Physics, 70*(11), 1081–1092.

Sokol, A., & Cranton, P. (1998, Spring). Transforming, not training. *Adult Learning, 9*(3), 14–17.

Sorcinelli, M. D. (2002). Ten principles of good practice in creating and sustaining teaching and learning centers. In K. H. Gillespie, L. R. Hilsen, & E. C. Wadsworth (Eds.), *A guide to faculty development: Practical advice, examples, and resources.* Bolton, MA: Anker.

Stanton, T., Giles, D., & Cruz, N. (1999). *Service-learning: A movement's pioneers reflect on its origins, practice and future.* San Francisco, CA: Jossey-Bass.

Steinert, Y. (2000, January). Faculty development in the new millennium: Key challenges and future directions. *Medical Teacher, 22,* 44–50.

Sternberg, R. J., & Grigorenko, E. L. (2002). The theory of successful intelligence as a basis for instruction and assessment in higher education. In D. F. Halpern & M. D. Hakel (Eds.), *New directions for teaching and learning: No. 89. Applying the science of learning to university teaching and beyond* (pp. 45–54). San Francisco, CA: Jossey-Bass.

Stone, T. E. (1996). Developing instructional objectives, lesson plans, and syllabi. In V. Bianco-Mathis & N. Chalofsky (Eds.), *The adjunct faculty handbook* (pp. 28–39). Thousand Oaks, CA: Sage.

Swail, W. S. (2002, July/August). Higher education and the new demographics: Questions for policy. *Change, 34*(4), 15–23.

Tagg, J. (2003). *The learning paradigm college.* Bolton, MA: Anker.

Tannen, D. (1998). *The argument culture: Stopping America's war of words.* New York, NY: Ballantine.

Taylor, E. W. (2000). Analyzing research on transformative learning theory. In J. Mezirow & Associates (Eds.), *Learning as transformation: Critical perspectives on a theory in progress.* San Francisco, CA: Jossey-Bass.

Teaching Partners Lunch Discussion. (2000, October 13). Unpublished tape transcript.

Tiberius, R. G. (2002). A brief history of educational development: Implications for teachers and developers. In D. Lieberman & C. Wehlburg (Eds.), *To improve the academy: Vol. 20. Resources for faculty, instructional, and organizational development* (pp. 20–37). Bolton, MA: Anker.

Tiberius, R. G., Sacklin, H. D., Janzen, K. R., & Preece, M. (1993). Alliances for change: A procedure for improving teaching through conversations with learners and partnerships with colleagues. *Journal of Staff, Program, and Organizational Development, 11*(1), 11–22.

Tierney, W. G. (1987). Facts and constructs: Defining reality in higher education organizations. *Review of Higher Education, 11*(1), 61–73.

Tierney, W. G. (1997). Organizational socialization in higher education. *Journal of Higher Education, 68*(1), 1–16.

Tierney, W. G., & Bensimon, E. M. (1996). *Promotion and tenure: Community and socialization in academe.* Albany, NY: State University of New York Press.

Tierney, W. G., & Rhoads, R. A. (1993). *Enhancing promotion, tenure and beyond: Faculty socialization as a cultural process* (ASHE-ERIC Higher Education Report No. 6). Washington, DC: George Washington University.

Trigwell, K., & Prosser, M. (1996). Congruence between intention and strategy in university science teachers' approaches to teaching. *Studies in Higher Education, 32,* 77–87.

Trosset, C. (1998, September/October). Obstacles to open discussion and critical thinking: The Grinnell College study. *Change, 30*(5), 44–49.

Turner, C. S. V. (2002). Women of color in academe: Living with multiple marginality. *Journal of Higher Education, 73*(1), 74–93.

Turner, C. S. V., & Myers, S. L., Jr. (2000). *Faculty of color in academe: Bittersweet success.* Needham Heights, MA: Allyn and Bacon.

Turner, C. S. V., & Thompson, R. J. (1993). Socializing women doctoral students: Minority and majority experiences. *Review of Higher Education, 16*(3), 355–370.

University of the Sciences in Philadelphia. (2002). *Tactical planning group report on creating a culture of student-centered learning and living.* Philadelphia, PA: Author.

U.S. Department of Education, National Center for Education Statistics. (1998). *Digest of education statistics.* Washington, DC: Author.

van der Bogert, V., Brinko, K. T., Atkins, S. S., & Arnold, E. L. (1990). Transformational faculty development: Integrating the feminine and the masculine. In L. Hilsen (Ed.), *To improve the academy: Vol. 9. Resources for student, faculty, and institutional development* (pp. 89–98). Stillwater, OK: New Forums Press.

Van Horn, C. E. (1995). *Enhancing the connection between higher education and the workplace: A survey of employers.* Denver, CO: State Higher Education Executive Officers and Education Commission of the States.

Walvoord, B. E., & Anderson, V. J. (1998). *Effective grading: A tool for learning and assessment.* San Francisco, CA: Jossey-Bass.

Ward, K. (1998). Addressing academic culture: Service learning, organizations, and faculty work. In R. A. Rhoads & J. Howard (Eds.), *Academic service learning: A pedagogy of action and reflection* (pp. 73–80). San Francisco, CA: Jossey-Bass.

Warren, R., & Plumb, E. (1999). Survey of distinguished teacher award schemes in higher education. *Journal of Further and Higher Education, 23*(2), 245–255.

Waters, T., Marzano, R. J., & McNulty, B. (2003). *Balanced leadership: What 30 years of research tells us about the effect of leadership on student achievement.* Aurora, CO: Mid-continent Research for Education and Learning.

Wehlburg, C. M. (2000, Fall). Respecting students and faculty: The need for "intrusive" assessment. *The Department Chair, 11*(2), 20–22.

Wehlburg, C. M. (2002). More than a thermometer: Using assessment effectively. In G. S. Wheeler (Ed.), *Teaching and learning in college: A resource for educators* (4th ed., pp. 177–199). Elyria, OH: Info–Tec.

Weigert, K. (1998). Academic service learning: Its meaning and relevance. In R. A. Rhoads & J. Howard (Eds.), *Academic service learning: A pedagogy of action and reflection* (pp. 3–10). San Francisco, CA: Jossey-Bass.

Weimer, M. (2002). *Learner-centered teaching: Five key changes to practice.* San Francisco, CA: Jossey-Bass.

Wenger, E. (1998). *Communities of practice: Learning, meaning and identity.* New York, NY: Cambridge University Press.

Wenger, E., McDermott, R., & Snyder, W. M. (2002). *Cultivating communities of practice: A guide to managing knowledge.* Boston, MA: Harvard Business School Press.

Wergin, J. F. (2003). *Departments that work: Building and sustaining cultures of excellence in academic programs.* Bolton, MA: Anker.

Westacott, B., & Hegeman, C. (Eds.). (1996). *Service learning in elder care: A resource manual.* Albany, NY: Foundation for Long Term Care.

Wiggins, G. (1996, Winter). Embracing accountability. *New Schools, New Communities, 12*(2), 4–10.

Wilber, K. (1998). *The marriage of sense and soul: Integrating science and religion.* New York, NY: Random House.

Wilcox, S. (1997). Becoming a faculty developer. In P. Cranton (Ed.), *New directions for adult and continuing education: No. 74. Transformative learning in action: Insights from practice* (pp. 23–32). San Francisco, CA: Jossey-Bass.

Williams, J. (1986). *A study of professional development practices of part-time instructors at selected League for Innovation community colleges.* Los Angeles, CA: League for Innovation in the Community College.

Wright, D. L. (2000). Faculty development centers in research universities: A study of resources and programs. In M. Kaplan & D. Lieberman (Eds.), *To improve the academy: Vol. 18. Resources for faculty, instructional, and organizational development* (pp. 291–301). Bolton, MA: Anker.

Wunsch, M. A. (1994). New directions for mentoring: An organizational development perspective. In M. A. Wunsch, R. J. Menges, & M. D. Svinicki (Eds.), *New directions for teaching and learning: No. 57. Mentoring revisited: Making an impact on individuals and institutions* (pp. 9–13). San Francisco, CA: Jossey-Bass.

Wyles, B. (1998). Adjunct faculty in the community college: Realities and challenges. In D. W. Leslie (Ed.), *New directions for higher education: No. 104. The growing use of part-time faculty: Understanding causes and effects* (pp. 89–93). San Francisco, CA: Jossey-Bass.

Zemsky, R. (1989). *Structure and coherence: Measuring the undergraduate curriculum.* Washington, DC: Association of American Colleges.

Zimmerman, M. (1986). The evolution-creation controversy: Opinions from students in a "liberal" liberal arts college. *Ohio Journal of Science, 86*(4), 134–139.

Zlotkowski, E. (1996). Foreword. In L. Adler-Kassner, R. Crooks, & A. Watters (Eds.), *Composition—Writing the community: Concepts and models for service-learning in composition* (pp. v–vii). Washington, DC: American Association for Higher Education.

Zull, J. (2002). *The art of changing the brain.* Sterling, VA: Stylus.